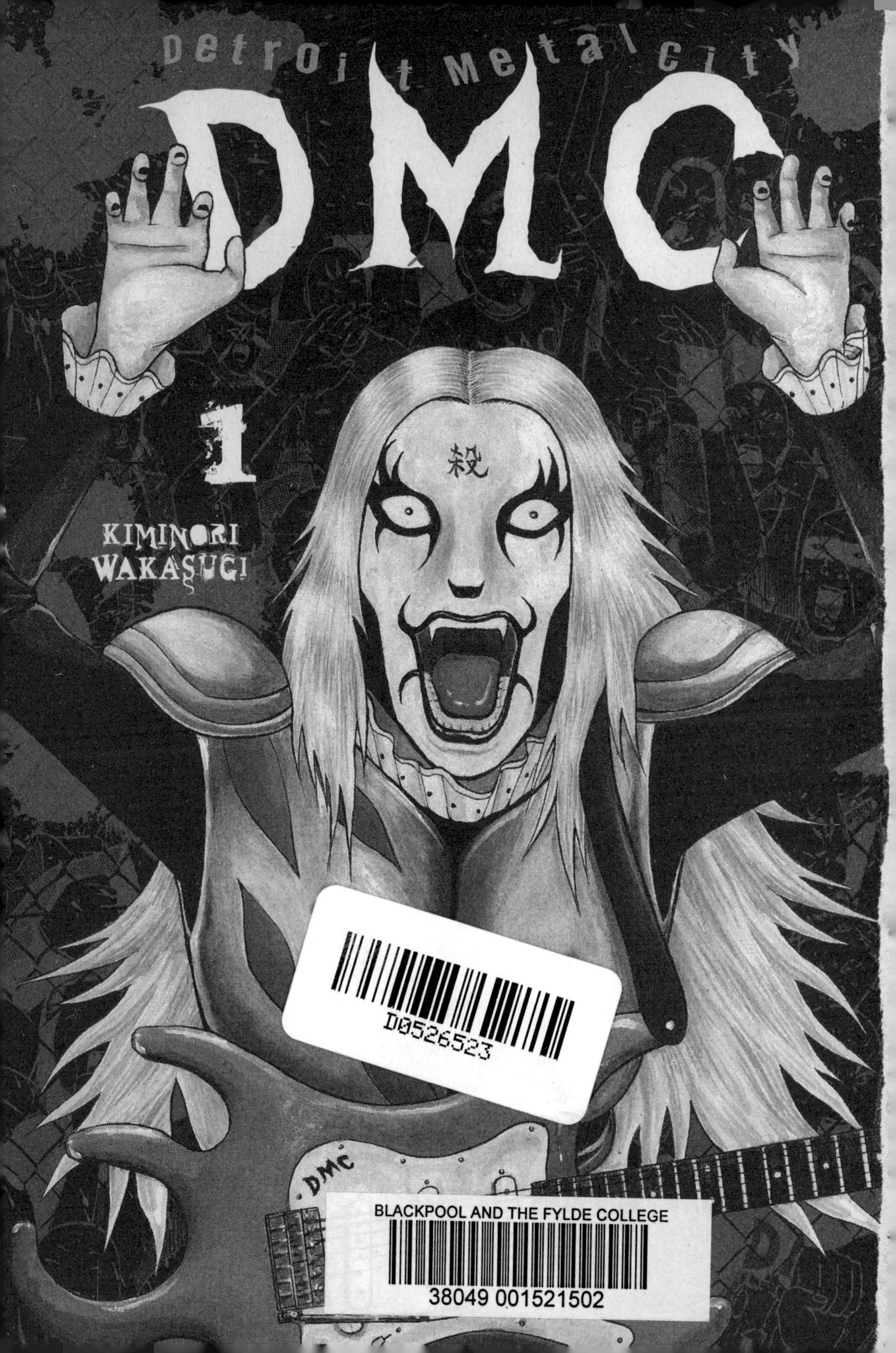
Detroit Metal City
DMC
1
KIMINORI
WAKASUGI
殺
DMC
DMC

Detroit Metal City

DMC

WARNING!
THIS ALBUM CONTAINS NOTHING BUT THE MOST PROFANE OF PROFANITIES! LISTEN AT THE RISK OF YOUR IMMORTAL SOUL.

DETROIT METAL CITY IS
KRAUSER II (LEAD GUITAR, VOCALS) CAMUS (DRUMS) JAGI (VOCALS AND BASS)

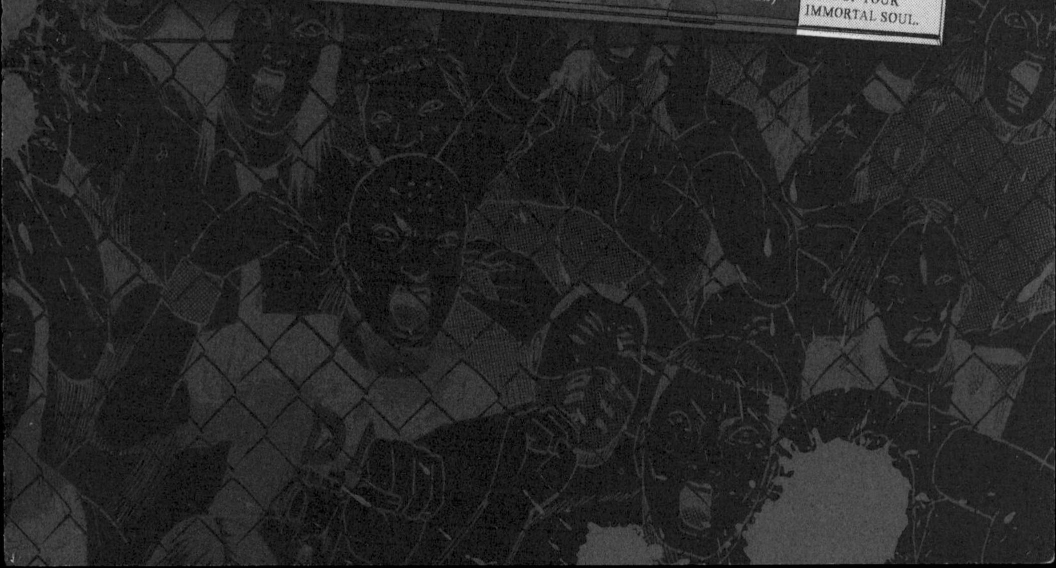

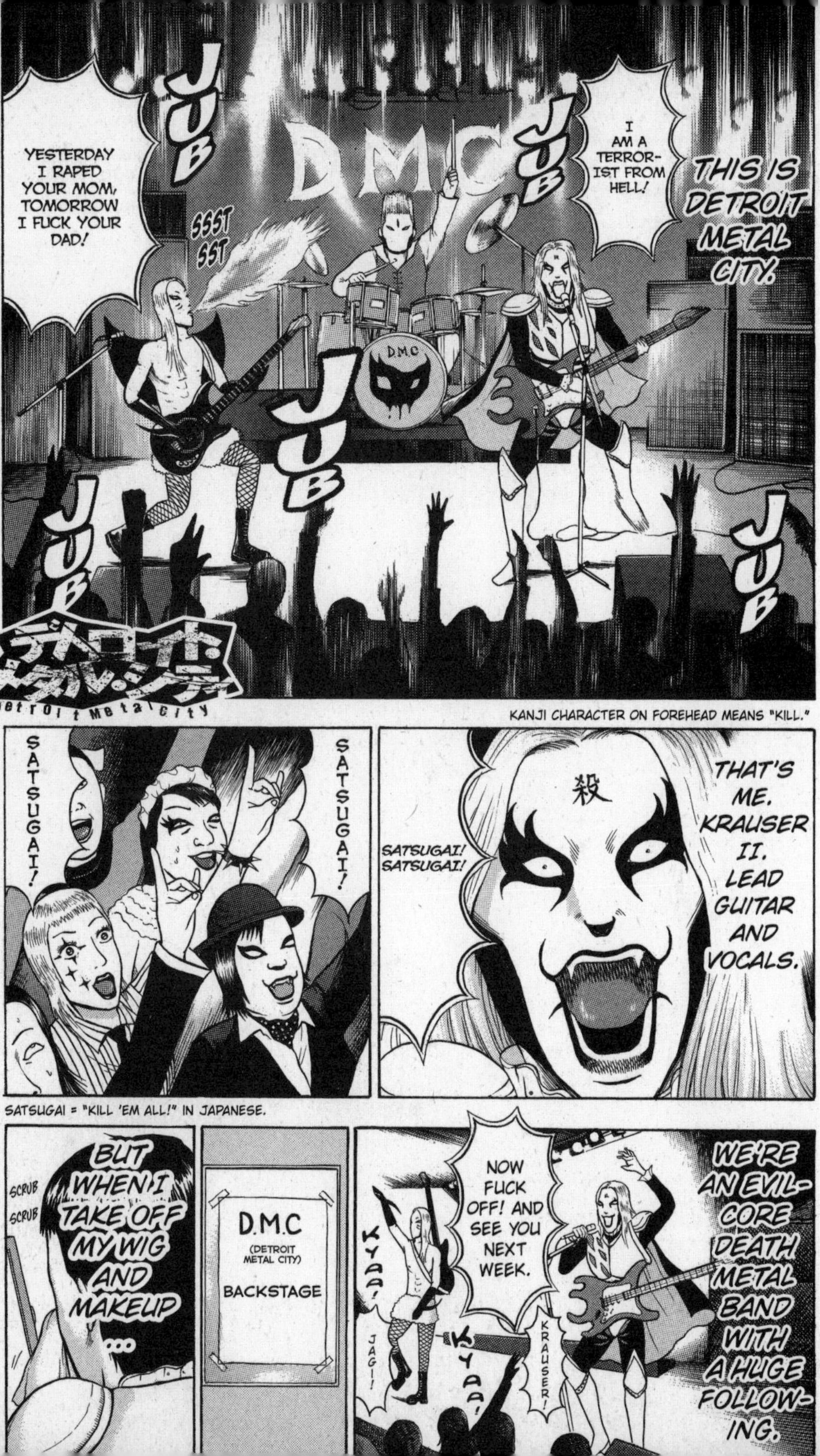
THIS IS DETROIT METAL CITY.
I AM A TERRORIST FROM HELL!
JUB JUB
YESTERDAY I RAPED YOUR MOM, TOMORROW I FUCK YOUR DAD!
JUB
SSST SST
JUB JUB JUB
Detroit Metal City
KANJI CHARACTER ON FOREHEAD MEANS "KILL."
THAT'S ME. KRAUSER II. LEAD GUITAR AND VOCALS.
殺
SATSUGAI! SATSUGAI!
SATSUGAI!
SATSUGAI!
SATSUGAI = "KILL 'EM ALL!" IN JAPANESE.
WE'RE AN EVIL-CORE DEATH METAL BAND WITH A HUGE FOLLOWING.
NOW FUCK OFF! AND SEE YOU NEXT WEEK.
KRAUSER!
KYAA!
JAGI!
KYAA!
D.M.C
(DETROIT METAL CITY)
BACKSTAGE
BUT WHEN I TAKE OFF MY WIG AND MAKEUP...
SCRUB
SCRUB

デトロイト・メタル・シティ
Detroit Metal City

TRACK 1 DMC

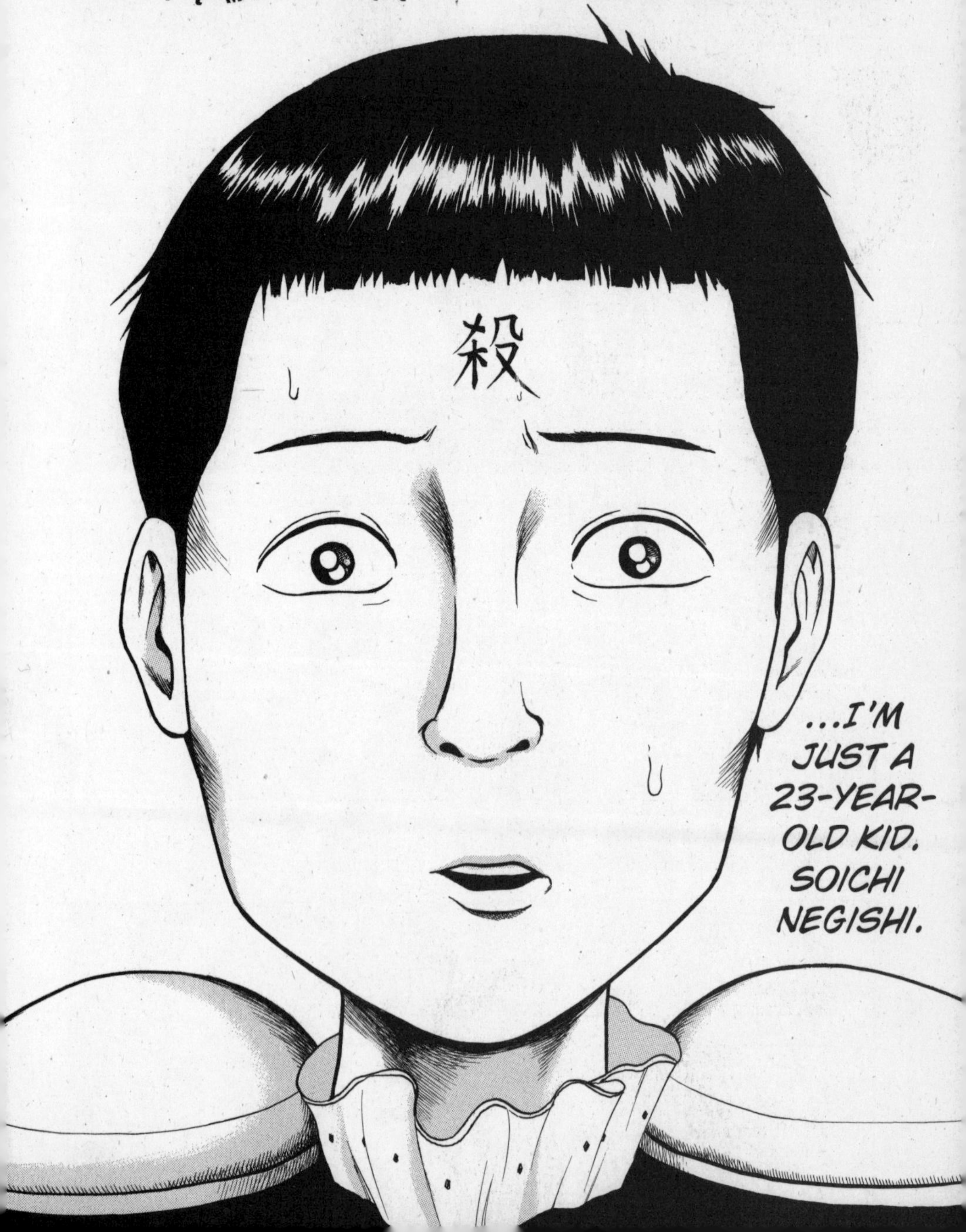
殺
...I'M JUST A 23-YEAR-OLD KID. SOICHI NEGISHI.

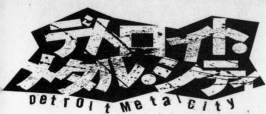

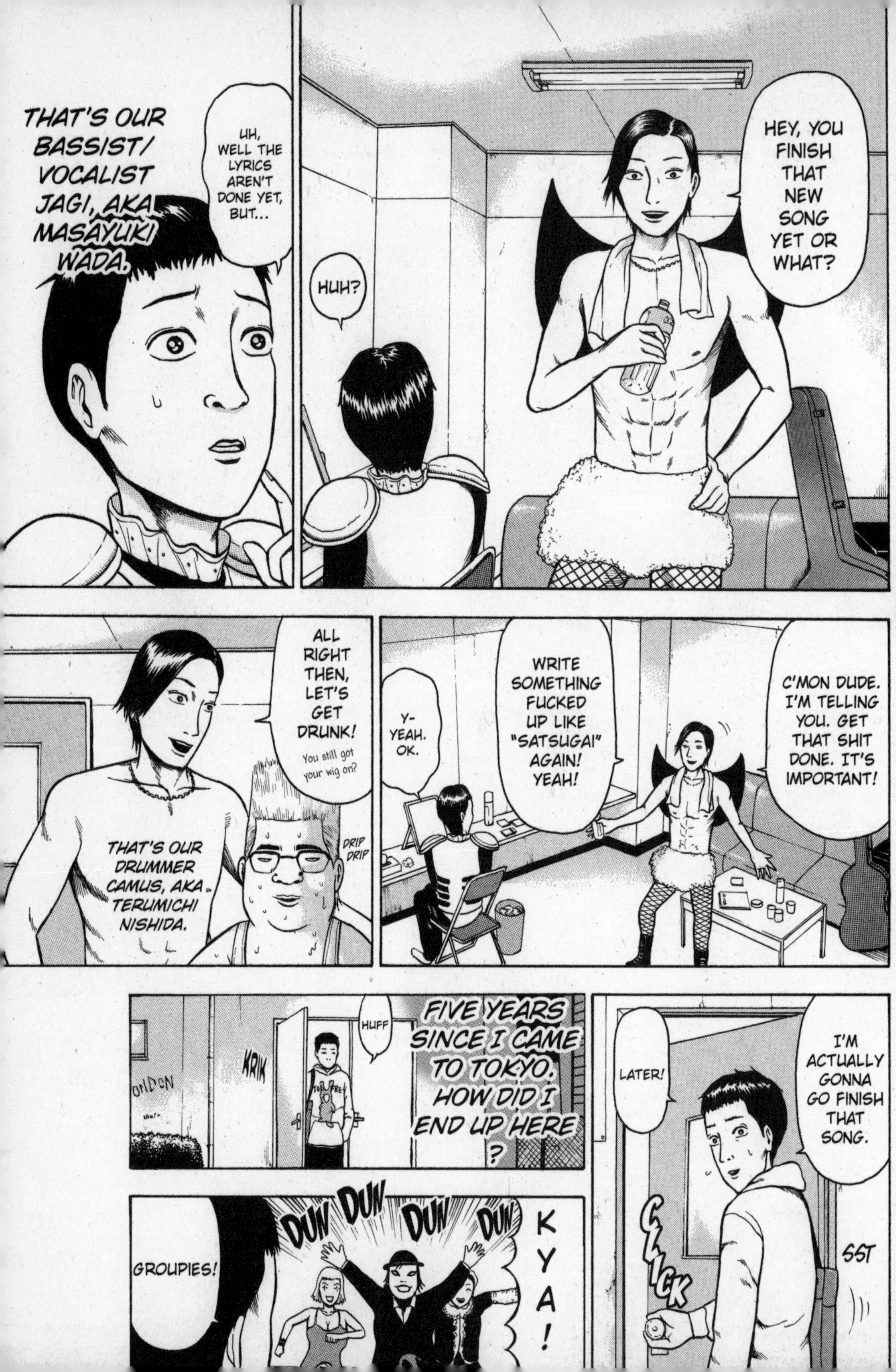
HEY, YOU FINISH THAT NEW SONG YET OR WHAT?
HUH?
UH, WELL THE LYRICS AREN'T DONE YET, BUT...
THAT'S OUR BASSIST/ VOCALIST JAGI, AKA MASAYUKI WADA.
C'MON DUDE. I'M TELLING YOU. GET THAT SHIT DONE. IT'S IMPORTANT!
WRITE SOMETHING FUCKED UP LIKE "SATSUGAI" AGAIN! YEAH!
Y-YEAH. OK.
ALL RIGHT THEN, LET'S GET DRUNK!
You still got your wig on?
DRIP DRIP
THAT'S OUR DRUMMER CAMUS, AKA TERUMICHI NISHIDA.
I'M ACTUALLY GONNA GO FINISH THAT SONG.
LATER!
CLICK
SST
FIVE YEARS SINCE I CAME TO TOKYO. HOW DID I END UP HERE?
HUFF
KRIK
KYA!
DUN DUN DUN DUN
GROUPIES!

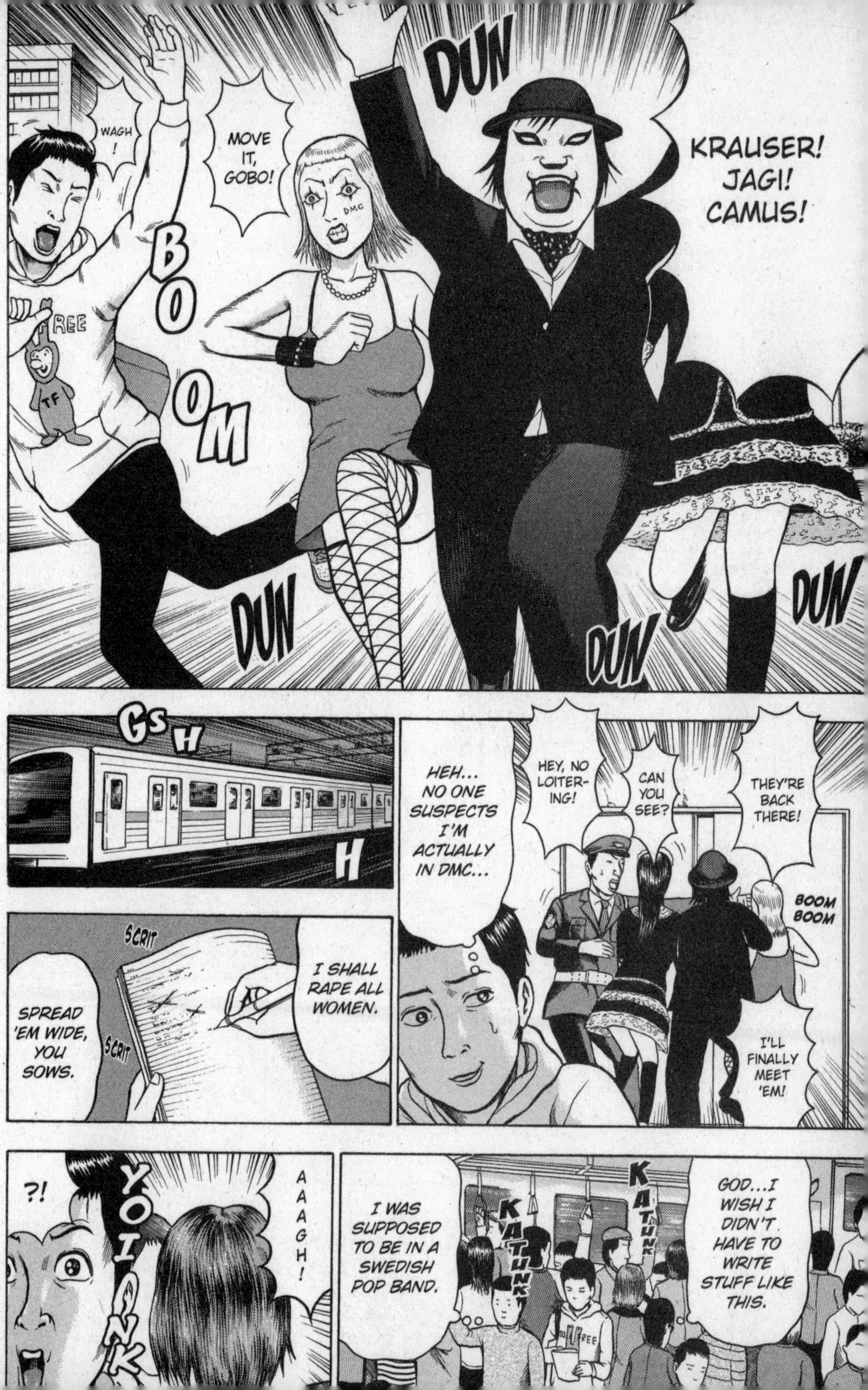
KRAUSER! JAGI! CAMUS!
DUN
MOVE IT, GOBO!
WAGH!
BOOM
DUN
DUN
DUN
THEY'RE BACK THERE!
CAN YOU SEE?
HEY, NO LOITERING!
HEH... NO ONE SUSPECTS I'M ACTUALLY IN DMC...
BOOM BOOM
I'LL FINALLY MEET 'EM!
GSH
H
I SHALL RAPE ALL WOMEN.
SCRIT
SPREAD 'EM WIDE, YOU SOWS.
SCRIT
GOD...I WISH I DIDN'T HAVE TO WRITE STUFF LIKE THIS.
KATUNK
KATUNK
I WAS SUPPOSED TO BE IN A SWEDISH POP BAND.
AAAGH!
YOINK
?!

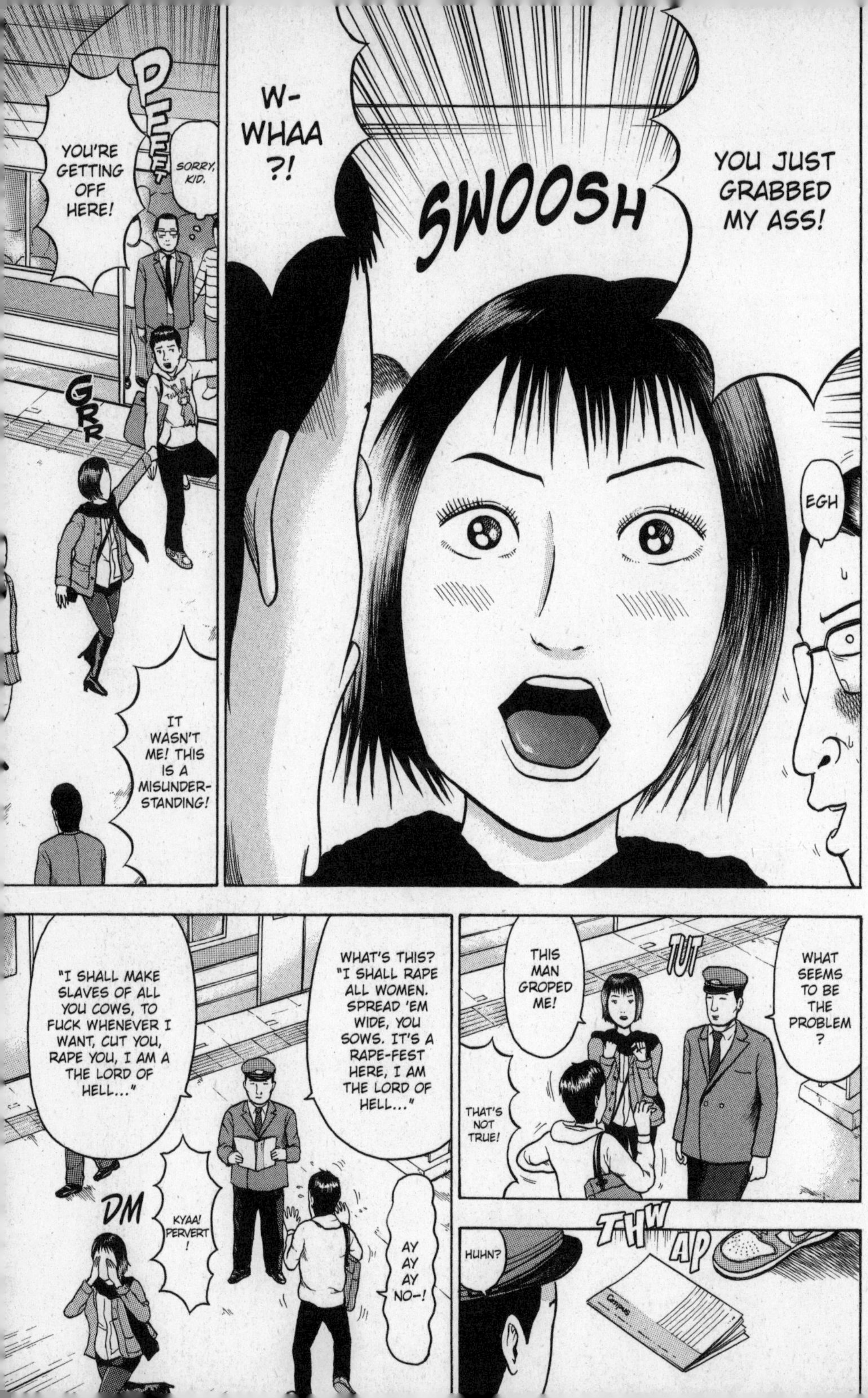

YOU JUST GRABBED MY ASS!
SWOOSH
W-WHAA?!
EGH
YOU'RE GETTING OFF HERE!
PFFFT
SORRY, KID.
GRR
IT WASN'T ME! THIS IS A MISUNDERSTANDING!
WHAT SEEMS TO BE THE PROBLEM?
TUT
THIS MAN GROPED ME!
THAT'S NOT TRUE!
THWAP
HUHN?
WHAT'S THIS? "I SHALL RAPE ALL WOMEN. SPREAD 'EM WIDE, YOU SOWS. IT'S A RAPE-FEST HERE, I AM THE LORD OF HELL..."
"I SHALL MAKE SLAVES OF ALL YOU COWS, TO FUCK WHENEVER I WANT, CUT YOU, RAPE YOU, I AM A THE LORD OF HELL..."
AY AY AY NO-!
KYAA! PERVERT!
DM

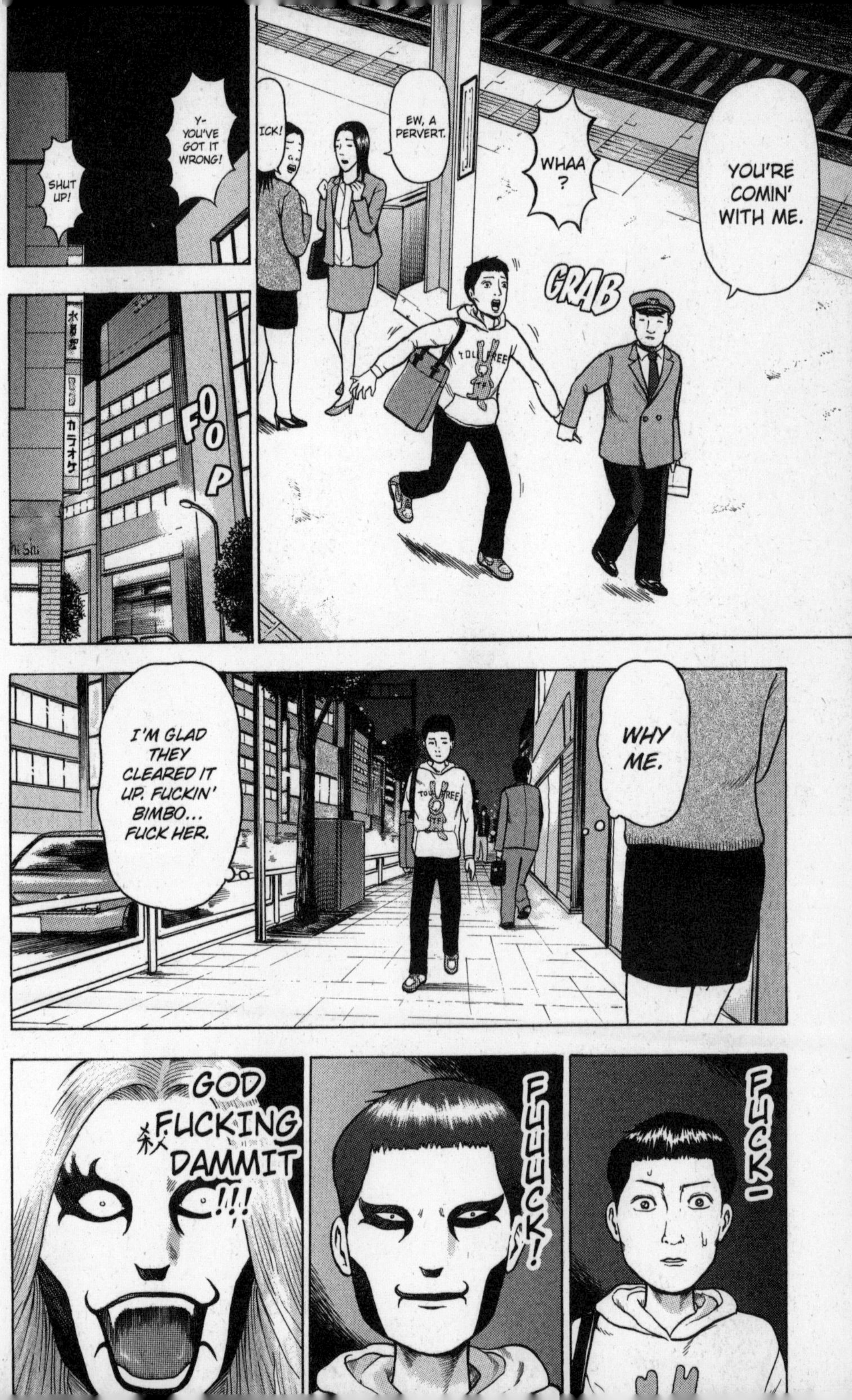
YOU'RE COMIN' WITH ME.
WHAA?
GRAB
EW, A PERVERT.
ICK!
Y- YOU'VE GOT IT WRONG!
SHUT UP!
FOOP
カラオケ
WHY ME.
I'M GLAD THEY CLEARED IT UP. FUCKIN' BIMBO... FUCK HER.
FUCK!
FUUUCK!
GOD 殺 FUCKING DAMMIT!!!

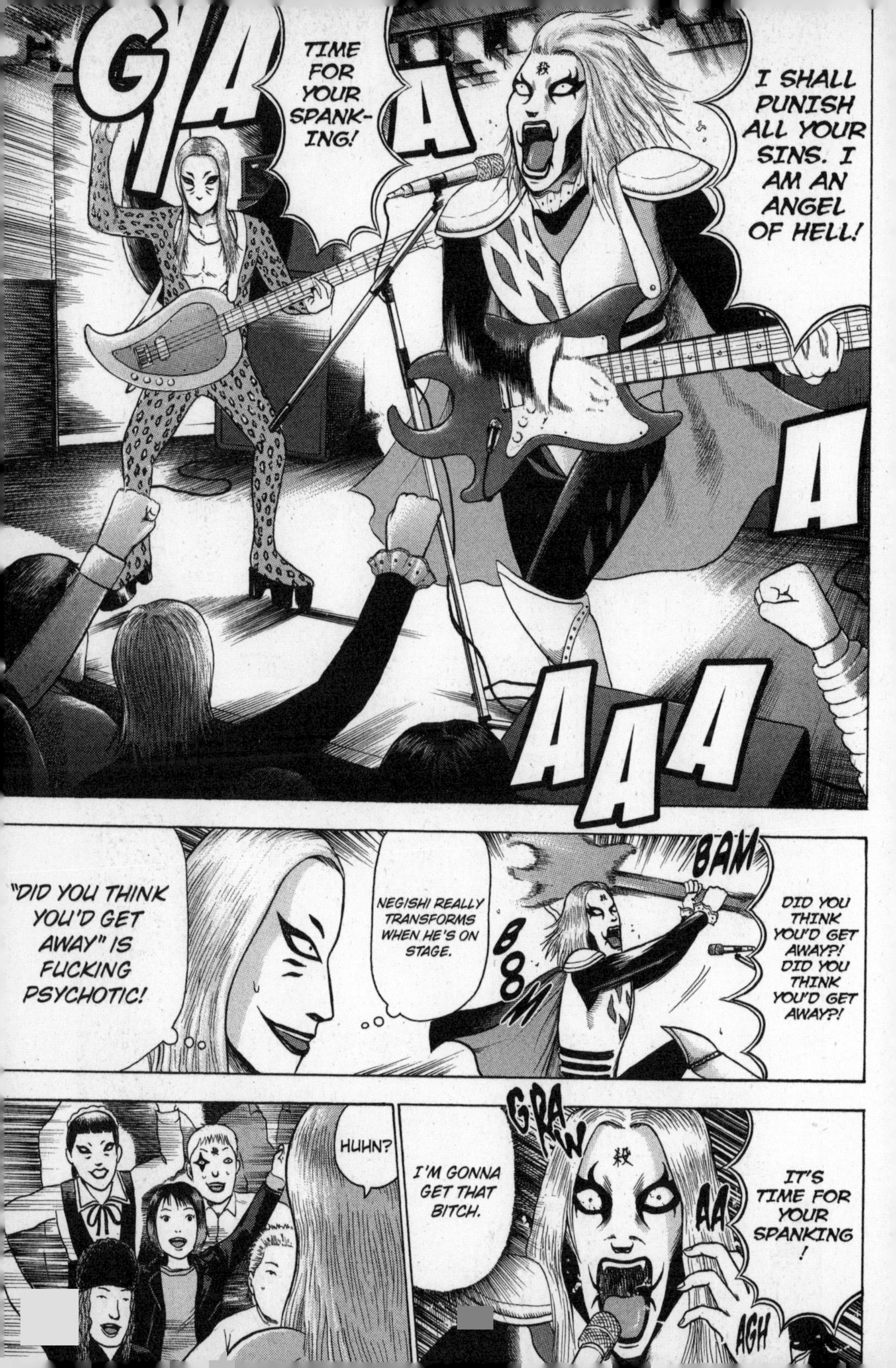
I SHALL PUNISH ALL YOUR SINS. I AM AN ANGEL OF HELL!
TIME FOR YOUR SPANK-ING!
GYA
A
A
A
AAA
BAM
BOOM
DID YOU THINK YOU'D GET AWAY?! DID YOU THINK YOU'D GET AWAY?!
NEGISHI REALLY TRANSFORMS WHEN HE'S ON STAGE.
"DID YOU THINK YOU'D GET AWAY" IS FUCKING PSYCHOTIC!
GRAW
AA
IT'S TIME FOR YOUR SPANKING!
AGH
HUHN?
I'M GONNA GET THAT BITCH.

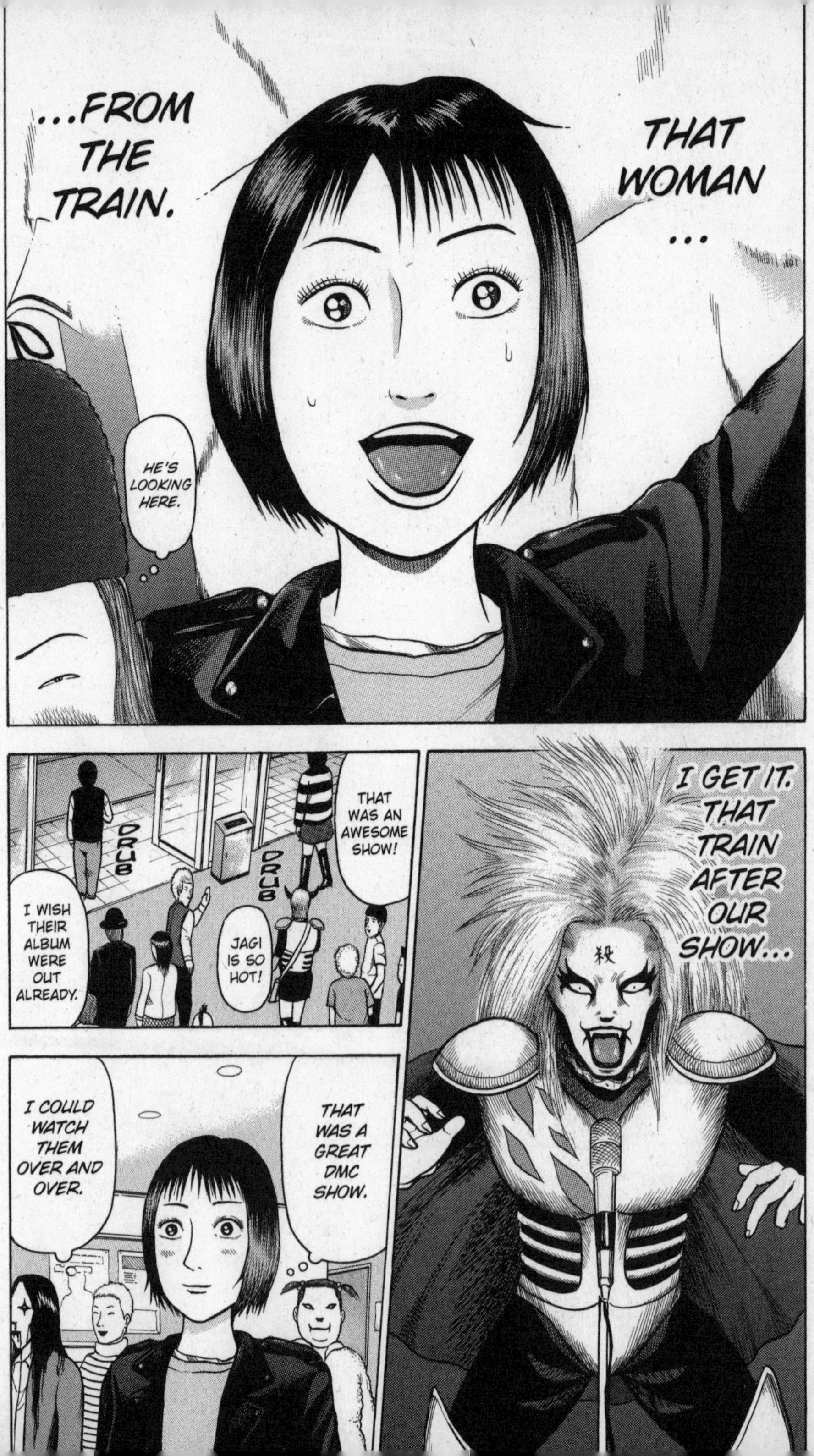
THAT WOMAN ...
...FROM THE TRAIN.
HE'S LOOKING HERE.
I GET IT. THAT TRAIN AFTER OUR SHOW...
THAT WAS AN AWESOME SHOW!
DRUB
DRUB
JAGI IS SO HOT!
I WISH THEIR ALBUM WERE OUT ALREADY.
THAT WAS A GREAT DMC SHOW.
I COULD WATCH THEM OVER AND OVER.

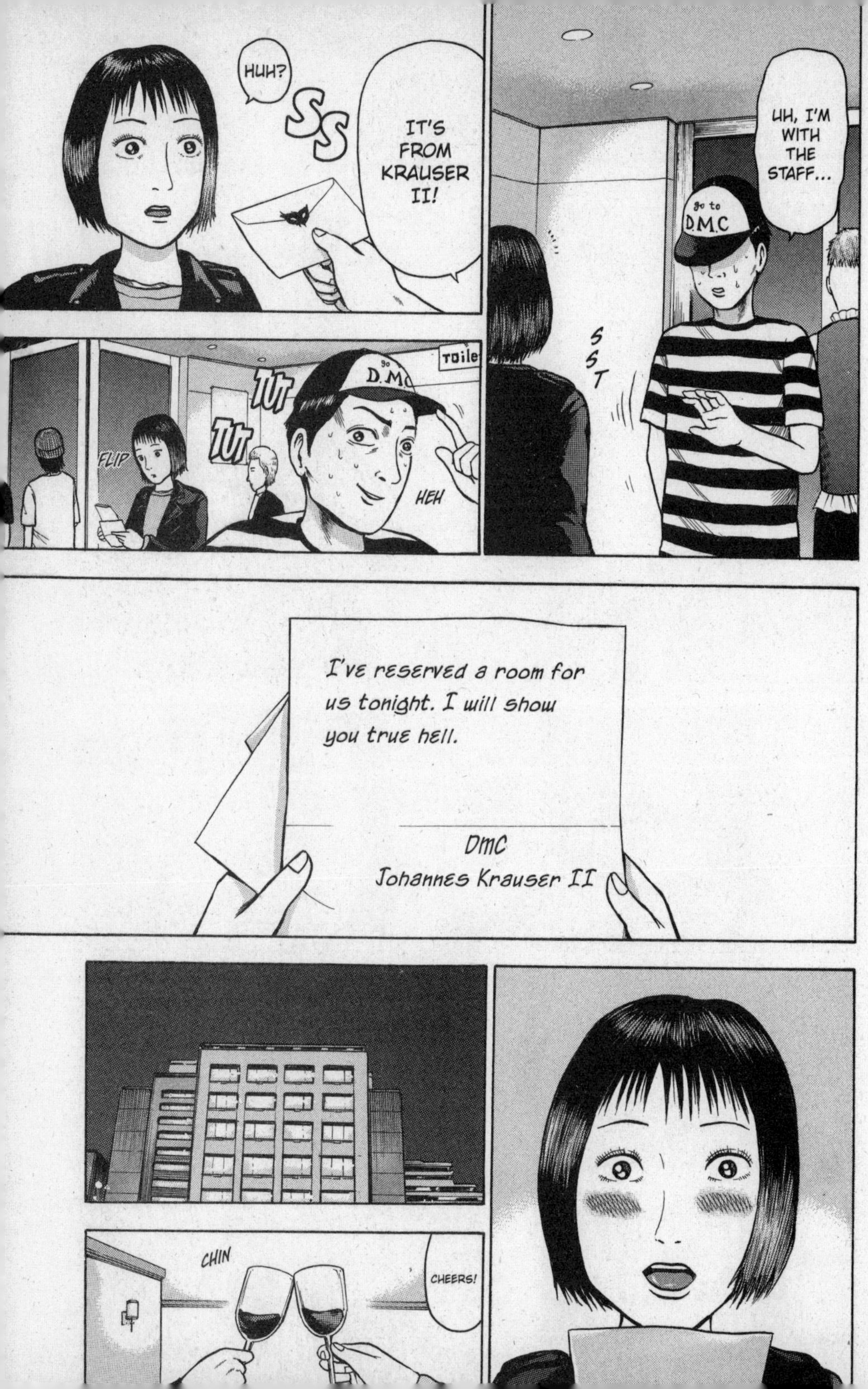
UH, I'M WITH THE STAFF...
go to D.M.C
SST
IT'S FROM KRAUSER II!
SS
HUH?
Toile
TUT
TUT
D.MC
HEH
FLIP
I've reserved a room for us tonight. I will show you true hell.
DMC
Johannes Krauser II
CHEERS!
CHIN

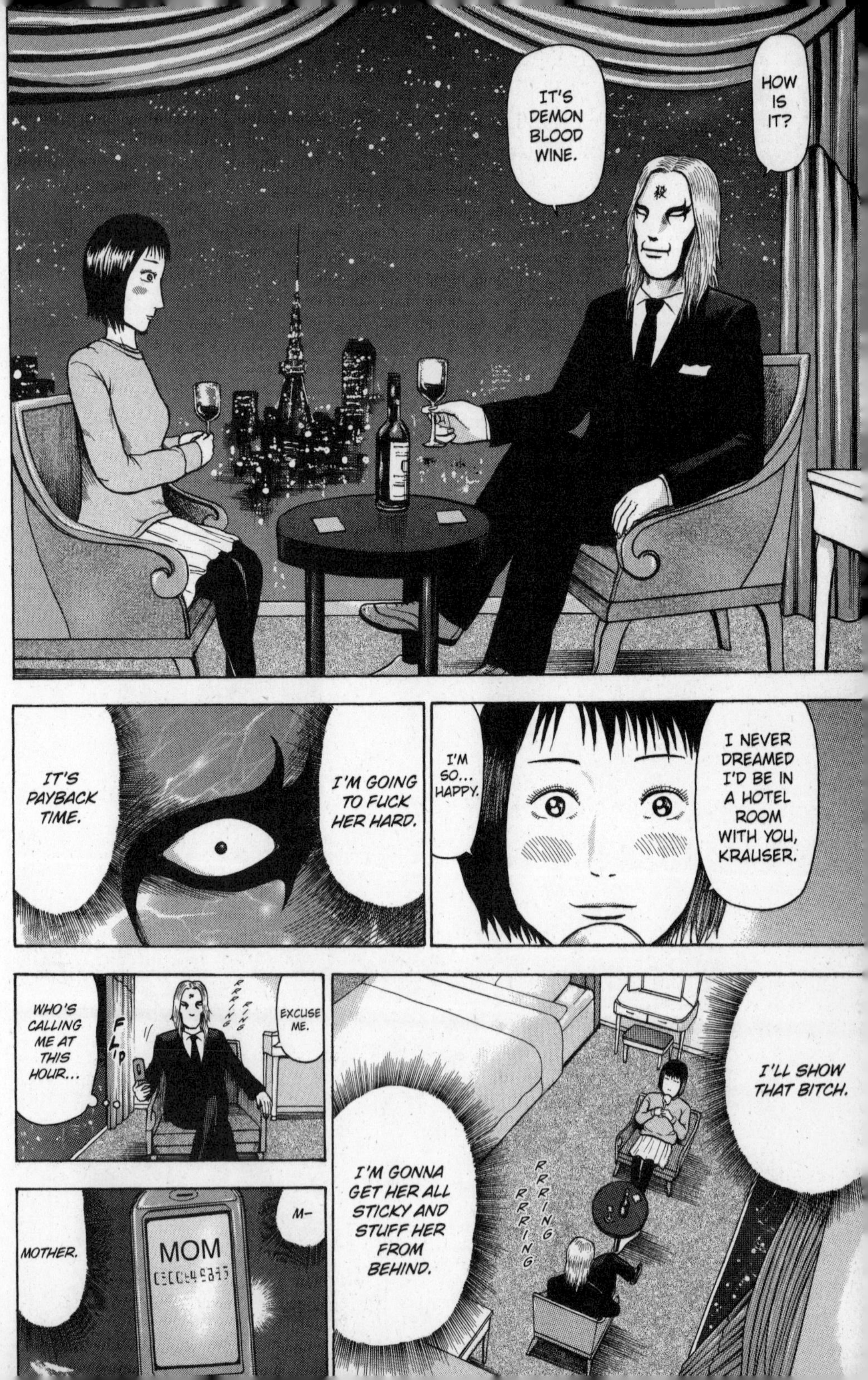
HOW IS IT?
IT'S DEMON BLOOD WINE.
I NEVER DREAMED I'D BE IN A HOTEL ROOM WITH YOU, KRAUSER.
I'M SO... HAPPY.
I'M GOING TO FUCK HER HARD.
IT'S PAYBACK TIME.
I'LL SHOW THAT BITCH.
RRRING
RRRING
I'M GONNA GET HER ALL STICKY AND STUFF HER FROM BEHIND.
EXCUSE ME.
RRRING RING
FLIP
WHO'S CALLING ME AT THIS HOUR...
M—
MOM
MOTHER.

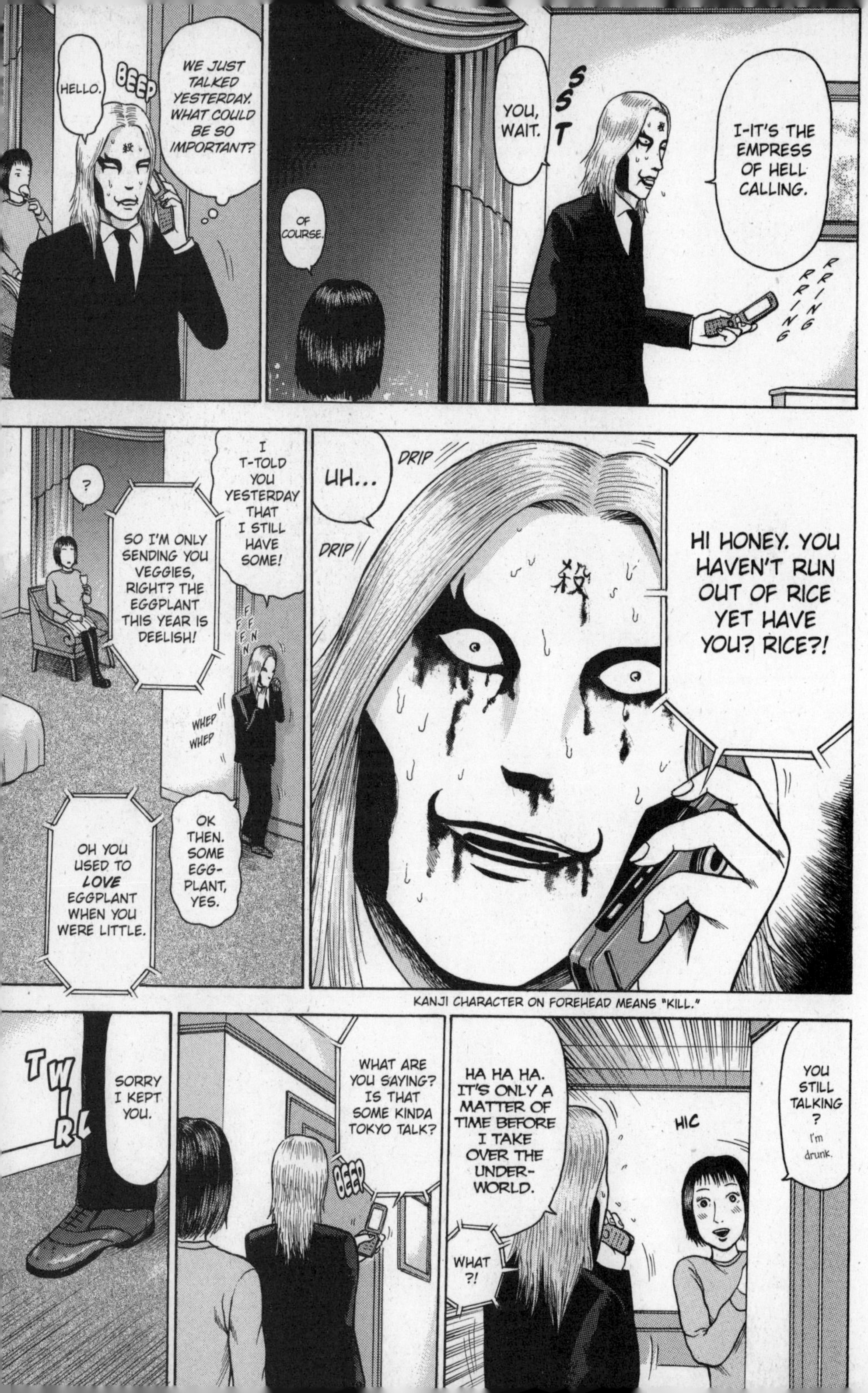
I-IT'S THE EMPRESS OF HELL CALLING.
RRING RRING
SST
YOU, WAIT.
OF COURSE.
BEEP
HELLO.
WE JUST TALKED YESTERDAY. WHAT COULD BE SO IMPORTANT?
HI HONEY. YOU HAVEN'T RUN OUT OF RICE YET HAVE YOU? RICE?!
UH...
DRIP
DRIP
I T-TOLD YOU YESTERDAY THAT I STILL HAVE SOME!
?
SO I'M ONLY SENDING YOU VEGGIES, RIGHT? THE EGGPLANT THIS YEAR IS DEELISH!
FFFN
WHEP WHEP
OK THEN. SOME EGG-PLANT, YES.
OH YOU USED TO LOVE EGGPLANT WHEN YOU WERE LITTLE.
KANJI CHARACTER ON FOREHEAD MEANS "KILL."
YOU STILL TALKING ?
I'm drunk.
HIC
HA HA HA. IT'S ONLY A MATTER OF TIME BEFORE I TAKE OVER THE UNDER-WORLD.
WHAT ?!
WHAT ARE YOU SAYING? IS THAT SOME KINDA TOKYO TALK?
BEEP
SORRY I KEPT YOU.
TWIRL

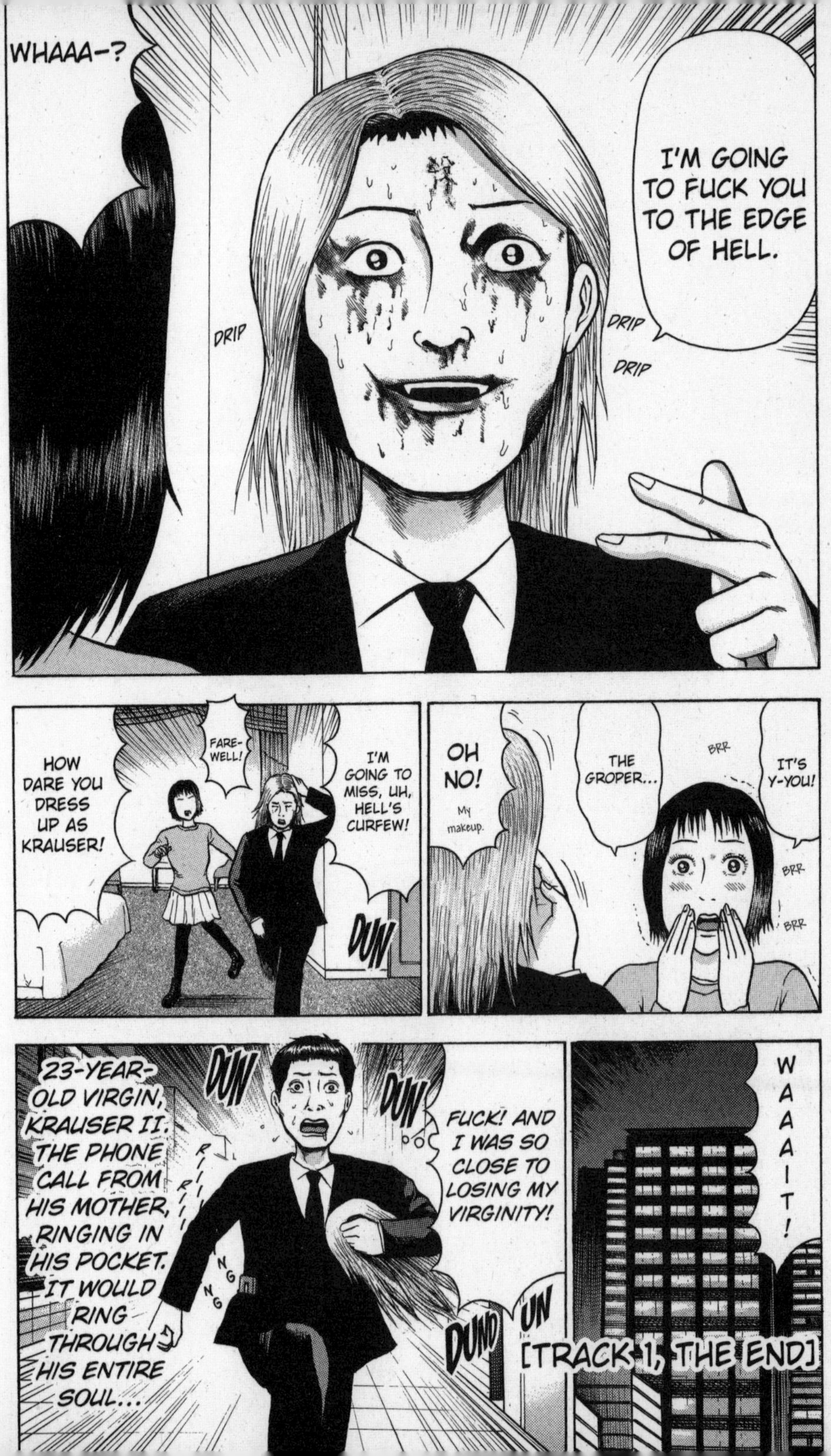
I'M GOING TO FUCK YOU TO THE EDGE OF HELL.
DRIP
DRIP
WHAAA-?
DRIP
IT'S Y-YOU!
BRR
THE GROPER...
OH NO!
My makeup.
BRR
BRR
I'M GOING TO MISS, UH, HELL'S CURFEW!
FAREWELL!
HOW DARE YOU DRESS UP AS KRAUSER!
DUN
WAAAAIT!
[TRACK 1, THE END]
FUCK! AND I WAS SO CLOSE TO LOSING MY VIRGINITY!
DUN
DUN
23-YEAR-OLD VIRGIN, KRAUSER II. THE PHONE CALL FROM HIS MOTHER, RINGING IN HIS POCKET. IT WOULD RING THROUGH HIS ENTIRE SOUL...
RIIII
NG NG
DUNDUN

DMC LEXICON

GOBO

A word used to signify a diminutive man. Gobo originally refers to an edible root of the Chrysanthemum genus. Because it is so thin, the term is also used to refer to skinny men. Spelled out in Chinese characters it reads "Bovine Weed," giving it a wild nuance.

Usage: Jenny, your man's such a gobo!

デトロイト・メタル・シティ

Detroit Metal City

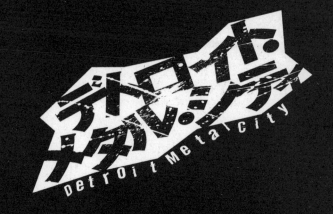

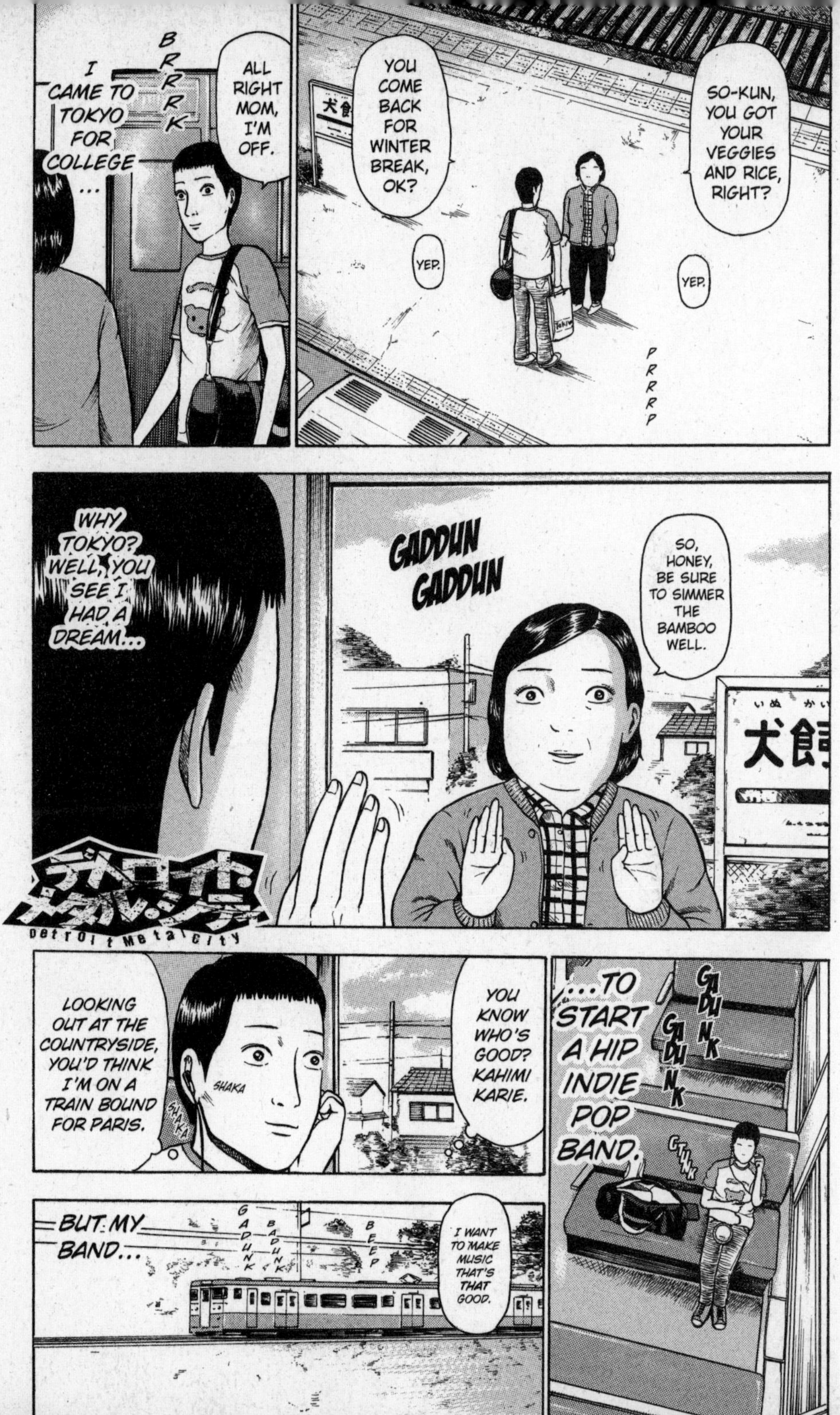
SO-KUN, YOU GOT YOUR VEGGIES AND RICE, RIGHT?
YEP.
YOU COME BACK FOR WINTER BREAK, OK?
YEP.
PRRRP
ALL RIGHT MOM, I'M OFF.
BRRRK
I CAME TO TOKYO FOR COLLEGE...
SO, HONEY, BE SURE TO SIMMER THE BAMBOO WELL.
GADDUN GADDUN
WHY TOKYO? WELL, YOU SEE I HAD A DREAM...
Detroit Metal City
...TO START A HIP INDIE POP BAND.
GADUNK
GADUNK
GTUNK
YOU KNOW WHO'S GOOD? KAHIMI KARIE.
LOOKING OUT AT THE COUNTRYSIDE, YOU'D THINK I'M ON A TRAIN BOUND FOR PARIS.
SHAKA
SHAKA
I WANT TO MAKE MUSIC THAT'S THAT GOOD.
BEEP
BADUNK
GADUNK
BUT MY BAND...

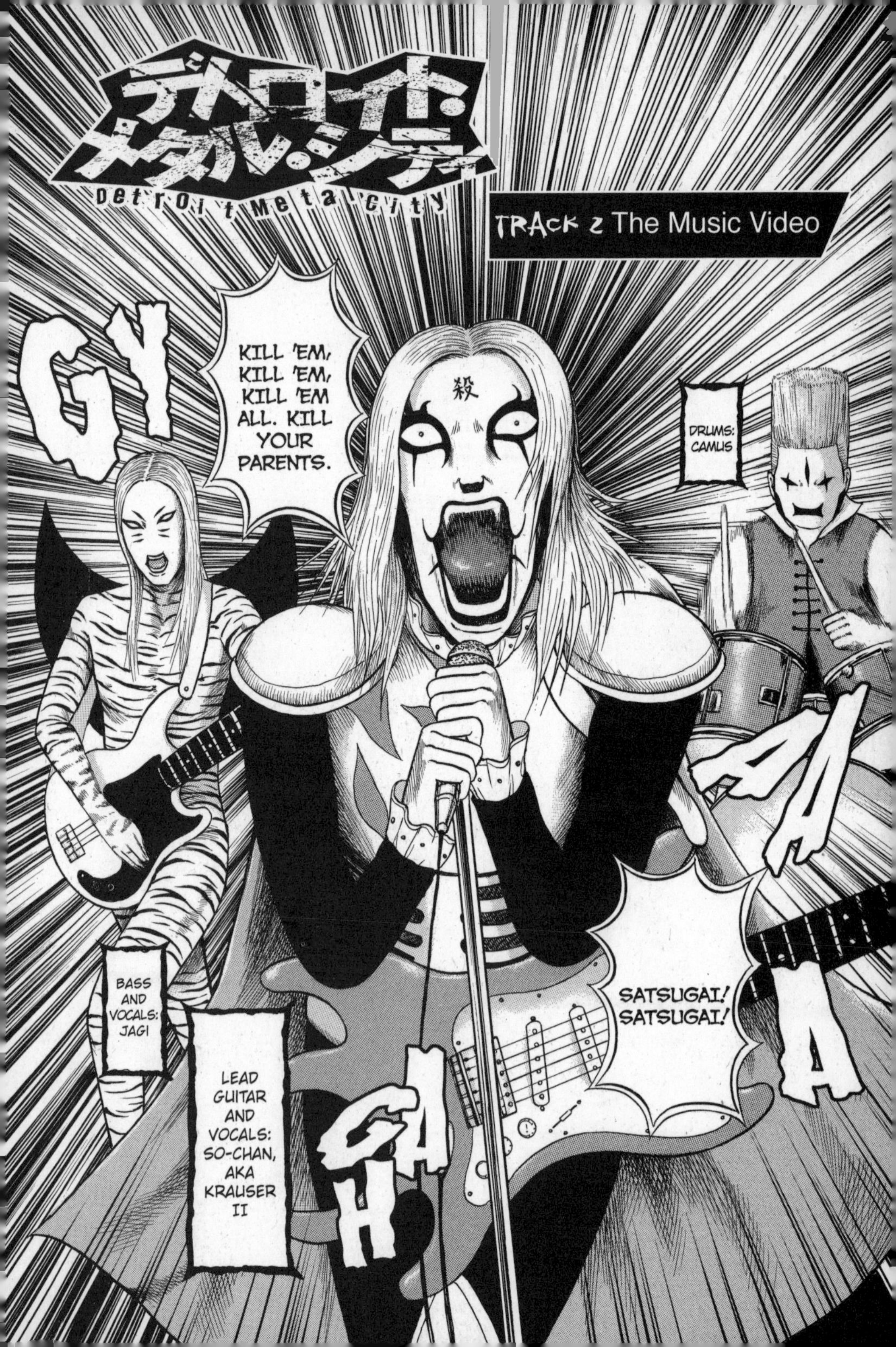
TRACK 2 The Music Video
デトロイト・メタル・シティ
DETROIT METAL CITY
DRUMS: CAMUS
KILL 'EM, KILL 'EM, KILL 'EM ALL. KILL YOUR PARENTS.
GY
AA
A
SATSUGAI! SATSUGAI!
BASS AND VOCALS: JAGI
LEAD GUITAR AND VOCALS: SO-CHAN, AKA KRAUSER II
GAH

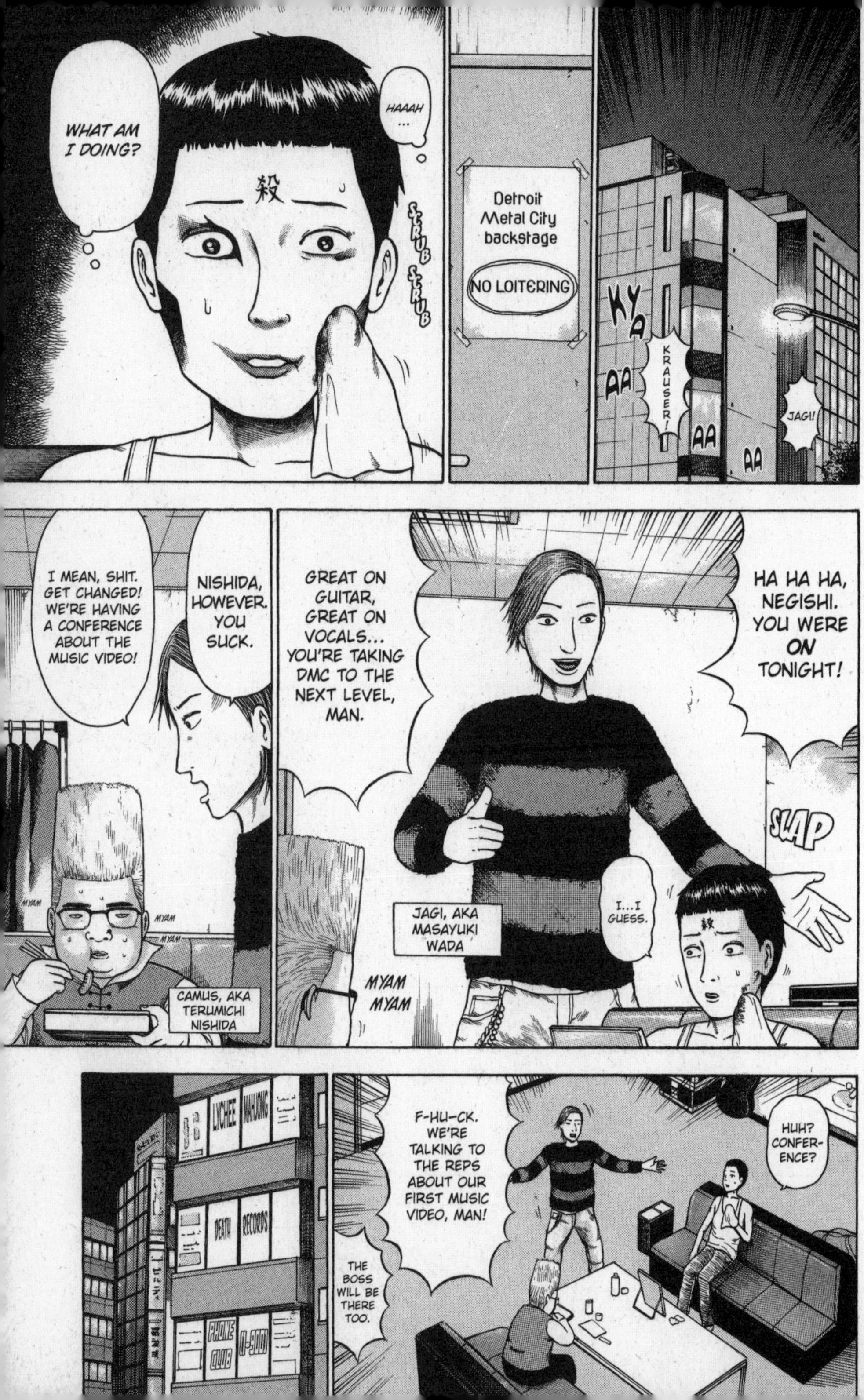
KYAA
AA
AA
AA
KRAUSER!
JAGI!
Detroit Metal City backstage
NO LOITERING
HAAAH...
SCRUB SCRUB
WHAT AM I DOING?
HA HA HA, NEGISHI. YOU WERE ON TONIGHT!
SLAP
GREAT ON GUITAR, GREAT ON VOCALS... YOU'RE TAKING DMC TO THE NEXT LEVEL, MAN.
I...I GUESS.
JAGI, AKA MASAYUKI WADA
MYAM MYAM
NISHIDA, HOWEVER. YOU SUCK.
I MEAN, SHIT. GET CHANGED! WE'RE HAVING A CONFERENCE ABOUT THE MUSIC VIDEO!
MYAM
MYAM
MYAM
CAMUS, AKA TERUMICHI NISHIDA
HUH? CONFERENCE?
F-HU-CK. WE'RE TALKING TO THE REPS ABOUT OUR FIRST MUSIC VIDEO, MAN!
THE BOSS WILL BE THERE TOO.
LYCHEE
MAHJONG
DEATH
RECORDS
PHONE CLUB

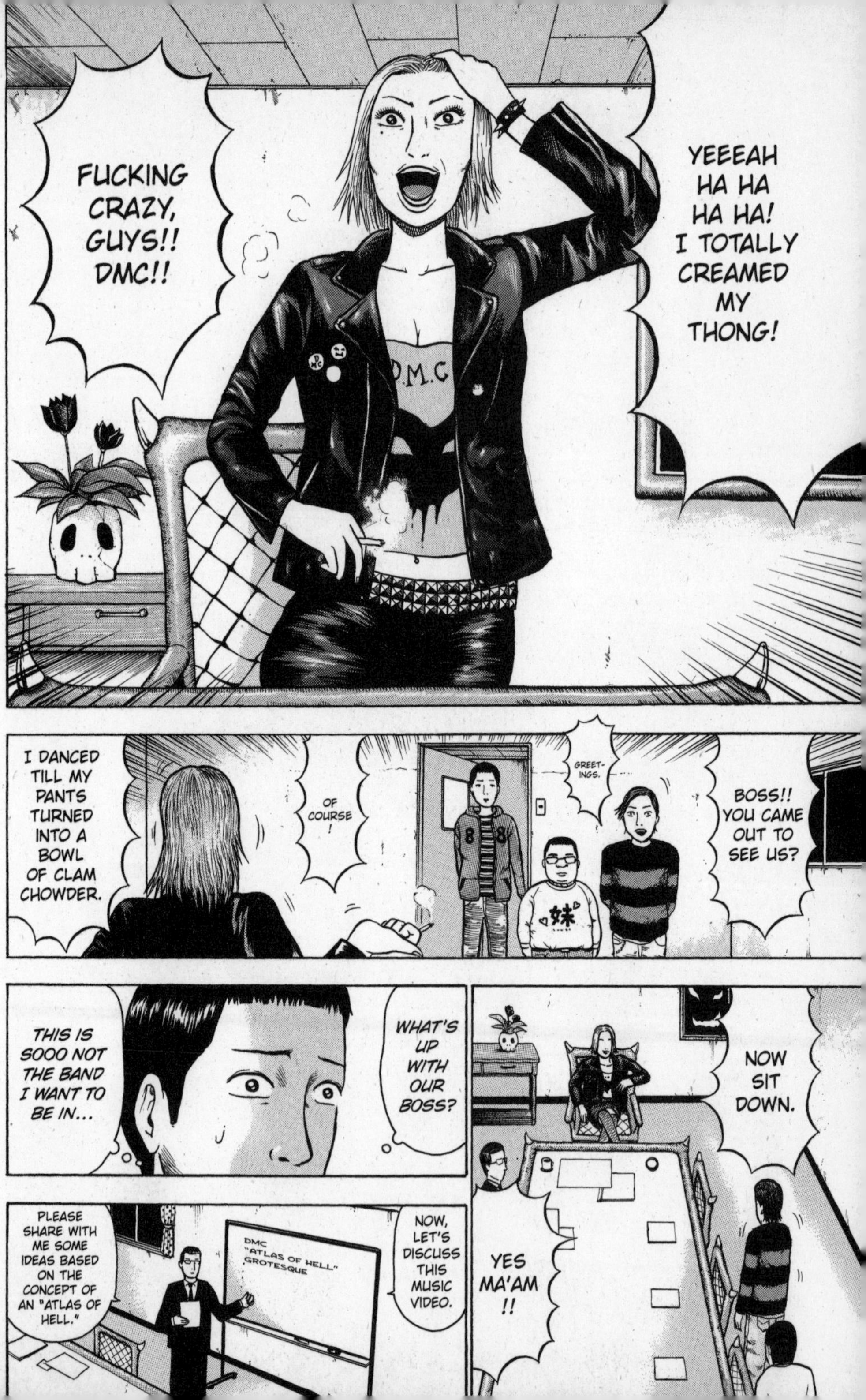
YEEEAH HA HA HA HA! I TOTALLY CREAMED MY THONG!
FUCKING CRAZY, GUYS!! DMC!!
BOSS!! YOU CAME OUT TO SEE US?
GREET-INGS.
OF COURSE!
I DANCED TILL MY PANTS TURNED INTO A BOWL OF CLAM CHOWDER.
NOW SIT DOWN.
YES MA'AM!!
WHAT'S UP WITH OUR BOSS?
THIS IS SOOO NOT THE BAND I WANT TO BE IN...
NOW, LET'S DISCUSS THIS MUSIC VIDEO.
DMC "ATLAS OF HELL" GROTESQUE
PLEASE SHARE WITH ME SOME IDEAS BASED ON THE CONCEPT OF AN "ATLAS OF HELL."

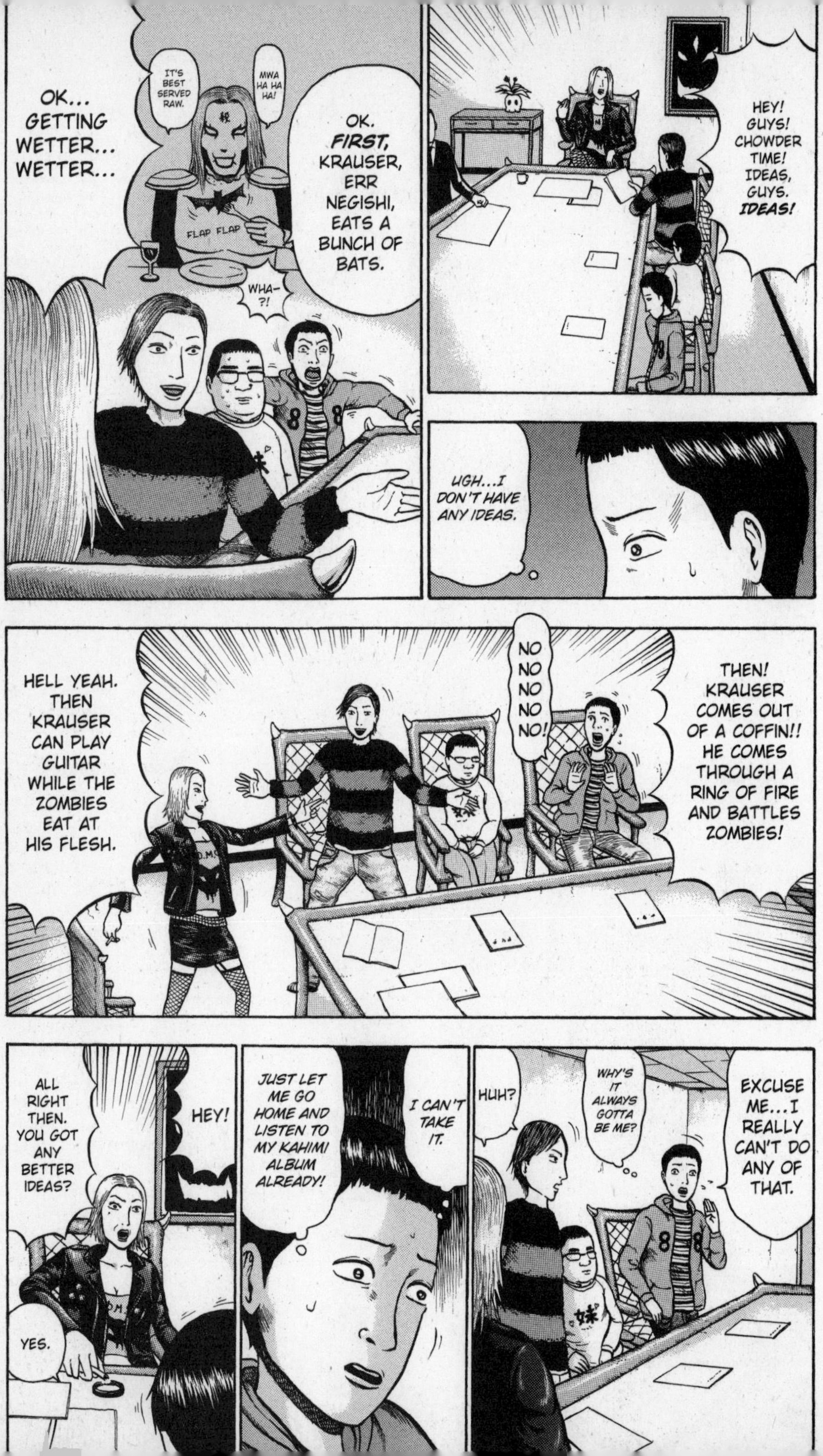
HEY! GUYS! CHOWDER TIME! IDEAS, GUYS. IDEAS!
UGH...I DON'T HAVE ANY IDEAS.
OK. FIRST, KRAUSER, ERR NEGISHI, EATS A BUNCH OF BATS.
MWA HA HA HA!
IT'S BEST SERVED RAW.
FLAP FLAP
OK... GETTING WETTER... WETTER...
WHA-?!
THEN! KRAUSER COMES OUT OF A COFFIN!! HE COMES THROUGH A RING OF FIRE AND BATTLES ZOMBIES!
NO NO NO NO NO!
HELL YEAH. THEN KRAUSER CAN PLAY GUITAR WHILE THE ZOMBIES EAT AT HIS FLESH.
EXCUSE ME...I REALLY CAN'T DO ANY OF THAT.
WHY'S IT ALWAYS GOTTA BE ME?
HUH?
I CAN'T TAKE IT.
JUST LET ME GO HOME AND LISTEN TO MY KAHIMI ALBUM ALREADY!
HEY!
ALL RIGHT THEN. YOU GOT ANY BETTER IDEAS?
YES.

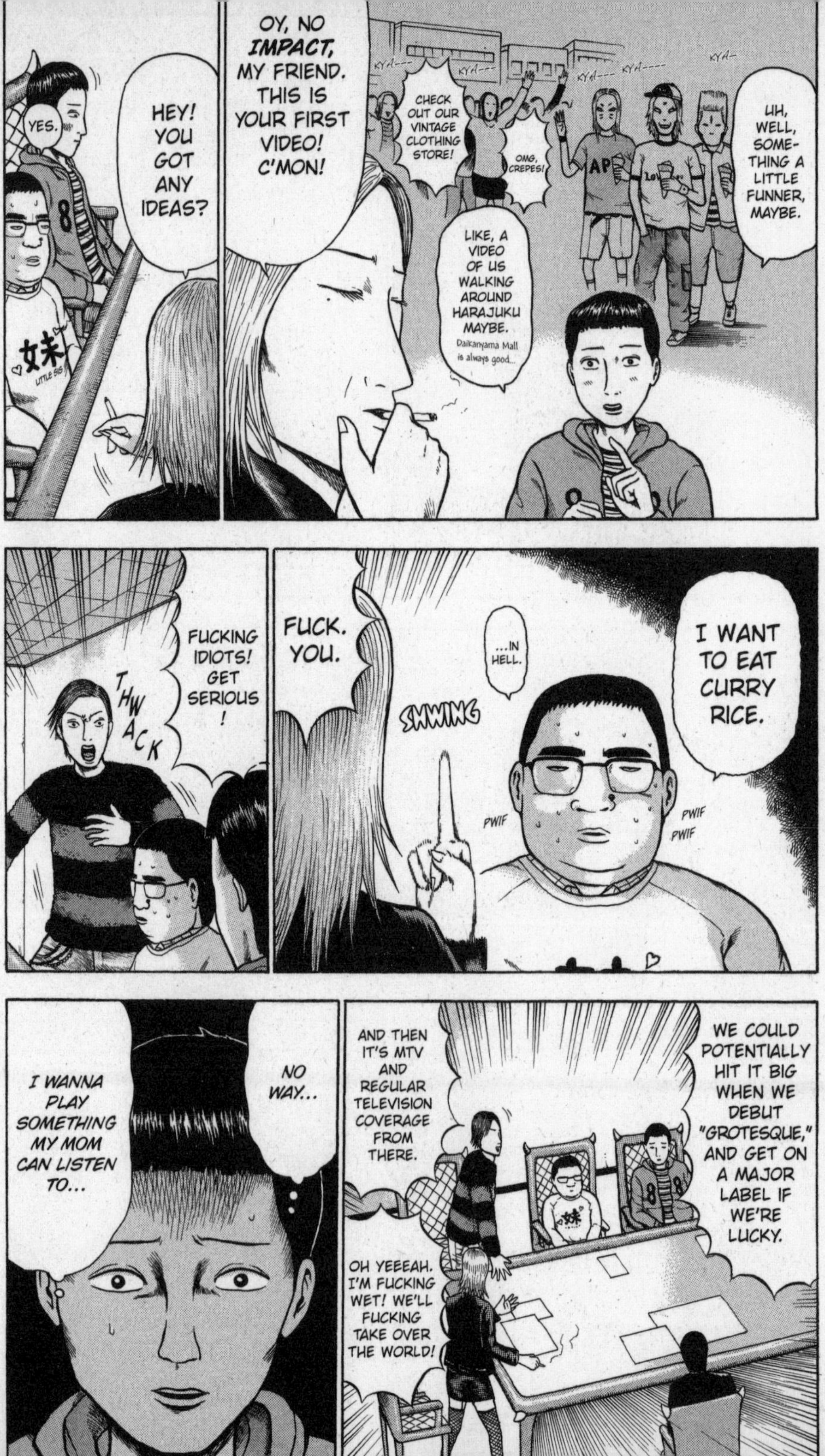

UH, WELL, SOME- THING A LITTLE FUNNER, MAYBE.
KYA— KYA—— KYA—— KYA—— KYA——
CHECK OUT OUR VINTAGE CLOTHING STORE!
OMG, CREPES!
OY, NO *IMPACT,* MY FRIEND. THIS IS YOUR FIRST VIDEO! C'MON!
LIKE, A VIDEO OF US WALKING AROUND HARAJUKU MAYBE.
Daikanyama Mall is always good...
HEY! YOU GOT ANY IDEAS?
YES.
I WANT TO EAT CURRY RICE.
PWIF PWIF PWIF
...IN HELL.
SHWING
FUCK. YOU.
FUCKING IDIOTS! GET SERIOUS!
THWACK
WE COULD POTENTIALLY HIT IT BIG WHEN WE DEBUT "GROTESQUE," AND GET ON A MAJOR LABEL IF WE'RE LUCKY.
AND THEN IT'S MTV AND REGULAR TELEVISION COVERAGE FROM THERE.
OH YEEEAH. I'M FUCKING WET! WE'LL FUCKING TAKE OVER THE WORLD!
NO WAY...
I WANNA PLAY SOMETHING MY MOM CAN LISTEN TO...

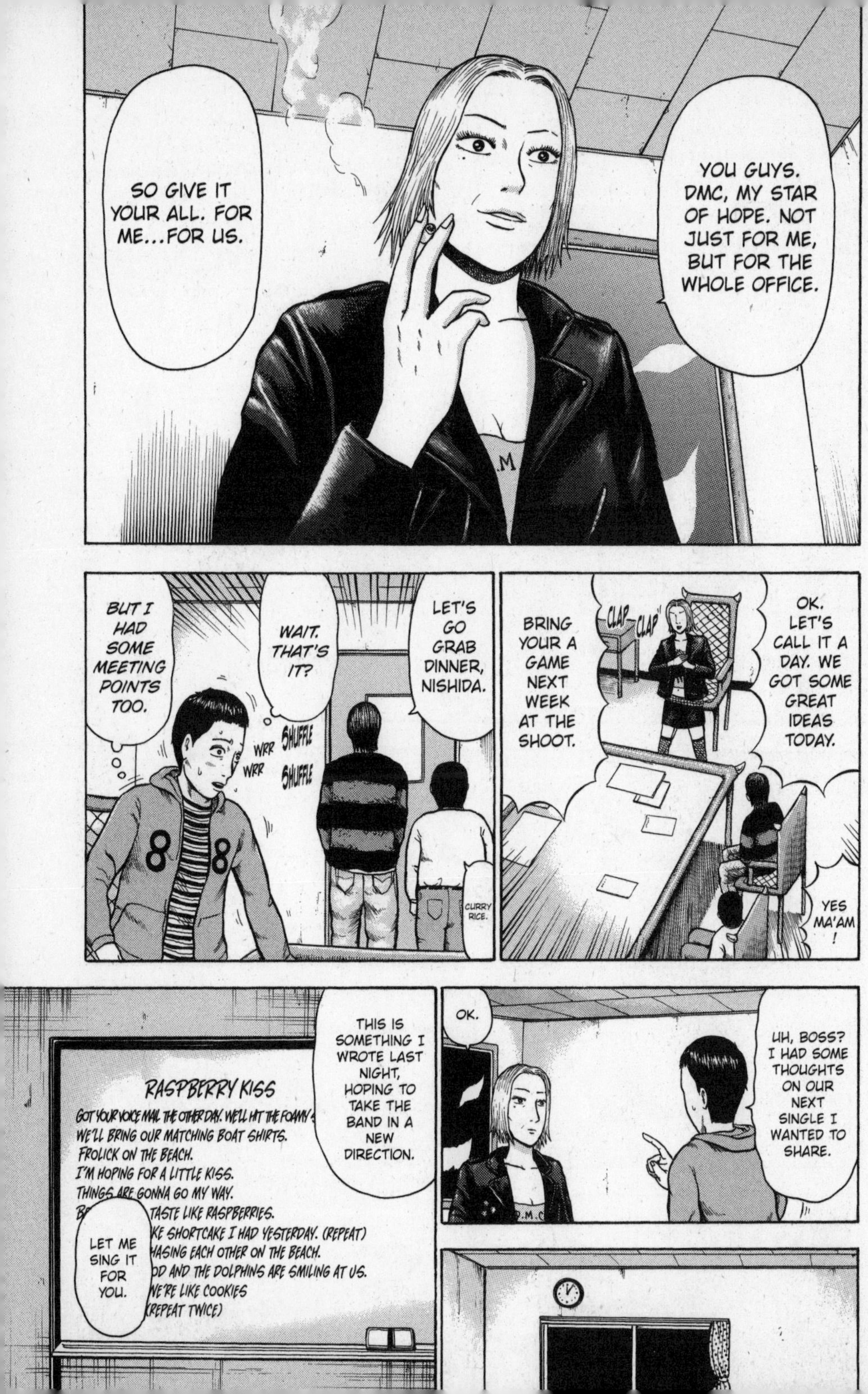

YOU GUYS. DMC, MY STAR OF HOPE. NOT JUST FOR ME, BUT FOR THE WHOLE OFFICE.
SO GIVE IT YOUR ALL. FOR ME...FOR US.
OK. LET'S CALL IT A DAY. WE GOT SOME GREAT IDEAS TODAY.
CLAP CLAP
BRING YOUR A GAME NEXT WEEK AT THE SHOOT.
YES MA'AM!
LET'S GO GRAB DINNER, NISHIDA.
CURRY RICE.
WAIT. THAT'S IT?
SHUFFLE SHUFFLE
WRR WRR
BUT I HAD SOME MEETING POINTS TOO.
UH, BOSS? I HAD SOME THOUGHTS ON OUR NEXT SINGLE I WANTED TO SHARE.
OK.
THIS IS SOMETHING I WROTE LAST NIGHT, HOPING TO TAKE THE BAND IN A NEW DIRECTION.
RASPBERRY KISS
GOT YOUR VOICE MAIL THE OTHER DAY. WE'LL HIT THE FOAMY
WE'LL BRING OUR MATCHING BOAT SHIRTS.
FROLICK ON THE BEACH.
I'M HOPING FOR A LITTLE KISS.
THINGS ARE GONNA GO MY WAY.
TASTE LIKE RASPBERRIES.
KE SHORTCAKE I HAD YESTERDAY. (REPEAT)
HASING EACH OTHER ON THE BEACH.
OD AND THE DOLPHINS ARE SMILING AT US.
WE'RE LIKE COOKIES
(REPEAT TWICE)
LET ME SING IT FOR YOU.

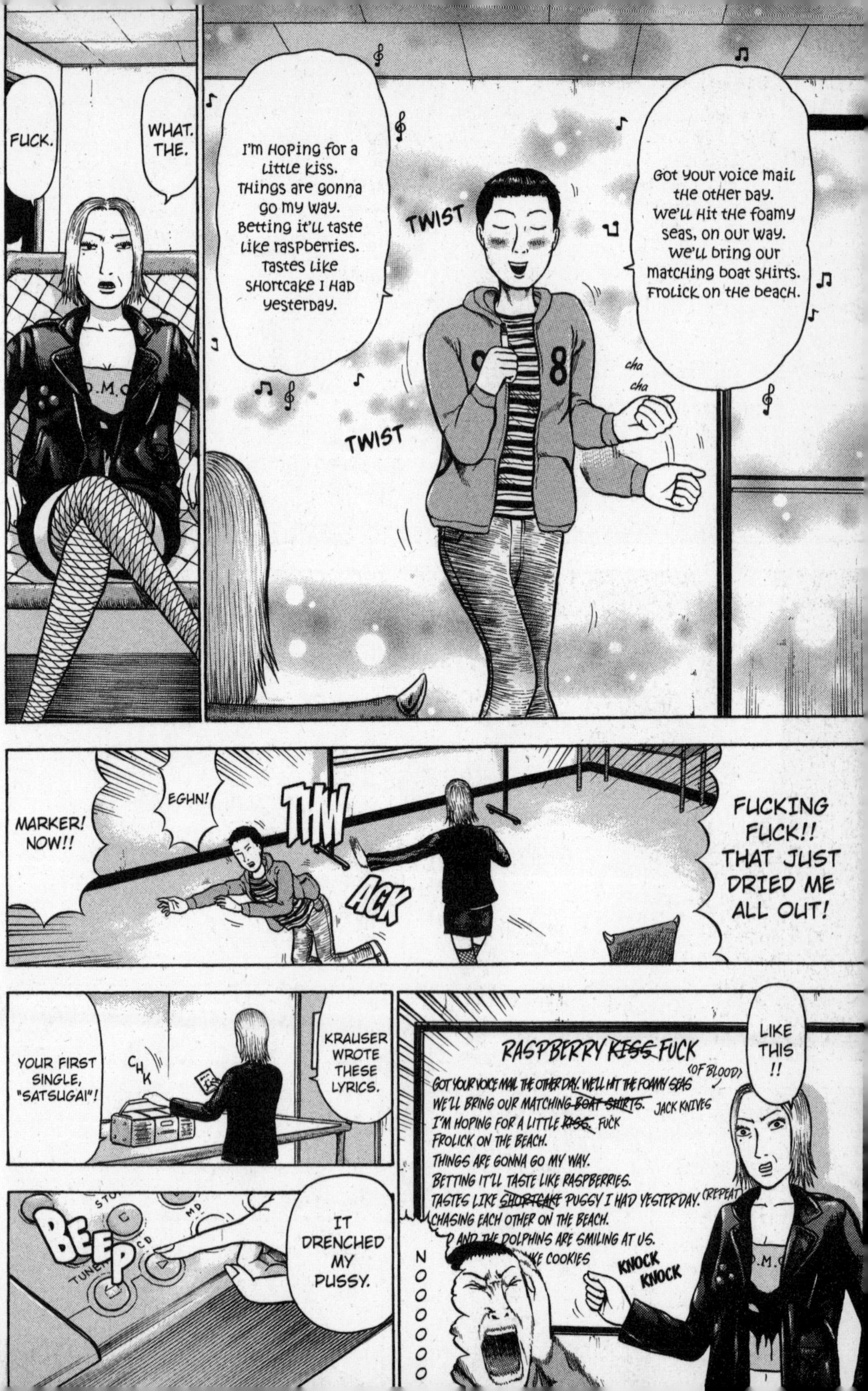

Got your voice mail the other day. We'll hit the foamy seas, on our way. We'll bring our matching boat shirts. Frolick on the beach.
I'm hoping for a little kiss. Things are gonna go my way. Betting it'll taste like raspberries. Tastes like shortcake I had yesterday.
TWIST
cha cha
TWIST
WHAT. THE.
FUCK.
FUCKING FUCK!! THAT JUST DRIED ME ALL OUT!
THW
ACK
EGHN!
MARKER! NOW!!
LIKE THIS !!
RASPBERRY ~~KISS~~ FUCK
(OF BLOOD)
GOT YOUR VOICE MAIL THE OTHER DAY. WE'LL HIT THE FOAMY SEAS
WE'LL BRING OUR MATCHING ~~BOAT SHIRTS.~~ JACK KNIVES
I'M HOPING FOR A LITTLE ~~KISS.~~ FUCK
FROLICK ON THE BEACH.
THINGS ARE GONNA GO MY WAY.
BETTING IT'LL TASTE LIKE RASPBERRIES.
TASTES LIKE ~~SHORTCAKE~~ PUSSY I HAD YESTERDAY. (REPEAT
CHASING EACH OTHER ON THE BEACH.
KNOCK KNOCK
NOOOOOOO
KRAUSER WROTE THESE LYRICS.
CHK
YOUR FIRST SINGLE, "SATSUGAI"!
IT DRENCHED MY PUSSY.
MD
CD
BEEP

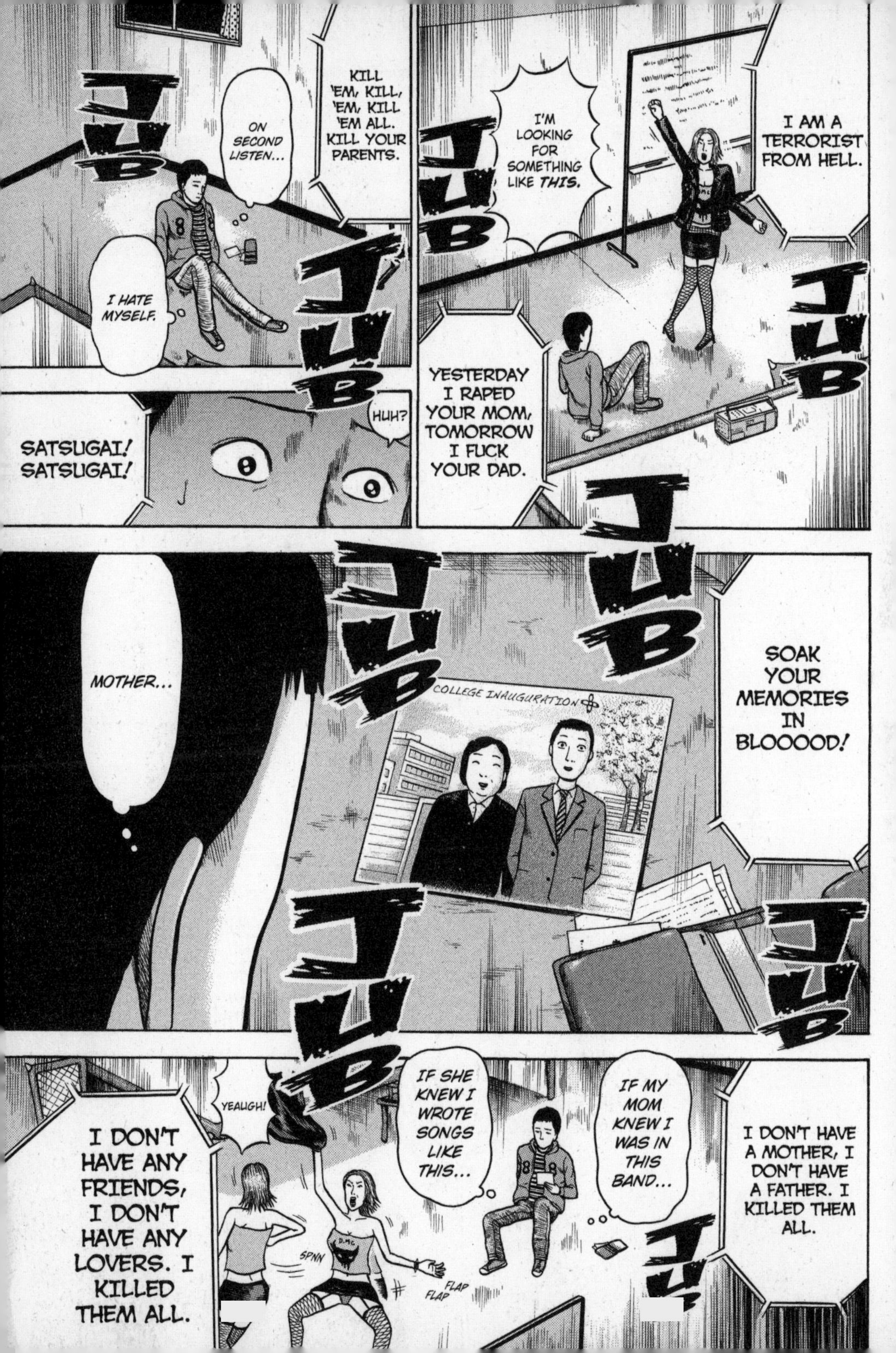
I AM A TERRORIST FROM HELL.
JUB
I'M LOOKING FOR SOMETHING LIKE THIS.
JUB
JUB
YESTERDAY I RAPED YOUR MOM, TOMORROW I FUCK YOUR DAD.
KILL 'EM, KILL 'EM, KILL 'EM ALL. KILL YOUR PARENTS.
ON SECOND LISTEN...
JUB
I HATE MYSELF.
JUB
HUH?
SATSUGAI! SATSUGAI!
JUB
SOAK YOUR MEMORIES IN BLOOOOD!
JUB
COLLEGE INAUGURATION
MOTHER...
JUB
JUB
I DON'T HAVE A MOTHER, I DON'T HAVE A FATHER. I KILLED THEM ALL.
IF MY MOM KNEW I WAS IN THIS BAND...
IF SHE KNEW I WROTE SONGS LIKE THIS...
YEAUGH!
FLAP FLAP
SPNN
I DON'T HAVE ANY FRIENDS, I DON'T HAVE ANY LOVERS. I KILLED THEM ALL.

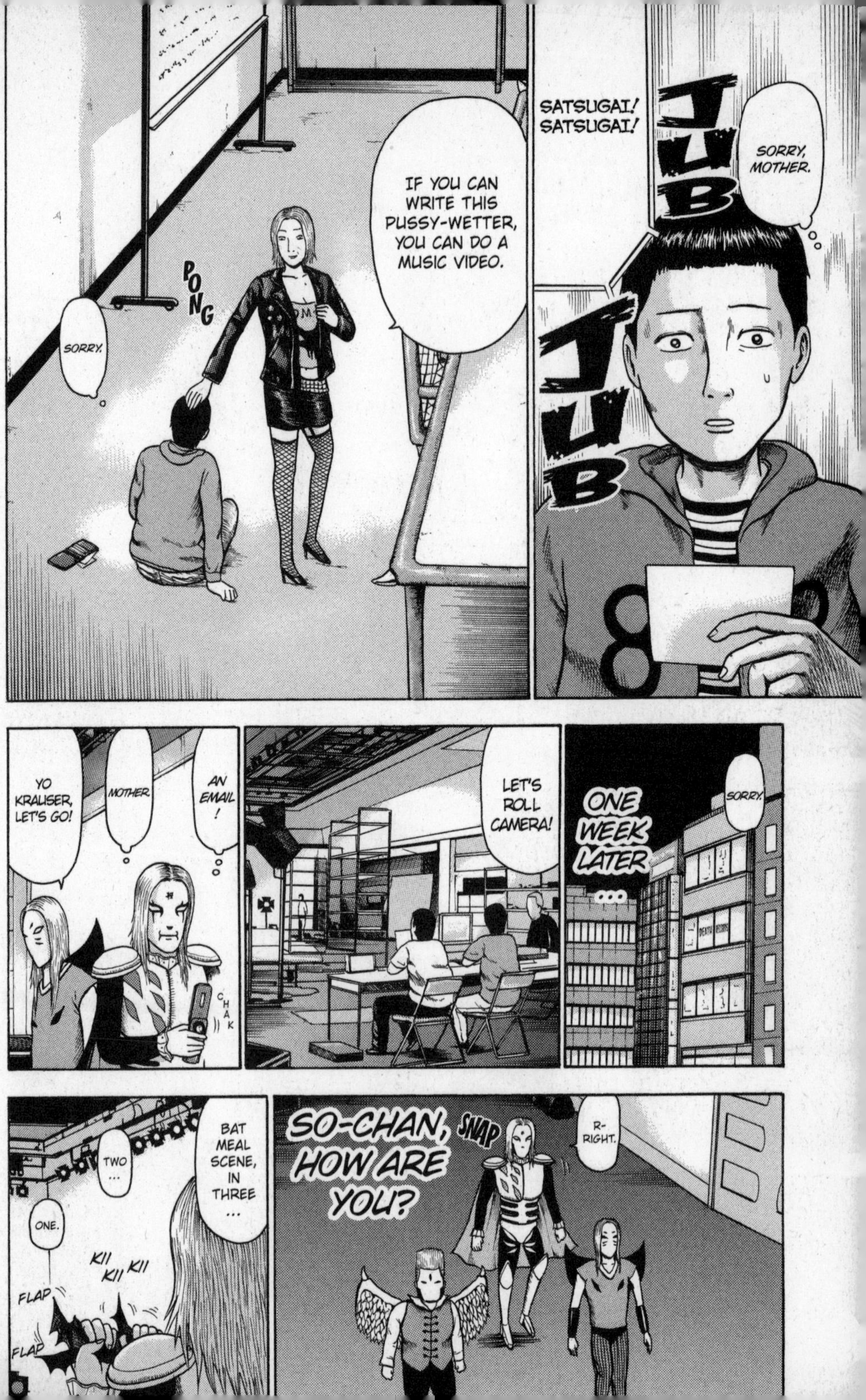
SATSUGAI! SATSUGAI!
SORRY, MOTHER.
JUB JUB
IF YOU CAN WRITE THIS PUSSY-WETTER, YOU CAN DO A MUSIC VIDEO.
PONG
SORRY.
SORRY.
ONE WEEK LATER...
LET'S ROLL CAMERA!
AN EMAIL!
MOTHER.
YO KRAUSER, LET'S GO!
CHAK
R-RIGHT.
SNAP
SO-CHAN, HOW ARE YOU?
BAT MEAL SCENE, IN THREE...
TWO...
ONE.
KII KII KII
FLAP
FLAP

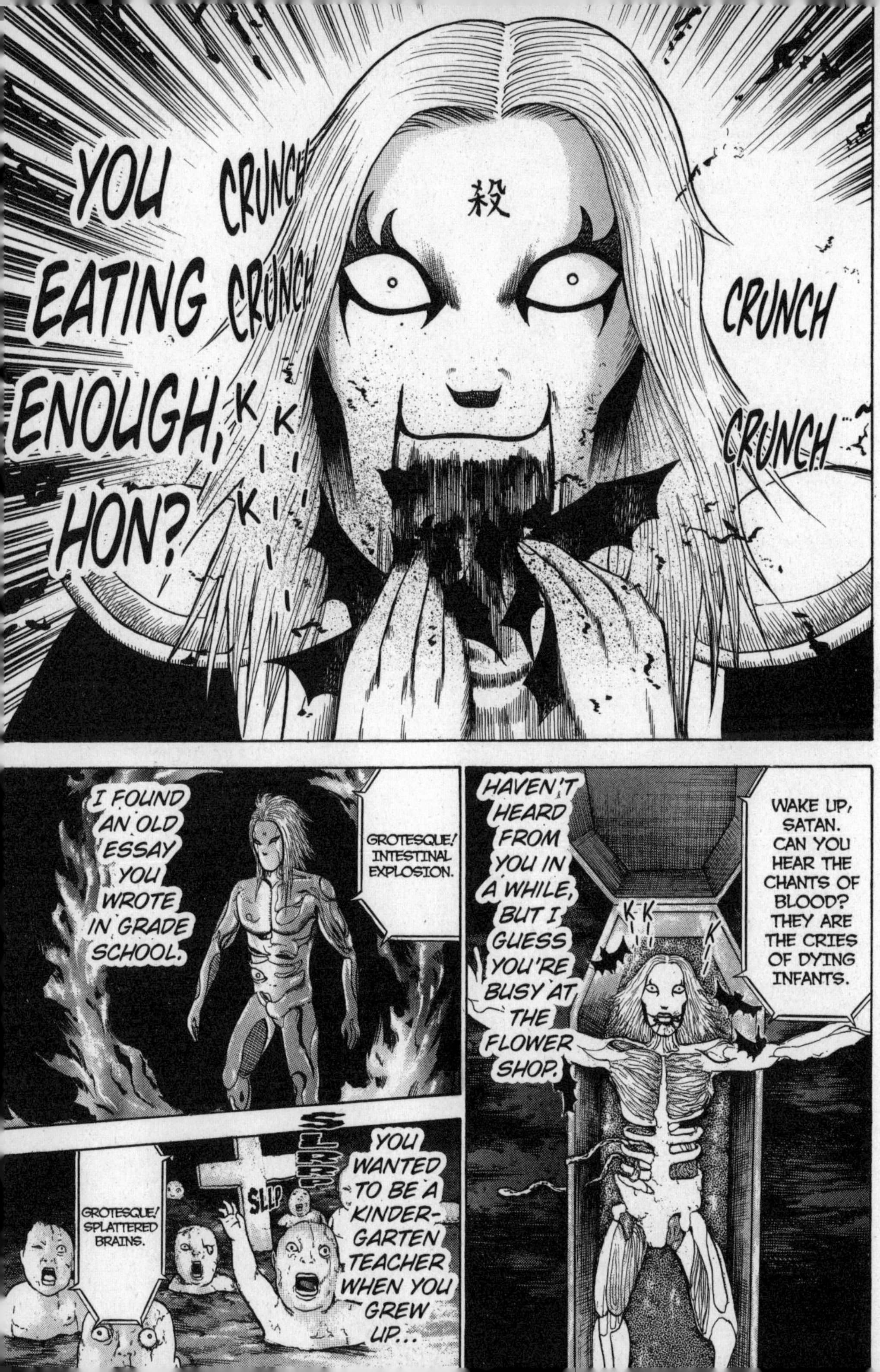
CRUNCH
CRUNCH
殺
CRUNCH
CRUNCH
K K K
YOU EATING ENOUGH, HON?
WAKE UP, SATAN. CAN YOU HEAR THE CHANTS OF BLOOD? THEY ARE THE CRIES OF DYING INFANTS.
HAVEN'T HEARD FROM YOU IN A WHILE, BUT I GUESS YOU'RE BUSY AT THE FLOWER SHOP.
K K K
GROTESQUE! INTESTINAL EXPLOSION.
I FOUND AN OLD ESSAY YOU WROTE IN GRADE SCHOOL.
SLRRP
YOU WANTED TO BE A KINDER-GARTEN TEACHER WHEN YOU GREW UP...
SLLP
GROTESQUE! SPLATTERED BRAINS.

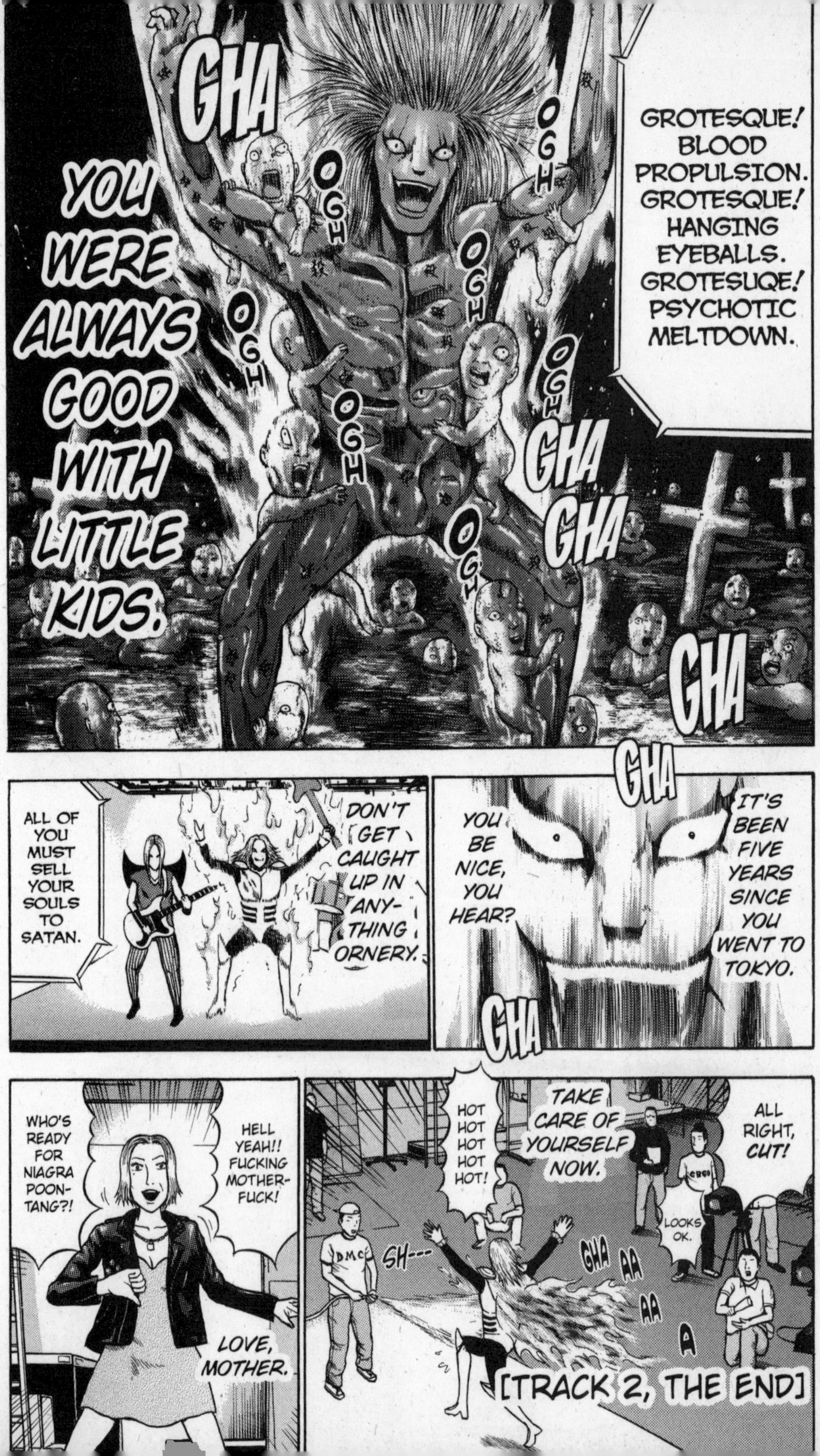
GROTESQUE! BLOOD PROPULSION. GROTESQUE! HANGING EYEBALLS. GROTESUQE! PSYCHOTIC MELTDOWN.
GHA
OGH
YOU WERE ALWAYS GOOD WITH LITTLE KIDS.
OGH
OGH
OGH
OGH
OGH
OGH
GHA
GHA
GHA
GHA
IT'S BEEN FIVE YEARS SINCE YOU WENT TO TOKYO.
YOU BE NICE, YOU HEAR?
GHA
DON'T GET CAUGHT UP IN ANY-THING ORNERY.
ALL OF YOU MUST SELL YOUR SOULS TO SATAN.
ALL RIGHT, CUT!
TAKE CARE OF YOURSELF NOW.
HOT HOT HOT HOT HOT!
LOOKS OK.
GHA AA AA A
SH---
[TRACK 2, THE END]
HELL YEAH!! FUCKING MOTHER-FUCK!
WHO'S READY FOR NIAGRA POON-TANG?!
LOVE, MOTHER.

DMC LEXICON

🎭 PARIS

Capital of chic. Designers and artists have been living here from long ago, calling it the city of lights. It is the capital of France. Every year, all kinds of chic things are launched here. Hum "Champs Elysée" for effect.

Usage: Wow, you've lived in Paris?! How chic!

デトロイト・メタル・シティ

Detroit Metal City

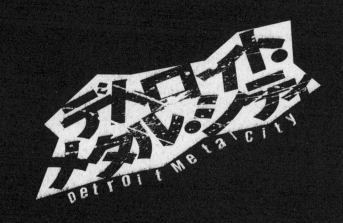

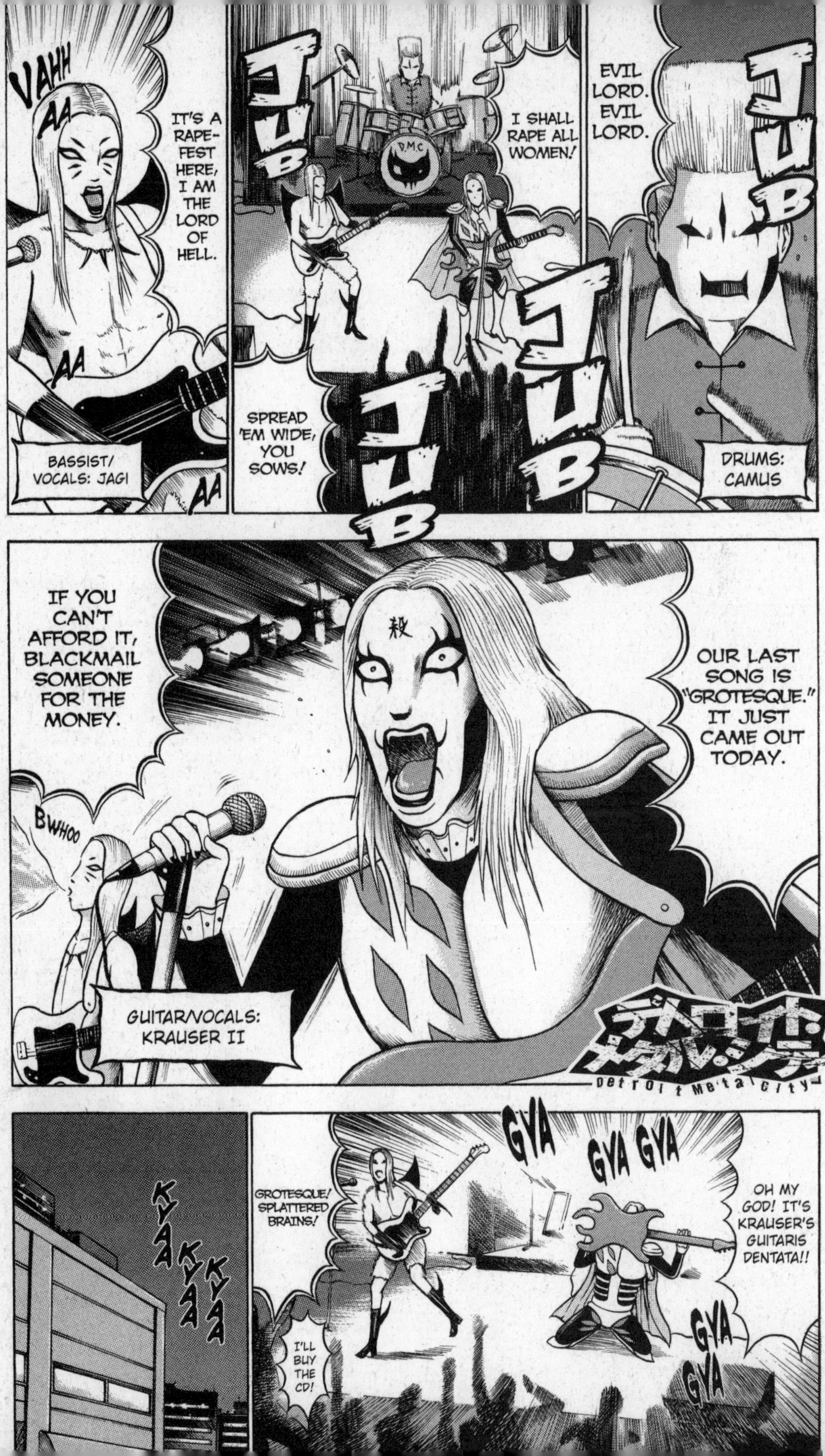
EVIL LORD. EVIL LORD.
JUB
DRUMS: CAMUS
I SHALL RAPE ALL WOMEN!
JUB
SPREAD 'EM WIDE, YOU SOWS!
JUB JUB
JUB
VAHH AA
IT'S A RAPE-FEST HERE, I AM THE LORD OF HELL.
AA
BASSIST/ VOCALS: JAGI
AA
OUR LAST SONG IS "GROTESQUE." IT JUST CAME OUT TODAY.
IF YOU CAN'T AFFORD IT, BLACKMAIL SOMEONE FOR THE MONEY.
BWHOO
GUITAR/VOCALS: KRAUSER II
GYA
GYA GYA
OH MY GOD! IT'S KRAUSER'S GUITARIS DENTATA!!
GROTESQUE! SPLATTERED BRAINS!
GYA GYA
I'LL BUY THE CD!
KYAA KYAA KYAA

Detroit Metal City

TRACK 3 Sick Murderer

D.M.C
(DETROIT METAL CITY)
DMC
GROTESQUE
C/W EVIL LORD
I worship music. If it weren't for music, I would have become a deranged killer.
—Krauser II
Death Records
Stereo
MSRP 1,260 yen
(1200 before tax)

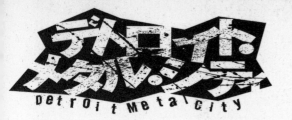

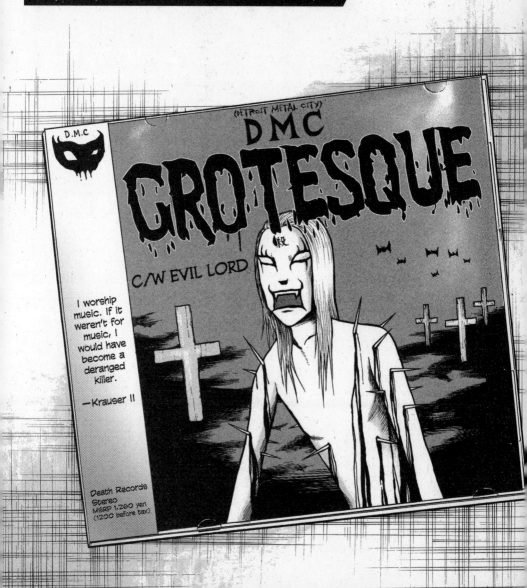

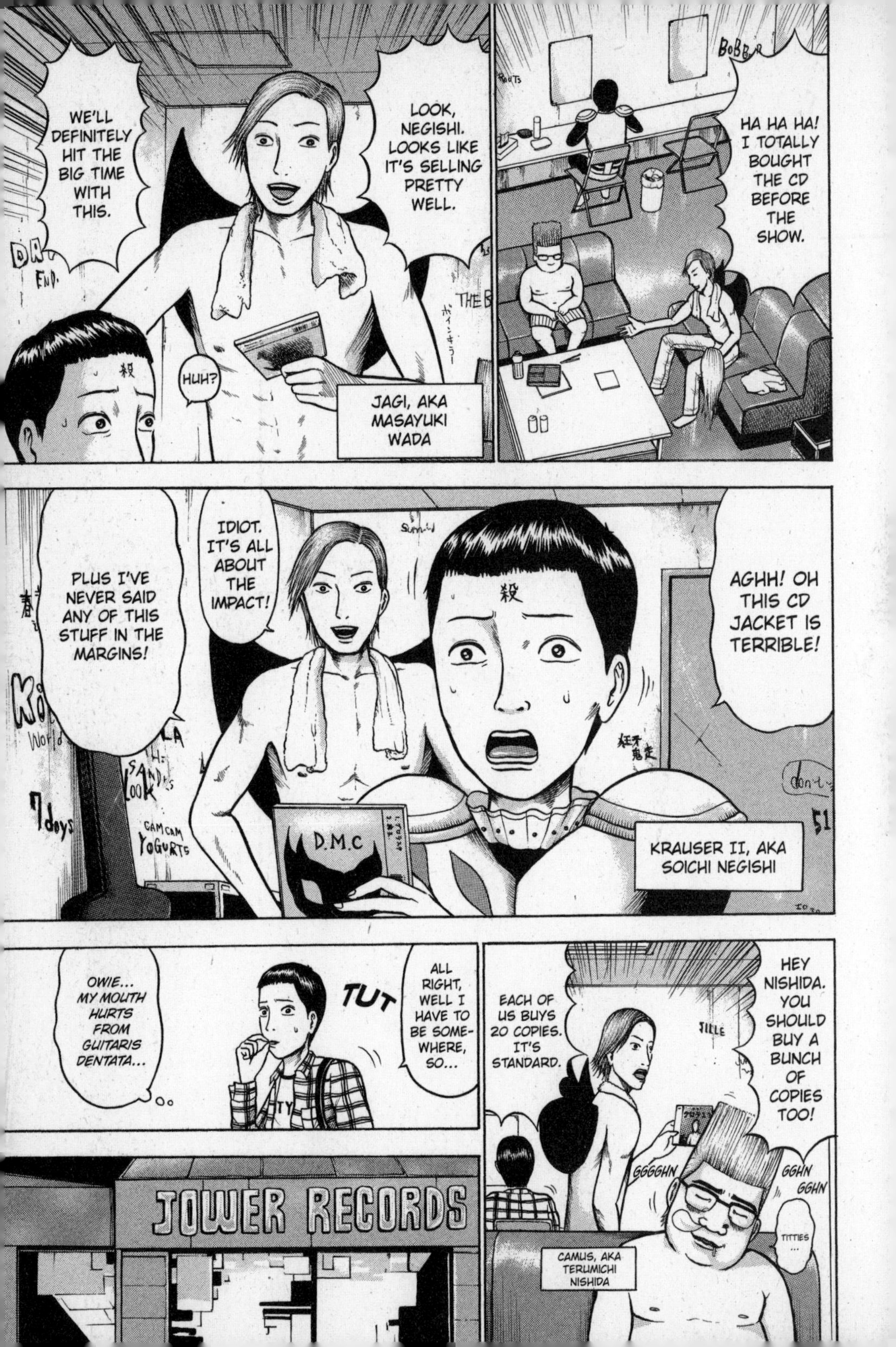

HA HA HA! I TOTALLY BOUGHT THE CD BEFORE THE SHOW.
LOOK, NEGISHI. LOOKS LIKE IT'S SELLING PRETTY WELL.
WE'LL DEFINITELY HIT THE BIG TIME WITH THIS.
HUH?
JAGI, AKA MASAYUKI WADA
AGHH! OH THIS CD JACKET IS TERRIBLE!
IDIOT. IT'S ALL ABOUT THE IMPACT!
PLUS I'VE NEVER SAID ANY OF THIS STUFF IN THE MARGINS!
D.M.C
KRAUSER II, AKA SOICHI NEGISHI
HEY NISHIDA. YOU SHOULD BUY A BUNCH OF COPIES TOO!
EACH OF US BUYS 20 COPIES. IT'S STANDARD.
GGHN GGHN
GGGGHN
TITTIES...
CAMUS, AKA TERUMICHI NISHIDA
ALL RIGHT, WELL I HAVE TO BE SOME-WHERE, SO...
TUT
OWIE... MY MOUTH HURTS FROM GUITARIS DENTATA...
JOWER RECORDS

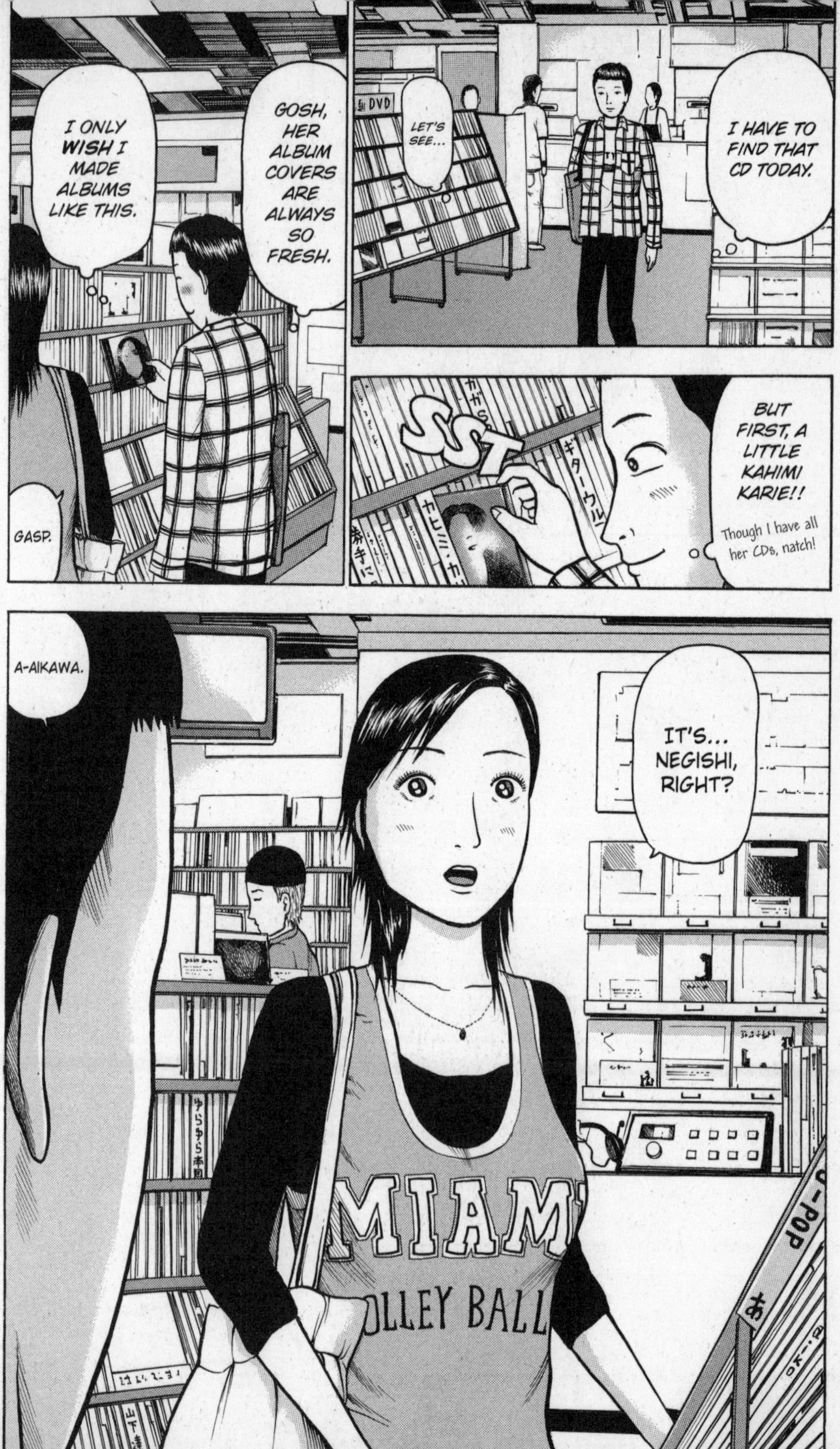
I HAVE TO FIND THAT CD TODAY.
LET'S SEE...
DVD
SST
BUT FIRST, A LITTLE KAHIMI KARIE!!
Though I have all her CDs, natch!
GOSH, HER ALBUM COVERS ARE ALWAYS SO FRESH.
I ONLY **WISH** I MADE ALBUMS LIKE THIS.
GASP.
IT'S... NEGISHI, RIGHT?
A-AIKAWA.

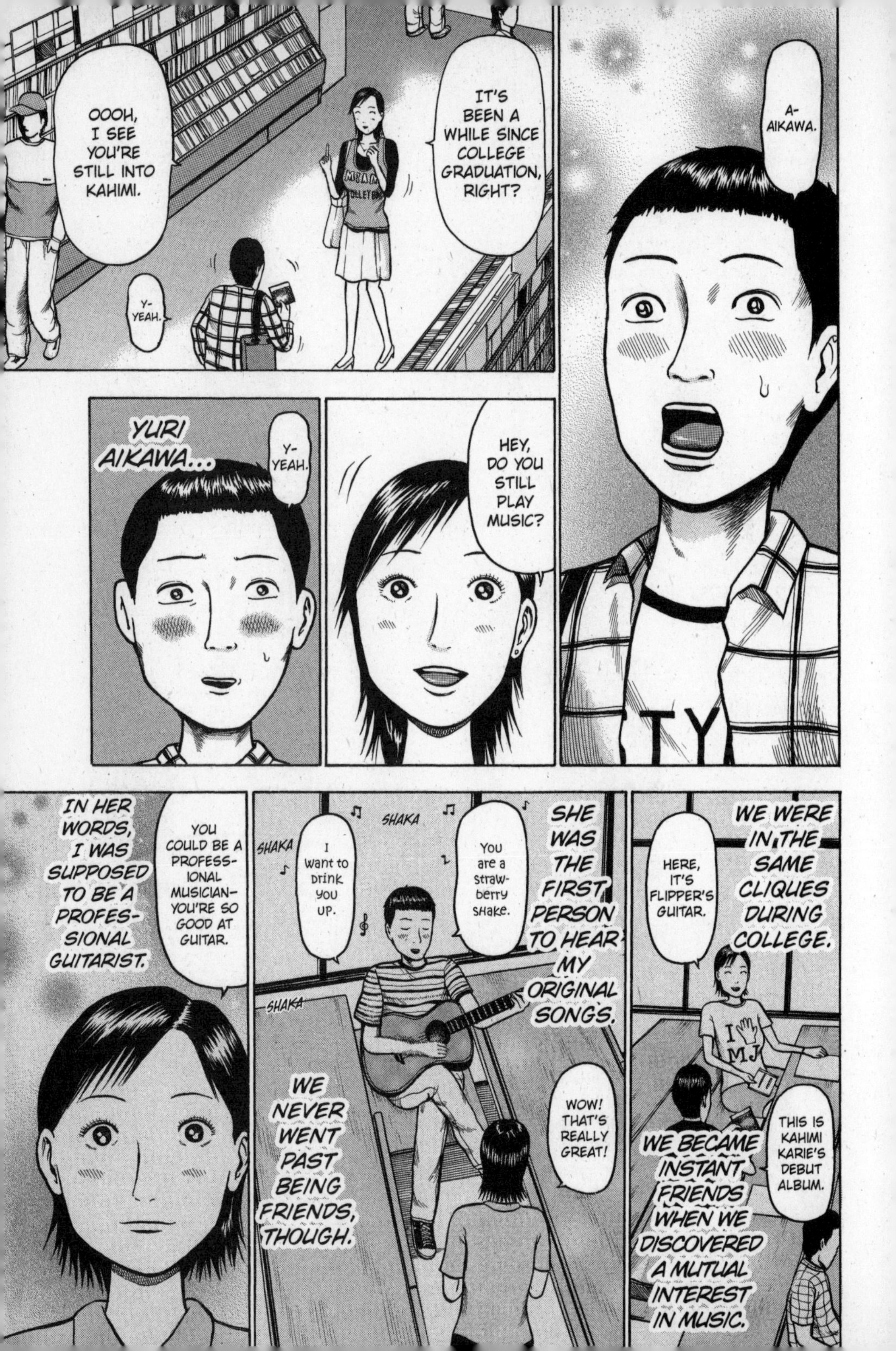
A-AIKAWA.
IT'S BEEN A WHILE SINCE COLLEGE GRADUATION, RIGHT?
OOOH, I SEE YOU'RE STILL INTO KAHIMI.
Y-YEAH.
HEY, DO YOU STILL PLAY MUSIC?
Y-YEAH.
YURI AIKAWA...
WE WERE IN THE SAME CLIQUES DURING COLLEGE.
HERE, IT'S FLIPPER'S GUITAR.
THIS IS KAHIMI KARIE'S DEBUT ALBUM.
WE BECAME INSTANT FRIENDS WHEN WE DISCOVERED A MUTUAL INTEREST IN MUSIC.
SHE WAS THE FIRST PERSON TO HEAR MY ORIGINAL SONGS.
You are a strawberry shake.
SHAKA
I want to drink you up.
SHAKA
SHAKA
WOW! THAT'S REALLY GREAT!
WE NEVER WENT PAST BEING FRIENDS, THOUGH.
YOU COULD BE A PROFESSIONAL MUSICIAN— YOU'RE SO GOOD AT GUITAR.
IN HER WORDS, I WAS SUPPOSED TO BE A PROFESSIONAL GUITARIST.

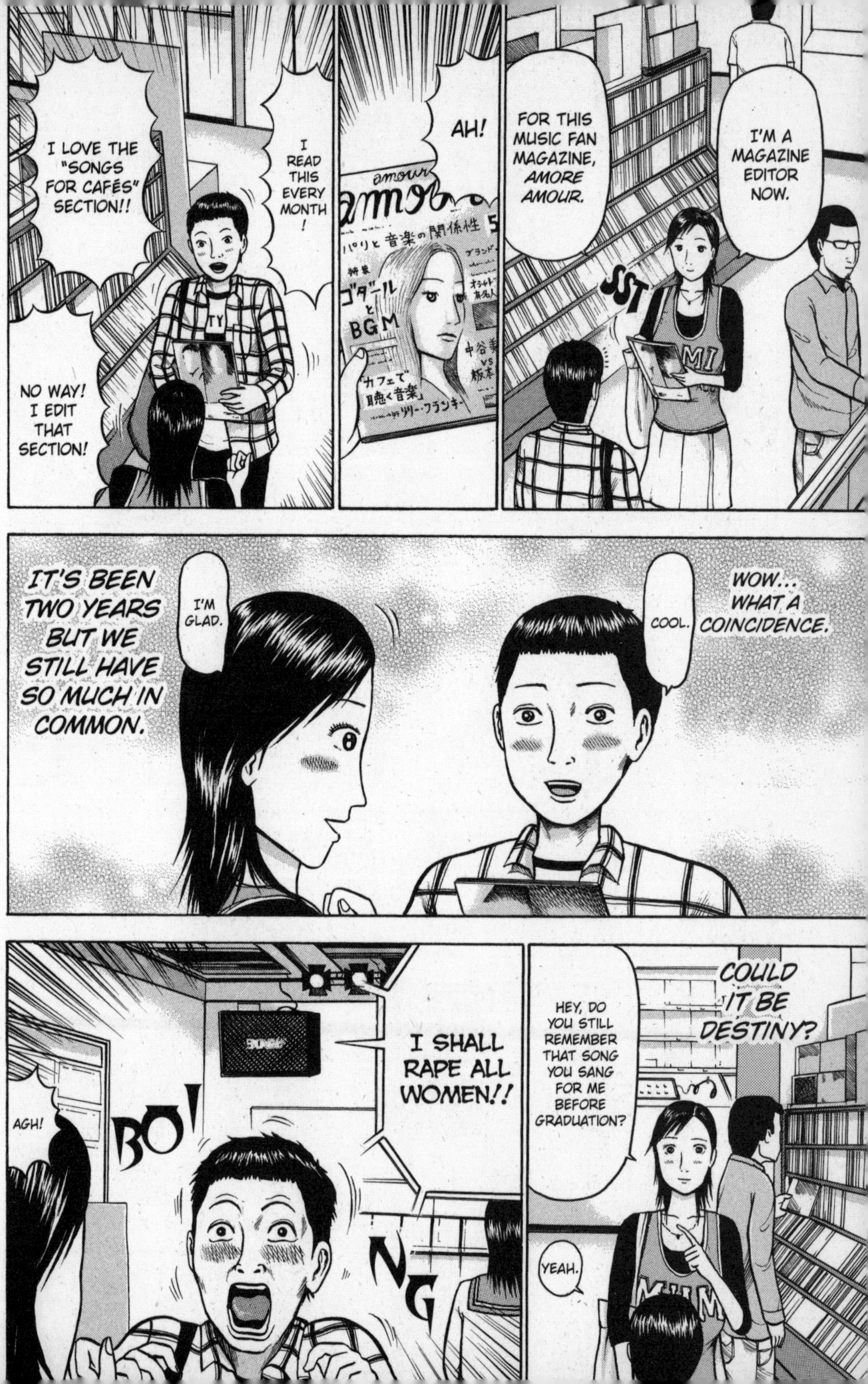
I'M A MAGAZINE EDITOR NOW.
FOR THIS MUSIC FAN MAGAZINE, AMORE AMOUR.
SST
AH!
amour
パリと音楽の関係性 5
特集 ゴダールとBGM
「カフェで聴く音楽」
I READ THIS EVERY MONTH!
I LOVE THE "SONGS FOR CAFÉS" SECTION!!
NO WAY! I EDIT THAT SECTION!
WOW... WHAT A COINCIDENCE.
COOL.
I'M GLAD.
IT'S BEEN TWO YEARS BUT WE STILL HAVE SO MUCH IN COMMON.
COULD IT BE DESTINY?
HEY, DO YOU STILL REMEMBER THAT SONG YOU SANG FOR ME BEFORE GRADUATION?
YEAH.
I SHALL RAPE ALL WOMEN!!
BOING
AGH!

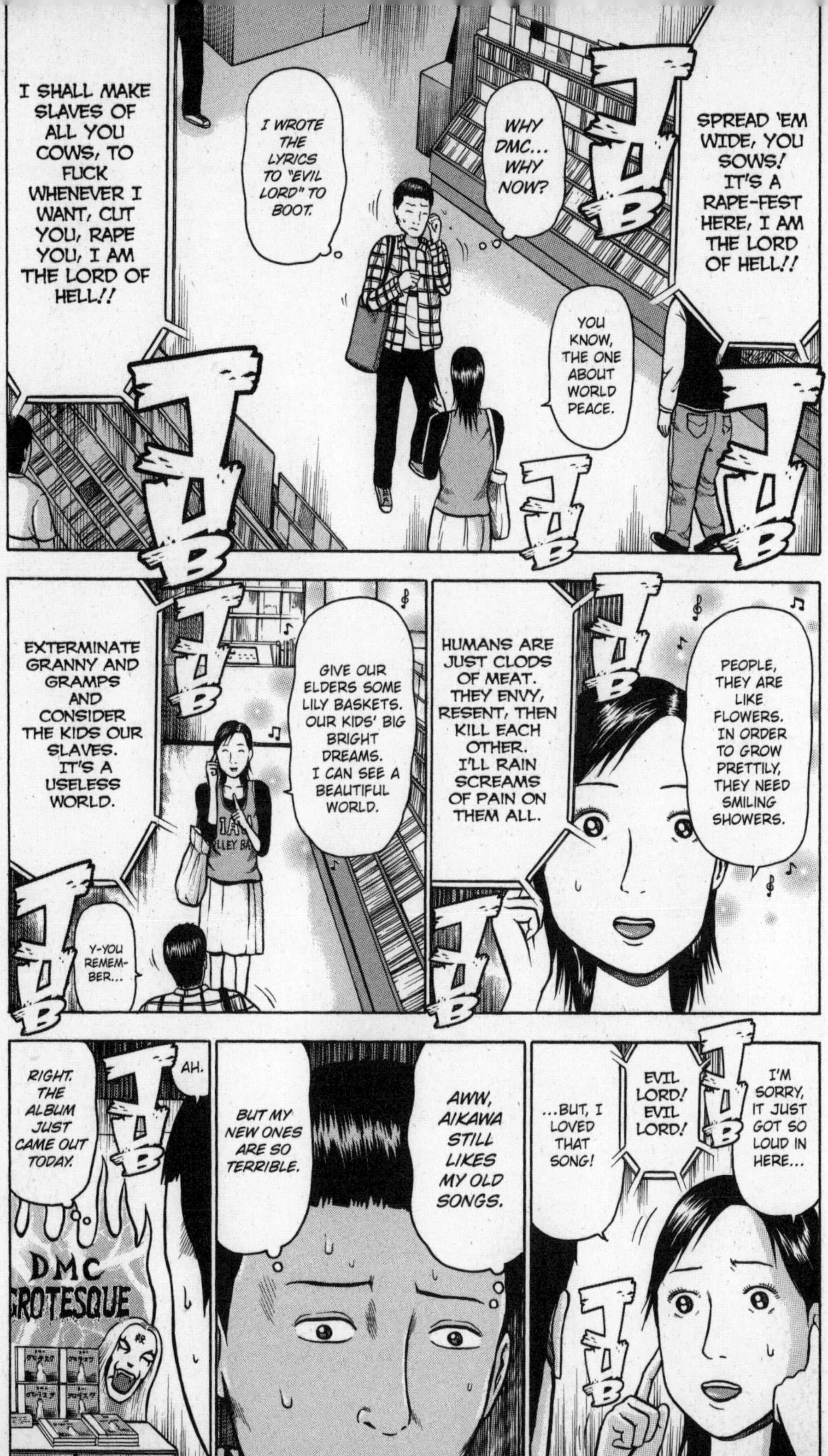
SPREAD 'EM WIDE, YOU SOWS! IT'S A RAPE-FEST HERE, I AM THE LORD OF HELL!!
WHY DMC... WHY NOW?
I WROTE THE LYRICS TO "EVIL LORD" TO BOOT.
I SHALL MAKE SLAVES OF ALL YOU COWS, TO FUCK WHENEVER I WANT, CUT YOU, RAPE YOU, I AM THE LORD OF HELL!!
YOU KNOW, THE ONE ABOUT WORLD PEACE.
PEOPLE, THEY ARE LIKE FLOWERS. IN ORDER TO GROW PRETTILY, THEY NEED SMILING SHOWERS.
HUMANS ARE JUST CLODS OF MEAT. THEY ENVY, RESENT, THEN KILL EACH OTHER. I'LL RAIN SCREAMS OF PAIN ON THEM ALL.
GIVE OUR ELDERS SOME LILY BASKETS. OUR KIDS' BIG BRIGHT DREAMS. I CAN SEE A BEAUTIFUL WORLD.
EXTERMINATE GRANNY AND GRAMPS AND CONSIDER THE KIDS OUR SLAVES. IT'S A USELESS WORLD.
Y-YOU REMEMBER...
I'M SORRY, IT JUST GOT SO LOUD IN HERE...
EVIL LORD! EVIL LORD!
...BUT, I LOVED THAT SONG!
AWW, AIKAWA STILL LIKES MY OLD SONGS.
BUT MY NEW ONES ARE SO TERRIBLE.
AH.
RIGHT. THE ALBUM JUST CAME OUT TODAY.
DMC GROTESQUE

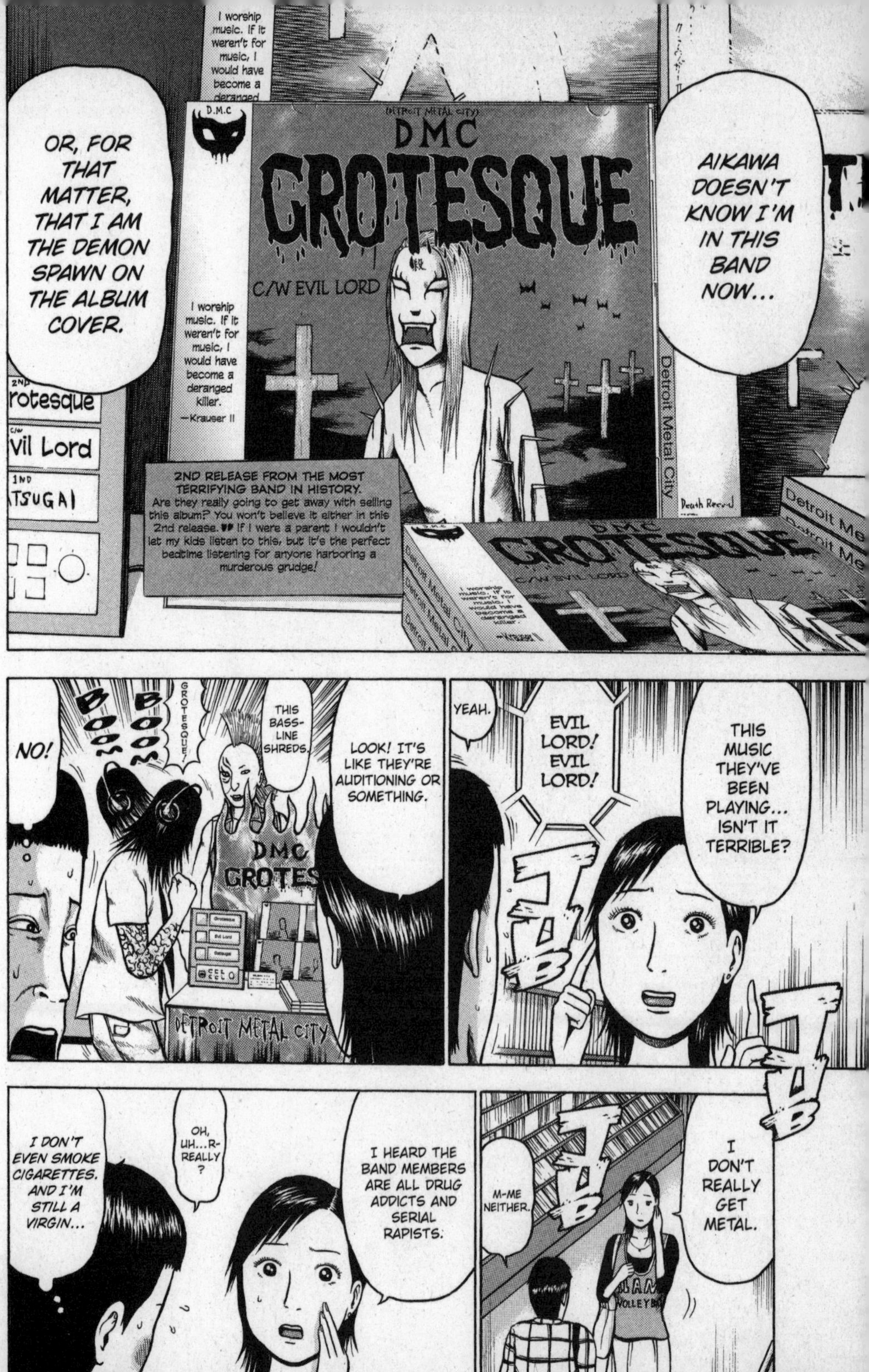
AIKAWA DOESN'T KNOW I'M IN THIS BAND NOW...
OR, FOR THAT MATTER, THAT I AM THE DEMON SPAWN ON THE ALBUM COVER.
D.M.C
DMC
GROTESQUE
C/W EVIL LORD
I worship music. If it weren't for music, I would have become a deranged killer.
—Krauser II
Detroit Metal City
Death Record
2ND RELEASE FROM THE MOST TERRIFYING BAND IN HISTORY.
Are they really going to get away with selling this album? You won't believe it either in this 2nd release. If I were a parent I wouldn't let my kids listen to this, but it's the perfect bedtime listening for anyone harboring a murderous grudge!
2ND Grotesque
C/W Evil Lord
1ND SATSUGAI
THIS MUSIC THEY'VE BEEN PLAYING... ISN'T IT TERRIBLE?
EVIL LORD! EVIL LORD!
YEAH.
LOOK! IT'S LIKE THEY'RE AUDITIONING OR SOMETHING.
THIS BASS-LINE SHREDS.
GROTESQUE!
DMC GROTES
DETROIT METAL CITY
BOOM BOOM
NO!
I DON'T REALLY GET METAL.
M-ME NEITHER.
I HEARD THE BAND MEMBERS ARE ALL DRUG ADDICTS AND SERIAL RAPISTS.
OH, UH...R-REALLY?
I DON'T EVEN SMOKE CIGARETTES. AND I'M STILL A VIRGIN...

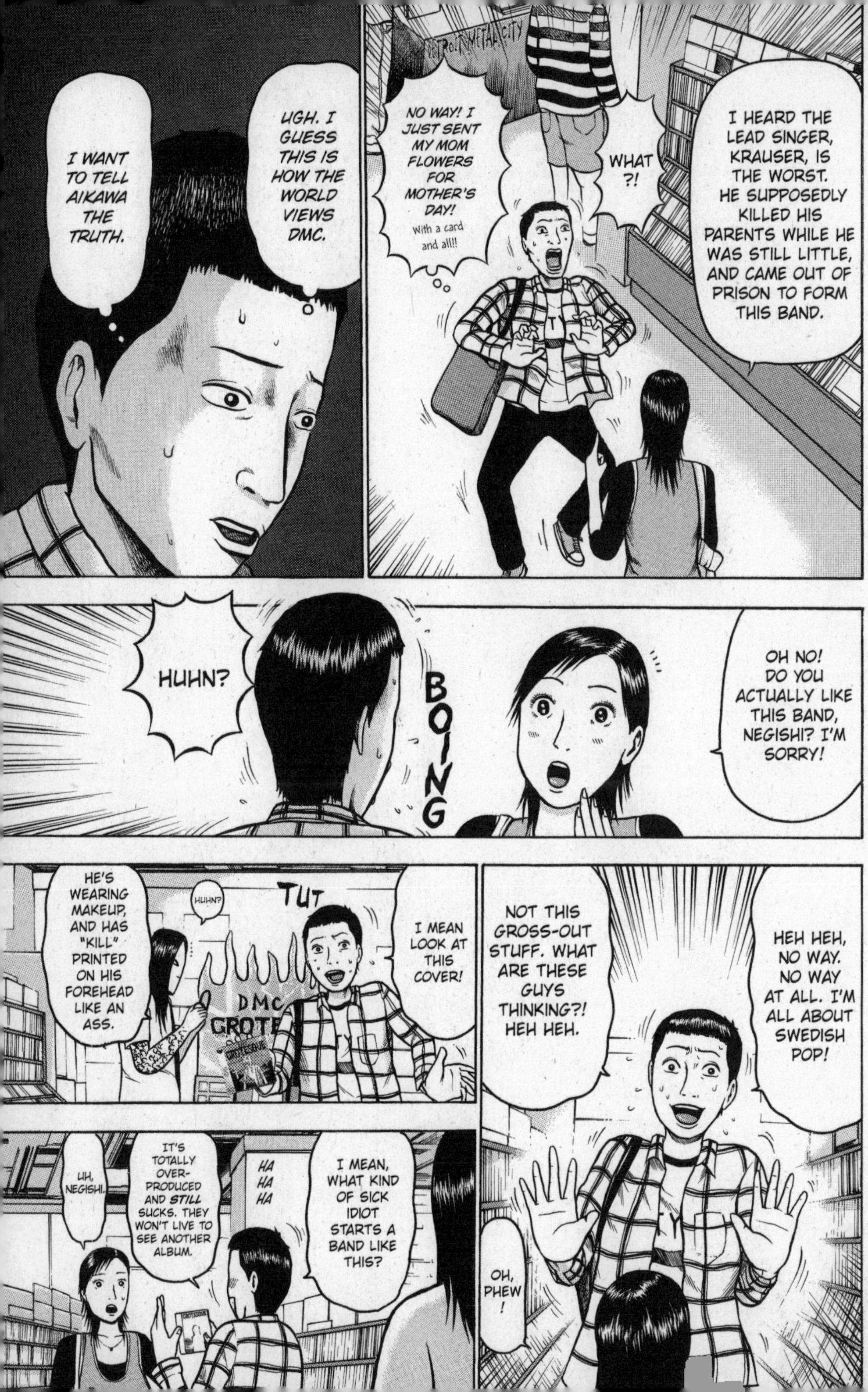
DETROIT METAL CITY
I HEARD THE LEAD SINGER, KRAUSER, IS THE WORST. HE SUPPOSEDLY KILLED HIS PARENTS WHILE HE WAS STILL LITTLE, AND CAME OUT OF PRISON TO FORM THIS BAND.
WHAT?!
NO WAY! I JUST SENT MY MOM FLOWERS FOR MOTHER'S DAY!
With a card and all!!
UGH. I GUESS THIS IS HOW THE WORLD VIEWS DMC.
I WANT TO TELL AIKAWA THE TRUTH.
OH NO! DO YOU ACTUALLY LIKE THIS BAND, NEGISHI? I'M SORRY!
BOING
HUHN?
HEH HEH, NO WAY. NO WAY AT ALL. I'M ALL ABOUT SWEDISH POP!
NOT THIS GROSS-OUT STUFF. WHAT ARE THESE GUYS THINKING?! HEH HEH.
OH, PHEW!
I MEAN LOOK AT THIS COVER!
TUT
DMC GROTE
HUHN?
HE'S WEARING MAKEUP, AND HAS "KILL" PRINTED ON HIS FOREHEAD LIKE AN ASS.
I MEAN, WHAT KIND OF SICK IDIOT STARTS A BAND LIKE THIS?
HA HA HA
IT'S TOTALLY OVER-PRODUCED AND STILL SUCKS. THEY WON'T LIVE TO SEE ANOTHER ALBUM.
UH, NEGISHI.

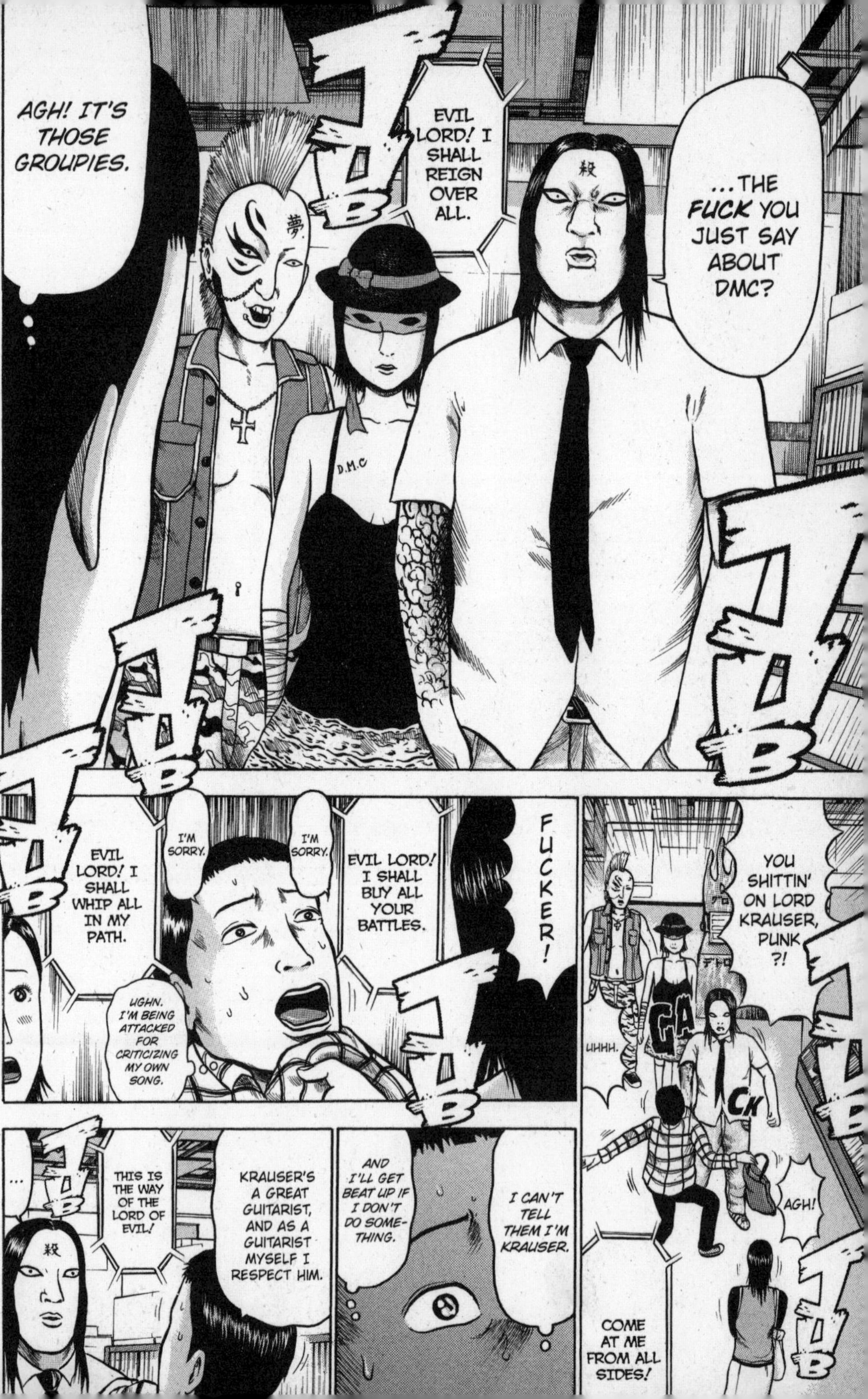
...THE FUCK YOU JUST SAY ABOUT DMC?
EVIL LORD! I SHALL REIGN OVER ALL.
AGH! IT'S THOSE GROUPIES.
D.M.C
YOU SHITTIN' ON LORD KRAUSER, PUNK ?!
GA
CK
UHHH.
AGH!
COME AT ME FROM ALL SIDES!
FUCKER!
EVIL LORD! I SHALL BUY ALL YOUR BATTLES.
I'M SORRY.
I'M SORRY.
EVIL LORD! I SHALL WHIP ALL IN MY PATH.
UGHN. I'M BEING ATTACKED FOR CRITICIZING MY OWN SONG.
I CAN'T TELL THEM I'M KRAUSER.
AND I'LL GET BEAT UP IF I DON'T DO SOMETHING.
KRAUSER'S A GREAT GUITARIST, AND AS A GUITARIST MYSELF I RESPECT HIM.
THIS IS THE WAY OF THE LORD OF EVIL!
...

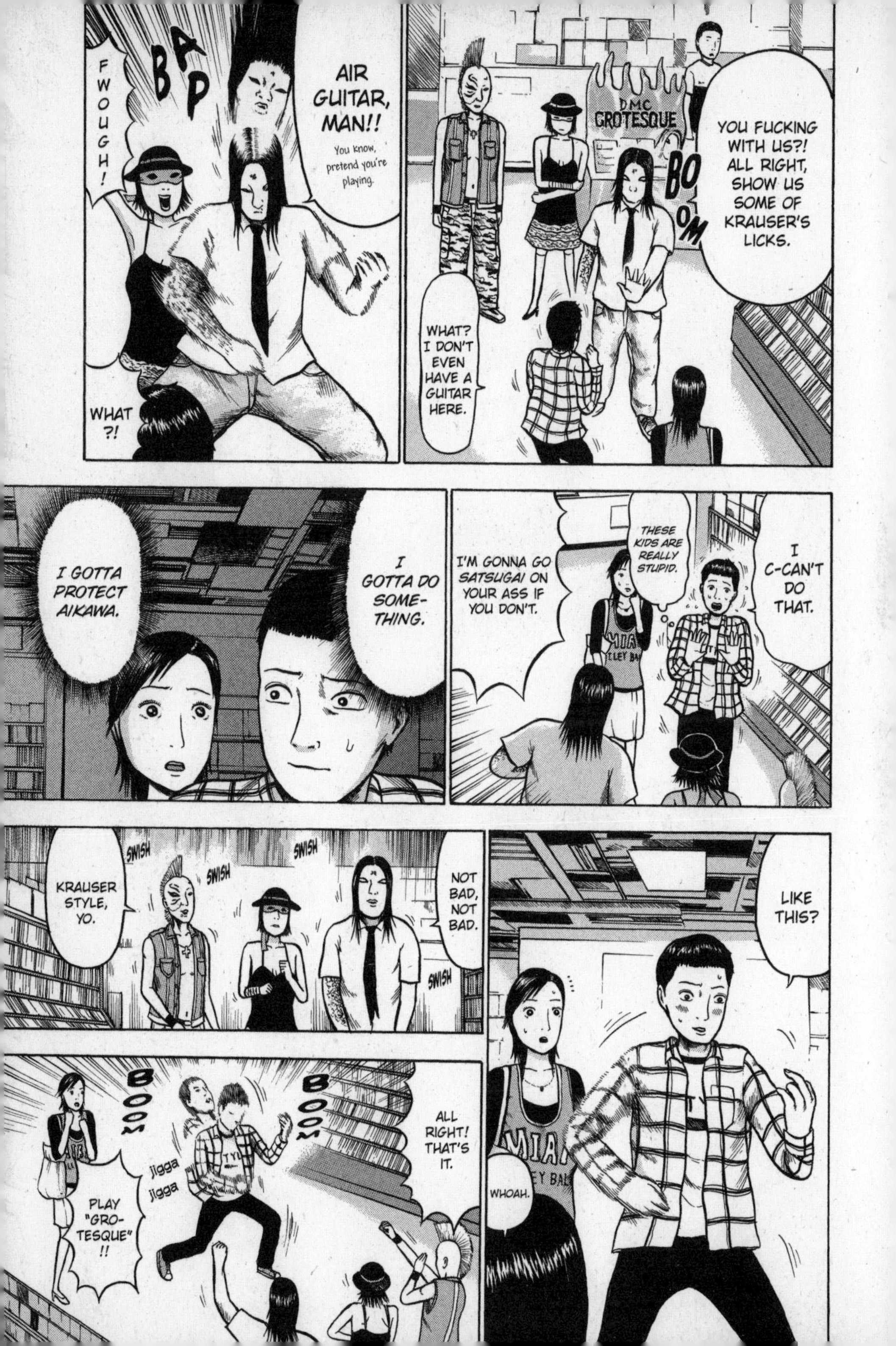

DMC GROTESQUE
YOU FUCKING WITH US?! ALL RIGHT, SHOW US SOME OF KRAUSER'S LICKS.
BOOM
WHAT? I DON'T EVEN HAVE A GUITAR HERE.
BAP
FWOUGH!
AIR GUITAR, MAN!!
You know, pretend you're playing.
WHAT?!
I C-CAN'T DO THAT.
THESE KIDS ARE REALLY STUPID.
I'M GONNA GO SATSUGAI ON YOUR ASS IF YOU DON'T.
I GOTTA DO SOME-THING.
I GOTTA PROTECT AIKAWA.
LIKE THIS?
WHOAH.
NOT BAD, NOT BAD.
SWISH
SWISH
SWISH
KRAUSER STYLE, YO.
ALL RIGHT! THAT'S IT.
BOOM
BOOM
jigga jigga
PLAY "GRO-TESQUE" !!

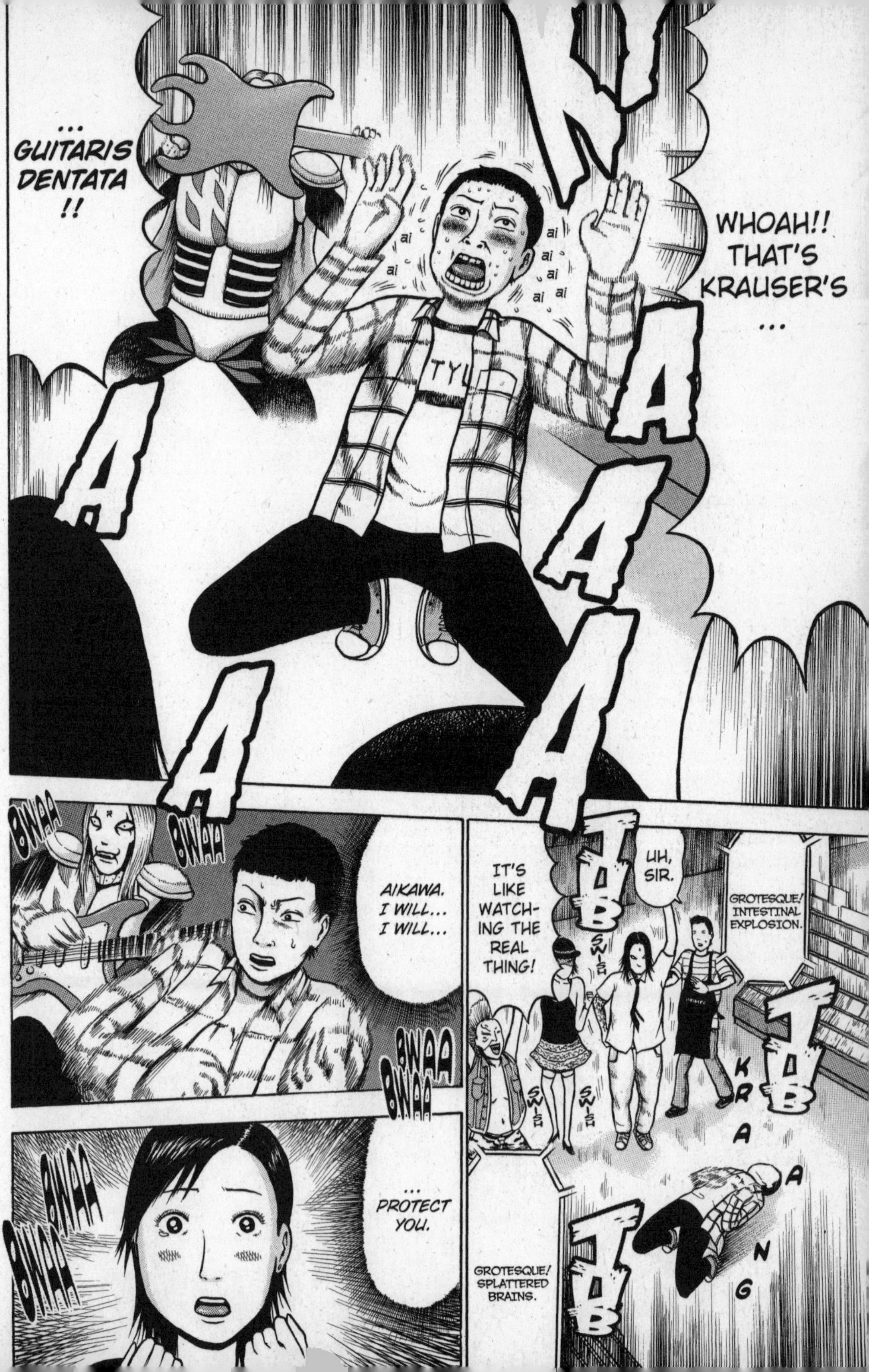
WHOAH!! THAT'S KRAUSER'S ...
NYAAAAAA
ai ai ai ai ai ai ai ai
... GUITARIS DENTATA !!
TOB
UH, SIR.
IT'S LIKE WATCHING THE REAL THING!
SWISH
GROTESQUE! INTESTINAL EXPLOSION.
TOB
SWISH
SWISH
KRAANG
TOB
GROTESQUE! SPLATTERED BRAINS.
BWAA
BWAA
AIKAWA. I WILL... I WILL...
BWAA
BWAA
BWAA
BWAA
... PROTECT YOU.

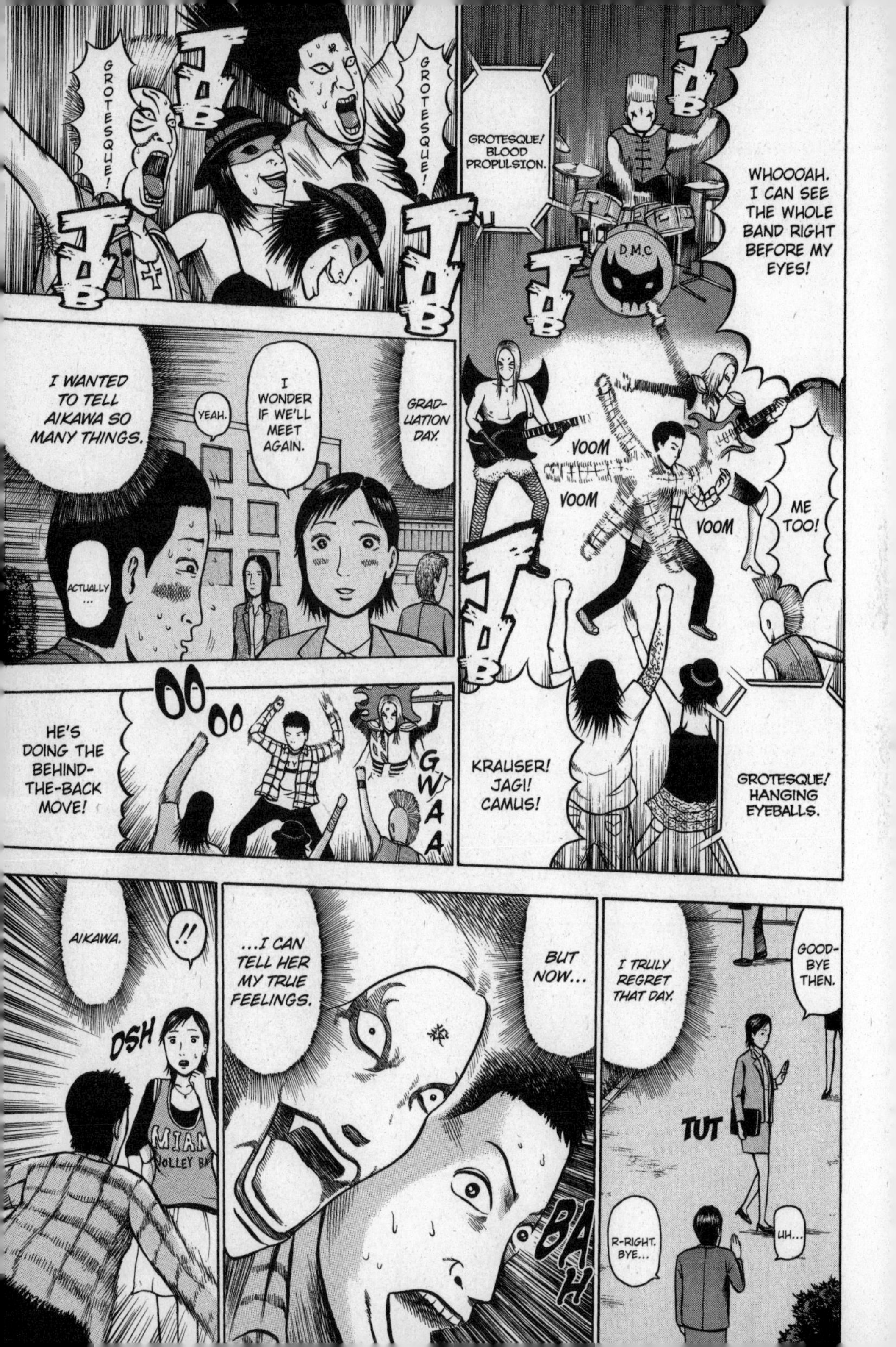
WHOOOAH. I CAN SEE THE WHOLE BAND RIGHT BEFORE MY EYES!
GROTESQUE! BLOOD PROPULSION.
VOOM
VOOM
VOOM
ME TOO!
GROTESQUE! HANGING EYEBALLS.
KRAUSER! JAGI! CAMUS!
GROTESQUE!
GROTESQUE!
GRAD-UATION DAY.
I WONDER IF WE'LL MEET AGAIN.
YEAH.
I WANTED TO TELL AIKAWA SO MANY THINGS.
ACTUALLY...
GWAA
OOOO
HE'S DOING THE BEHIND-THE-BACK MOVE!
GOOD-BYE THEN.
I TRULY REGRET THAT DAY.
TUT
UH...
R-RIGHT. BYE...
BUT NOW...
...I CAN TELL HER MY TRUE FEELINGS.
BAH
!!
AIKAWA.
DSH

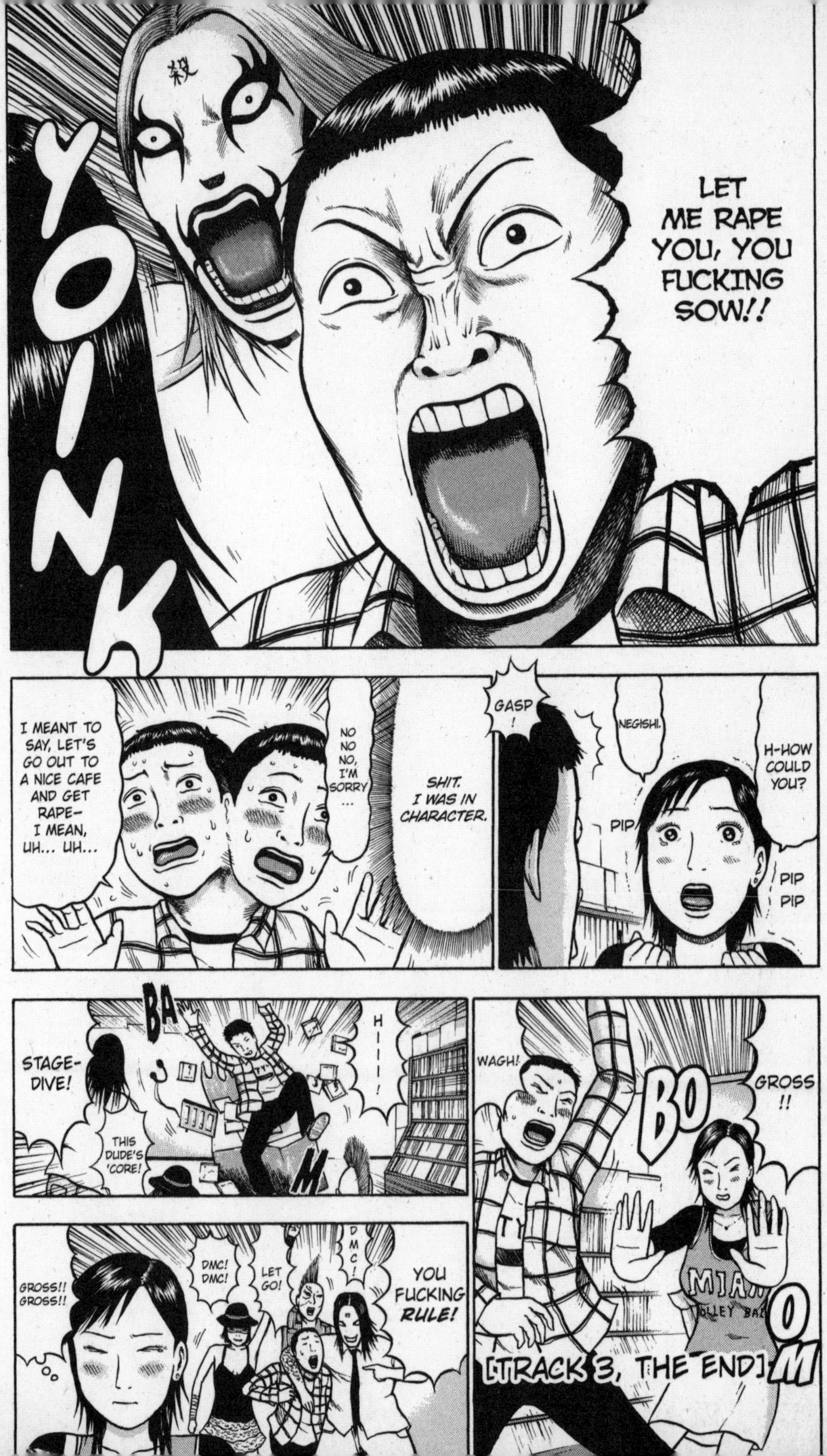
LET ME RAPE YOU, YOU FUCKING SOW!!
YOINK
H-HOW COULD YOU?
NEGISHI.
GASP!
PIP
PIP PIP
NO NO NO, I'M SORRY...
SHIT. I WAS IN CHARACTER.
I MEANT TO SAY, LET'S GO OUT TO A NICE CAFE AND GET RAPE— I MEAN, UH... UH...
GROSS!!
BO
WAGH!
O
M
[TRACK 3, THE END]
H-!!!
BA
STAGE-DIVE!
THIS DUDE'S 'CORE!
M
YOU FUCKING RULE!
DMC!
LET GO!
DMC! DMC!
GROSS!! GROSS!!

DMC LEXICON
GUITARIS DENTATA

When one plays an instrument with their teeth. One recalls Jimi Hendrix's iconic oral performance at Woodstock, but Krauser II is the first to take it to its summit with his "Guitaris Dentata." Those with cavities should avoid this move.

Usage: He's doing it! Krauser's doing the Guitaris Dentata!

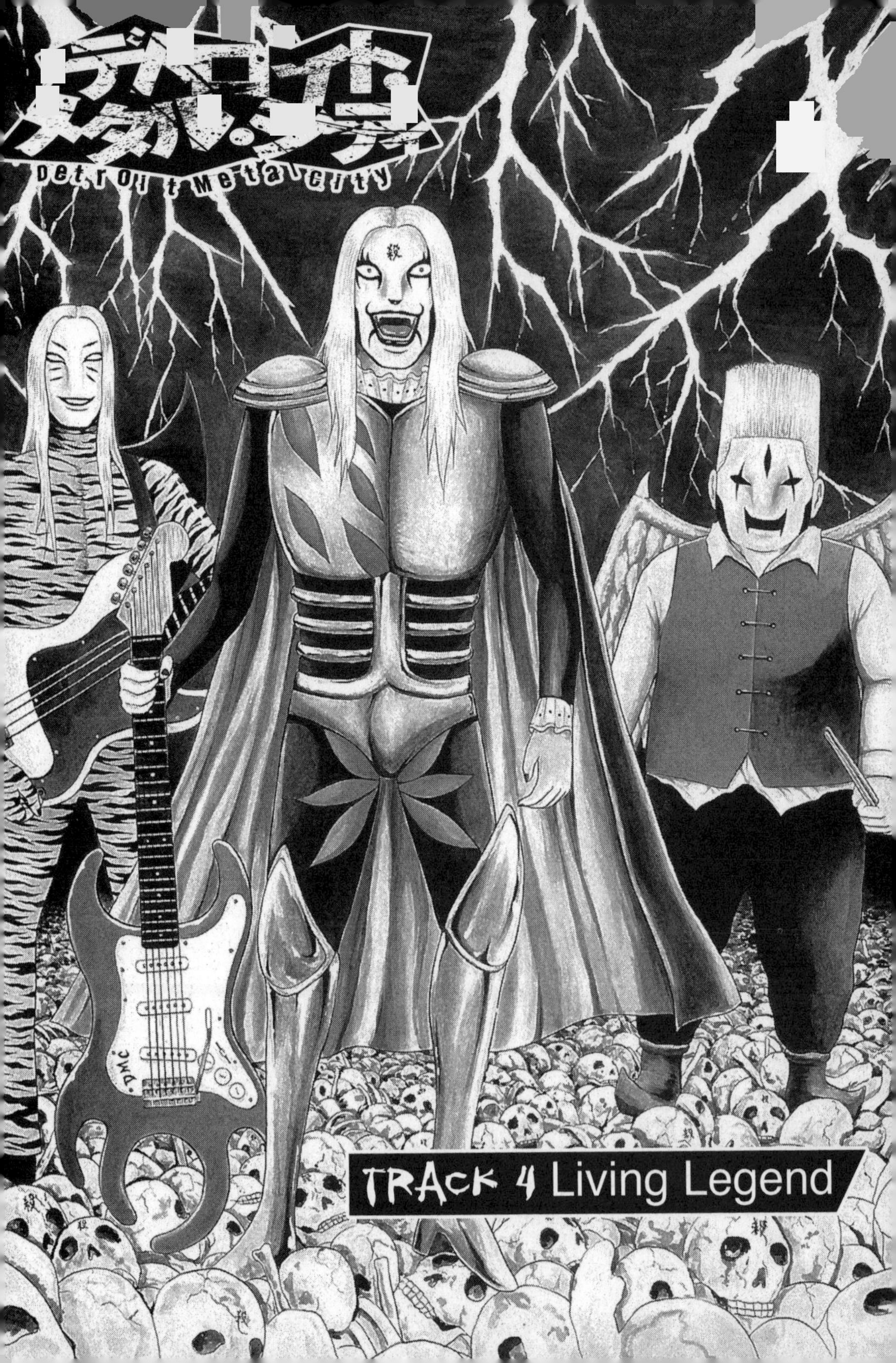
Detroit Metal City
TRACK 4 Living Legend

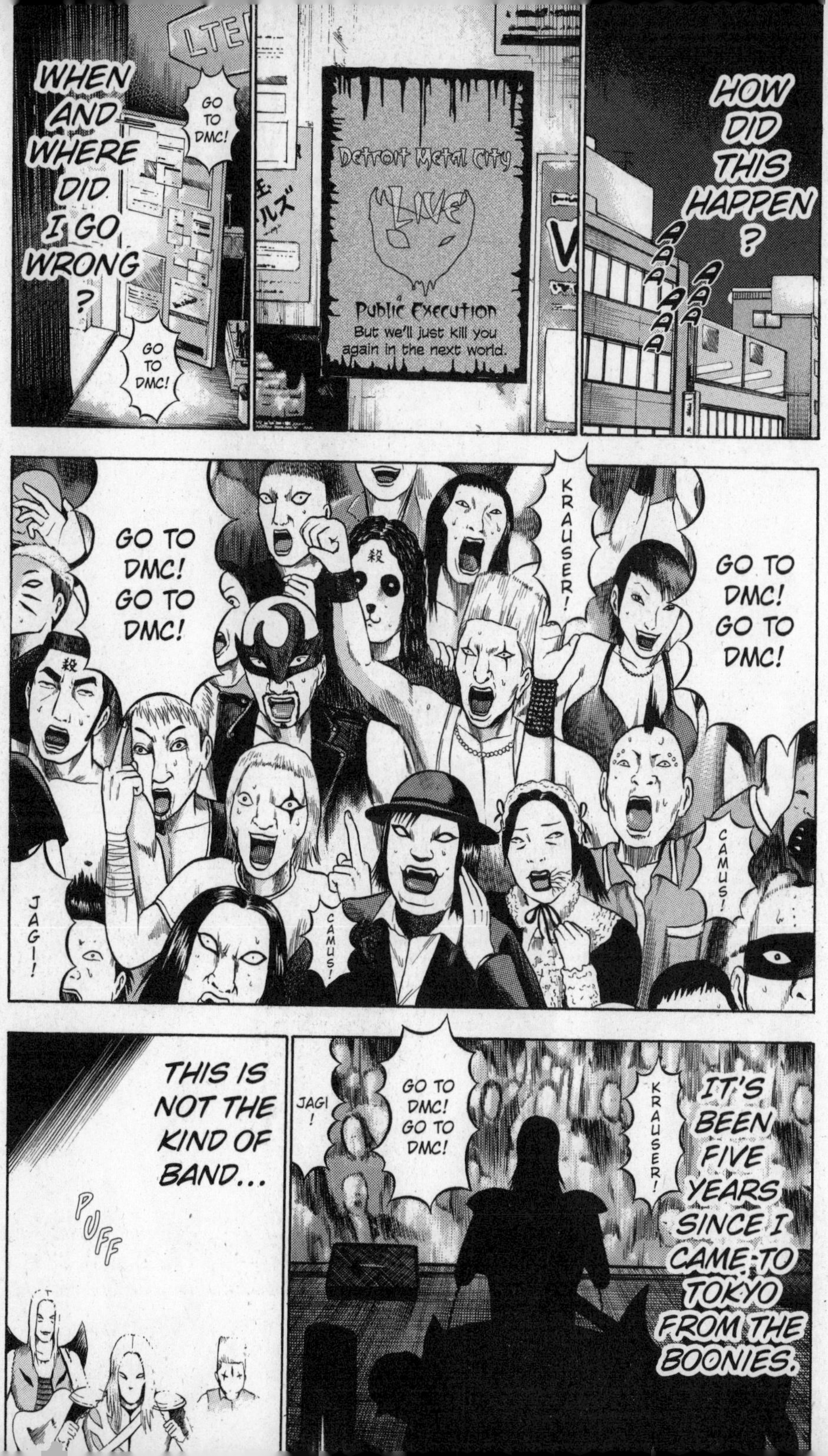
HOW DID THIS HAPPEN?
AAAAAAA
AAAA
Detroit Metal City
LIVE
Public Execution
But we'll just kill you again in the next world.
GO TO DMC!
WHEN AND WHERE DID I GO WRONG?
GO TO DMC!
GO TO DMC! GO TO DMC!
KRAUSER!
GO TO DMC! GO TO DMC!
CAMUS!
CAMUS!
JAGI!
IT'S BEEN FIVE YEARS SINCE I CAME TO TOKYO FROM THE BOONIES.
KRAUSER!
GO TO DMC! GO TO DMC!
JAGI!
THIS IS NOT THE KIND OF BAND...
PUFF

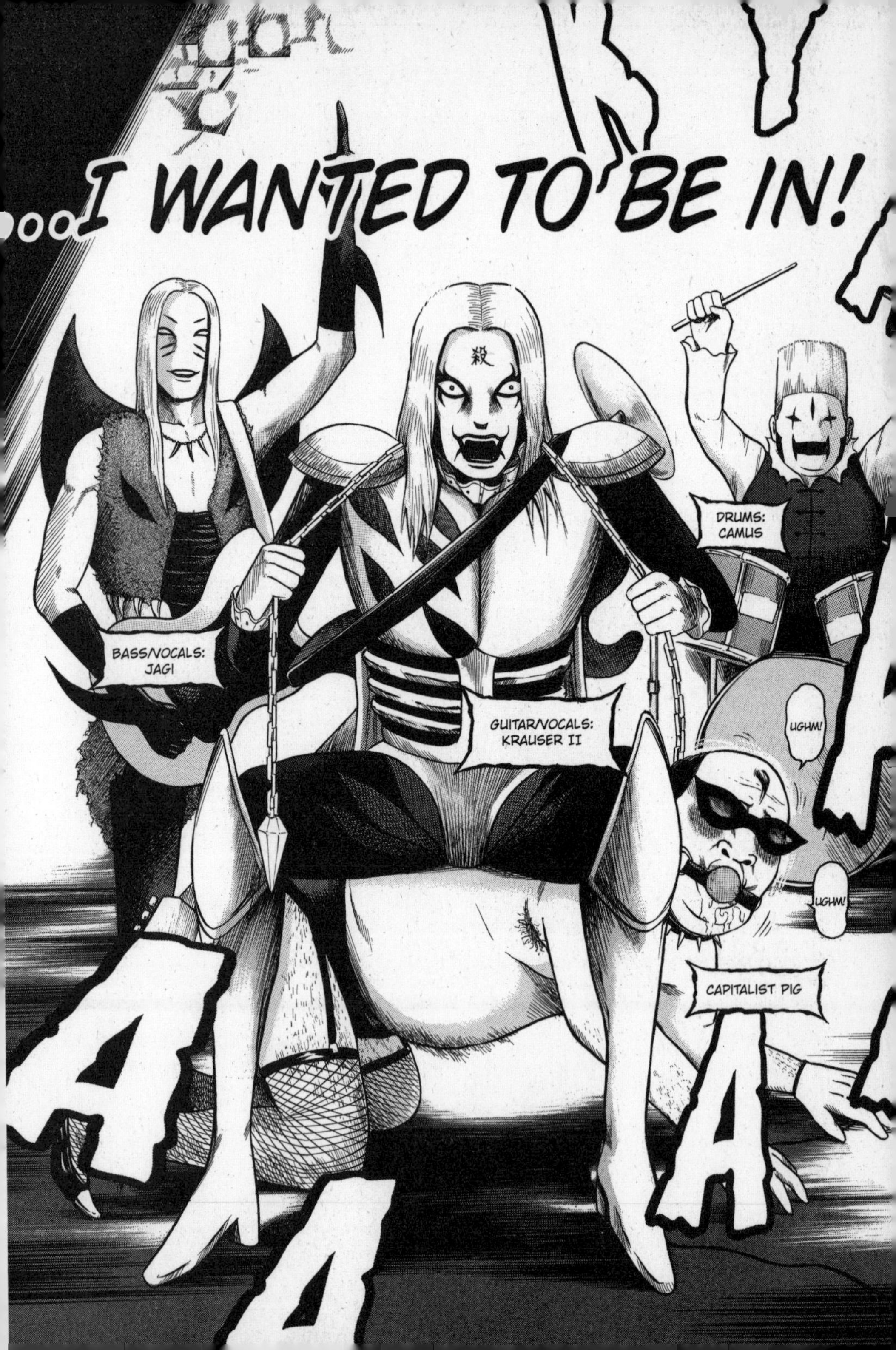
...I WANTED TO BE IN!
DRUMS: CAMUS
BASS/VOCALS: JAGI
GUITAR/VOCALS: KRAUSER II
UGHM!
UGHM!
CAPITALIST PIG

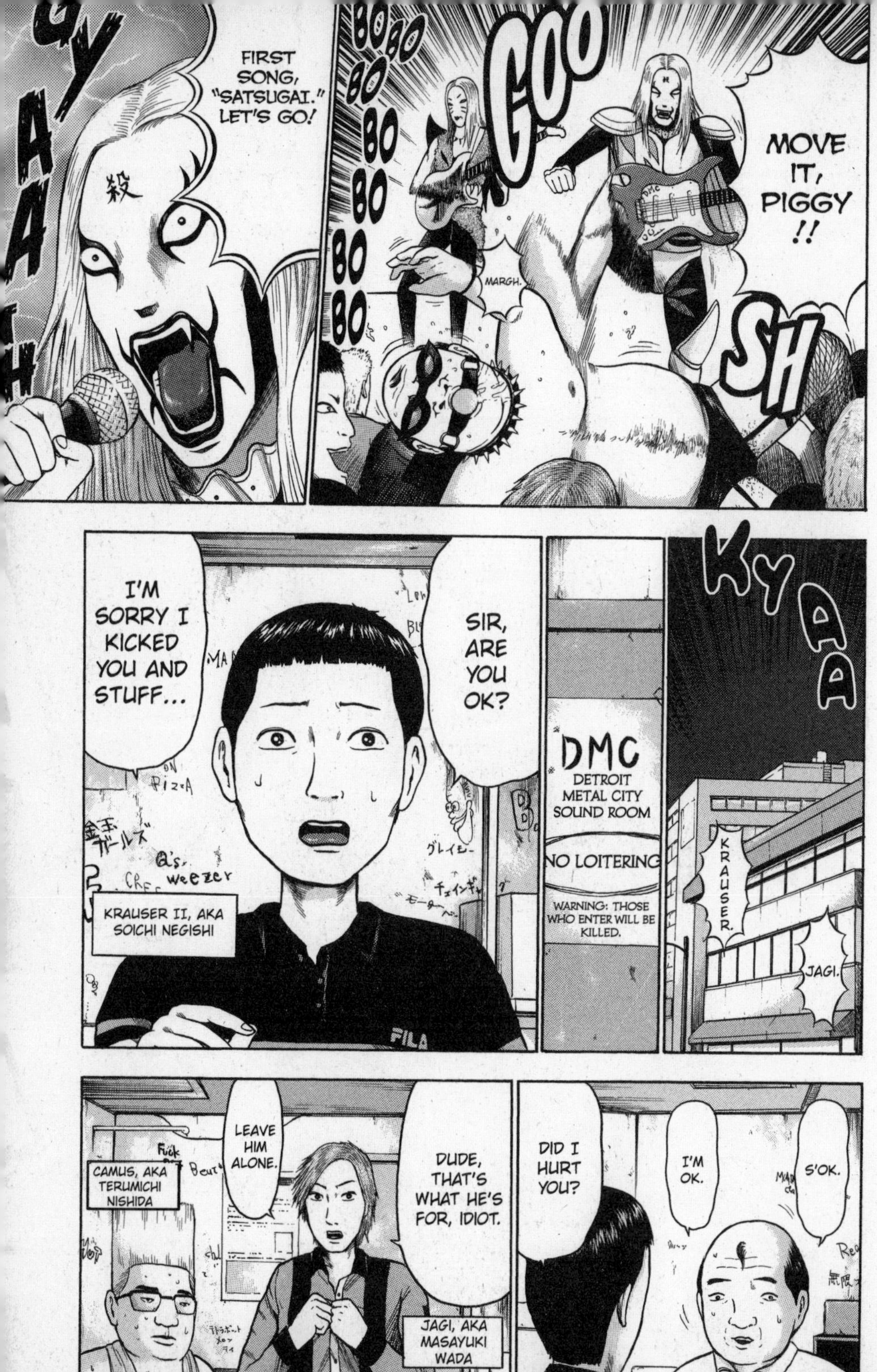
GOO
BO BO BO BO BO BO BO BO BO BO
MOVE IT, PIGGY!!
MARGH.
SH
FIRST SONG, "SATSUGAI." LET'S GO!
殺
KYAA
KRAUSER.
JAGI.
DMC
DETROIT METAL CITY SOUND ROOM
NO LOITERING
WARNING: THOSE WHO ENTER WILL BE KILLED.
SIR, ARE YOU OK?
I'M SORRY I KICKED YOU AND STUFF...
weezer
KRAUSER II, AKA SOICHI NEGISHI
FILA
S'OK.
I'M OK.
DID I HURT YOU?
DUDE, THAT'S WHAT HE'S FOR, IDIOT.
LEAVE HIM ALONE.
CAMUS, AKA TERUMICHI NISHIDA
JAGI, AKA MASAYUKI WADA

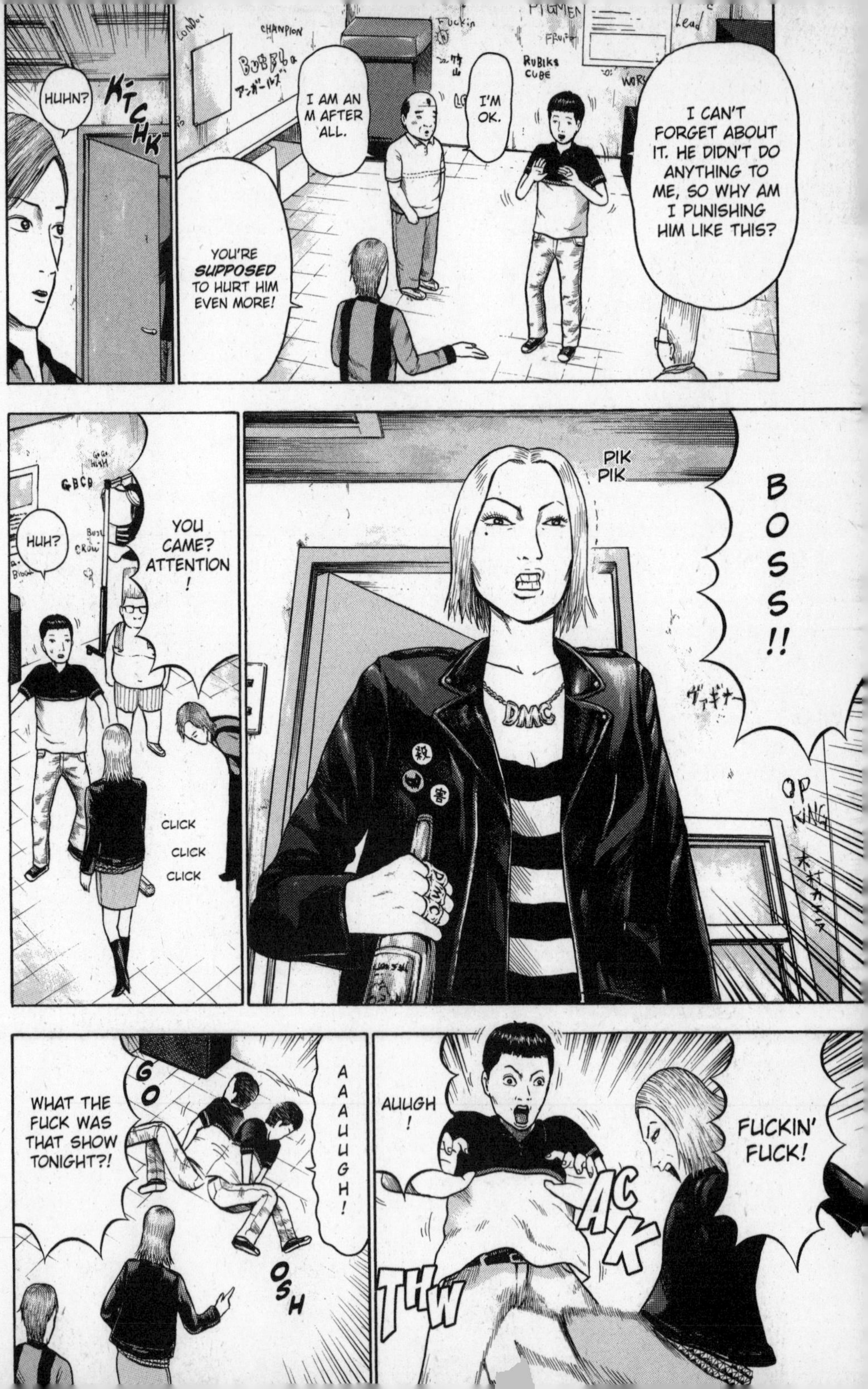

I CAN'T FORGET ABOUT IT. HE DIDN'T DO ANYTHING TO ME, SO WHY AM I PUNISHING HIM LIKE THIS?
I'M OK.
I AM AN M AFTER ALL.
YOU'RE SUPPOSED TO HURT HIM EVEN MORE!
K-TCHK
HUHN?
BOSS!!
PIK PIK
YOU CAME? ATTENTION!
HUH?
CLICK
CLICK
CLICK
FUCKIN' FUCK!
AUUGH!
ACK
THW
AAAUUGH!
GO
WHAT THE FUCK WAS THAT SHOW TONIGHT?!
OSH

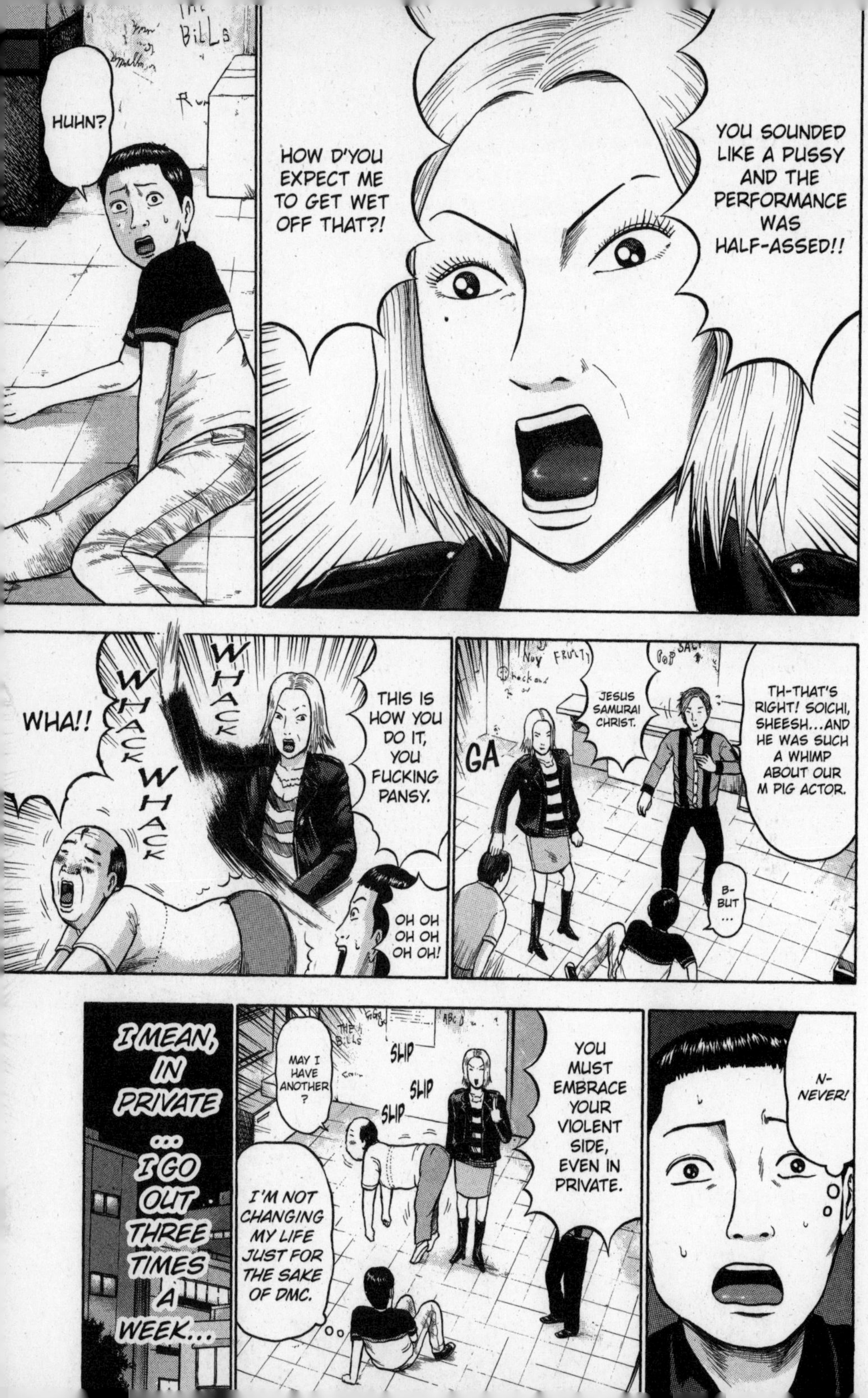
YOU SOUNDED LIKE A PUSSY AND THE PERFORMANCE WAS HALF-ASSED!!
HOW D'YOU EXPECT ME TO GET WET OFF THAT?!
HUHN?
TH-THAT'S RIGHT! SOICHI, SHEESH...AND HE WAS SUCH A WHIMP ABOUT OUR M PIG ACTOR.
JESUS SAMURAI CHRIST.
GA
B-BUT ...
THIS IS HOW YOU DO IT, YOU FUCKING PANSY.
WHACK
WHACK
WHACK
WHA!!
OH OH OH OH OH OH!
N-NEVER!
YOU MUST EMBRACE YOUR VIOLENT SIDE, EVEN IN PRIVATE.
MAY I HAVE ANOTHER?
SLIP
SLIP
SLIP
I'M NOT CHANGING MY LIFE JUST FOR THE SAKE OF DMC.
I MEAN, IN PRIVATE ... I GO OUT THREE TIMES A WEEK...

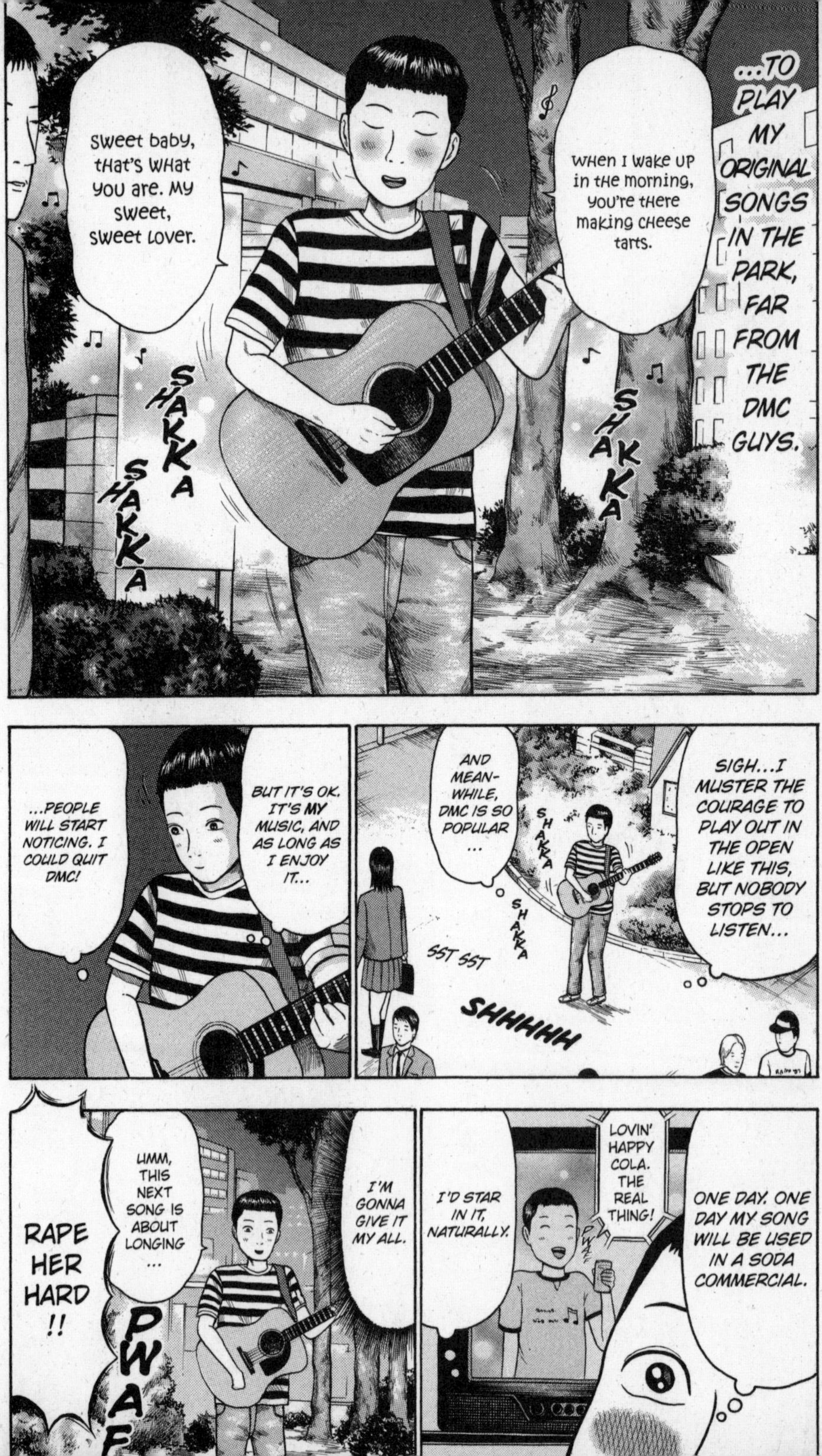
...TO PLAY MY ORIGINAL SONGS IN THE PARK, FAR FROM THE DMC GUYS.
When I wake up in the morning, you're there making cheese tarts.
SHAKKA
Sweet baby, that's what you are. My sweet, sweet lover.
SHAKKA
SHAKKA
SIGH...I MUSTER THE COURAGE TO PLAY OUT IN THE OPEN LIKE THIS, BUT NOBODY STOPS TO LISTEN...
AND MEAN-WHILE, DMC IS SO POPULAR ...
SHAKKA
SHAKKA
SST SST
SHHHHHH
BUT IT'S OK. IT'S MY MUSIC, AND AS LONG AS I ENJOY IT...
...PEOPLE WILL START NOTICING. I COULD QUIT DMC!
ONE DAY. ONE DAY MY SONG WILL BE USED IN A SODA COMMERCIAL.
LOVIN' HAPPY COLA. THE REAL THING!
PWAF
I'D STAR IN IT, NATURALLY.
I'M GONNA GIVE IT MY ALL.
UMM, THIS NEXT SONG IS ABOUT LONGING ...
RAPE HER HARD !!
PWAF

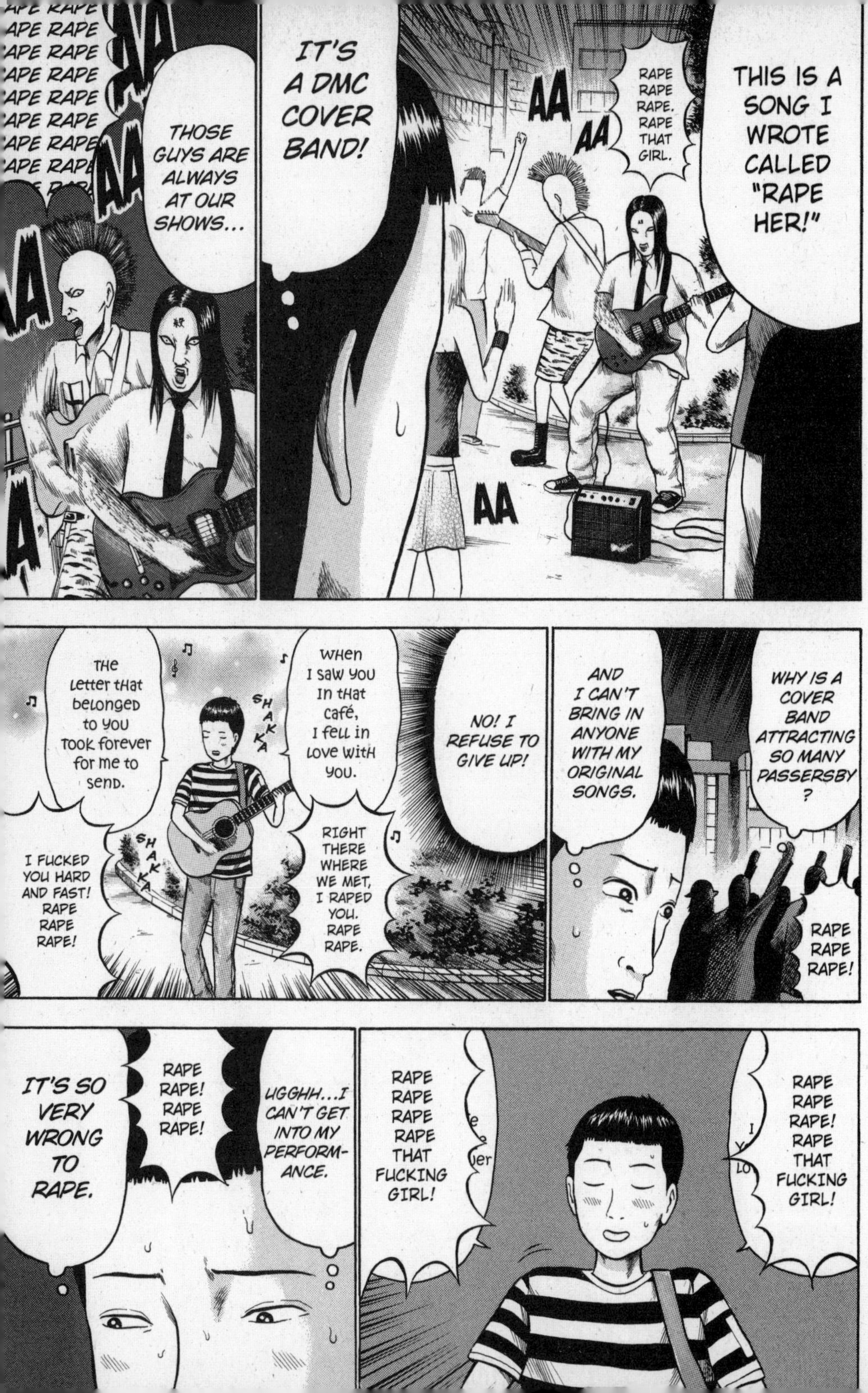
THIS IS A SONG I WROTE CALLED "RAPE HER!"
RAPE RAPE RAPE. RAPE THAT GIRL.
AA
AA
AA
IT'S A DMC COVER BAND!
THOSE GUYS ARE ALWAYS AT OUR SHOWS...
AA
AA
WHY IS A COVER BAND ATTRACTING SO MANY PASSERSBY?
AND I CAN'T BRING IN ANYONE WITH MY ORIGINAL SONGS.
RAPE RAPE RAPE!
NO! I REFUSE TO GIVE UP!
When I saw you in that café, I fell in love with you.
The letter that belonged to you took forever for me to send.
SHAKA
SHAKA
RIGHT THERE WHERE WE MET, I RAPED YOU. RAPE RAPE.
I FUCKED YOU HARD AND FAST! RAPE RAPE RAPE!
RAPE RAPE RAPE! RAPE THAT FUCKING GIRL!
RAPE RAPE RAPE RAPE THAT FUCKING GIRL!
UGGHH...I CAN'T GET INTO MY PERFORMANCE.
RAPE RAPE! RAPE RAPE!
IT'S SO VERY WRONG TO RAPE.

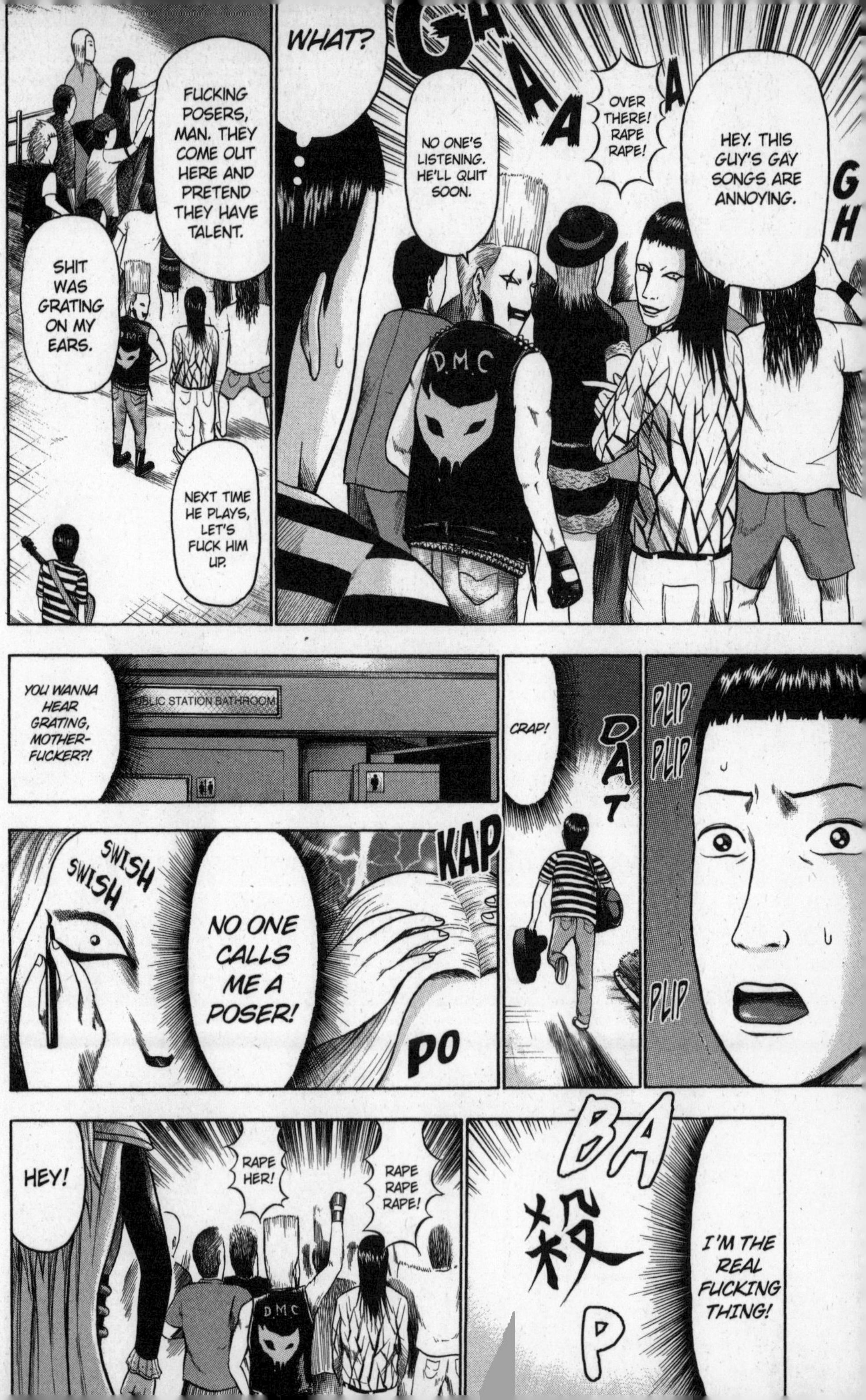
GH
HEY. THIS GUY'S GAY SONGS ARE ANNOYING.
A
OVER THERE! RAPE RAPE!
GAA
NO ONE'S LISTENING. HE'LL QUIT SOON.
WHAT?
FUCKING POSERS, MAN. THEY COME OUT HERE AND PRETEND THEY HAVE TALENT.
SHIT WAS GRATING ON MY EARS.
NEXT TIME HE PLAYS, LET'S FUCK HIM UP.
PLIP PLIP
PLIP
DAT
CRAP!
BLIC STATION BATHROOM
YOU WANNA HEAR GRATING, MOTHER-FUCKER?!
KAP
NO ONE CALLS ME A POSER!
SWISH SWISH
PO
BA
殺
P
I'M THE REAL FUCKING THING!
RAPE RAPE RAPE!
RAPE HER!
HEY!

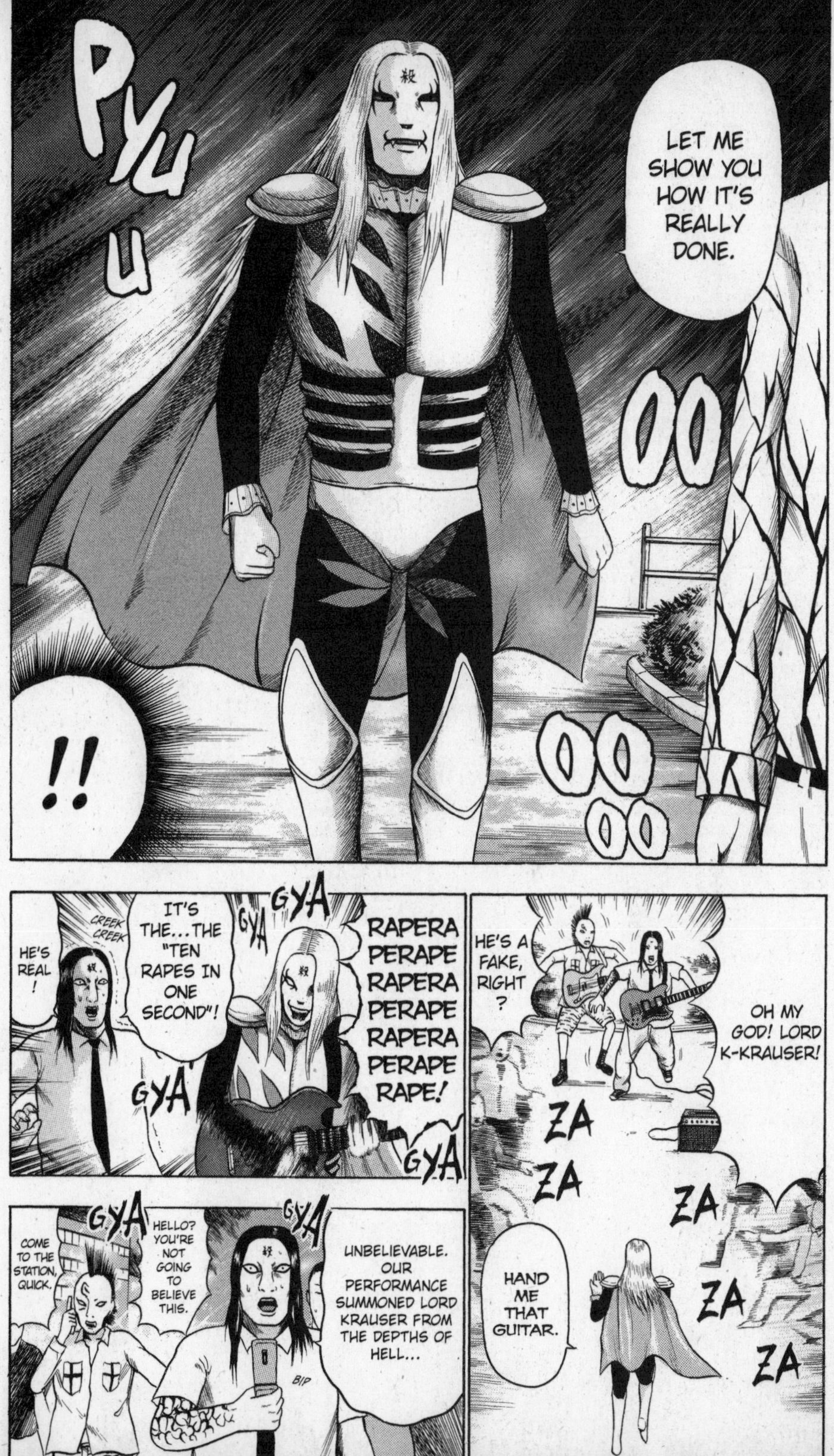
LET ME SHOW YOU HOW IT'S REALLY DONE.
Pyuu
u
OO
OO
OO
OO
!!
OH MY GOD! LORD K-KRAUSER!
HE'S A FAKE, RIGHT?
ZA
ZA
ZA
ZA
ZA
HAND ME THAT GUITAR.
RAPERA PERAPE RAPERA PERAPE RAPERA PERAPE RAPE!
GYA
GYA
IT'S THE... THE "TEN RAPES IN ONE SECOND"!
CREEK CREEK
HE'S REAL!
GYA
GYA
UNBELIEVABLE. OUR PERFORMANCE SUMMONED LORD KRAUSER FROM THE DEPTHS OF HELL...
GYA
BIP
HELLO? YOU'RE NOT GOING TO BELIEVE THIS.
GYA
COME TO THE STATION, QUICK.

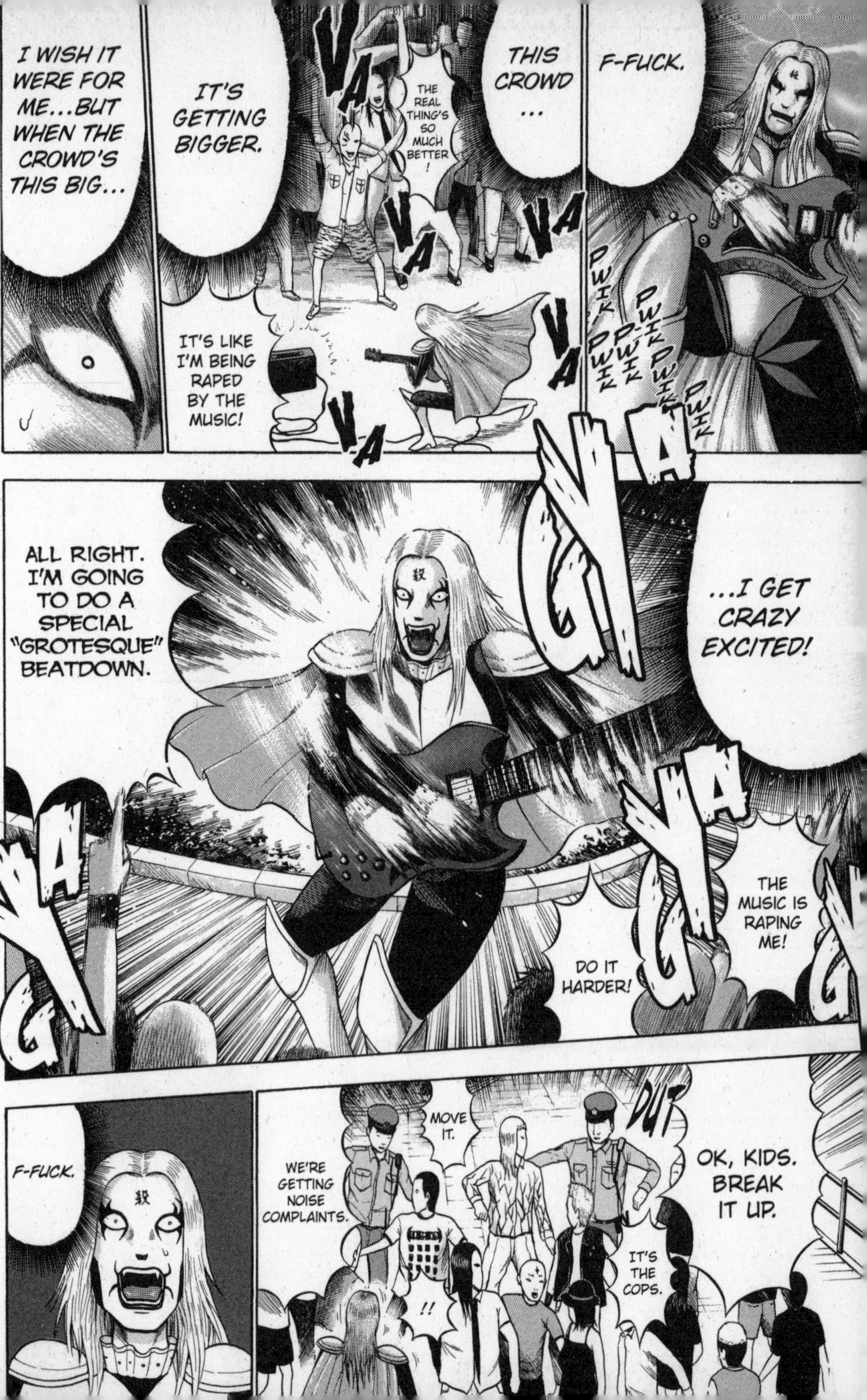
F-FUCK.
PWIK PWIK P-PWIK PWIK PWIK PWIK
THIS CROWD ...
THE REAL THING'S SO MUCH BETTER!
IT'S GETTING BIGGER.
VA VA VA VA VA VA
IT'S LIKE I'M BEING RAPED BY THE MUSIC!
I WISH IT WERE FOR ME...BUT WHEN THE CROWD'S THIS BIG...
GYA
...I GET CRAZY EXCITED!
ALL RIGHT. I'M GOING TO DO A SPECIAL "GROTESQUE" BEATDOWN.
GYA
THE MUSIC IS RAPING ME!
DO IT HARDER!
GYA
DUT
OK, KIDS. BREAK IT UP.
MOVE IT.
WE'RE GETTING NOISE COMPLAINTS.
IT'S THE COPS.
!!
F-FUCK.

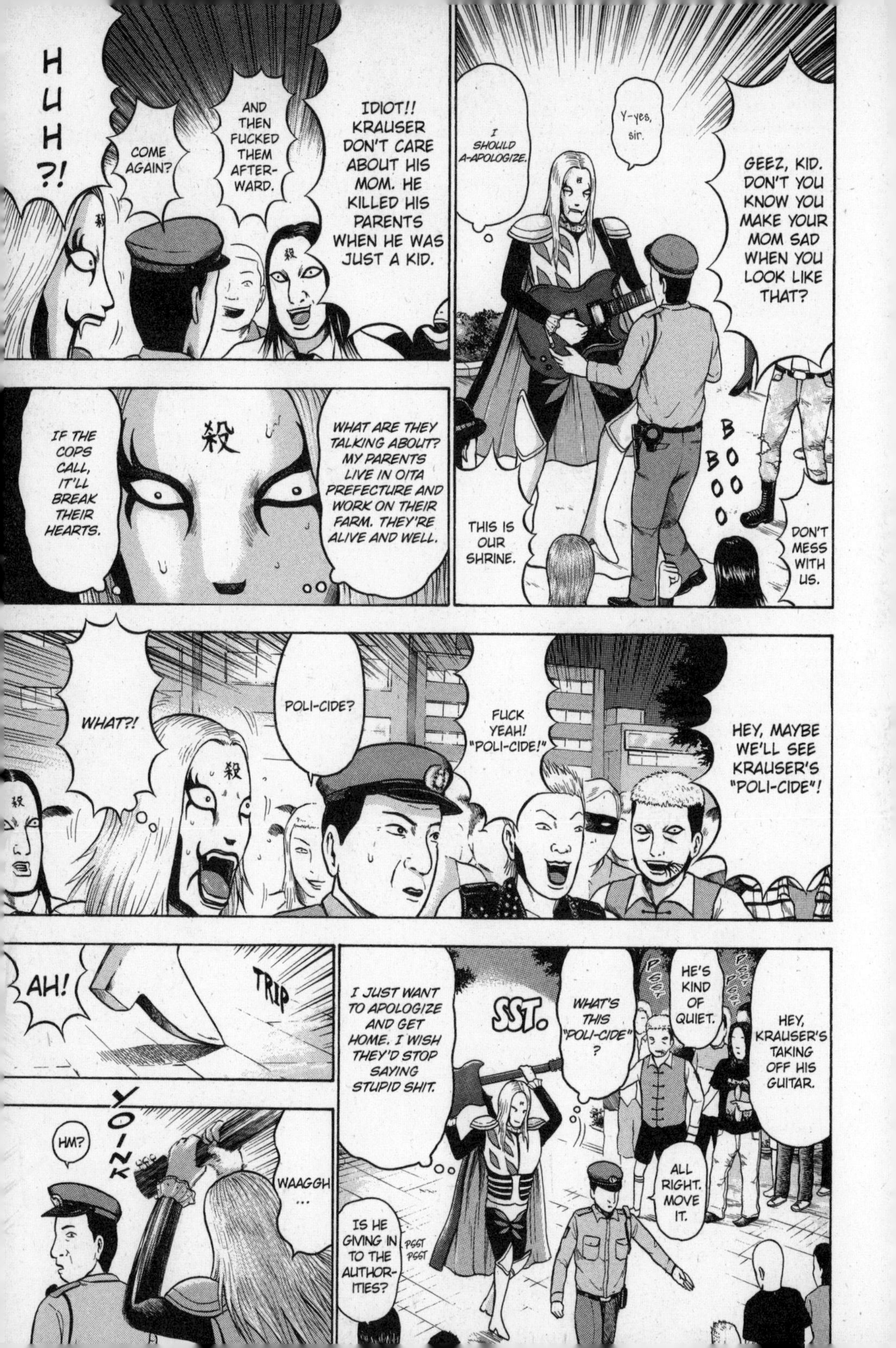
GEEZ, KID. DON'T YOU KNOW YOU MAKE YOUR MOM SAD WHEN YOU LOOK LIKE THAT?
Y-yes, sir.
I SHOULD A-APOLOGIZE.
DON'T MESS WITH US.
BOOOOO
THIS IS OUR SHRINE.
IDIOT!! KRAUSER DON'T CARE ABOUT HIS MOM. HE KILLED HIS PARENTS WHEN HE WAS JUST A KID.
AND THEN FUCKED THEM AFTER-WARD.
COME AGAIN?
HUH?!
WHAT ARE THEY TALKING ABOUT? MY PARENTS LIVE IN OITA PREFECTURE AND WORK ON THEIR FARM. THEY'RE ALIVE AND WELL.
IF THE COPS CALL, IT'LL BREAK THEIR HEARTS.
HEY, MAYBE WE'LL SEE KRAUSER'S "POLI-CIDE"!
FUCK YEAH! "POLI-CIDE!"
POLI-CIDE?
WHAT?!
HEY, KRAUSER'S TAKING OFF HIS GUITAR.
HE'S KIND OF QUIET.
PSST PSST
WHAT'S THIS "POLI-CIDE"?
SST.
I JUST WANT TO APOLOGIZE AND GET HOME. I WISH THEY'D STOP SAYING STUPID SHIT.
ALL RIGHT. MOVE IT.
PSST PSST
IS HE GIVING IN TO THE AUTHOR-ITIES?
TRIP
AH!
WAAGGH...
YOINK
HM?

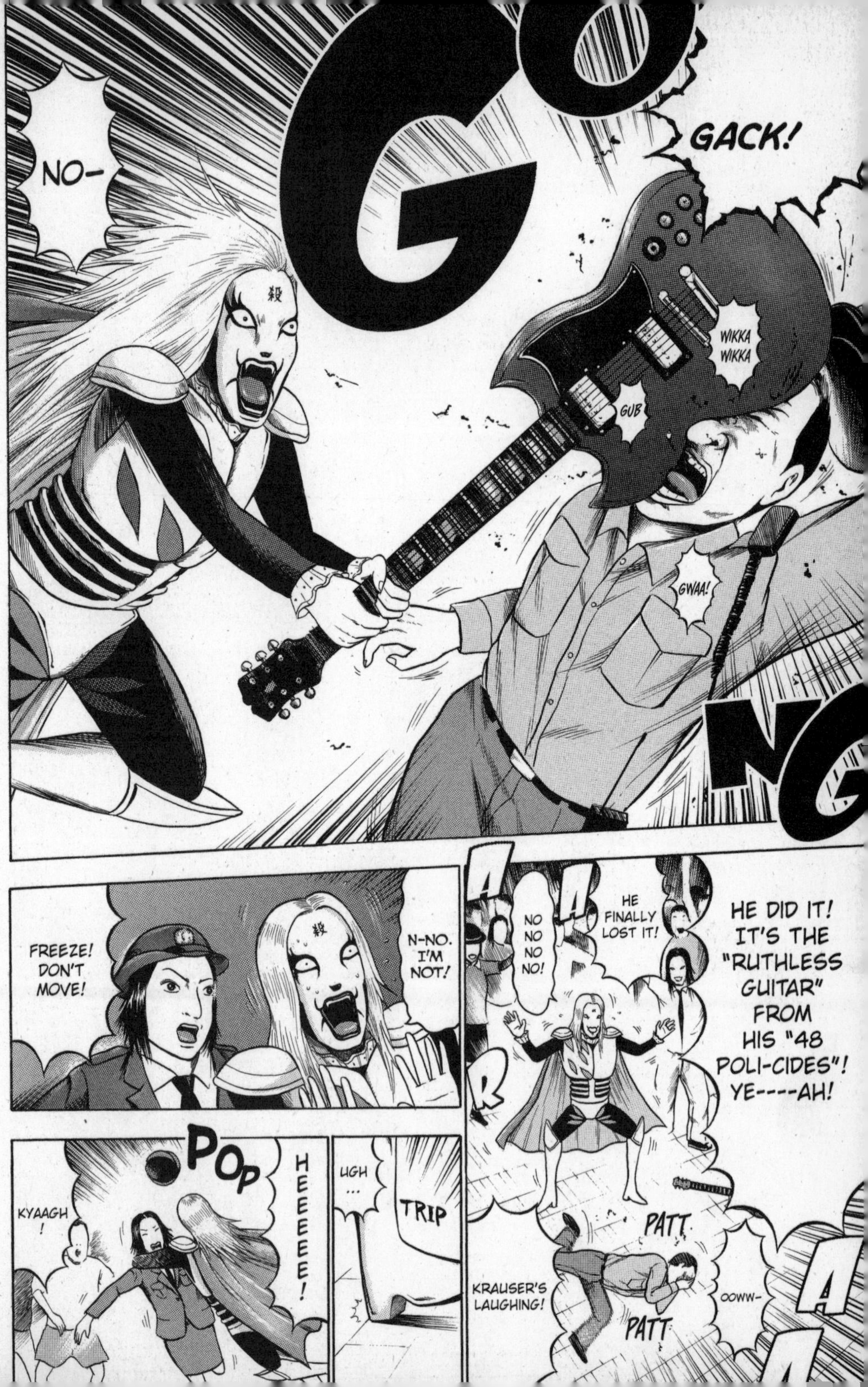
GO
GACK!
WIKKA WIKKA
NO-
GUB
GWAA!
NG
HE DID IT! IT'S THE "RUTHLESS GUITAR" FROM HIS "48 POLI-CIDES"! YE----AH!
HE FINALLY LOST IT!
NO NO NO NO NO!
PATT
OOWW-
PATT
KRAUSER'S LAUGHING!
N-NO. I'M NOT!
FREEZE! DON'T MOVE!
UGH ...
TRIP
POP
HEEEEEE!
KYAAGH!

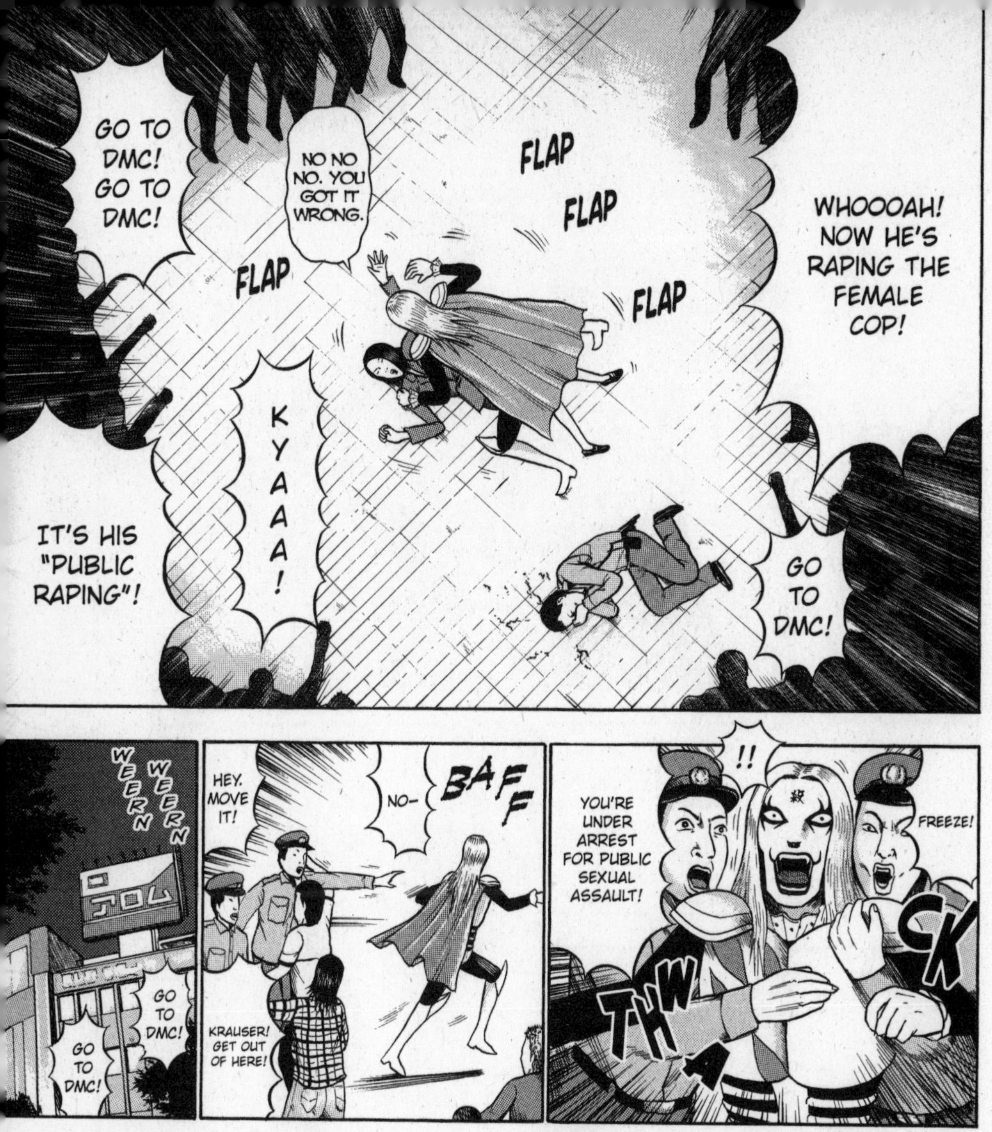
WHOOOAH! NOW HE'S RAPING THE FEMALE COP!
FLAP
FLAP
NO NO NO. YOU GOT IT WRONG.
GO TO DMC! GO TO DMC!
FLAP
FLAP
KYAAAA!
GO TO DMC!
IT'S HIS "PUBLIC RAPING"!
!!
FREEZE!
YOU'RE UNDER ARREST FOR PUBLIC SEXUAL ASSAULT!
THWACK
BAFF
NO–
HEY. MOVE IT!
KRAUSER! GET OUT OF HERE!
WEERN WEERN
GO TO DMC!
GO TO DMC!

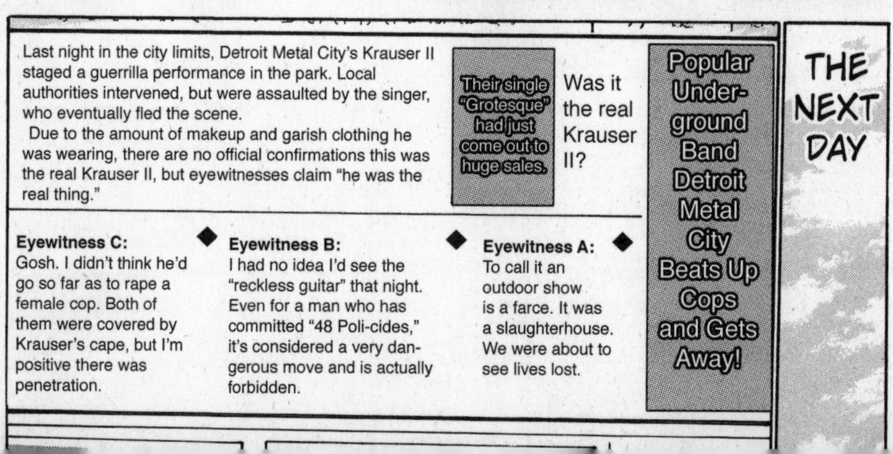
THE NEXT DAY

Popular Underground Band Detroit Metal City Beats Up Cops and Gets Away!

Was it the real Krauser II?

Their single "Grotesque" had just come out to huge sales.

Last night in the city limits, Detroit Metal City's Krauser II staged a guerrilla performance in the park. Local authorities intervened, but were assaulted by the singer, who eventually fled the scene.

Due to the amount of makeup and garish clothing he was wearing, there are no official confirmations this was the real Krauser II, but eyewitnesses claim "he was the real thing."

◆ **Eyewitness A:** To call it an outdoor show is a farce. It was a slaughterhouse. We were about to see lives lost.

◆ **Eyewitness B:** I had no idea I'd see the "reckless guitar" that night. Even for a man who has committed "48 Poli-cides," it's considered a very dangerous move and is actually forbidden.

◆ **Eyewitness C:** Gosh. I didn't think he'd go so far as to rape a female cop. Both of them were covered by Krauser's cape, but I'm positive there was penetration.

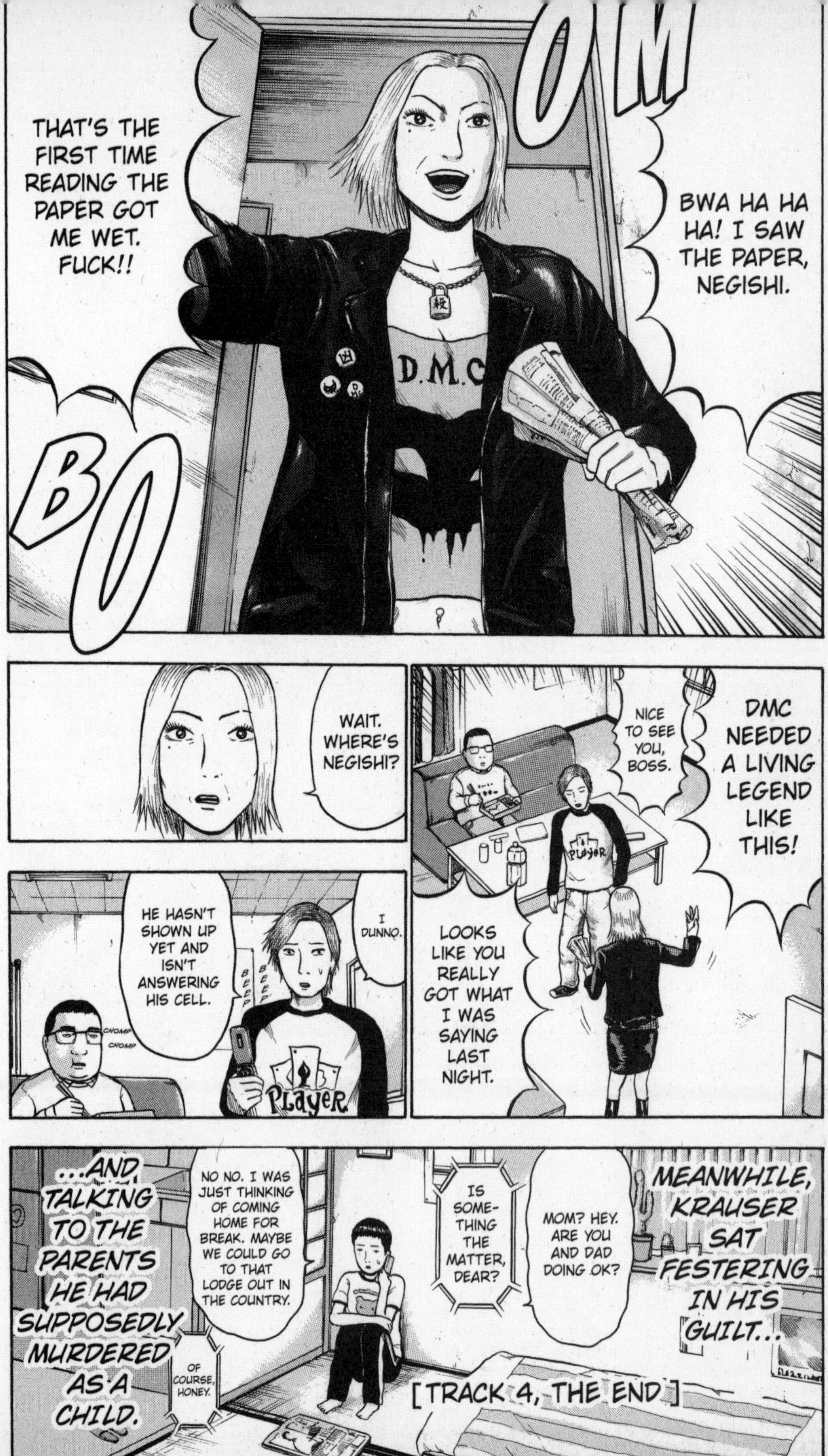
BOOM
BWA HA HA HA! I SAW THE PAPER, NEGISHI.
THAT'S THE FIRST TIME READING THE PAPER GOT ME WET. FUCK!!
D.M.C
DMC NEEDED A LIVING LEGEND LIKE THIS!
NICE TO SEE YOU, BOSS.
PLAYER
LOOKS LIKE YOU REALLY GOT WHAT I WAS SAYING LAST NIGHT.
WAIT. WHERE'S NEGISHI?
I DUNNO.
BEEP BEEP
HE HASN'T SHOWN UP YET AND ISN'T ANSWERING HIS CELL.
CHOMP CHOMP
PLAYER
MEANWHILE, KRAUSER SAT FESTERING IN HIS GUILT...
MOM? HEY. ARE YOU AND DAD DOING OK?
IS SOMETHING THE MATTER, DEAR?
NO NO. I WAS JUST THINKING OF COMING HOME FOR BREAK. MAYBE WE COULD GO TO THAT LODGE OUT IN THE COUNTRY.
...AND TALKING TO THE PARENTS HE HAD SUPPOSEDLY MURDERED AS A CHILD.
OF COURSE, HONEY.
[TRACK 4, THE END]

DMC LEXICON

 M

Someone who derives pleasure from being spanked and suffering humiliating attacks. Usually perpetrated by a master, who exercises harsher behavior than average. Neglect, humiliation, whipping, candling, enemas, gangbangs, whatever floats their boat.

Usage: You think this miserable excuse for an M costume will cut it? What will your subordinates think?

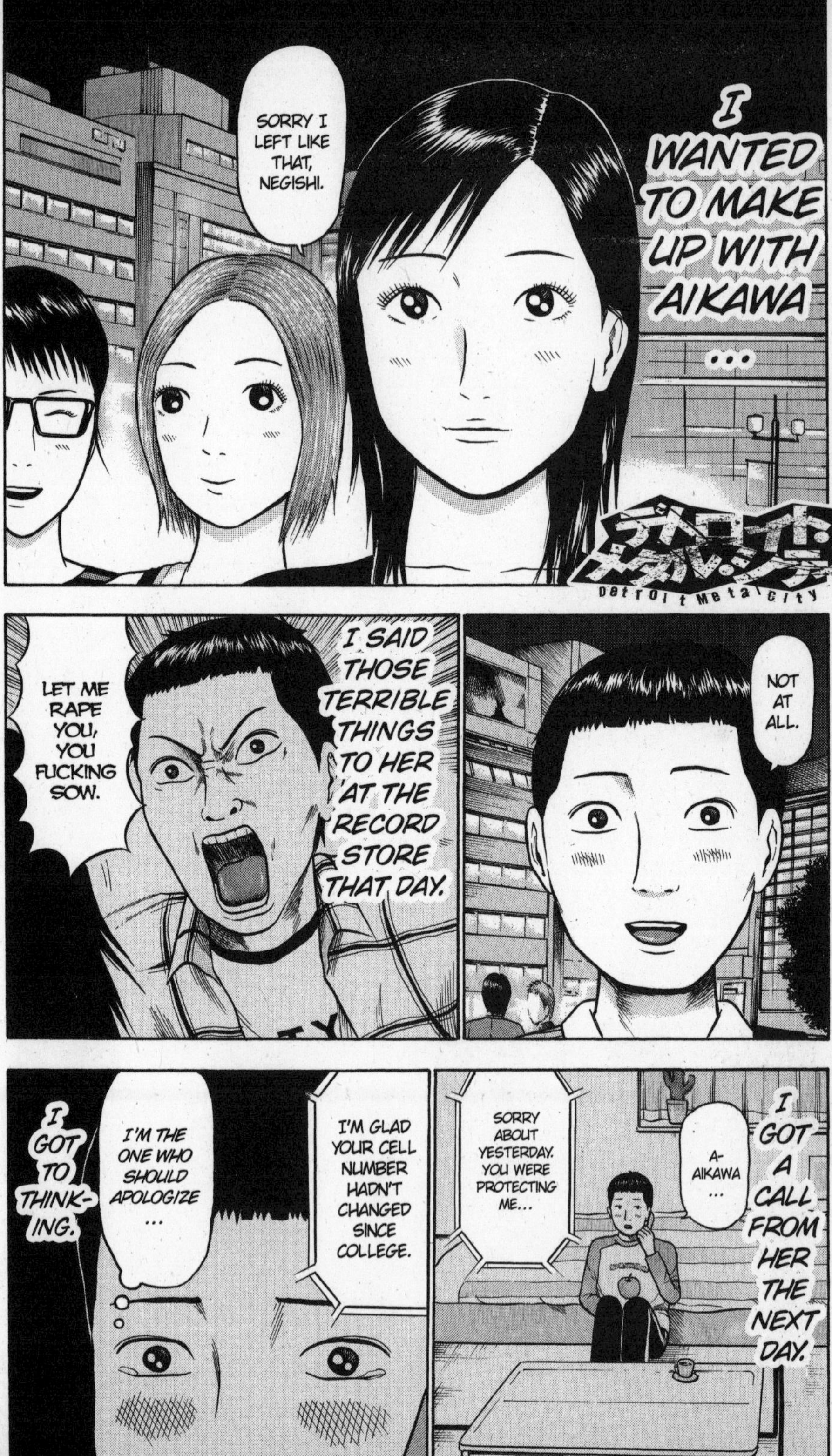
I WANTED TO MAKE UP WITH AIKAWA...
SORRY I LEFT LIKE THAT, NEGISHI.
Detroit Metal City
NOT AT ALL.
I SAID THOSE TERRIBLE THINGS TO HER AT THE RECORD STORE THAT DAY.
LET ME RAPE YOU, YOU FUCKING SOW.
I GOT A CALL FROM HER THE NEXT DAY.
A-AIKAWA...
SORRY ABOUT YESTERDAY. YOU WERE PROTECTING ME...
I'M GLAD YOUR CELL NUMBER HADN'T CHANGED SINCE COLLEGE.
I'M THE ONE WHO SHOULD APOLOGIZE...
I GOT TO THINKING.

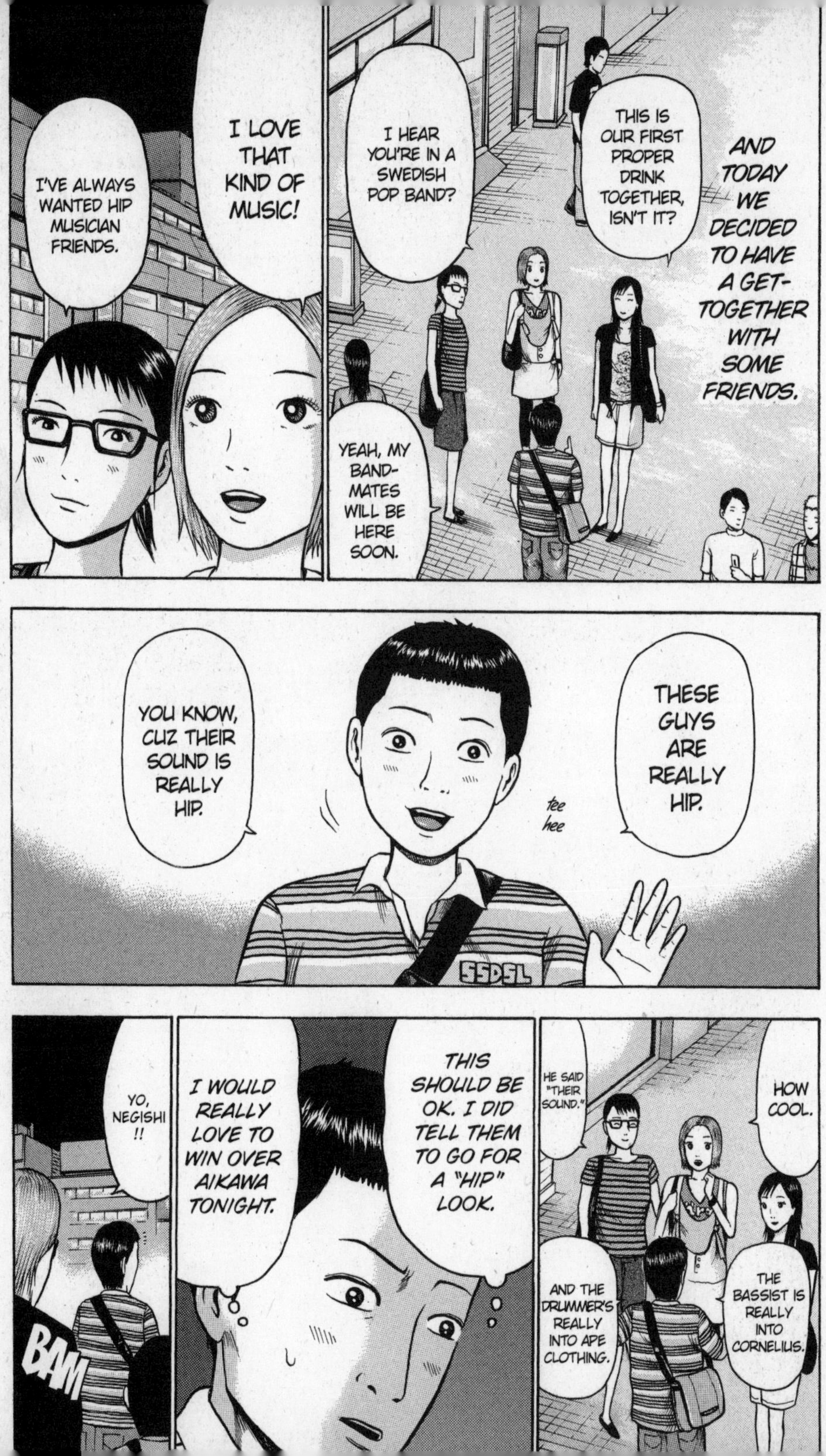
AND TODAY WE DECIDED TO HAVE A GET-TOGETHER WITH SOME FRIENDS.
THIS IS OUR FIRST PROPER DRINK TOGETHER, ISN'T IT?
I HEAR YOU'RE IN A SWEDISH POP BAND?
YEAH, MY BAND-MATES WILL BE HERE SOON.
I LOVE THAT KIND OF MUSIC!
I'VE ALWAYS WANTED HIP MUSICIAN FRIENDS.
THESE GUYS ARE REALLY HIP.
tee hee
YOU KNOW, CUZ THEIR SOUND IS REALLY HIP.
SSDSL
HOW COOL.
HE SAID "THEIR SOUND."
THE BASSIST IS REALLY INTO CORNELIUS.
AND THE DRUMMER'S REALLY INTO APE CLOTHING.
THIS SHOULD BE OK. I DID TELL THEM TO GO FOR A "HIP" LOOK.
I WOULD REALLY LOVE TO WIN OVER AIKAWA TONIGHT.
YO, NEGISHI !!
BAM

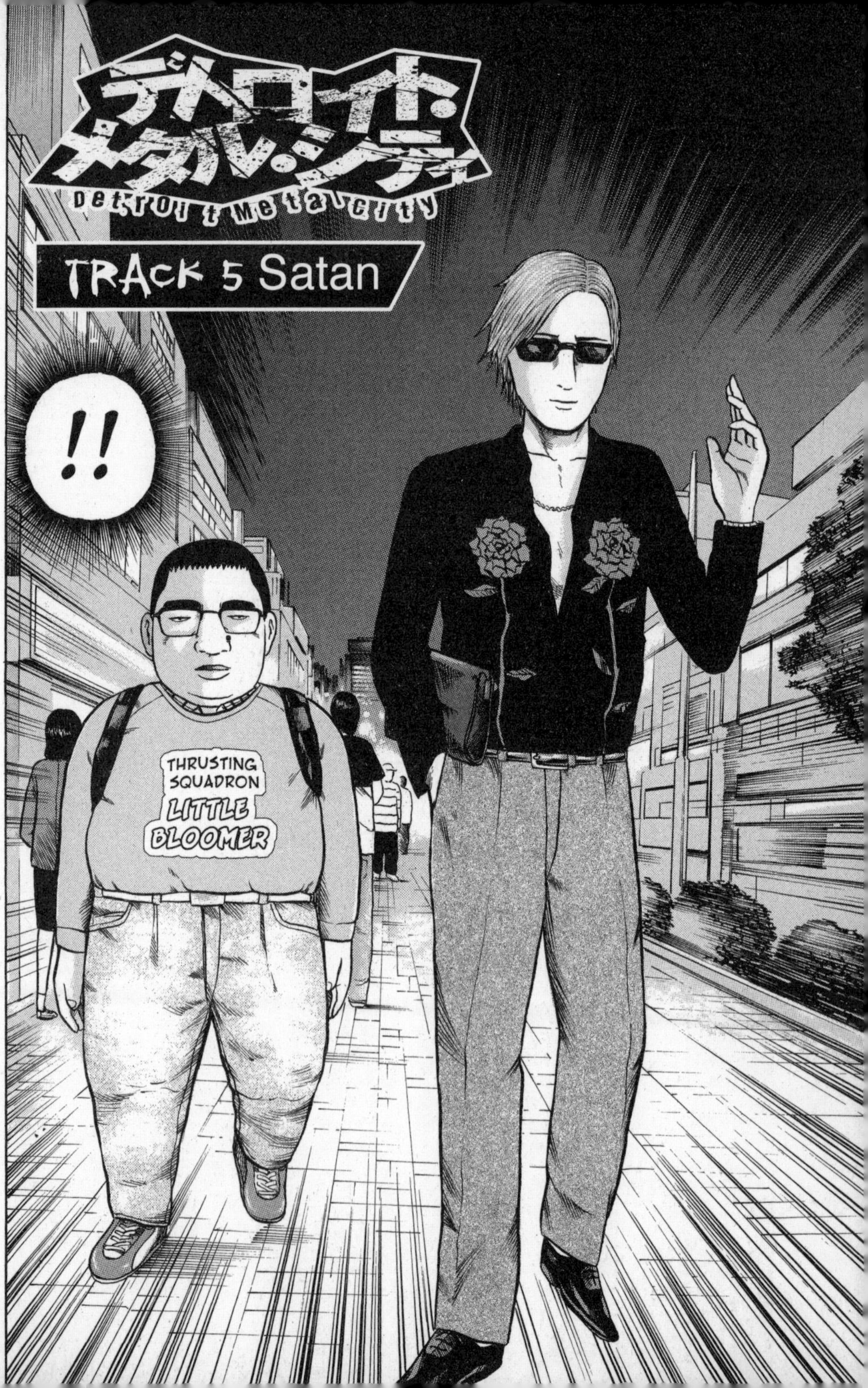
デトロイト・メタル・シティ
Detroit Metal City
TRACK 5 Satan
!!
THRUSTING SQUADRON LITTLE BLOOMER

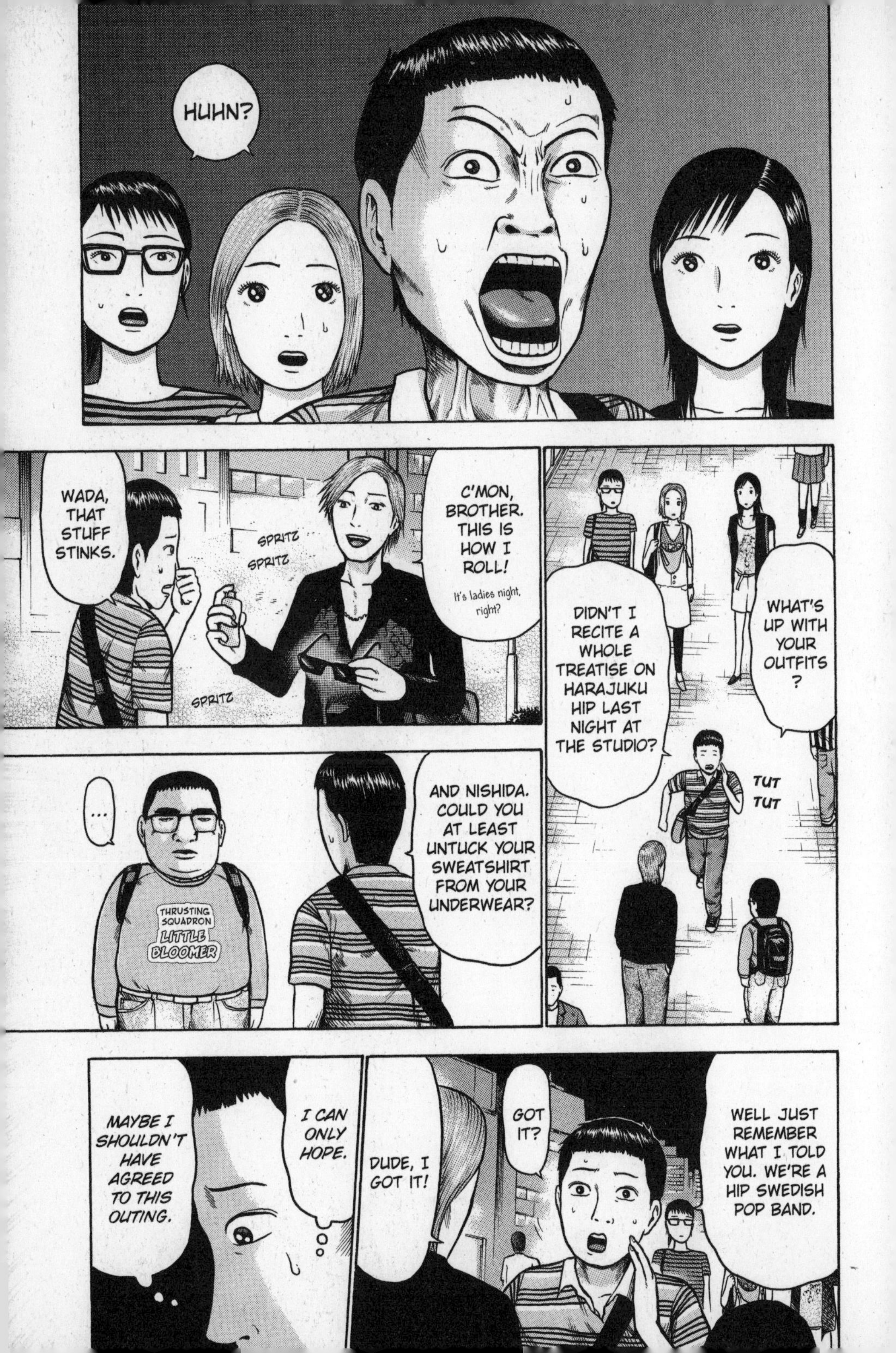
HUHN?
WHAT'S UP WITH YOUR OUTFITS?
DIDN'T I RECITE A WHOLE TREATISE ON HARAJUKU HIP LAST NIGHT AT THE STUDIO?
TUT TUT
C'MON, BROTHER. THIS IS HOW I ROLL!
It's ladies night, right?
SPRITZ
SPRITZ
WADA, THAT STUFF STINKS.
SPRITZ
AND NISHIDA. COULD YOU AT LEAST UNTUCK YOUR SWEATSHIRT FROM YOUR UNDERWEAR?
...
THRUSTING SQUADRON LITTLE BLOOMER
WELL JUST REMEMBER WHAT I TOLD YOU. WE'RE A HIP SWEDISH POP BAND.
GOT IT?
DUDE, I GOT IT!
I CAN ONLY HOPE.
MAYBE I SHOULDN'T HAVE AGREED TO THIS OUTING.

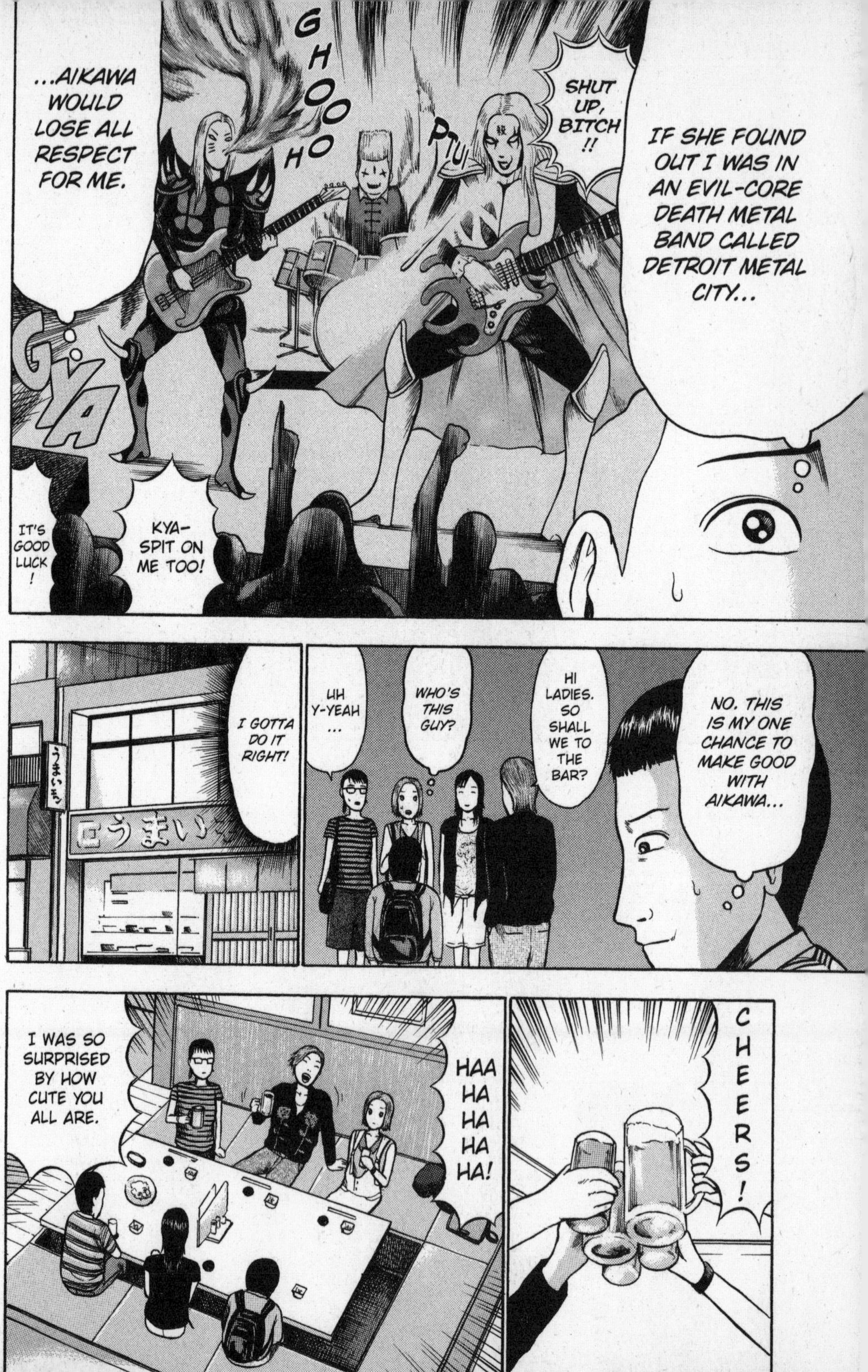
IF SHE FOUND OUT I WAS IN AN EVIL-CORE DEATH METAL BAND CALLED DETROIT METAL CITY...
SHUT UP, BITCH!!
PTUI
GHOOOH
...AIKAWA WOULD LOSE ALL RESPECT FOR ME.
GYA
KYA- SPIT ON ME TOO!
IT'S GOOD LUCK!
NO. THIS IS MY ONE CHANCE TO MAKE GOOD WITH AIKAWA...
HI LADIES. SO SHALL WE TO THE BAR?
WHO'S THIS GUY?
UH Y-YEAH ...
I GOTTA DO IT RIGHT!
CHEERS!
HAA HA HA HA HA!
I WAS SO SURPRISED BY HOW CUTE YOU ALL ARE.

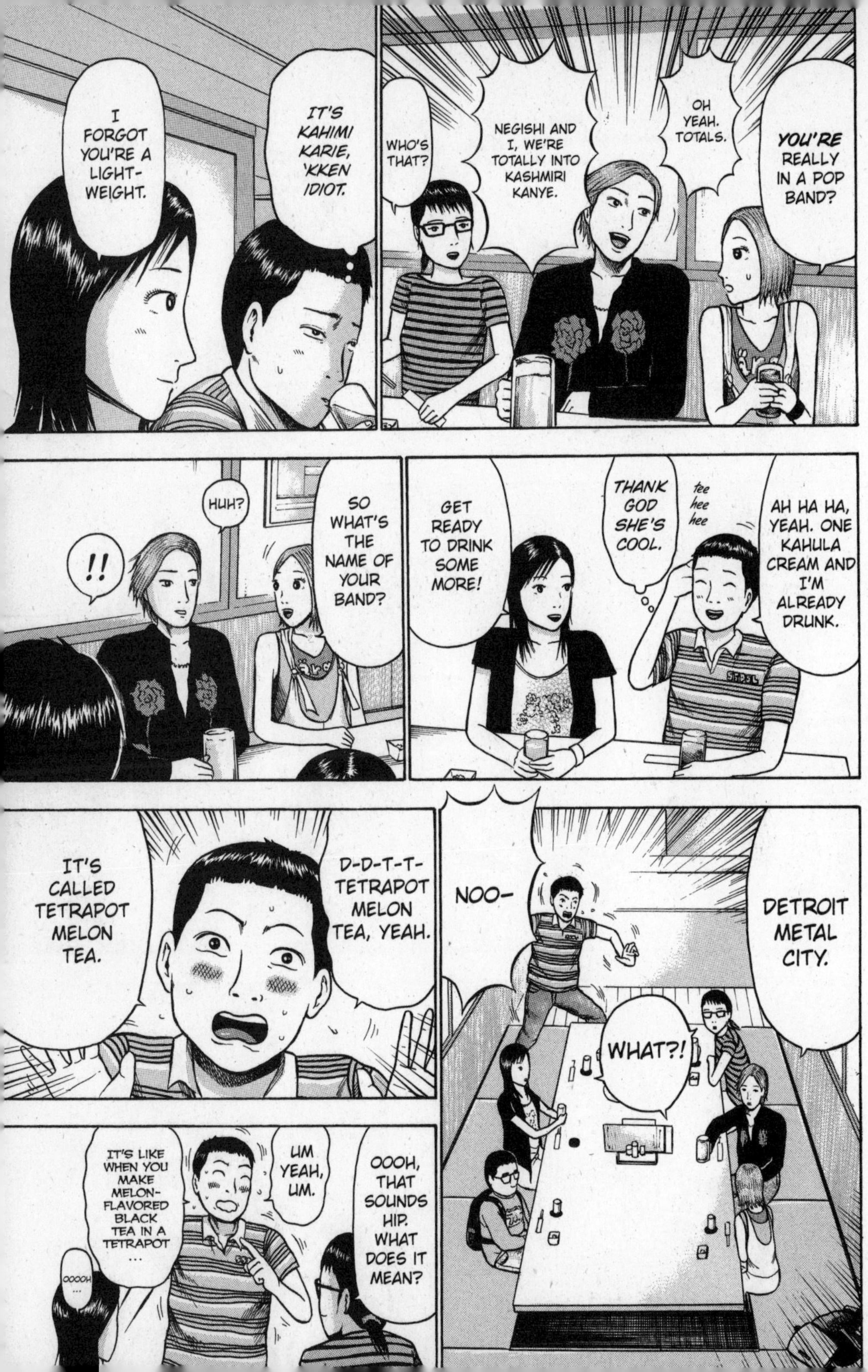
YOU'RE REALLY IN A POP BAND?
OH YEAH. TOTALS.
NEGISHI AND I, WE'RE TOTALLY INTO KASHMIRI KANYE.
WHO'S THAT?
IT'S KAHIMI KARIE, 'KKEN IDIOT.
I FORGOT YOU'RE A LIGHT-WEIGHT.
AH HA HA, YEAH. ONE KAHULA CREAM AND I'M ALREADY DRUNK.
tee hee hee
THANK GOD SHE'S COOL.
GET READY TO DRINK SOME MORE!
SO WHAT'S THE NAME OF YOUR BAND?
HUH?
!!
DETROIT METAL CITY.
NOO-
WHAT?!
D-D-T-T-TETRAPOT MELON TEA, YEAH.
IT'S CALLED TETRAPOT MELON TEA.
OOOH, THAT SOUNDS HIP. WHAT DOES IT MEAN?
UM YEAH, UM.
IT'S LIKE WHEN YOU MAKE MELON-FLAVORED BLACK TEA IN A TETRAPOT ...
OOOOH ...

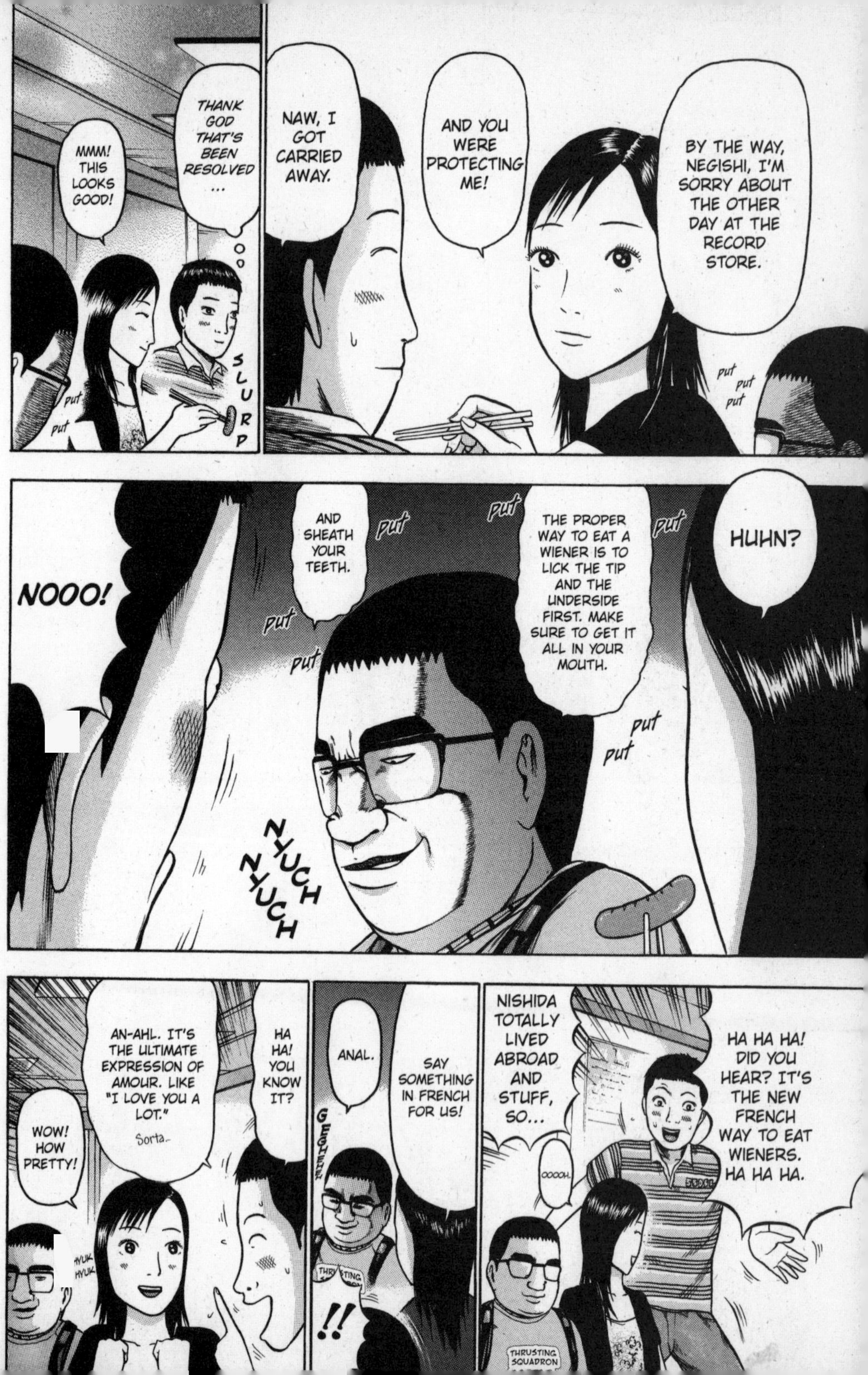
BY THE WAY, NEGISHI, I'M SORRY ABOUT THE OTHER DAY AT THE RECORD STORE.
AND YOU WERE PROTECTING ME!
NAW, I GOT CARRIED AWAY.
put put put
THANK GOD THAT'S BEEN RESOLVED ...
MMM! THIS LOOKS GOOD!
SLURP
put put
HUHN?
put
THE PROPER WAY TO EAT A WIENER IS TO LICK THE TIP AND THE UNDERSIDE FIRST. MAKE SURE TO GET IT ALL IN YOUR MOUTH.
put
AND SHEATH YOUR TEETH.
put
NOOO!
put
put
put put
NYUCH NYUCH
HA HA HA! DID YOU HEAR? IT'S THE NEW FRENCH WAY TO EAT WIENERS. HA HA HA.
NISHIDA TOTALLY LIVED ABROAD AND STUFF, SO...
OOOOH.
THRUSTING SQUADRON
SAY SOMETHING IN FRENCH FOR US!
ANAL.
GEGHEHE
!!
HA HA! YOU KNOW IT?
AN-AHL. IT'S THE ULTIMATE EXPRESSION OF AMOUR. LIKE "I LOVE YOU A LOT."
Sorta...
WOW! HOW PRETTY!
HYUK HYUK

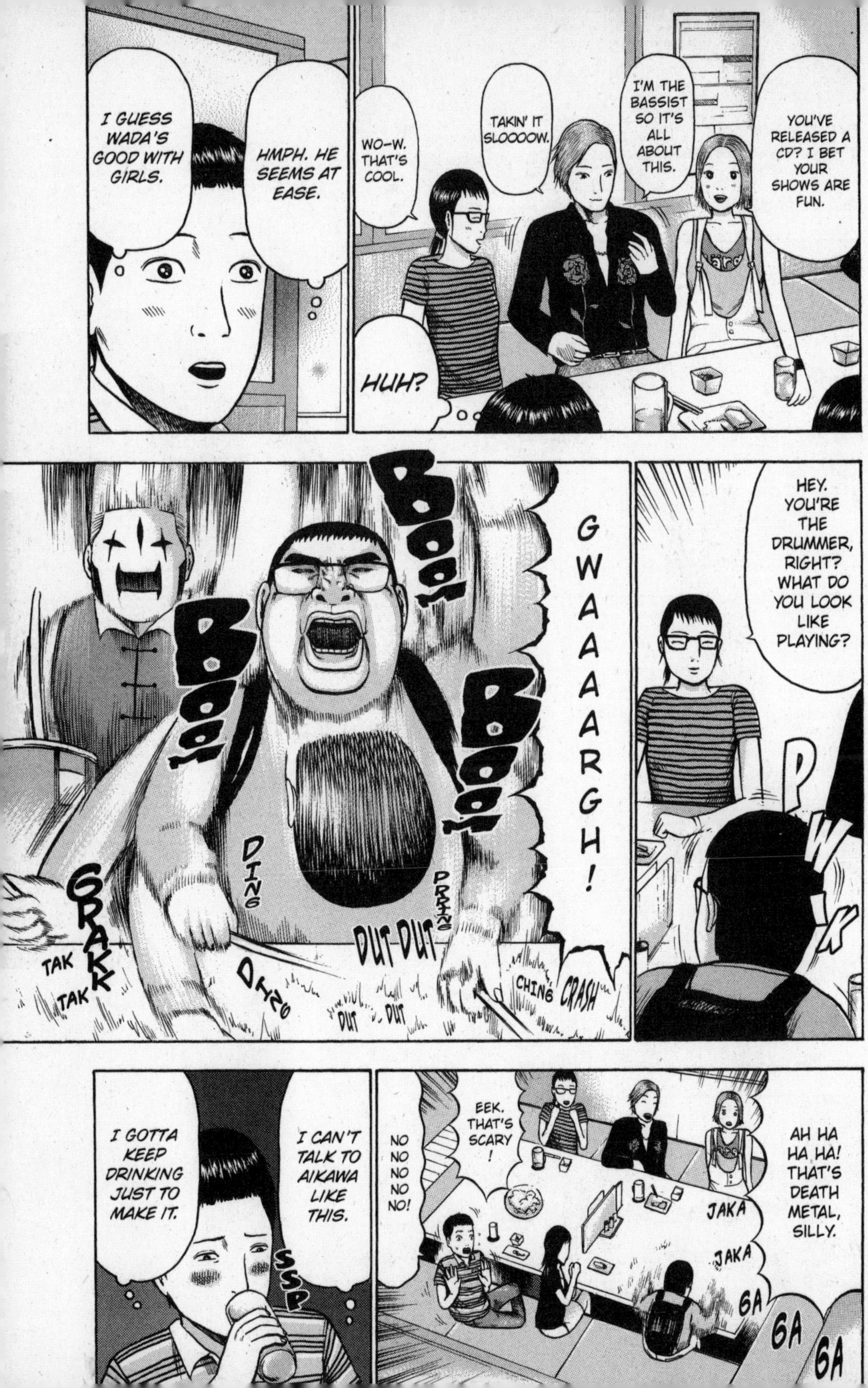
YOU'VE RELEASED A CD? I BET YOUR SHOWS ARE FUN.
I'M THE BASSIST SO IT'S ALL ABOUT THIS.
TAKIN' IT SLOOOOW.
WO-W. THAT'S COOL.
HUH?
HMPH. HE SEEMS AT EASE.
I GUESS WADA'S GOOD WITH GIRLS.
HEY. YOU'RE THE DRUMMER, RIGHT? WHAT DO YOU LOOK LIKE PLAYING?
PWK
GWAAAAARGH!
BOOOM
BOOOM
BOOOM
DING
PRRING
DUT DUT
CHING
CRASH
DUT DUT
GRAKK
TAK
TAK
AH HA HA HA! THAT'S DEATH METAL, SILLY.
EEK. THAT'S SCARY!
NO NO NO NO NO!
JAKA
JAKA
GA
GA
GA
I CAN'T TALK TO AIKAWA LIKE THIS.
I GOTTA KEEP DRINKING JUST TO MAKE IT.
SSP

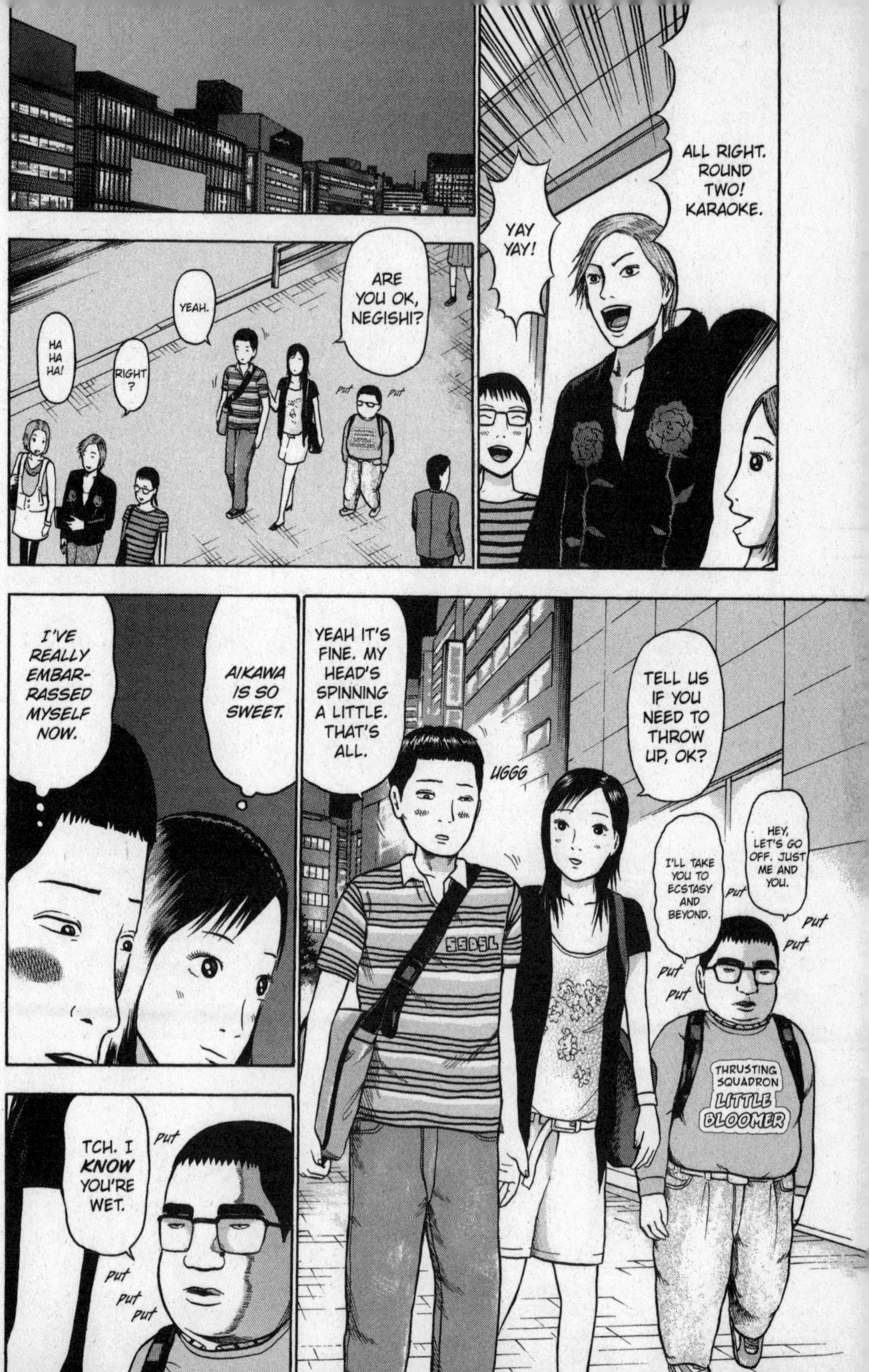

ALL RIGHT. ROUND TWO! KARAOKE.
YAY YAY!
ARE YOU OK, NEGISHI?
YEAH.
RIGHT?
HA HA HA!
put put
TELL US IF YOU NEED TO THROW UP, OK?
YEAH IT'S FINE. MY HEAD'S SPINNING A LITTLE. THAT'S ALL.
UGGG
HEY, LET'S GO OFF. JUST ME AND YOU.
I'LL TAKE YOU TO ECSTASY AND BEYOND.
put put put put put
THRUSTING SQUADRON LITTLE BLOOMER
AIKAWA IS SO SWEET.
I'VE REALLY EMBARRASSED MYSELF NOW.
TCH. I KNOW YOU'RE WET.
put
put put put

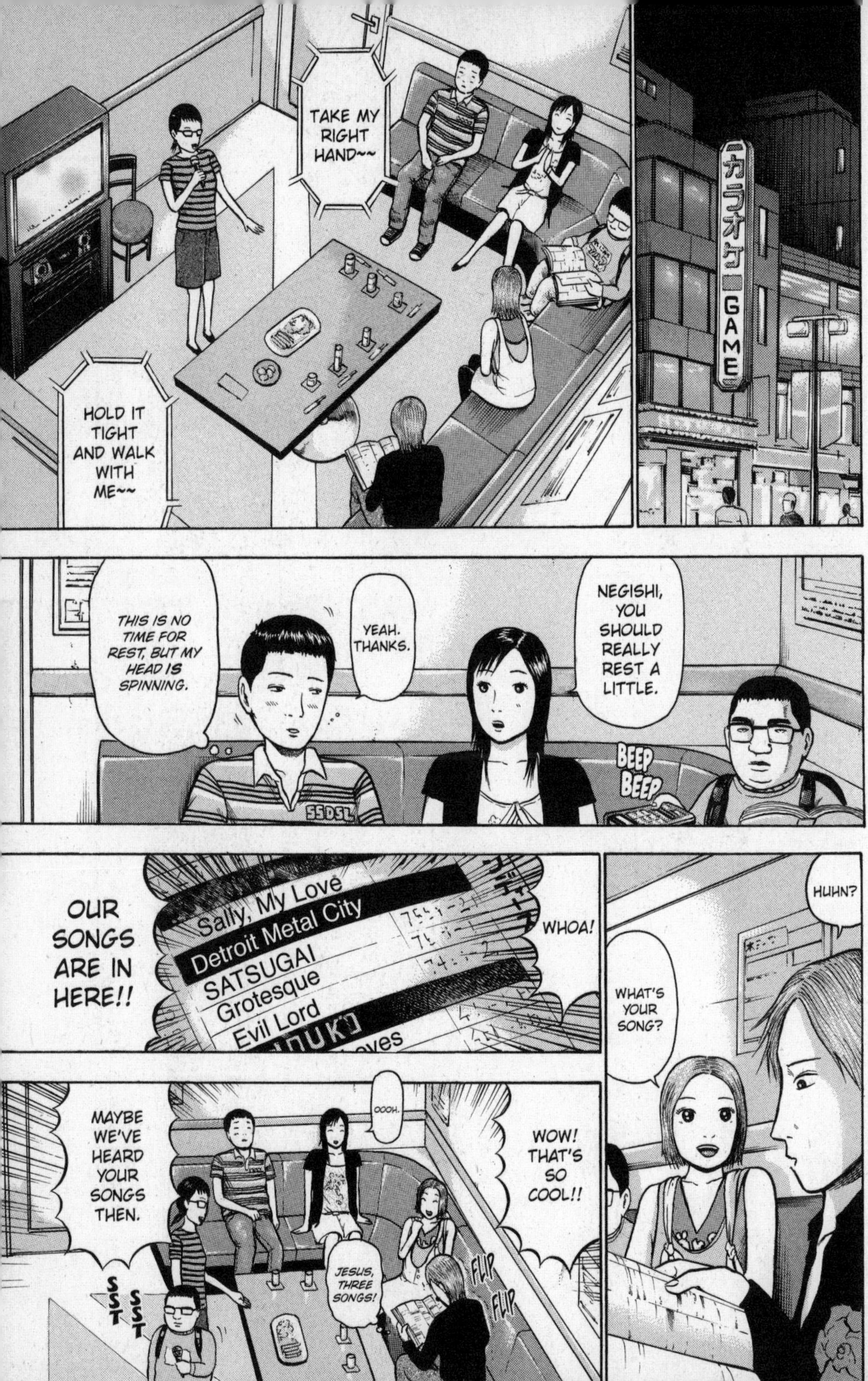
カラオケ
GAME
TAKE MY RIGHT HAND~~
HOLD IT TIGHT AND WALK WITH ME~~
NEGISHI, YOU SHOULD REALLY REST A LITTLE.
BEEP BEEP
YEAH. THANKS.
THIS IS NO TIME FOR REST, BUT MY HEAD IS SPINNING.
HUHN?
WHAT'S YOUR SONG?
WHOA!
Sally, My Love
Detroit Metal City
SATSUGAI
Grotesque
Evil Lord
OUR SONGS ARE IN HERE!!
WOW! THAT'S SO COOL!!
FLIP FLIP
OOOH.
JESUS, THREE SONGS!
MAYBE WE'VE HEARD YOUR SONGS THEN.
SST SST

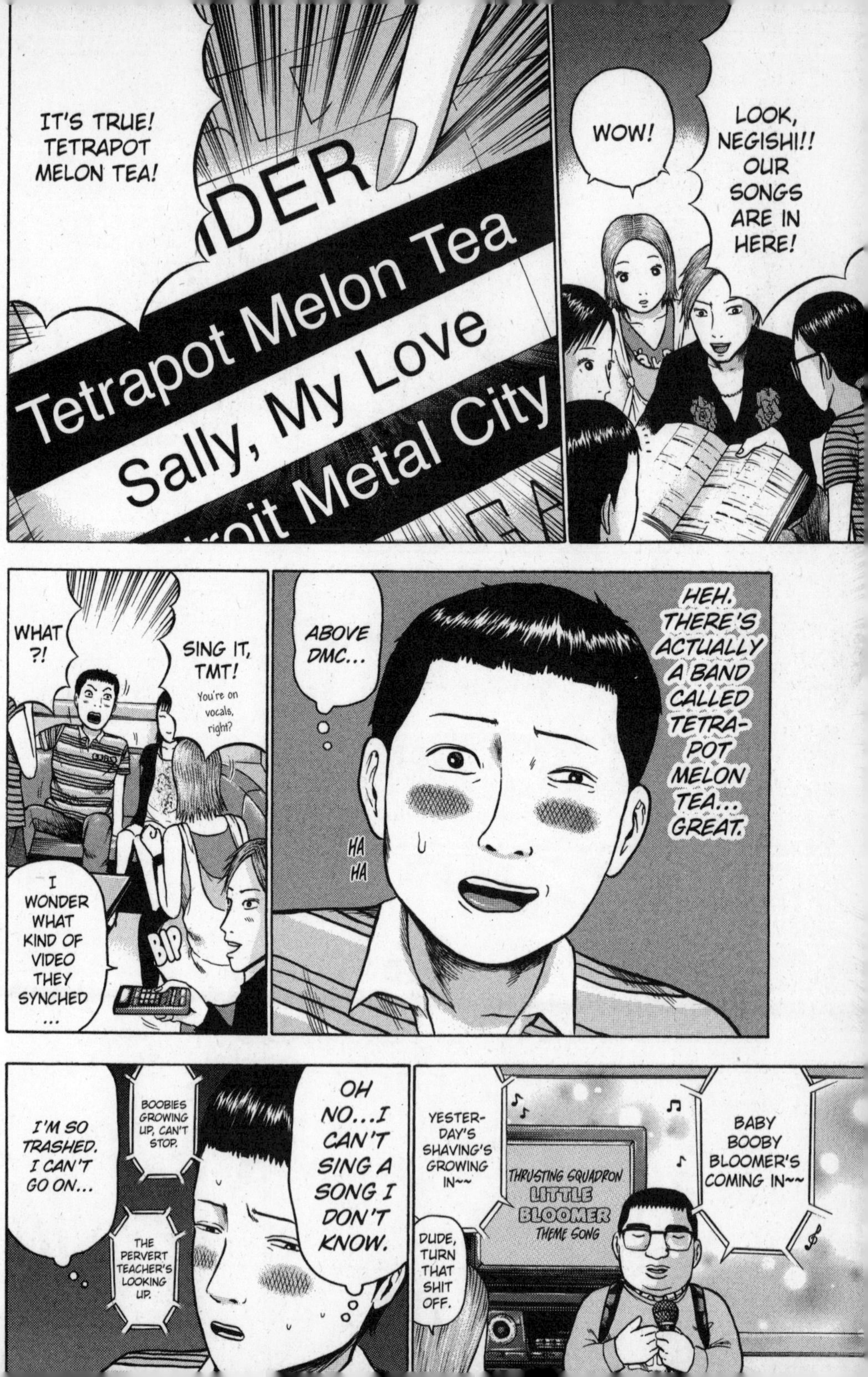
LOOK, NEGISHI!! OUR SONGS ARE IN HERE!
WOW!
IT'S TRUE! TETRAPOT MELON TEA!
DER
Tetrapot Melon Tea
Sally, My Love
roit Metal City
HEH. THERE'S ACTUALLY A BAND CALLED TETRA-POT MELON TEA... GREAT.
ABOVE DMC...
HA HA
SING IT, TMT!
You're on vocals, right?
WHAT ?!
I WONDER WHAT KIND OF VIDEO THEY SYNCHED ...
BIP
BABY BOOBY BLOOMER'S COMING IN~~
YESTER-DAY'S SHAVING'S GROWING IN~~
THRUSTING SQUADRON LITTLE BLOOMER THEME SONG
DUDE, TURN THAT SHIT OFF.
OH NO...I CAN'T SING A SONG I DON'T KNOW.
BOOBIES GROWING UP, CAN'T STOP.
I'M SO TRASHED. I CAN'T GO ON...
THE PERVERT TEACHER'S LOOKING UP.

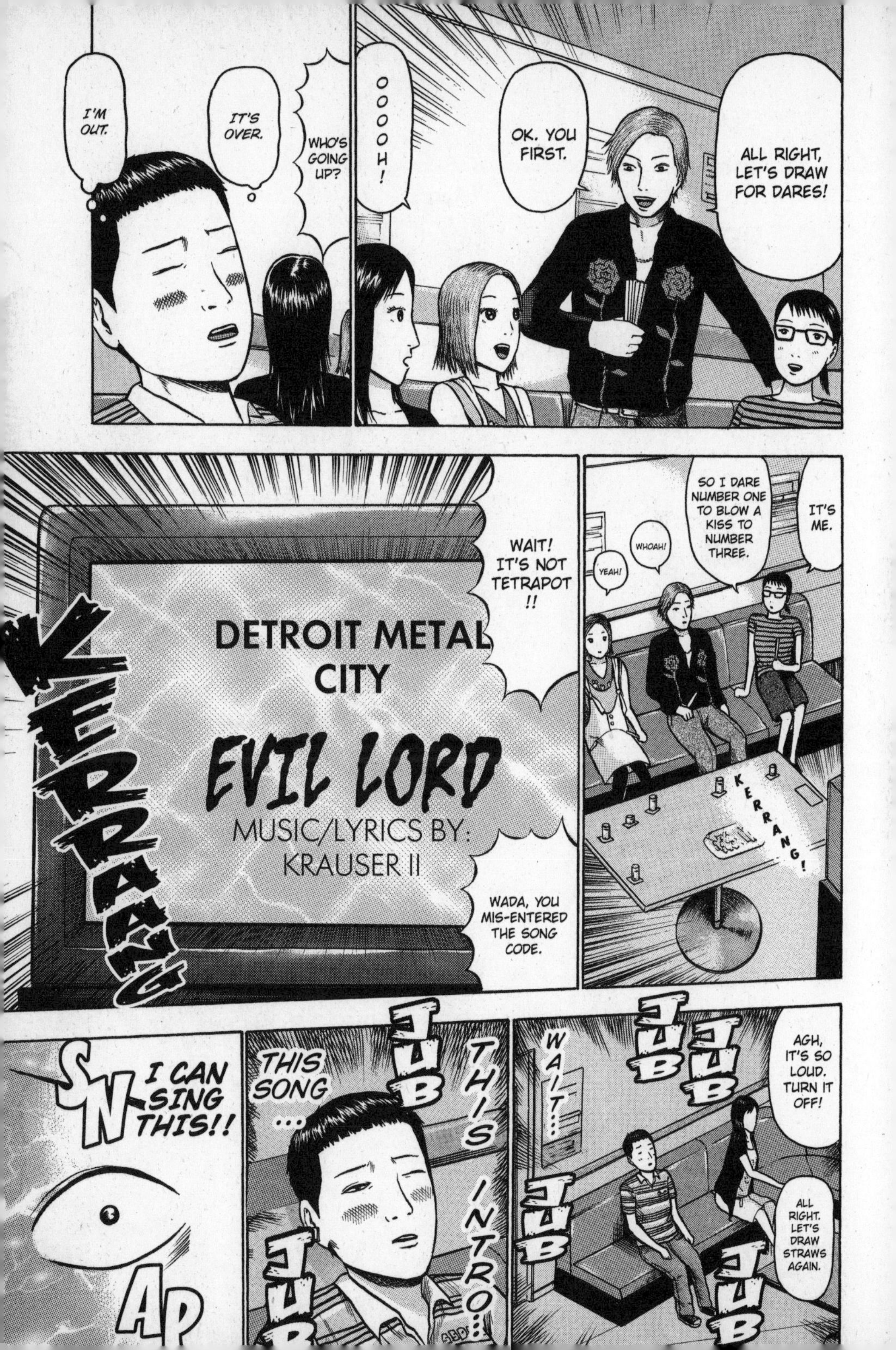
ALL RIGHT, LET'S DRAW FOR DARES!
OK. YOU FIRST.
OOOOOH!
WHO'S GOING UP?
IT'S OVER.
I'M OUT.
IT'S ME.
SO I DARE NUMBER ONE TO BLOW A KISS TO NUMBER THREE.
WHOAH!
YEAH!
KERRANG!
WAIT! IT'S NOT TETRAPOT!!
DETROIT METAL CITY
EVIL LORD
MUSIC/LYRICS BY: KRAUSER II
WADA, YOU MIS-ENTERED THE SONG CODE.
KERRANG
AGH, IT'S SO LOUD. TURN IT OFF!
JUB JUB
WAIT...
JUB
ALL RIGHT. LET'S DRAW STRAWS AGAIN.
JUB
JUB
THIS SONG...
THIS INTRO...
I CAN SING THIS!!
SNAP

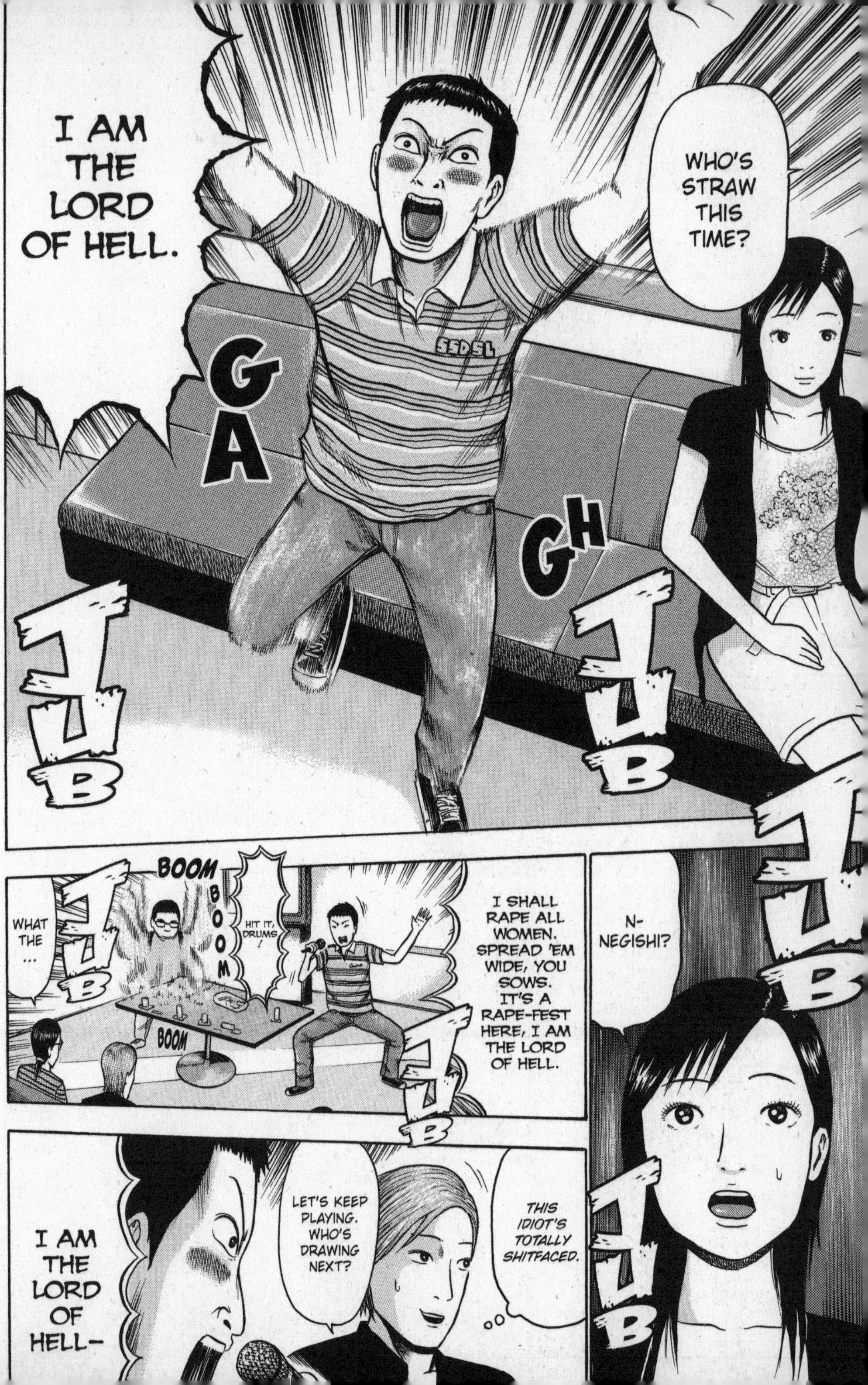
WHO'S STRAW THIS TIME?
I AM THE LORD OF HELL.
GAGH
JUB
JUB
JUB
N-NEGISHI?
JUB
I SHALL RAPE ALL WOMEN. SPREAD 'EM WIDE, YOU SOWS. IT'S A RAPE-FEST HERE, I AM THE LORD OF HELL.
JUB
HIT IT, DRUMS!
BOOM
BOOM
BOOM
WHAT THE ...
JUB
BOOM
THIS IDIOT'S TOTALLY SHITFACED.
LET'S KEEP PLAYING. WHO'S DRAWING NEXT?
I AM THE LORD OF HELL-

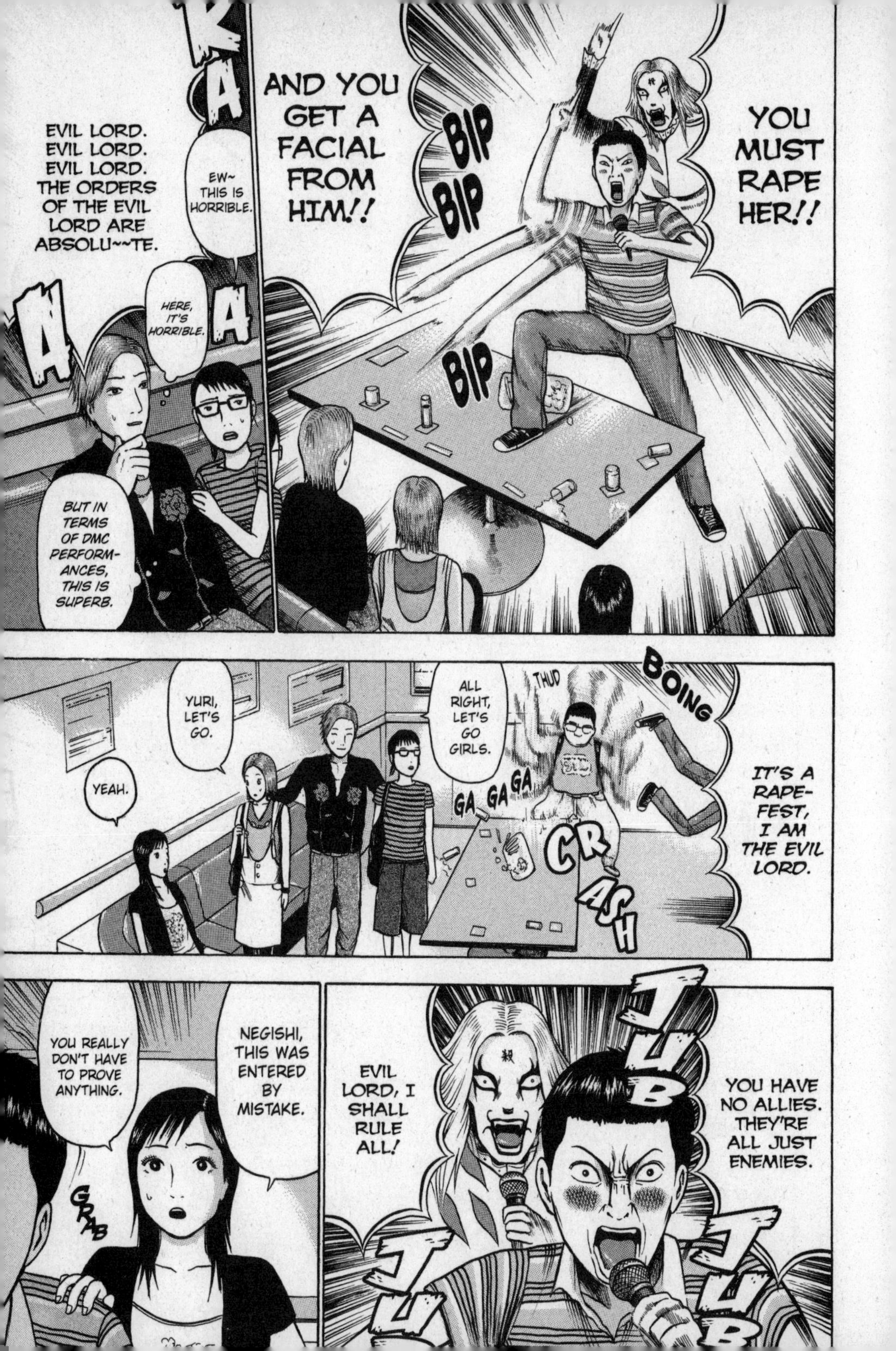
YOU MUST RAPE HER!!
BIP BIP
AND YOU GET A FACIAL FROM HIM!!
BIP
KA A A A
EVIL LORD. EVIL LORD. EVIL LORD. THE ORDERS OF THE EVIL LORD ARE ABSOLU~~TE.
EW~ THIS IS HORRIBLE.
HERE, IT'S HORRIBLE.
BUT IN TERMS OF DMC PERFORMANCES, THIS IS SUPERB.
BOING
IT'S A RAPE-FEST, I AM THE EVIL LORD.
THUD
ALL RIGHT, LET'S GO GIRLS.
GA GA GA
CRASH
YURI, LET'S GO.
YEAH.
YOU HAVE NO ALLIES. THEY'RE ALL JUST ENEMIES.
JUB JUB JUB
EVIL LORD, I SHALL RULE ALL!
NEGISHI, THIS WAS ENTERED BY MISTAKE.
YOU REALLY DON'T HAVE TO PROVE ANYTHING.
GRAB

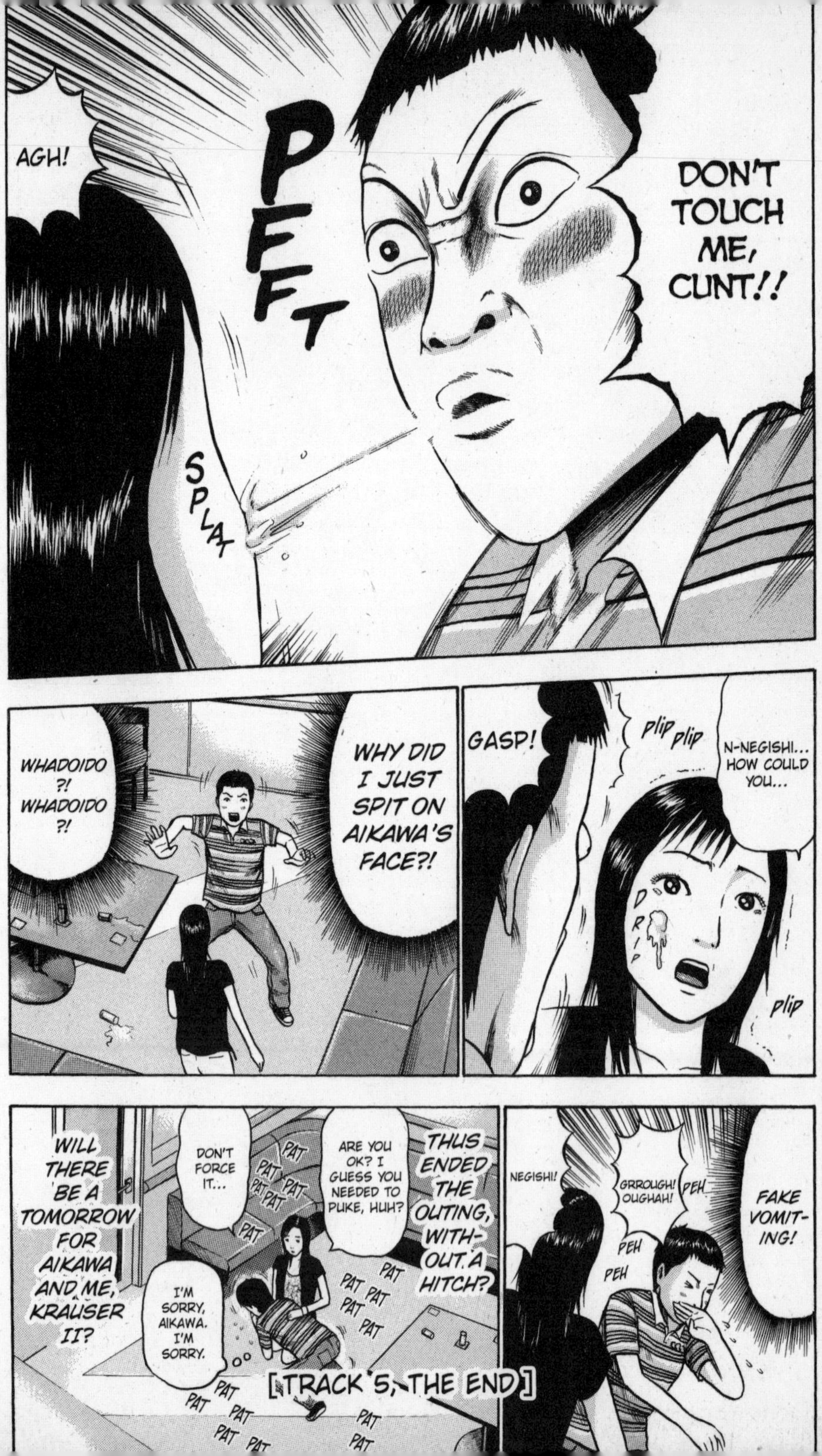
DON'T TOUCH ME, CUNT!!
PFFT
AGH!
SPLAT
N-NEGISHI... HOW COULD YOU...
plip plip
GASP!
DRIP
plip
WHY DID I JUST SPIT ON AIKAWA'S FACE?!
WHADOIDO?! WHADOIDO?!
FAKE VOMITING!
PEH
GRROUGH! OUGHAH!
NEGISHI!
PEH PEH
THUS ENDED THE OUTING, WITHOUT A HITCH?
ARE YOU OK? I GUESS YOU NEEDED TO PUKE, HUH?
PAT PAT PAT PAT PAT PAT
DON'T FORCE IT...
WILL THERE BE A TOMORROW FOR AIKAWA AND ME, KRAUSER II?
PAT PAT PAT PAT PAT
I'M SORRY, AIKAWA. I'M SORRY.
[TRACK 5, THE END]
PAT PAT PAT PAT PAT PAT PAT

DMC LEXICON

🦇 ANAL

The ultimate expression of amour. Meaning "I love you *very much*." The French don't generally have adjectival declensions to express comparative or superior emotion, and amour itself is a noun anyway, so anal may only be slang that's understood in Japan for now.

Usage: Ohh, mon anal!
(Oh, my true lover!)

デトロイト・メタル・シティ
Detroit Metal City

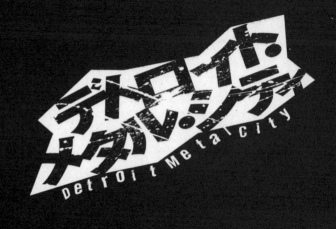

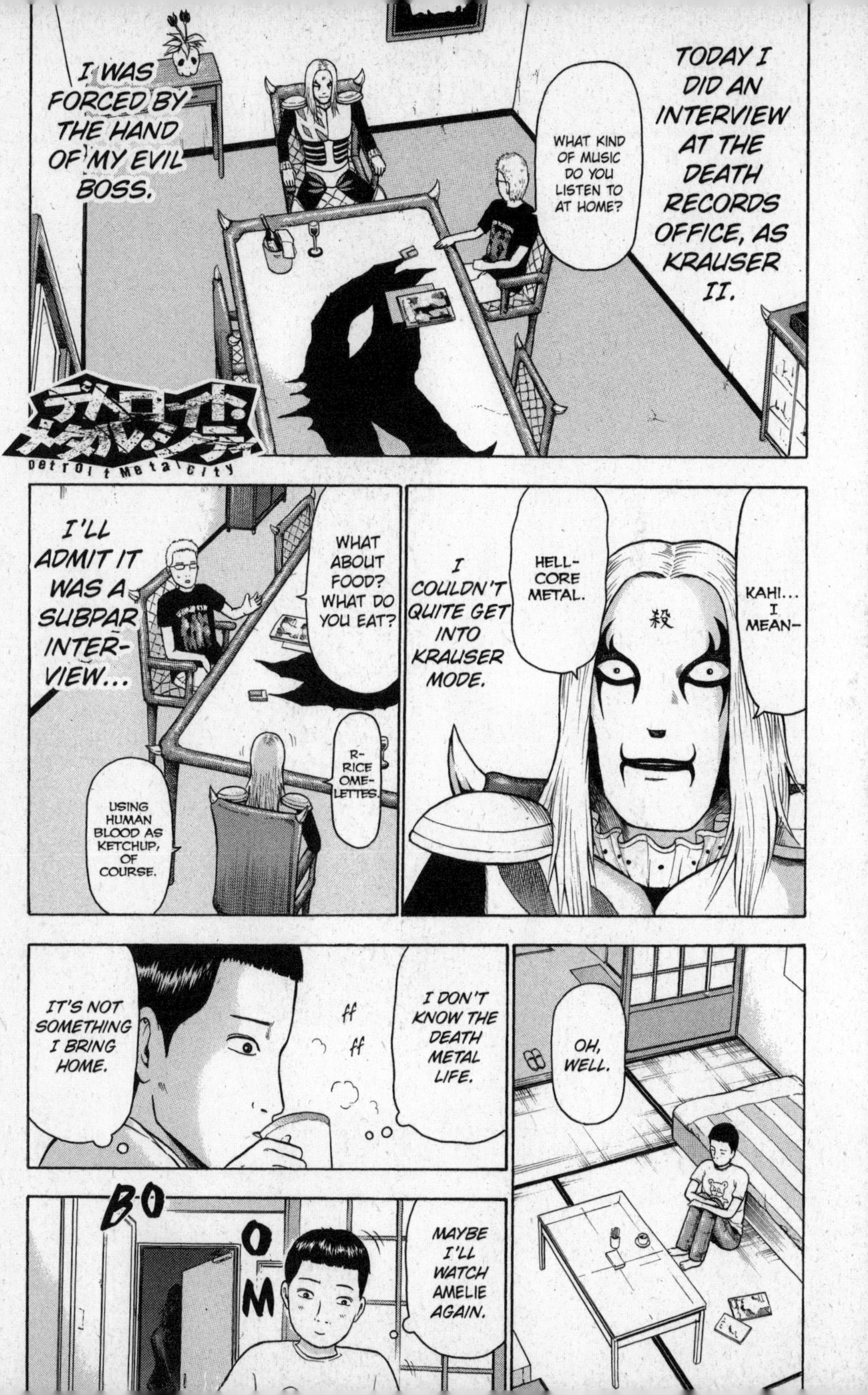
TODAY I DID AN INTERVIEW AT THE DEATH RECORDS OFFICE, AS KRAUSER II.
WHAT KIND OF MUSIC DO YOU LISTEN TO AT HOME?
I WAS FORCED BY THE HAND OF MY EVIL BOSS.
Detroit Metal City
KAHI... I MEAN-
HELL-CORE METAL.
I COULDN'T QUITE GET INTO KRAUSER MODE.
WHAT ABOUT FOOD? WHAT DO YOU EAT?
I'LL ADMIT IT WAS A SUBPAR INTERVIEW...
R-RICE OMELETTES.
USING HUMAN BLOOD AS KETCHUP, OF COURSE.
OH, WELL.
I DON'T KNOW THE DEATH METAL LIFE.
ff
ff
IT'S NOT SOMETHING I BRING HOME.
MAYBE I'LL WATCH AMELIE AGAIN.
BOOM

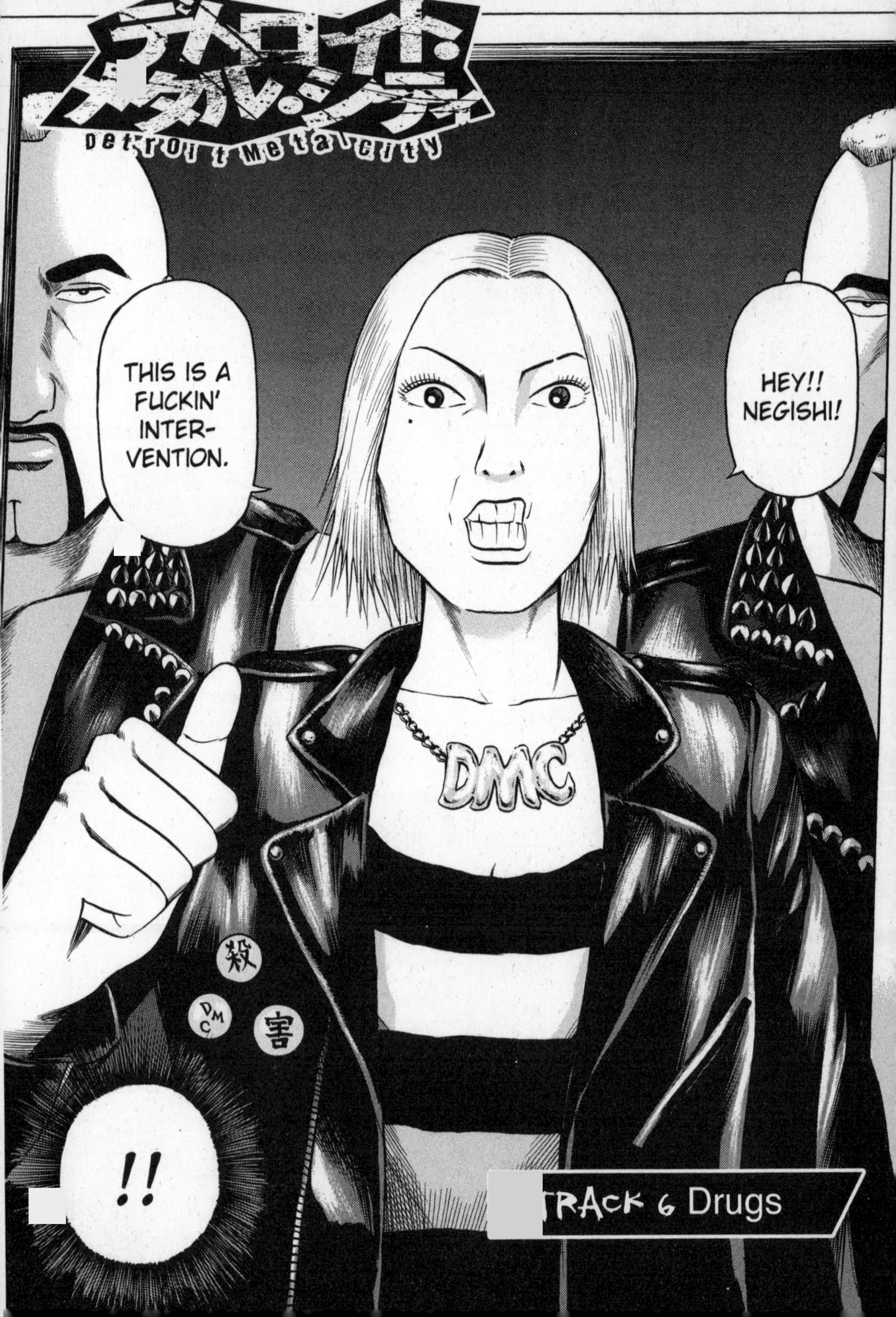
デトロイト・メタル・シティ
Detroit Metal City
HEY!! NEGISHI!
THIS IS A FUCKIN' INTER-VENTION.
DMC
殺
害
!!
TRACK 6 Drugs

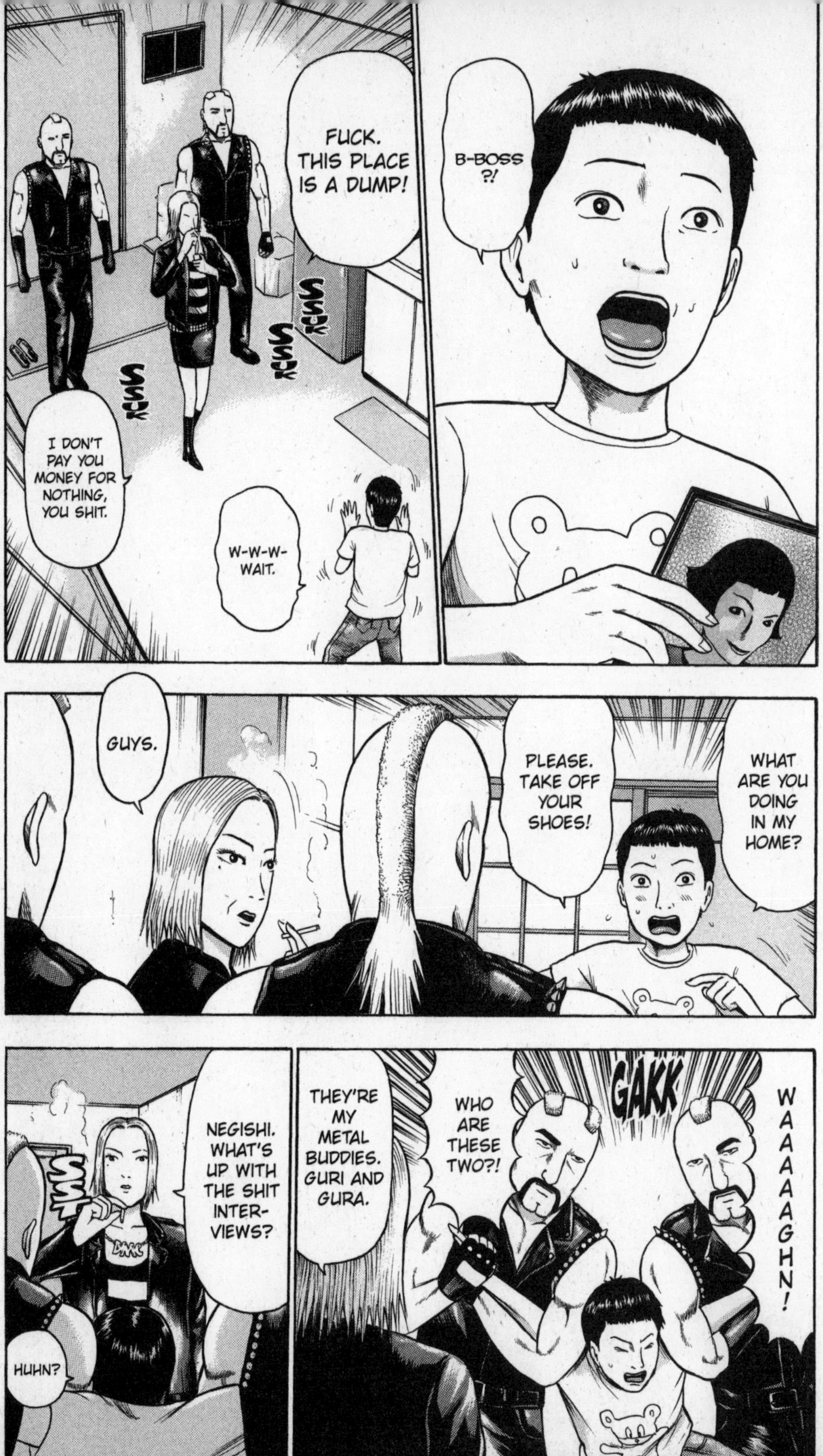
B-BOSS ?!
FUCK. THIS PLACE IS A DUMP!
SNUK
SNUK
SNUK
SNUK
W-W-W-WAIT.
I DON'T PAY YOU MONEY FOR NOTHING, YOU SHIT.
WHAT ARE YOU DOING IN MY HOME?
PLEASE. TAKE OFF YOUR SHOES!
GUYS.
WAAAAAGHN!
GAKK
WHO ARE THESE TWO?!
THEY'RE MY METAL BUDDIES. GURI AND GURA.
NEGISHI. WHAT'S UP WITH THE SHIT INTER-VIEWS?
HUHN?

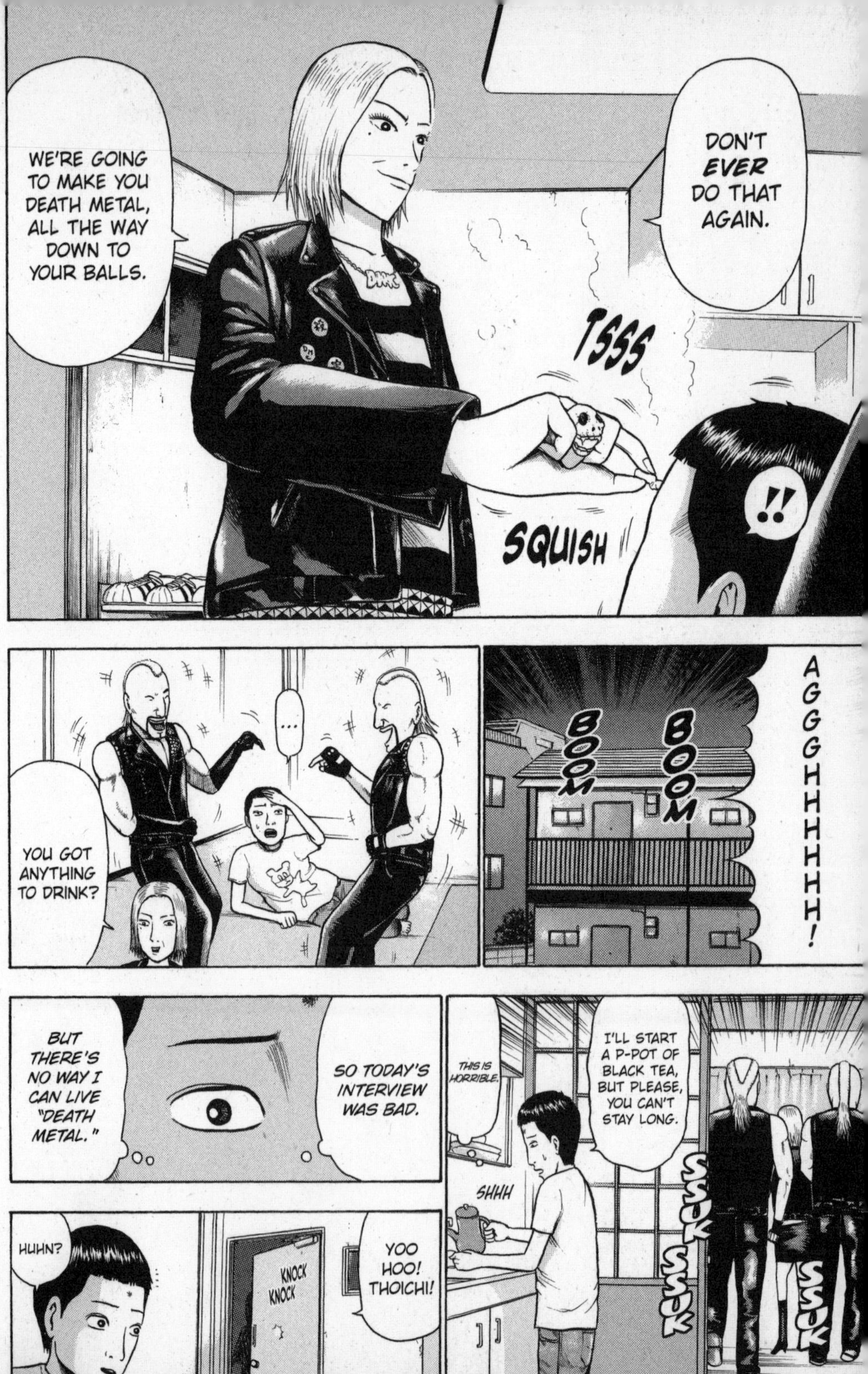
DON'T EVER DO THAT AGAIN.
WE'RE GOING TO MAKE YOU DEATH METAL, ALL THE WAY DOWN TO YOUR BALLS.
TSSS
!!
SQUISH
AGGGHHHHHHH!
BOOM
BOOM
...
YOU GOT ANYTHING TO DRINK?
I'LL START A P-POT OF BLACK TEA, BUT PLEASE, YOU CAN'T STAY LONG.
THIS IS HORRIBLE.
SHHH
SSUK
SSUK
SSUK
SO TODAY'S INTERVIEW WAS BAD.
BUT THERE'S NO WAY I CAN LIVE "DEATH METAL."
YOO HOO! THOICHI!
KNOCK KNOCK
HUHN?

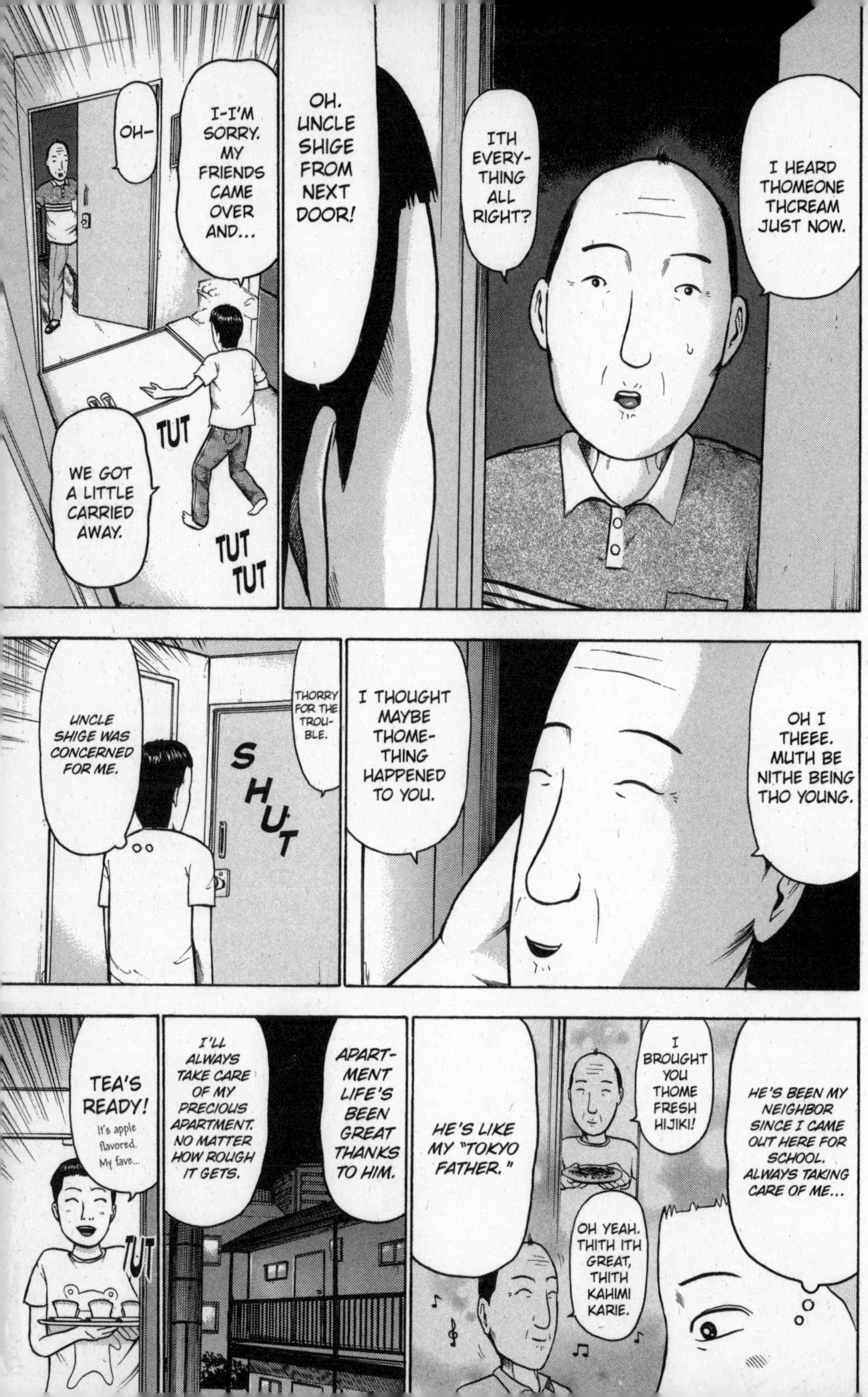

I HEARD THOMEONE THCREAM JUST NOW.
ITH EVERY-THING ALL RIGHT?
OH. UNCLE SHIGE FROM NEXT DOOR!
I-I'M SORRY. MY FRIENDS CAME OVER AND...
OH-
TUT
WE GOT A LITTLE CARRIED AWAY.
TUT TUT
OH I THEEE. MUTH BE NITHE BEING THO YOUNG.
I THOUGHT MAYBE THOME-THING HAPPENED TO YOU.
THORRY FOR THE TROU-BLE.
UNCLE SHIGE WAS CONCERNED FOR ME.
SHUT
HE'S BEEN MY NEIGHBOR SINCE I CAME OUT HERE FOR SCHOOL. ALWAYS TAKING CARE OF ME...
I BROUGHT YOU THOME FRESH HIJIKI!
OH YEAH. THITH ITH GREAT, THITH KAHIMI KARIE.
HE'S LIKE MY "TOKYO FATHER."
APART-MENT LIFE'S BEEN GREAT THANKS TO HIM.
I'LL ALWAYS TAKE CARE OF MY PRECIOUS APARTMENT. NO MATTER HOW ROUGH IT GETS.
TEA'S READY!
It's apple flavored. My fave...
TUT

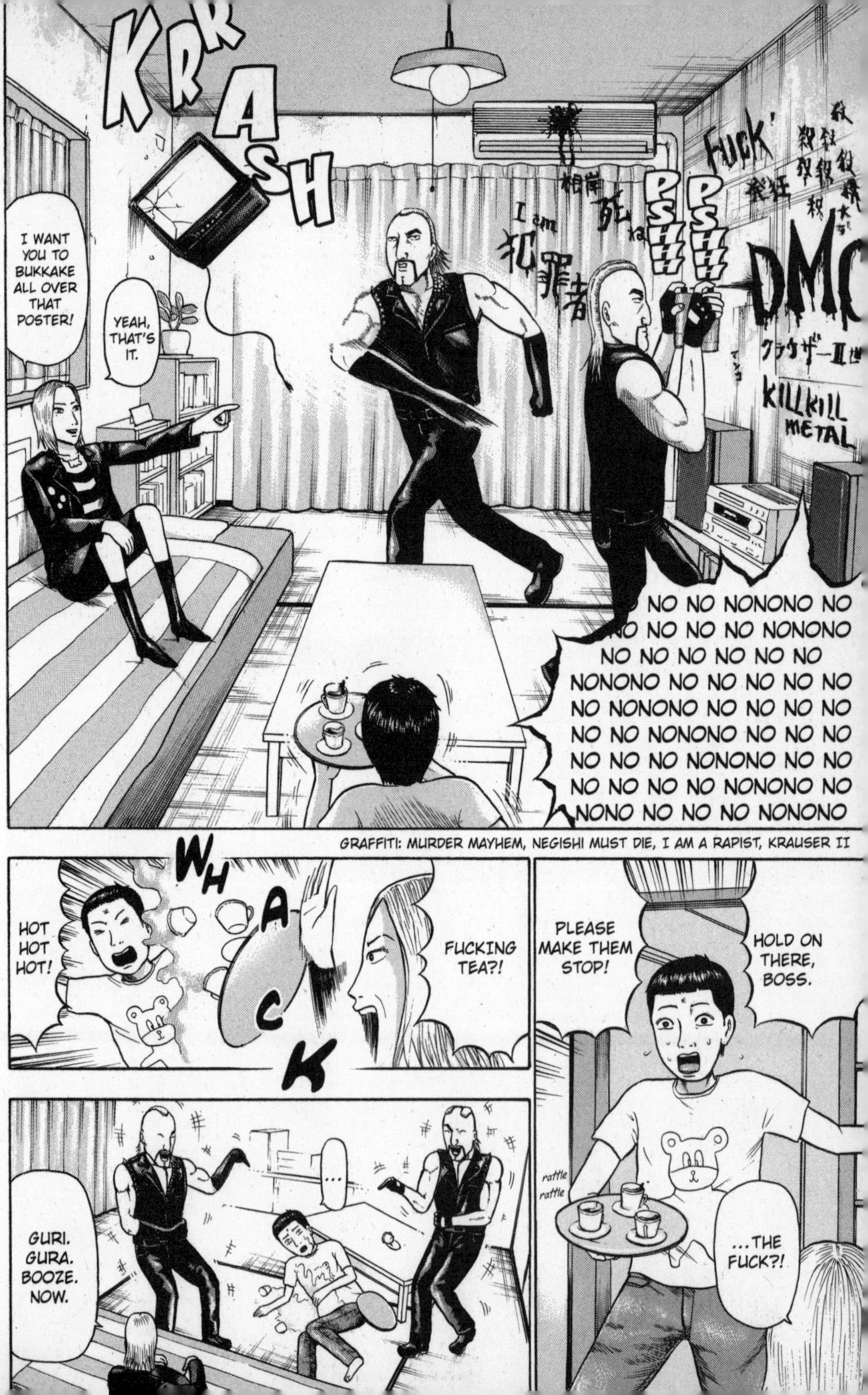

FUCK
DMC
KILLKILL METAL
PSSH PSSH
I am
KRKRASH
I WANT YOU TO BUKKAKE ALL OVER THAT POSTER!
YEAH, THAT'S IT.
NO NO NONONO NO NO NO NO NO NONONO NO NO NO NO NO NO NONONO NO NO NO NO NO NO NONONO NO NO NO NO NO NO NONONO NO NO NO NO NO NO NONONO NO NO NO NO NO NONONO NO NONO NO NO NO NONONO
GRAFFITI: MURDER MAYHEM, NEGISHI MUST DIE, I AM A RAPIST, KRAUSER II
HOLD ON THERE, BOSS.
PLEASE MAKE THEM STOP!
rattle rattle
...THE FUCK?!
FUCKING TEA?!
WHACK
HOT HOT HOT!
...
GURI. GURA. BOOZE. NOW.

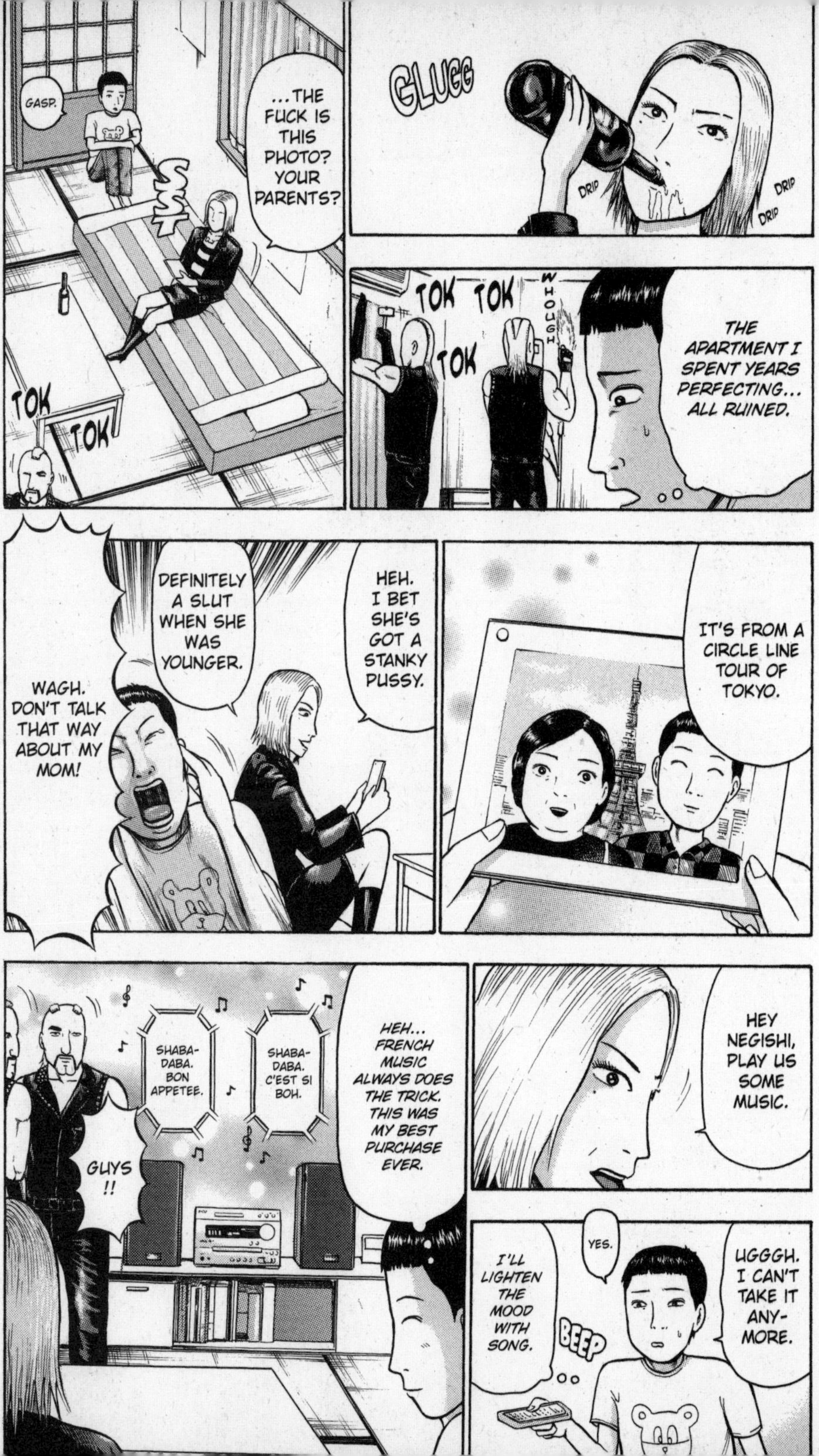
GLUGG
DRIP
DRIP
DRIP
TOK
TOK
WHOUGH
TOK
THE APARTMENT I SPENT YEARS PERFECTING... ALL RUINED.
...THE FUCK IS THIS PHOTO? YOUR PARENTS?
GASP.
TOK
TOK
IT'S FROM A CIRCLE LINE TOUR OF TOKYO.
HEH. I BET SHE'S GOT A STANKY PUSSY.
DEFINITELY A SLUT WHEN SHE WAS YOUNGER.
WAGH. DON'T TALK THAT WAY ABOUT MY MOM!
HEY NEGISHI, PLAY US SOME MUSIC.
UGGGH. I CAN'T TAKE IT ANY-MORE.
YES.
BEEP
I'LL LIGHTEN THE MOOD WITH SONG.
HEH... FRENCH MUSIC ALWAYS DOES THE TRICK. THIS WAS MY BEST PURCHASE EVER.
SHABA-DABA. C'EST SI BOH.
SHABA-DABA. BON APPETEE.
GUYS !!

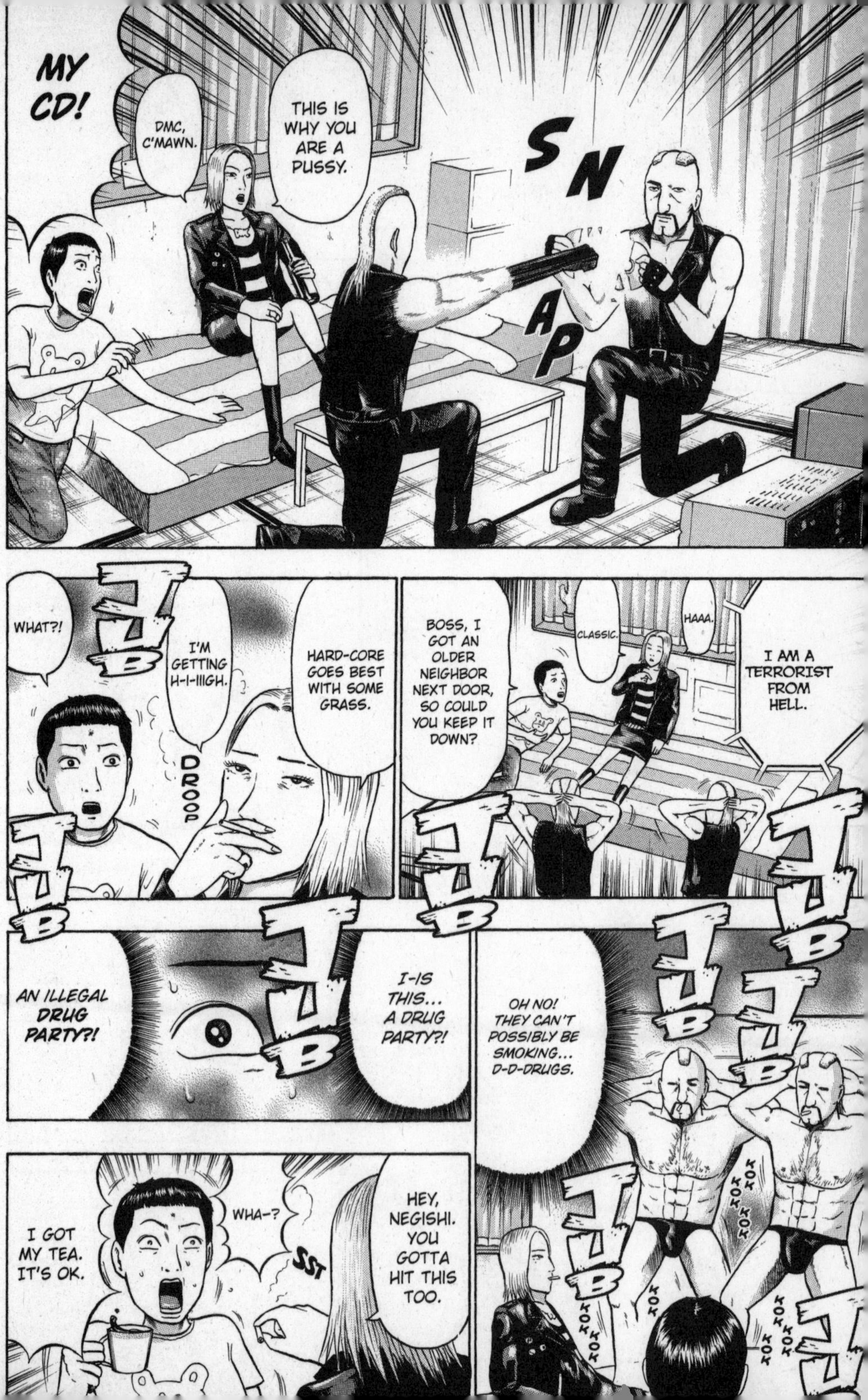
SNAP
THIS IS WHY YOU ARE A PUSSY.
DMC, C'MAWN.
MY CD!
I AM A TERRORIST FROM HELL.
HAAA.
CLASSIC.
BOSS, I GOT AN OLDER NEIGHBOR NEXT DOOR, SO COULD YOU KEEP IT DOWN?
JUB
JUB
HARD-CORE GOES BEST WITH SOME GRASS.
I'M GETTING H-I-IIIGH.
DROOP
WHAT?!
JUB
JUB
OH NO! THEY CAN'T POSSIBLY BE SMOKING... D-D-DRUGS.
JUB
JUB
KOK KOK KOK KOK
KOK KOK KOK KOK
I-IS THIS... A DRUG PARTY?!
AN ILLEGAL DRUG PARTY?!
JUB
HEY, NEGISHI. YOU GOTTA HIT THIS TOO.
SST
WHA-?
I GOT MY TEA. IT'S OK.

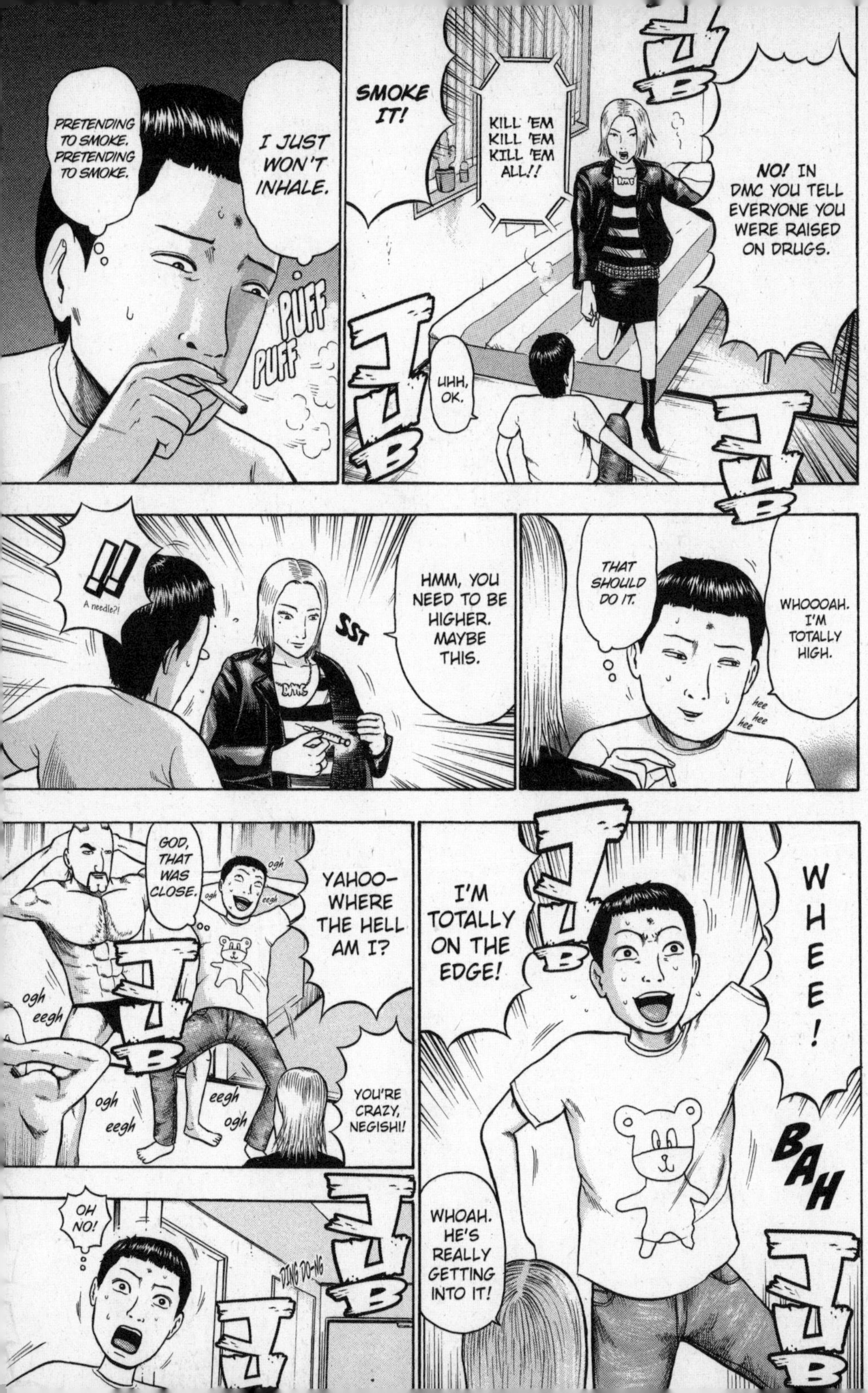
JUB
NO! IN DMC YOU TELL EVERYONE YOU WERE RAISED ON DRUGS.
SMOKE IT!
KILL 'EM KILL 'EM KILL 'EM ALL!!
UHH, OK.
JUB
JUB
I JUST WON'T INHALE.
PRETENDING TO SMOKE. PRETENDING TO SMOKE.
PUFF PUFF
WHOOOAH. I'M TOTALLY HIGH.
THAT SHOULD DO IT.
hee hee hee
HMM, YOU NEED TO BE HIGHER. MAYBE THIS.
SST
!!
A needle?!
WHEE!
I'M TOTALLY ON THE EDGE!
JUB
BAH
JUB
WHOAH. HE'S REALLY GETTING INTO IT!
YAHOO- WHERE THE HELL AM I?
GOD, THAT WAS CLOSE.
ogh eegh
JUB
ogh eegh
ogh eegh
eegh ogh
YOU'RE CRAZY, NEGISHI!
JUB
DING DO-NG
OH NO!
JU

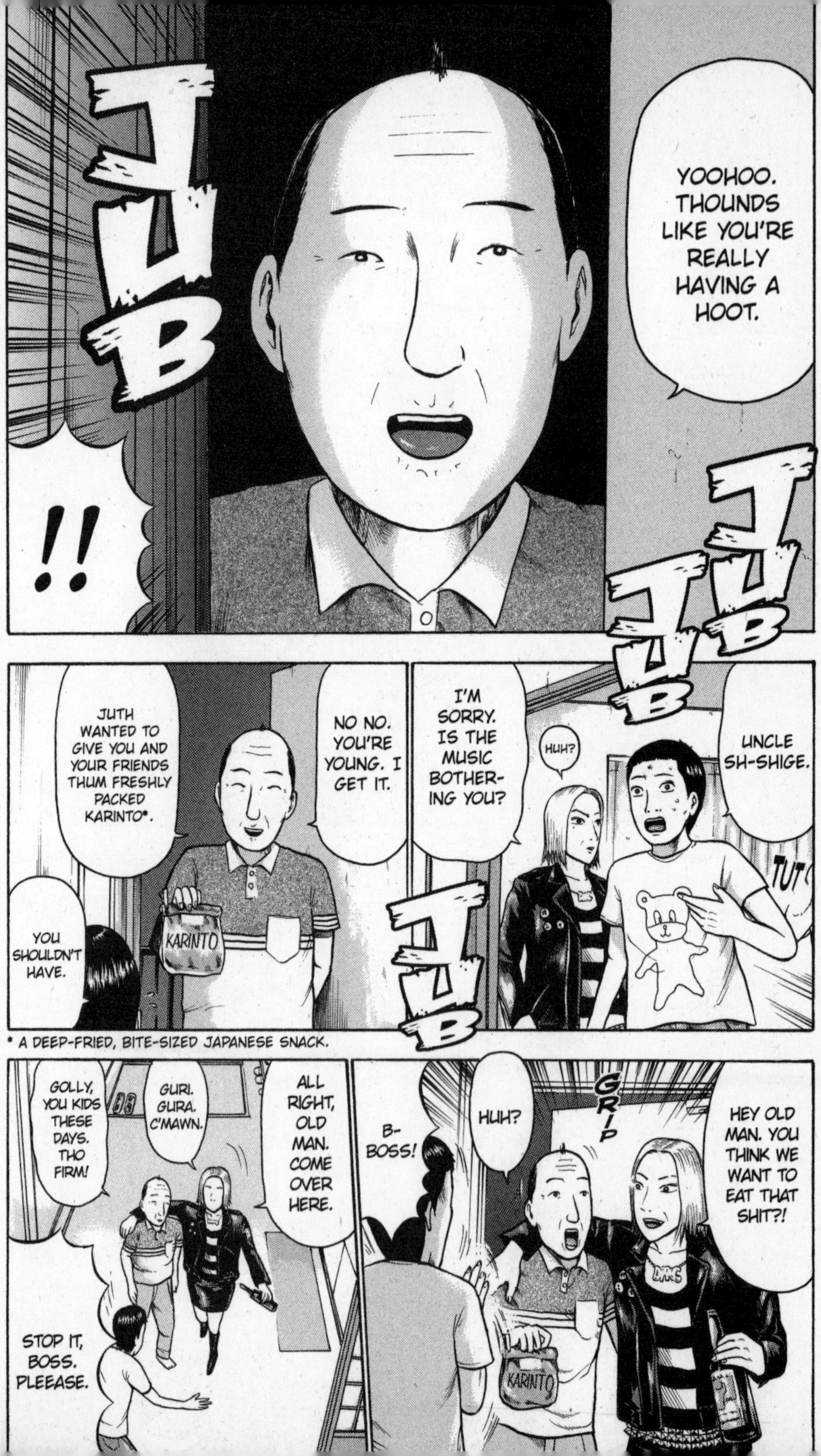
YOOHOO. THOUNDS LIKE YOU'RE REALLY HAVING A HOOT.
JUB
JUB
JUB
!!
UNCLE SH-SHIGE.
HUH?
TUT
I'M SORRY. IS THE MUSIC BOTHERING YOU?
JUB
NO NO. YOU'RE YOUNG. I GET IT.
JUTH WANTED TO GIVE YOU AND YOUR FRIENDS THUM FRESHLY PACKED KARINTO*.
KARINTO
YOU SHOULDN'T HAVE.
HEY OLD MAN. YOU THINK WE WANT TO EAT THAT SHIT?!
GRIP
HUH?
B- BOSS!
KARINTO
ALL RIGHT, OLD MAN. COME OVER HERE.
GURI. GURA. C'MAWN.
GOLLY, YOU KIDS THESE DAYS. THO FIRM!
STOP IT, BOSS. PLEEASE.

* A DEEP-FRIED, BITE-SIZED JAPANESE SNACK.

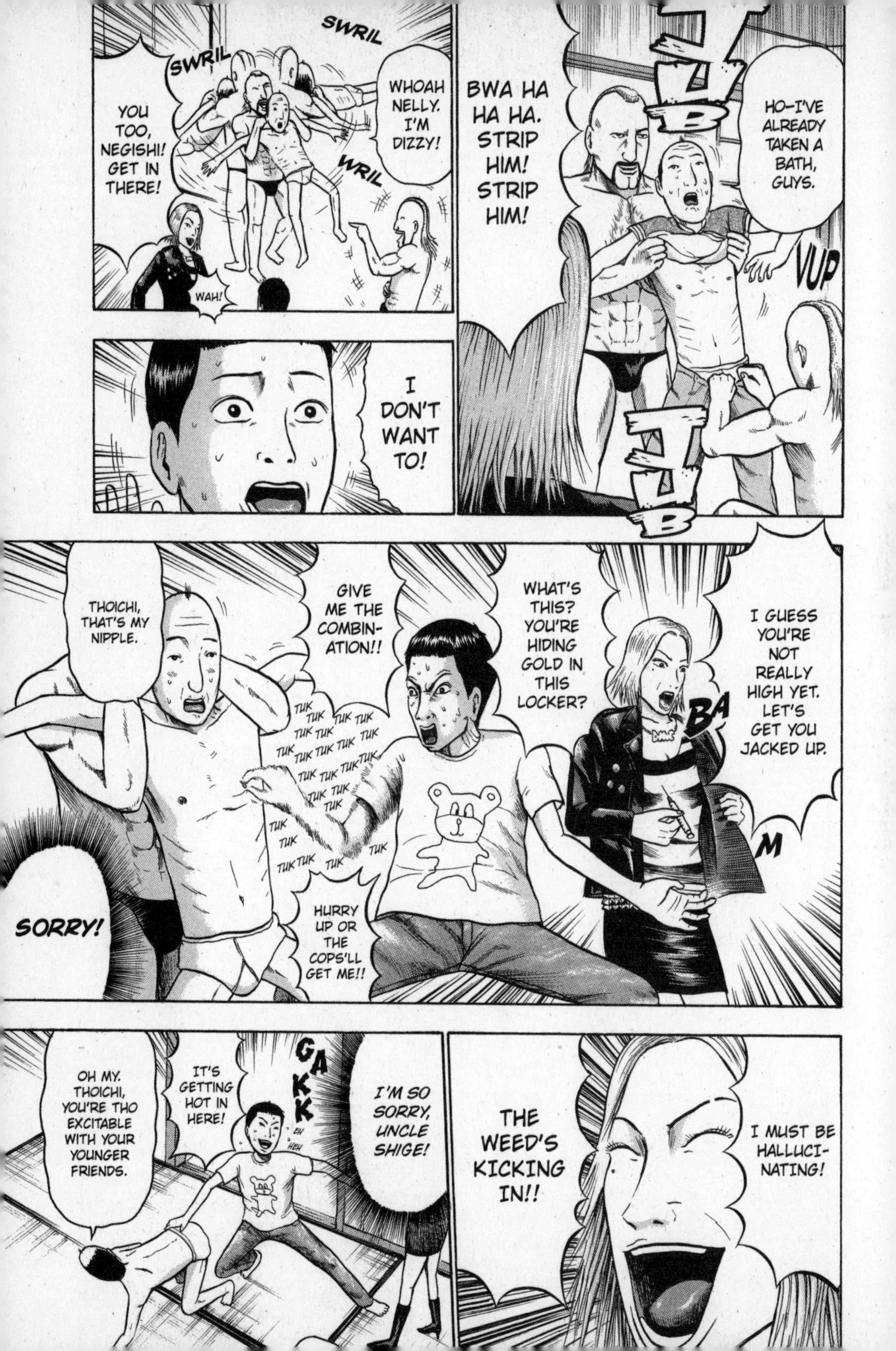

JUB
HO-I'VE ALREADY TAKEN A BATH, GUYS.
BWA HA HA HA. STRIP HIM! STRIP HIM!
VUP
JUB
SWRIL
WHOAH NELLY. I'M DIZZY!
SWRIL
YOU TOO, NEGISHI! GET IN THERE!
WRIL
WAH!
I DON'T WANT TO!
I GUESS YOU'RE NOT REALLY HIGH YET. LET'S GET YOU JACKED UP.
BAM
WHAT'S THIS? YOU'RE HIDING GOLD IN THIS LOCKER?
GIVE ME THE COMBINATION!!
TUK TUK TUK TUK TUK TUK TUK TUK TUK TUK TUK TUK TUK TUK TUK TUK TUK TUK TUK TUK TUK TUK TUK TUK TUK TUK
HURRY UP OR THE COPS'LL GET ME!!
THOICHI, THAT'S MY NIPPLE.
SORRY!
I MUST BE HALLUCINATING!
THE WEED'S KICKING IN!!
I'M SO SORRY, UNCLE SHIGE!
GAKK
EH HEH
IT'S GETTING HOT IN HERE!
OH MY. THOICHI, YOU'RE THO EXCITABLE WITH YOUR YOUNGER FRIENDS.

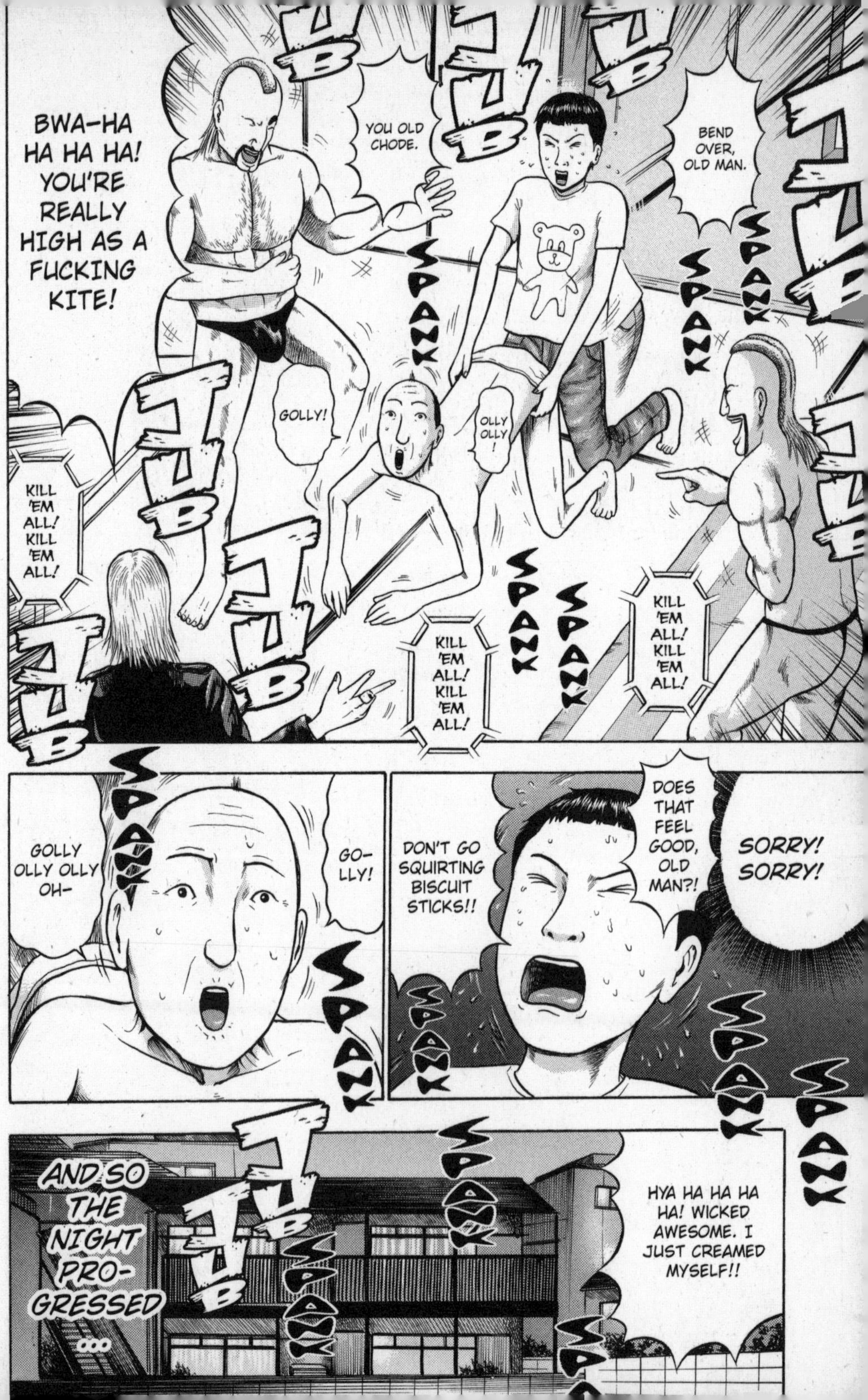
BEND OVER, OLD MAN.
SPANK
SPANK
YOU OLD CHODE.
BWA-HA HA HA HA! YOU'RE REALLY HIGH AS A FUCKING KITE!
SPANK
OLLY OLLY!
GOLLY!
KILL 'EM ALL! KILL 'EM ALL!
SPANK
SPANK
KILL 'EM ALL! KILL 'EM ALL!
KILL 'EM ALL! KILL 'EM ALL!
SORRY! SORRY!
DOES THAT FEEL GOOD, OLD MAN?!
DON'T GO SQUIRTING BISCUIT STICKS!!
SPANK
SPANK
GO-LLY!
GOLLY OLLY OLLY OH-
SPANK
SPANK
SPANK
HYA HA HA HA HA! WICKED AWESOME. I JUST CREAMED MYSELF!!
SPANK
AND SO THE NIGHT PRO-GRESSED...

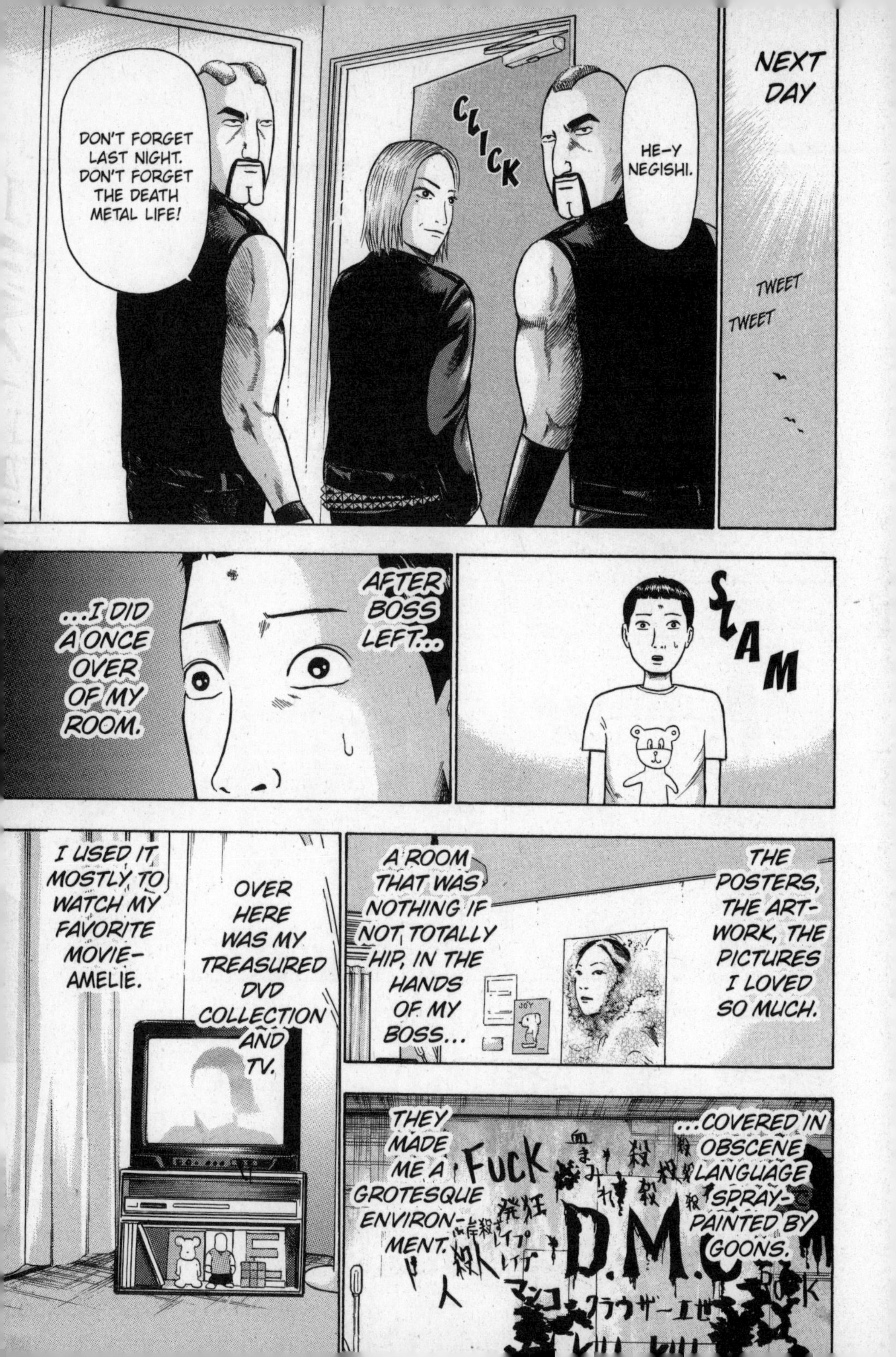
NEXT DAY
TWEET
TWEET
HE-Y NEGISHI.
CLICK
DON'T FORGET LAST NIGHT. DON'T FORGET THE DEATH METAL LIFE!
SLAM
AFTER BOSS LEFT...
...I DID A ONCE OVER OF MY ROOM.
THE POSTERS, THE ART-WORK, THE PICTURES I LOVED SO MUCH.
A ROOM THAT WAS NOTHING IF NOT TOTALLY HIP, IN THE HANDS OF MY BOSS...
...COVERED IN OBSCENE LANGUAGE SPRAY-PAINTED BY GOONS.
THEY MADE ME A GROTESQUE ENVIRONMENT.
FUCK
発狂
殺人
レイプ
D.M.C
マンコ
ROCK
OVER HERE WAS MY TREASURED DVD COLLECTION AND TV.
I USED IT MOSTLY TO WATCH MY FAVORITE MOVIE-AMELIE.

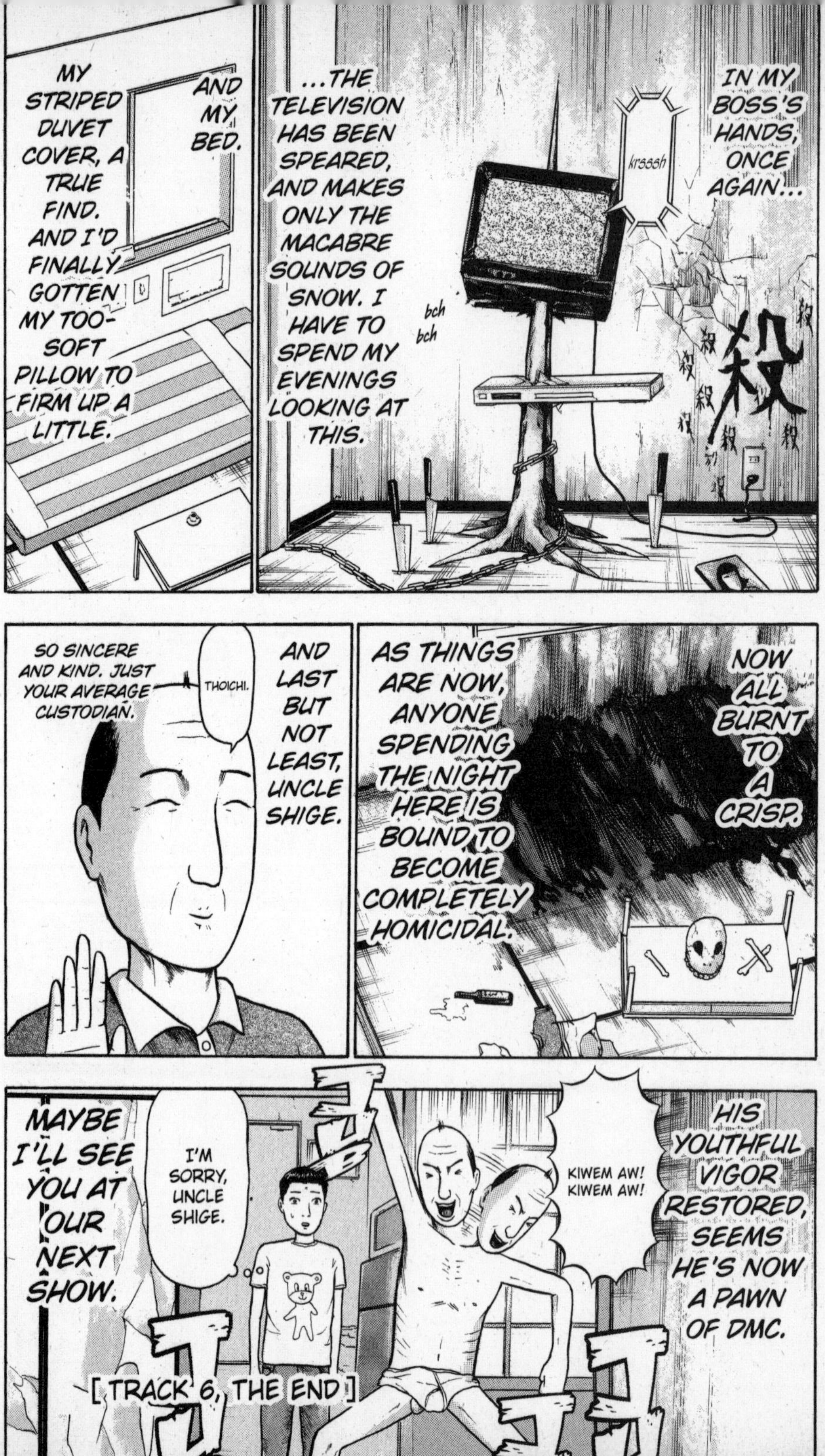
IN MY BOSS'S HANDS, ONCE AGAIN...
krsssh
...THE TELEVISION HAS BEEN SPEARED, AND MAKES ONLY THE MACABRE SOUNDS OF SNOW. I HAVE TO SPEND MY EVENINGS LOOKING AT THIS.
bch bch
殺
AND MY BED.
MY STRIPED DUVET COVER, A TRUE FIND. AND I'D FINALLY GOTTEN MY TOO-SOFT PILLOW TO FIRM UP A LITTLE.
NOW ALL BURNT TO A CRISP.
AS THINGS ARE NOW, ANYONE SPENDING THE NIGHT HERE IS BOUND TO BECOME COMPLETELY HOMICIDAL.
AND LAST BUT NOT LEAST, UNCLE SHIGE.
THOICHI.
SO SINCERE AND KIND. JUST YOUR AVERAGE CUSTODIAN.
HIS YOUTHFUL VIGOR RESTORED, SEEMS HE'S NOW A PAWN OF DMC.
KIWEM AW! KIWEM AW!
I'M SORRY, UNCLE SHIGE.
MAYBE I'LL SEE YOU AT OUR NEXT SHOW.
[TRACK 6, THE END]

DMC LEXICON

AMELIE

French film directed by Jean-Pierre Jeunet, starring
Audrey Tautou. From its lush cinematography to its
soundtrack, the film embues "hip" all the way. It is the
epitome of hip existence. A must-see if you're hip all the
way down to your bones.

Usage: Crème Brulée really has to be enjoyed after
cracking the shell, just like in Amelie!

デトロイト・メタル・シティ

Detroit Metal City

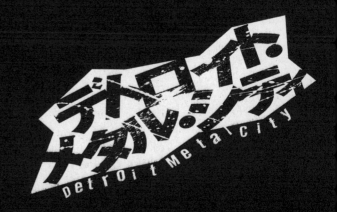

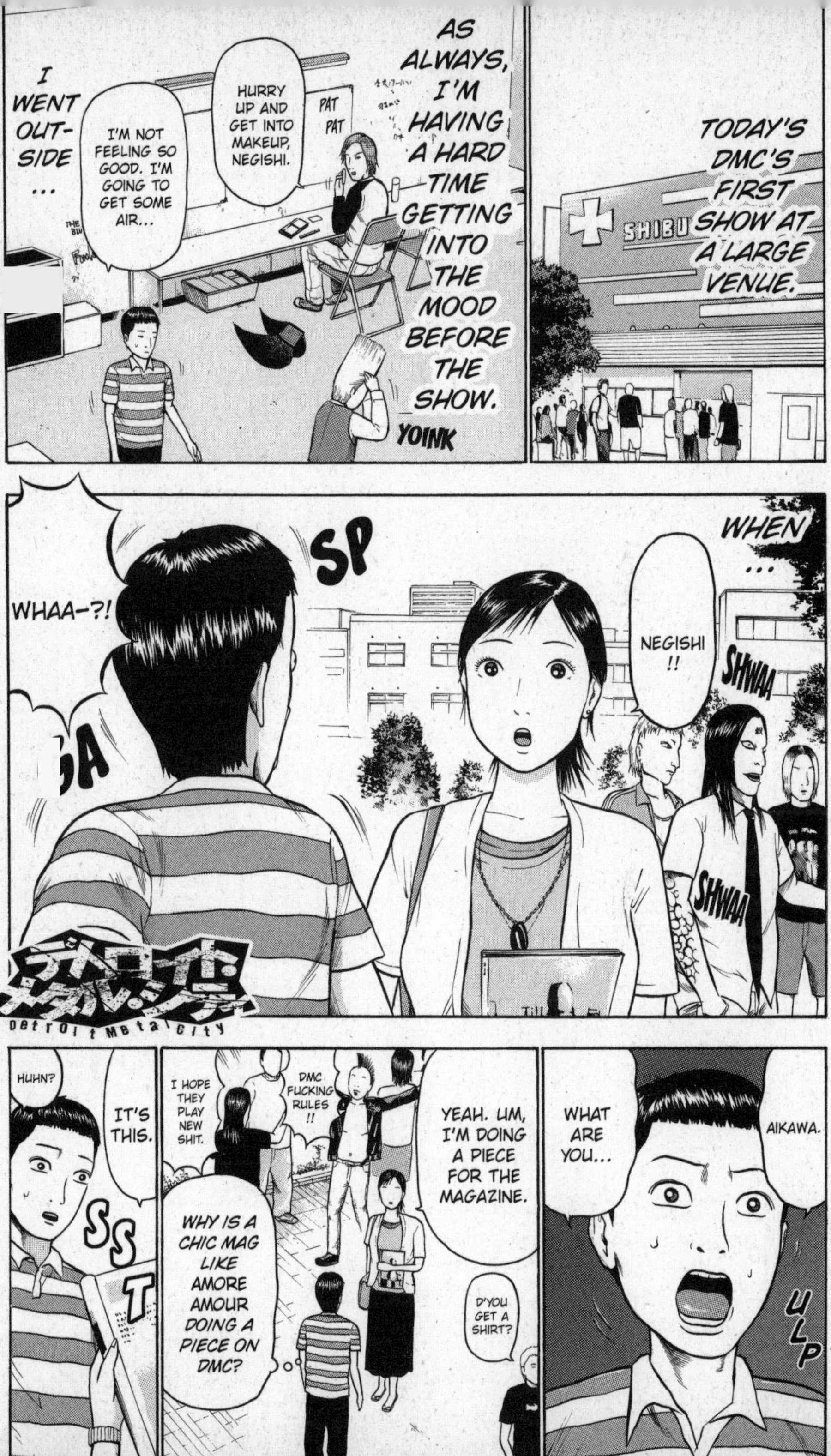

TODAY'S DMC'S FIRST SHOW AT A LARGE VENUE.
AS ALWAYS, I'M HAVING A HARD TIME GETTING INTO THE MOOD BEFORE THE SHOW.
PAT PAT
HURRY UP AND GET INTO MAKEUP, NEGISHI.
I'M NOT FEELING SO GOOD. I'M GOING TO GET SOME AIR...
I WENT OUTSIDE...
YOINK
WHEN...
NEGISHI!!
SHWAA
SHWAA
SP
WHAA-?!
GA
AIKAWA.
WHAT ARE YOU...
ULP
YEAH. UM, I'M DOING A PIECE FOR THE MAGAZINE.
DMC FUCKING RULES!!
I HOPE THEY PLAY NEW SHIT.
D'YOU GET A SHIRT?
WHY IS A CHIC MAG LIKE AMORE AMOUR DOING A PIECE ON DMC?
IT'S THIS.
HUHN?
SST

Detroit Metal City

Our First LIVE UNDERCOVER REPORT ON OTHER SCENES ★

Amore Amour readers voted on
the weirdest scenes:

① **Detroit Metal City**
(Death Metal) --- 1,246 Votes
Offensive lyrics! (Nurse, age 20)
Tacky makeup! (Student, age 16)
I dumped my friend when they became
a fan! (Secretary, age 26)

② **KIBA**
(Hip-hop) --- 89 Votes
They talk too much trash!
(Beautician, age 23)
That voice is gross! (Operator, age 21)

③ **Kintama Girls**
(Punk) --- 46 Votes
I don't understand this whole
"anti-male movement"!
(Secretary, age 25)
The singer's cute, but still...
(Student, age 17)

D etroit
C ity
M etal

Three demons joined to form this death metal

Launched with "Sats
Last month's "Grotes
of the Indie label char
All kinds of rumors ar
crazy fans abound.

!!

No surprises. No. 1 was  **DETROIT METAL CITY**

Gro~~ss!
No way!!

Next issue: Our own Amore Amour editor infiltrates the band's show!!!

Editor A: I normally go to shows for bands
like Stereolab. I don't really get death metal
so I'm really nervous.
Detroit Metal
Band webs

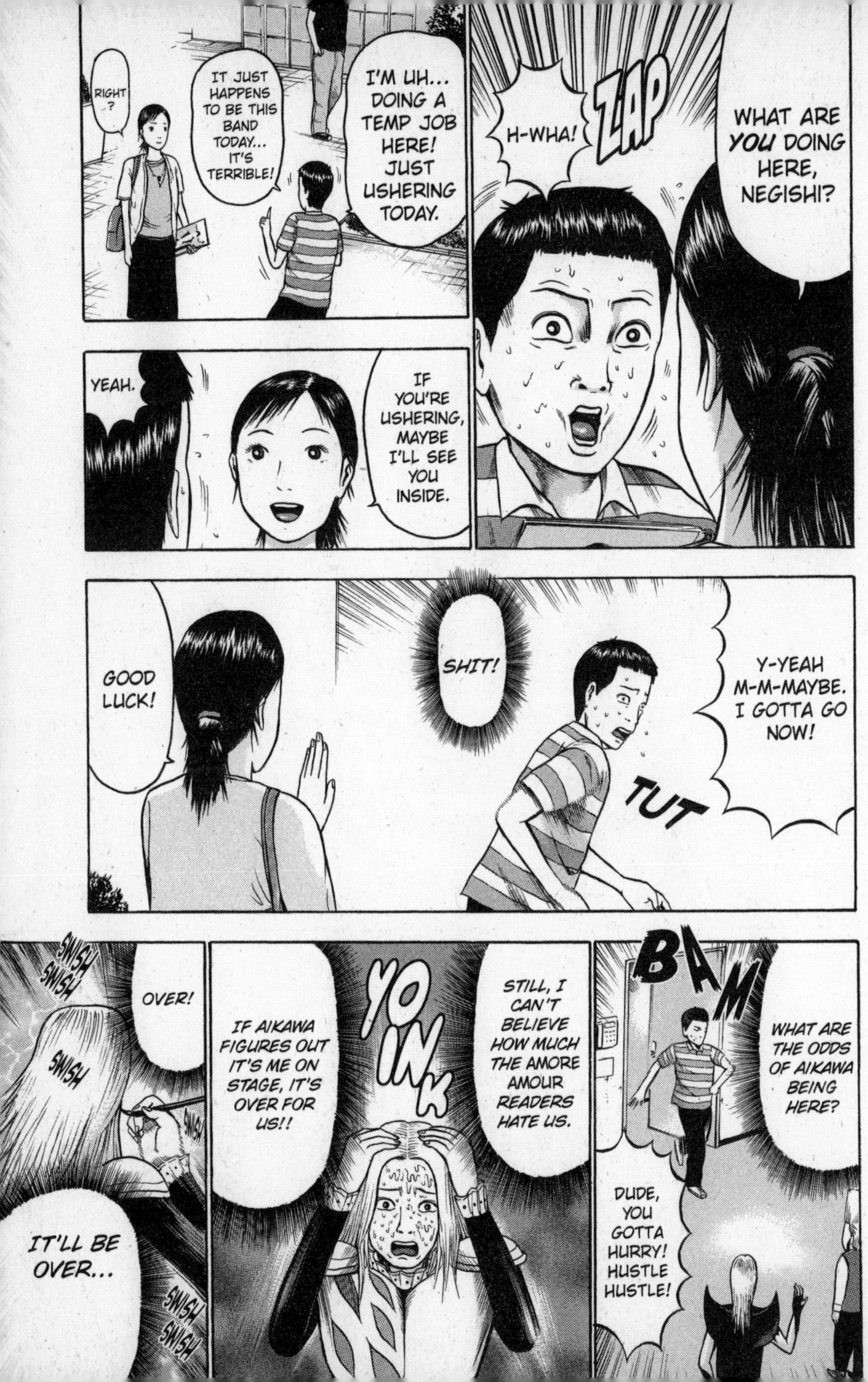
WHAT ARE YOU DOING HERE, NEGISHI?
ZAP
H-WHA!
I'M UH... DOING A TEMP JOB HERE! JUST USHERING TODAY.
IT JUST HAPPENS TO BE THIS BAND TODAY... IT'S TERRIBLE!
RIGHT?
IF YOU'RE USHERING, MAYBE I'LL SEE YOU INSIDE.
YEAH.
Y-YEAH M-M-MAYBE. I GOTTA GO NOW!
TUT
SHIT!
GOOD LUCK!
BAM
WHAT ARE THE ODDS OF AIKAWA BEING HERE?
DUDE, YOU GOTTA HURRY! HUSTLE HUSTLE!
STILL, I CAN'T BELIEVE HOW MUCH THE AMORE AMOUR READERS HATE US.
YOINK
IF AIKAWA FIGURES OUT IT'S ME ON STAGE, IT'S OVER FOR US!!
OVER!
SWISH SWISH
SWISH
IT'LL BE OVER...
SWISH SWISH

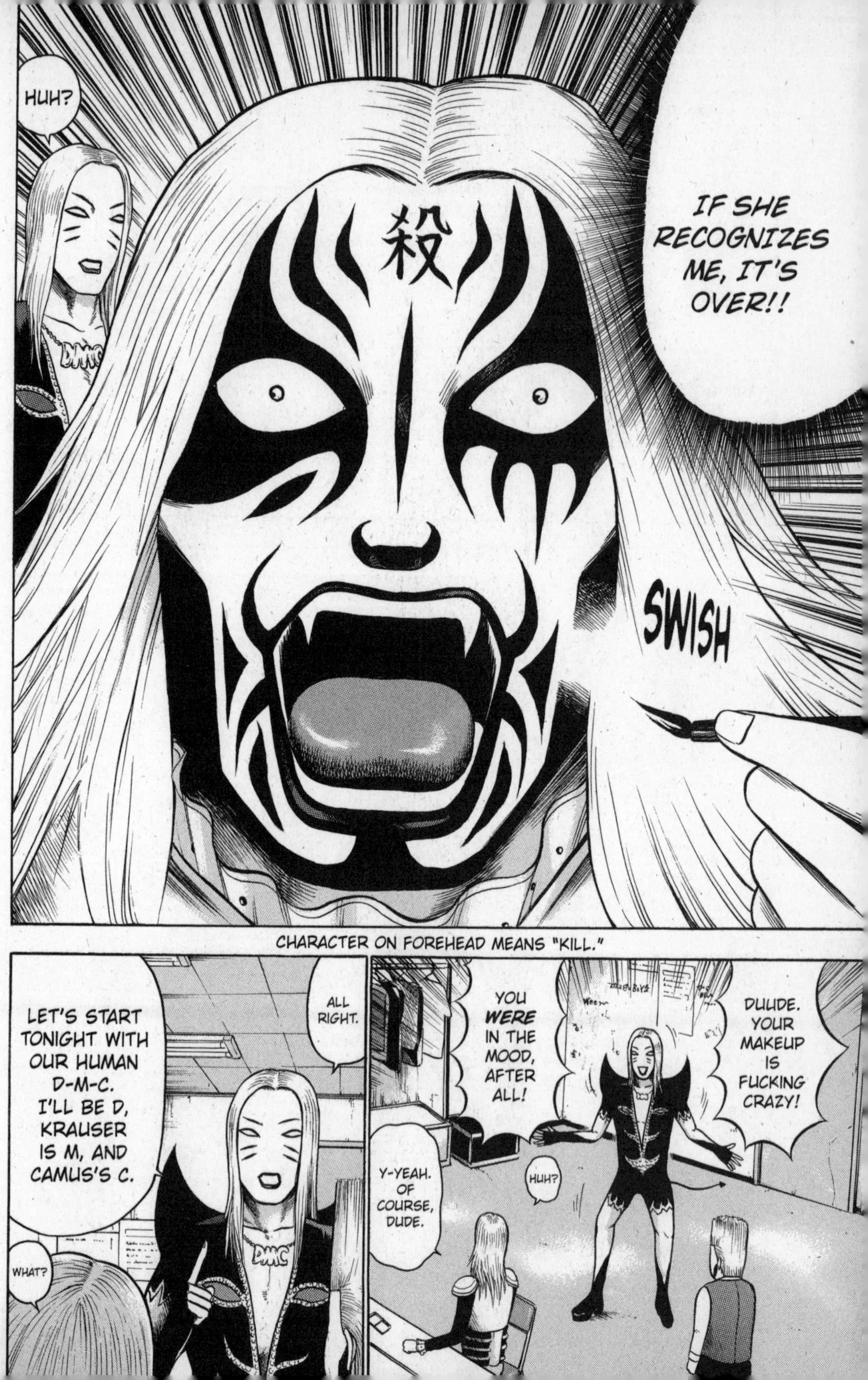
IF SHE RECOGNIZES ME, IT'S OVER!!
SWISH
HUH?
CHARACTER ON FOREHEAD MEANS "KILL."
DUUDE. YOUR MAKEUP IS FUCKING CRAZY!
YOU WERE IN THE MOOD, AFTER ALL!
HUH?
Y-YEAH. OF COURSE, DUDE.
ALL RIGHT.
LET'S START TONIGHT WITH OUR HUMAN D-M-C. I'LL BE D, KRAUSER IS M, AND CAMUS'S C.
WHAT?

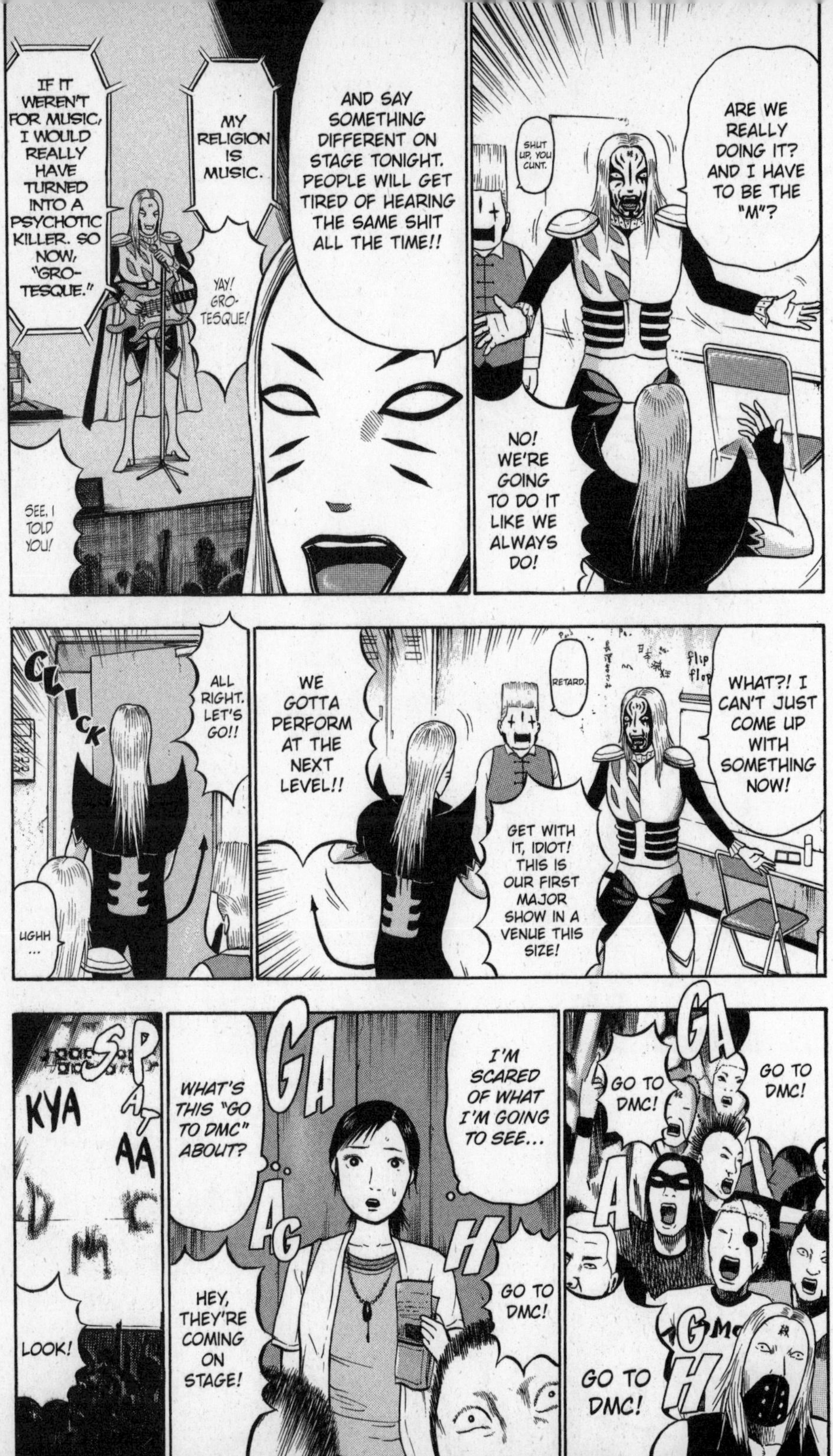

ARE WE REALLY DOING IT? AND I HAVE TO BE THE "M"?
SHUT UP, YOU CUNT.
NO! WE'RE GOING TO DO IT LIKE WE ALWAYS DO!
AND SAY SOMETHING DIFFERENT ON STAGE TONIGHT. PEOPLE WILL GET TIRED OF HEARING THE SAME SHIT ALL THE TIME!!
MY RELIGION IS MUSIC.
IF IT WEREN'T FOR MUSIC, I WOULD REALLY HAVE TURNED INTO A PSYCHOTIC KILLER. SO NOW, "GRO-TESQUE."
YAY! GRO-TESQUE!
SEE, I TOLD YOU!
WHAT?! I CAN'T JUST COME UP WITH SOMETHING NOW!
flip flop
RETARD.
WE GOTTA PERFORM AT THE NEXT LEVEL!!
GET WITH IT, IDIOT! THIS IS OUR FIRST MAJOR SHOW IN A VENUE THIS SIZE!
ALL RIGHT. LET'S GO!!
CLICK
UGHH ...
GA
GO TO DMC!
GO TO DMC!
A
GAGH
GO TO DMC!
I'M SCARED OF WHAT I'M GOING TO SEE...
GA
WHAT'S THIS "GO TO DMC" ABOUT?
AGH
GO TO DMC!
HEY, THEY'RE COMING ON STAGE!
SPAT
KYA
AA
D M C
LOOK!

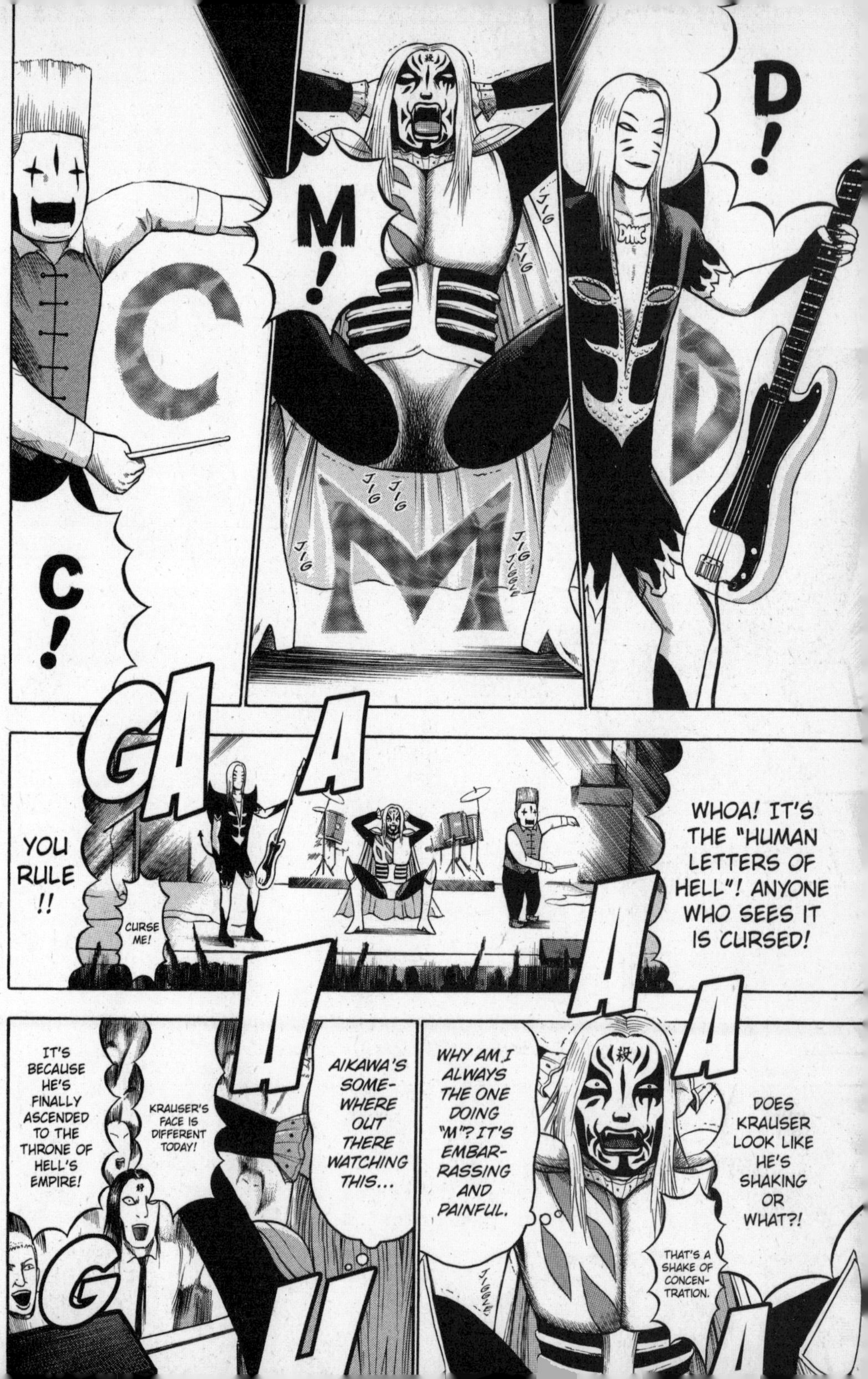
D!
JIG
M!
JIG JIG
JIG JIGGLE
C!
WHOA! IT'S THE "HUMAN LETTERS OF HELL"! ANYONE WHO SEES IT IS CURSED!
YOU RULE!!
CURSE ME!
GAAAAA
DOES KRAUSER LOOK LIKE HE'S SHAKING OR WHAT?!
THAT'S A SHAKE OF CONCEN-TRATION.
JIGGLE
WHY AM I ALWAYS THE ONE DOING "M"? IT'S EMBAR-RASSING AND PAINFUL.
AIKAWA'S SOME-WHERE OUT THERE WATCHING THIS...
KRAUSER'S FACE IS DIFFERENT TODAY!
IT'S BECAUSE HE'S FINALLY ASCENDED TO THE THRONE OF HELL'S EMPIRE!

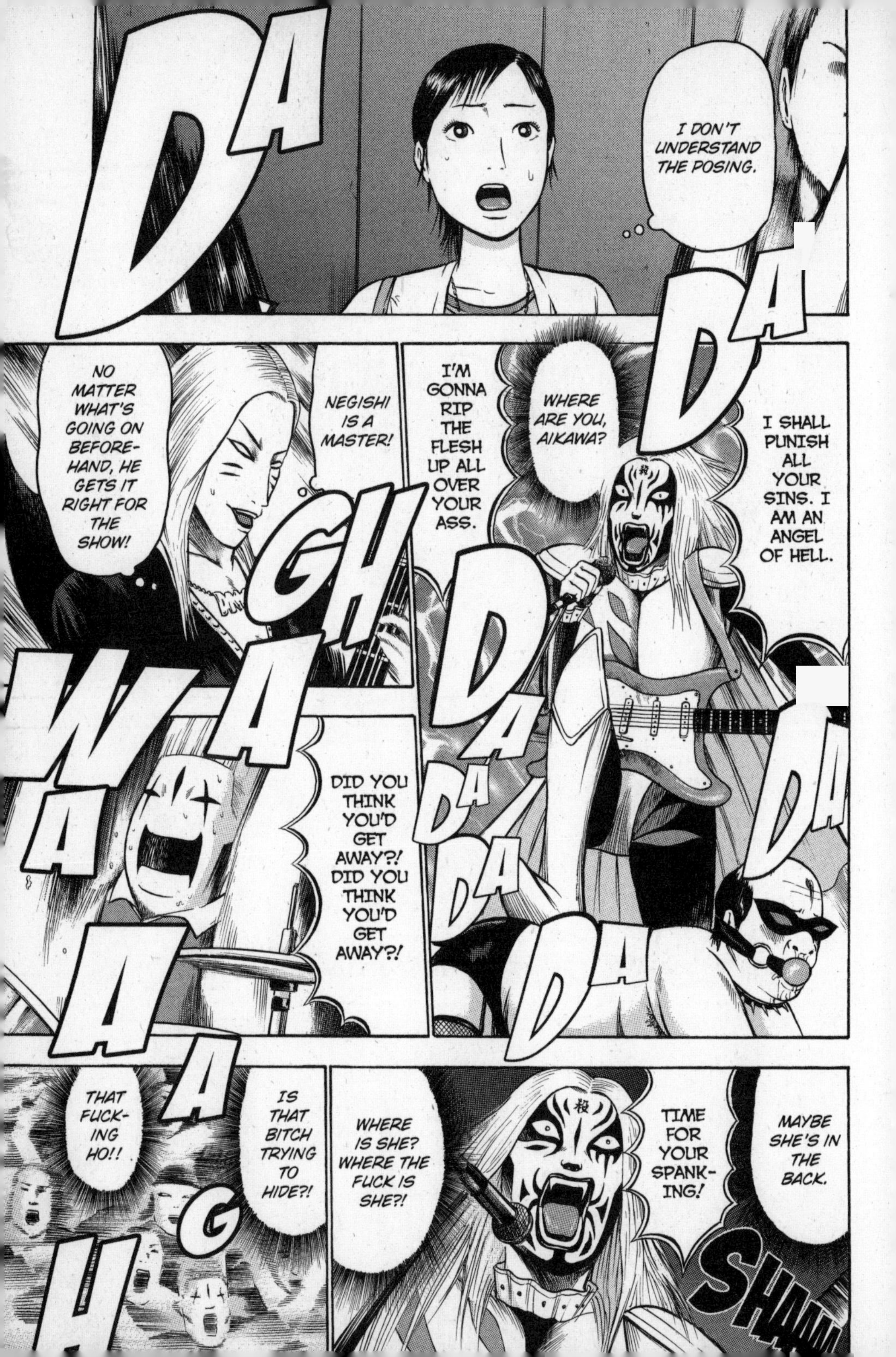
DA
I DON'T UNDERSTAND THE POSING.
DA
I SHALL PUNISH ALL YOUR SINS. I AM AN ANGEL OF HELL.
WHERE ARE YOU, AIKAWA?
I'M GONNA RIP THE FLESH UP ALL OVER YOUR ASS.
NEGISHI IS A MASTER!
NO MATTER WHAT'S GOING ON BEFORE-HAND, HE GETS IT RIGHT FOR THE SHOW!
GH
DA DA DA DA DA DA
DID YOU THINK YOU'D GET AWAY?! DID YOU THINK YOU'D GET AWAY?!
WA A A A A G H
MAYBE SHE'S IN THE BACK.
TIME FOR YOUR SPANK-ING!
WHERE IS SHE? WHERE THE FUCK IS SHE?!
SHAM
IS THAT BITCH TRYING TO HIDE?!
THAT FUCK-ING HO!!

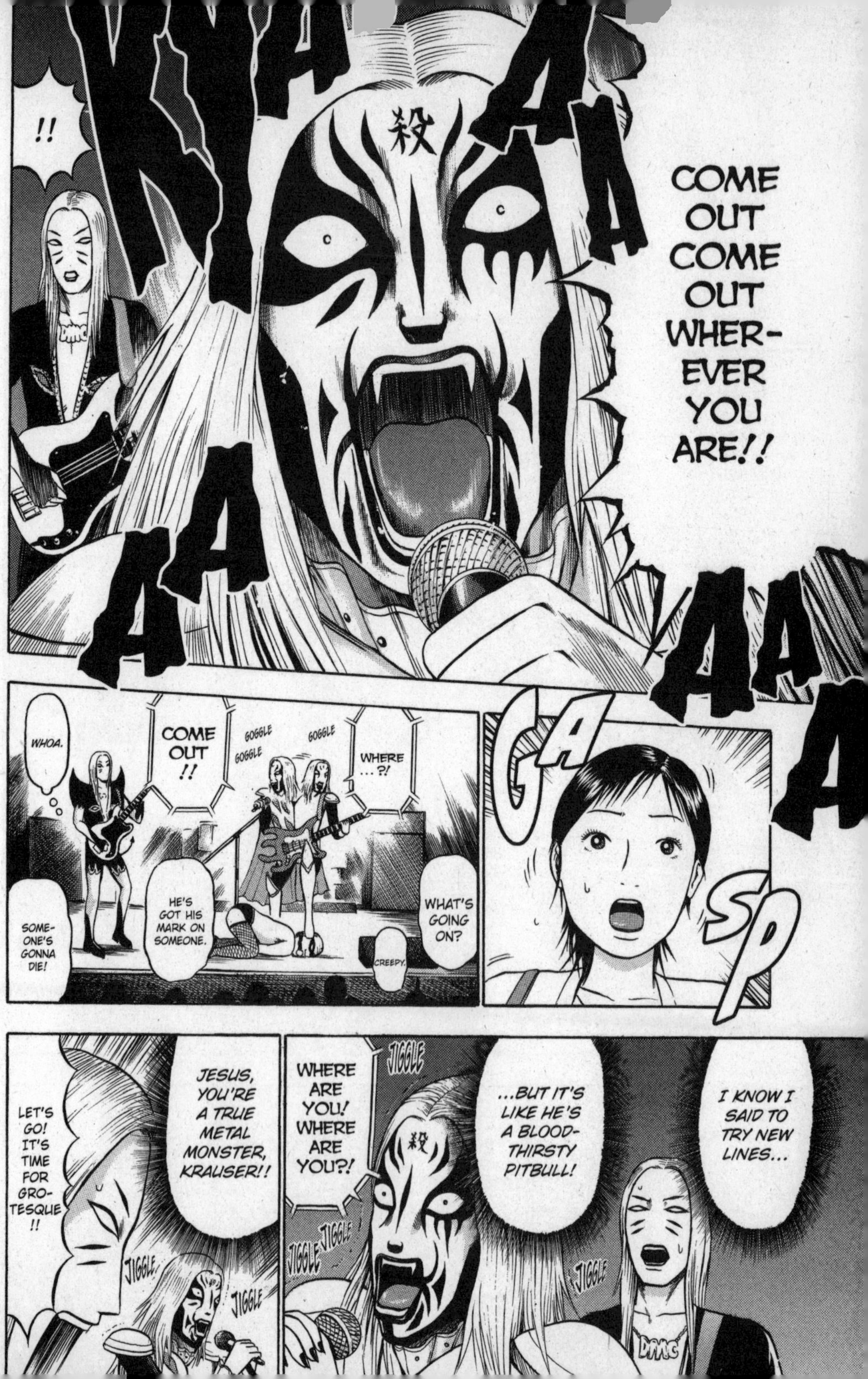
COME OUT COME OUT WHER-EVER YOU ARE!!
!!
GA
SP
WHERE …?!
WHAT'S GOING ON?
CREEPY.
GOGGLE
GOGGLE GOGGLE
COME OUT!!
HE'S GOT HIS MARK ON SOMEONE.
WHOA.
SOME-ONE'S GONNA DIE!
I KNOW I SAID TO TRY NEW LINES…
…BUT IT'S LIKE HE'S A BLOOD-THIRSTY PITBULL!
JIGGLE
WHERE ARE YOU! WHERE ARE YOU?!
JIGGLE
JIGGLE JIGGLE
JESUS, YOU'RE A TRUE METAL MONSTER, KRAUSER!!
LET'S GO! IT'S TIME FOR GRO-TESQUE!!
JIGGLE
JIGGLE

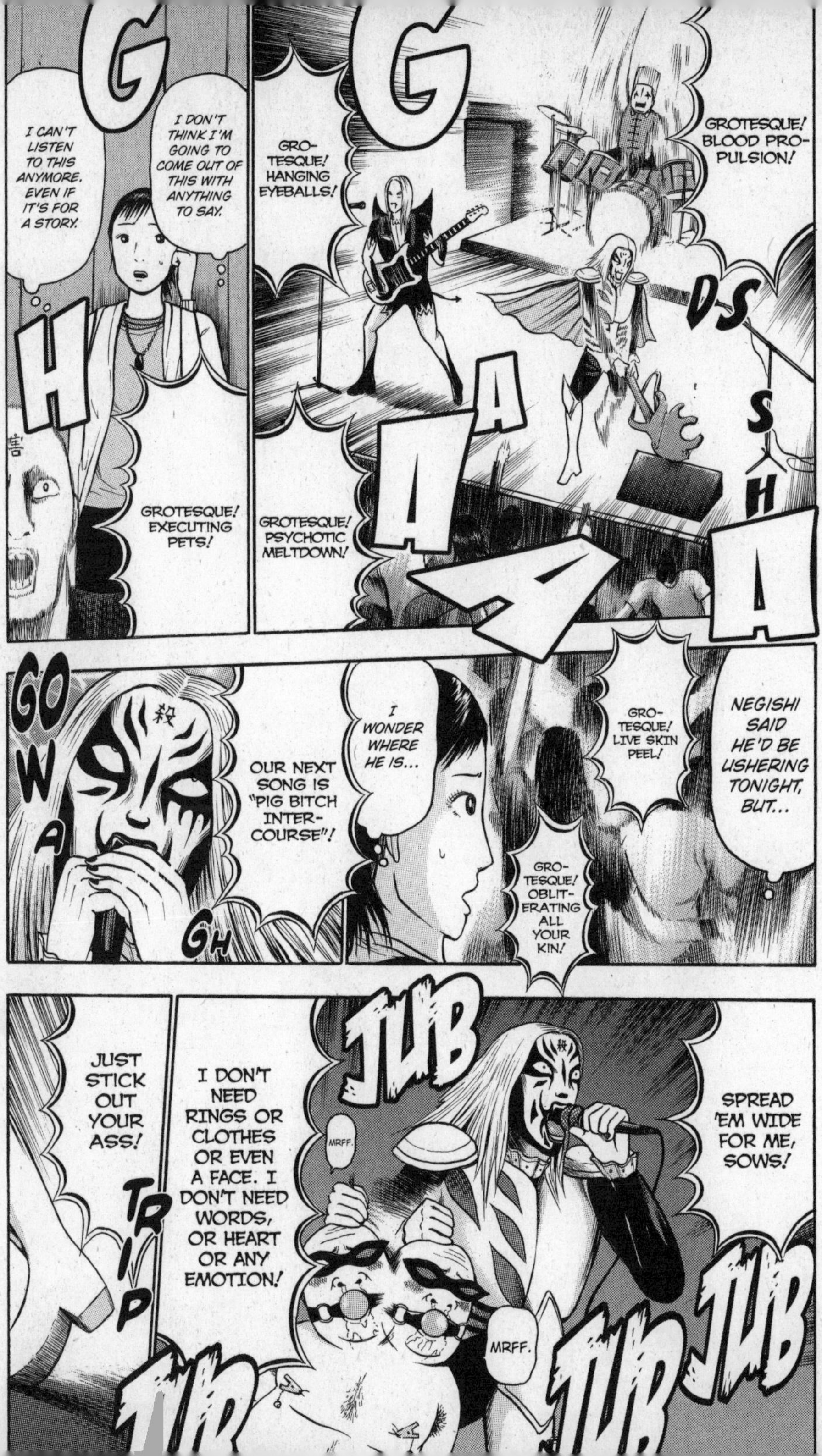

G
GROTESQUE! BLOOD PRO-PULSION!
GRO-TESQUE! HANGING EYEBALLS!
DS
S
H
A
A
A
A
GROTESQUE! PSYCHOTIC MELTDOWN!
G
I DON'T THINK I'M GOING TO COME OUT OF THIS WITH ANYTHING TO SAY.
I CAN'T LISTEN TO THIS ANYMORE. EVEN IF IT'S FOR A STORY.
H
害
GROTESQUE! EXECUTING PETS!
NEGISHI SAID HE'D BE USHERING TONIGHT, BUT...
GRO-TESQUE! LIVE SKIN PEEL!
GRO-TESQUE! OBLIT-ERATING ALL YOUR KIN!
I WONDER WHERE HE IS...
OUR NEXT SONG IS "PIG BITCH INTER-COURSE"!
GO
WA
殺
GH
SPREAD 'EM WIDE FOR ME, SOWS!
JUB
JUB
JUB
MRFF.
MRFF.
I DON'T NEED RINGS OR CLOTHES OR EVEN A FACE. I DON'T NEED WORDS, OR HEART OR ANY EMOTION!
JUB
JUST STICK OUT YOUR ASS!
TRIP

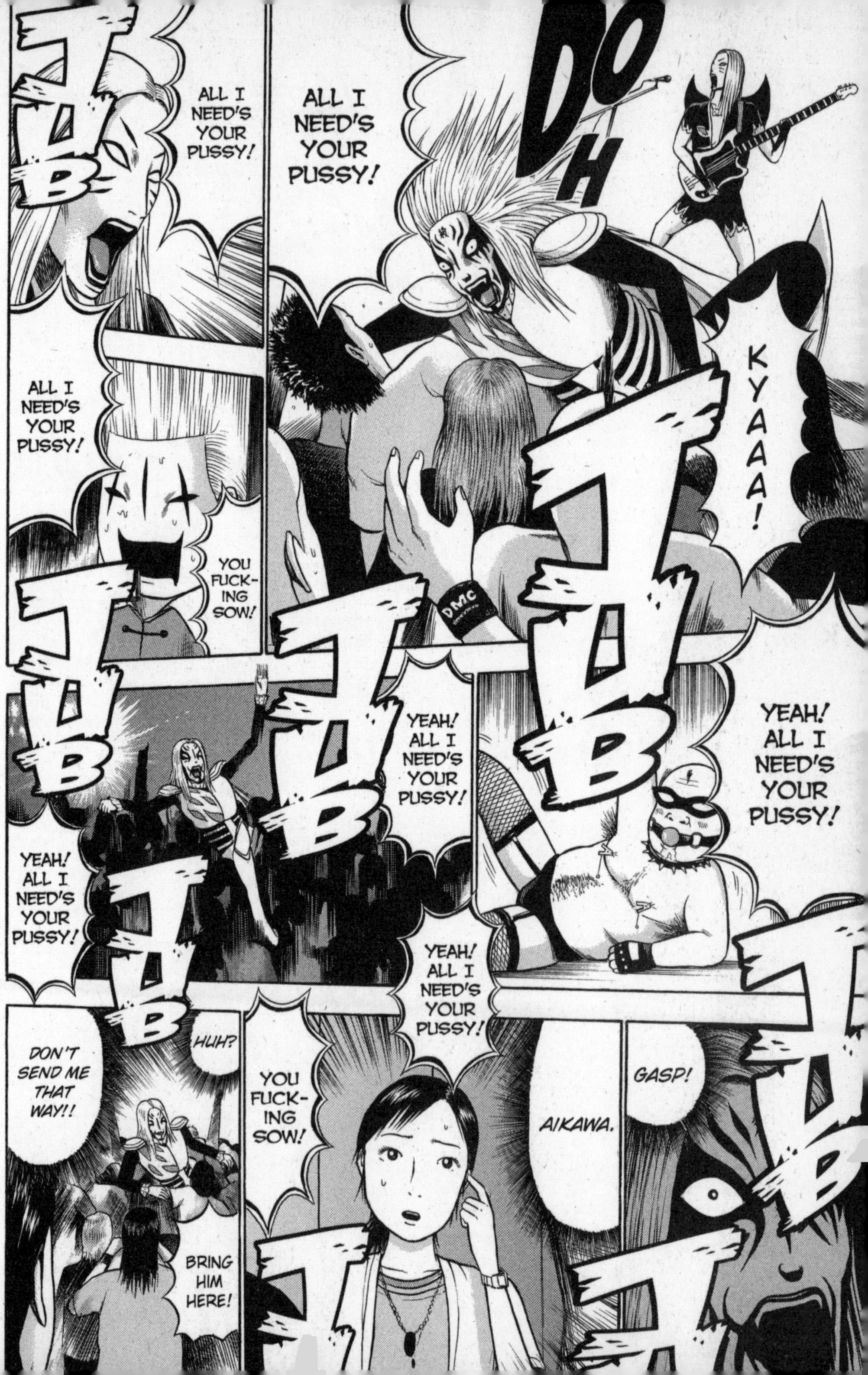
DOH
KYAAAA!
JUB
ALL I NEED'S YOUR PUSSY!
JUB
ALL I NEED'S YOUR PUSSY!
ALL I NEED'S YOUR PUSSY!
JUB
YOU FUCKING SOW!
YEAH! ALL I NEED'S YOUR PUSSY!
JUB
YEAH! ALL I NEED'S YOUR PUSSY!
JUB
YEAH! ALL I NEED'S YOUR PUSSY!
JUB
GASP!
AIKAWA.
JUB
YEAH! ALL I NEED'S YOUR PUSSY!
YOU FUCKING SOW!
HUH?
DON'T SEND ME THAT WAY!!
BRING HIM HERE!

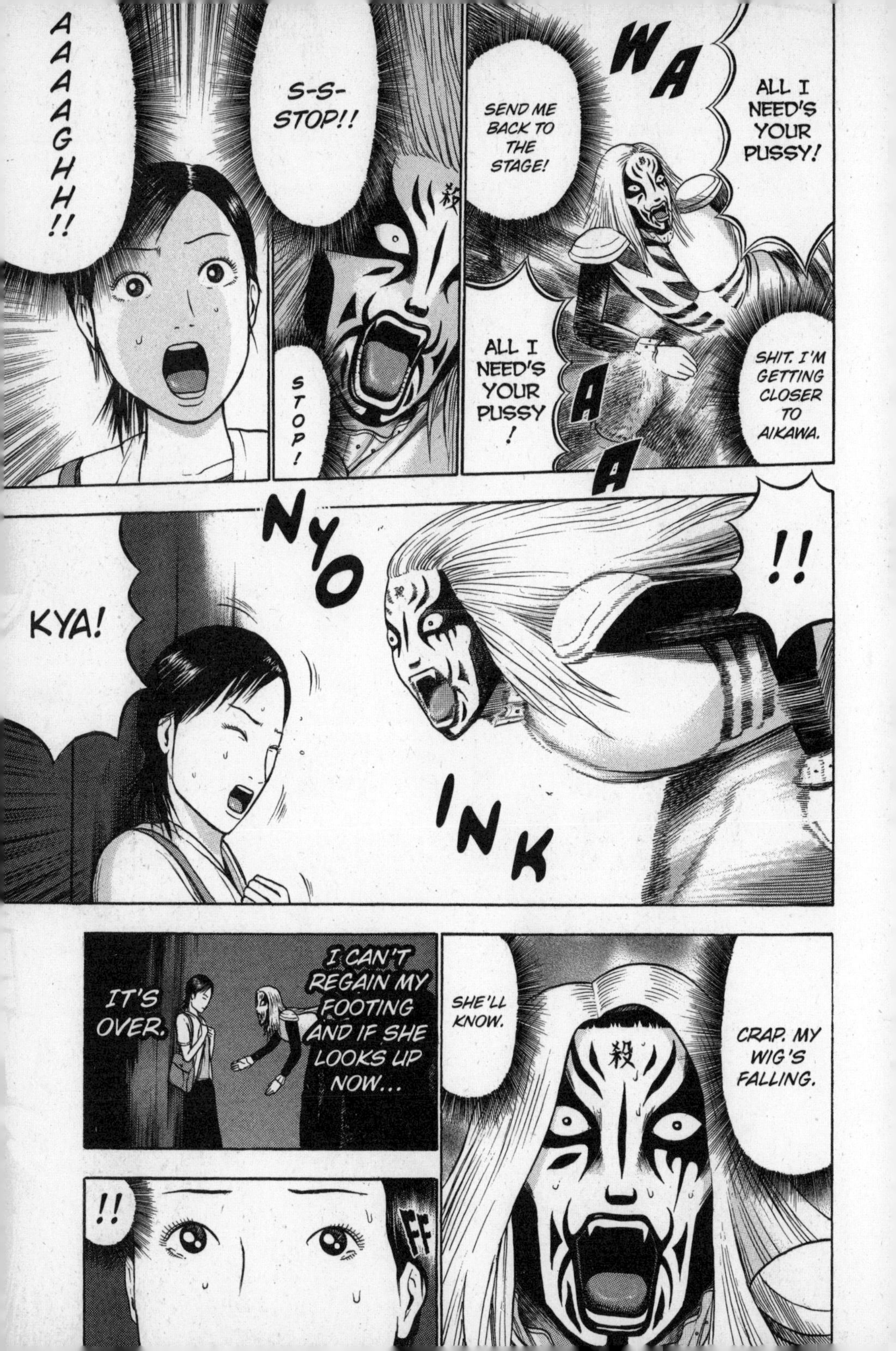
WA
ALL I NEED'S YOUR PUSSY!
SEND ME BACK TO THE STAGE!
SHIT. I'M GETTING CLOSER TO AIKAWA.
ALL I NEED'S YOUR PUSSY!
AAA
S-S-STOP!!
STOP!
AAAAGHH!!
!!
NYO
INK
KYA!
CRAP. MY WIG'S FALLING.
SHE'LL KNOW.
I CAN'T REGAIN MY FOOTING AND IF SHE LOOKS UP NOW...
IT'S OVER.
FF
!!

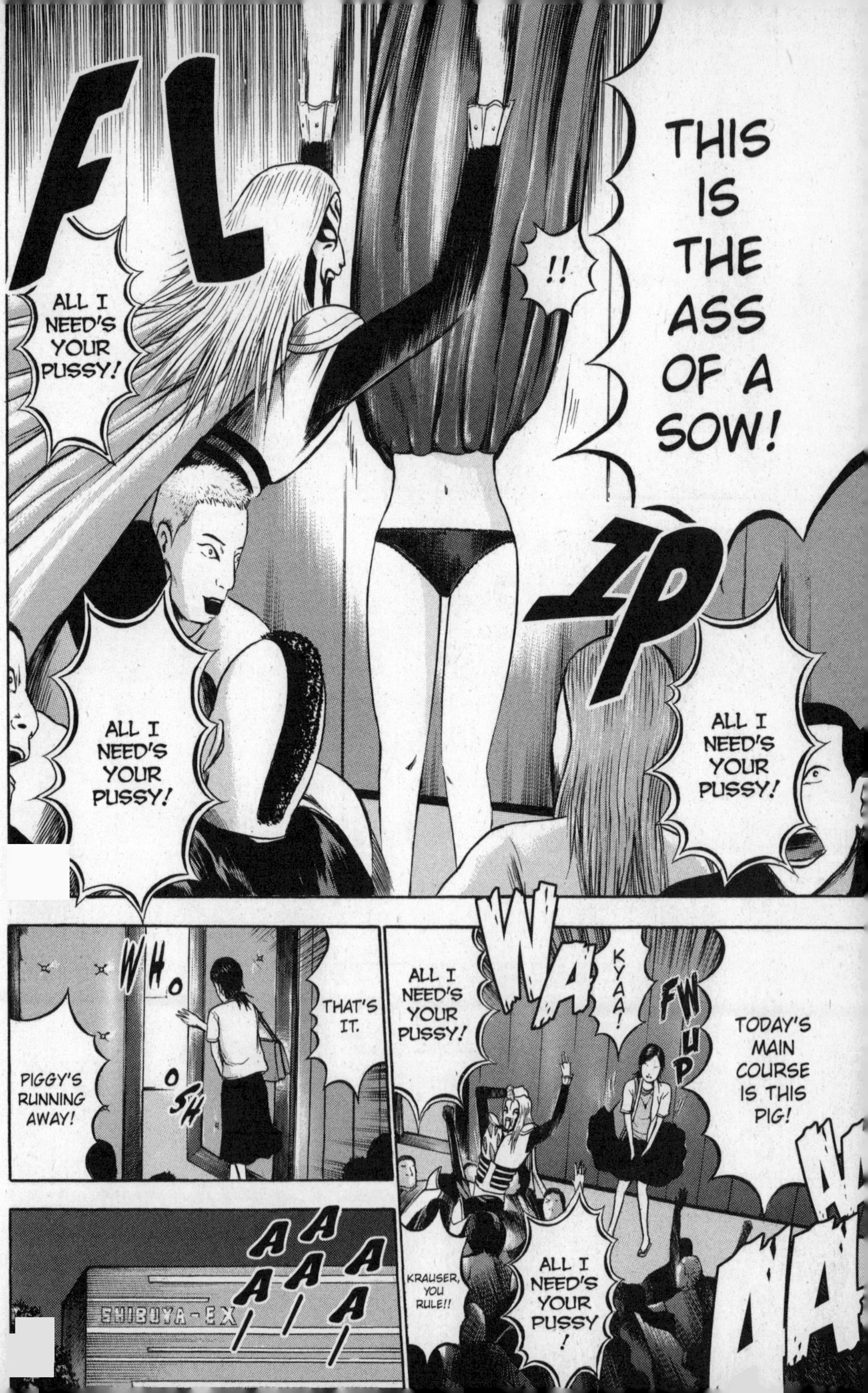
THIS IS THE ASS OF A SOW!
FL
!!
ALL I NEED'S YOUR PUSSY!
IP
ALL I NEED'S YOUR PUSSY!
ALL I NEED'S YOUR PUSSY!
WA
KYAA!
FWUP
TODAY'S MAIN COURSE IS THIS PIG!
ALL I NEED'S YOUR PUSSY!
ALL I NEED'S YOUR PUSSY!
KRAUSER, YOU RULE!!
THAT'S IT.
WHOOSH
PIGGY'S RUNNING AWAY!
AAAAAAAA
SHIBUYA-EX

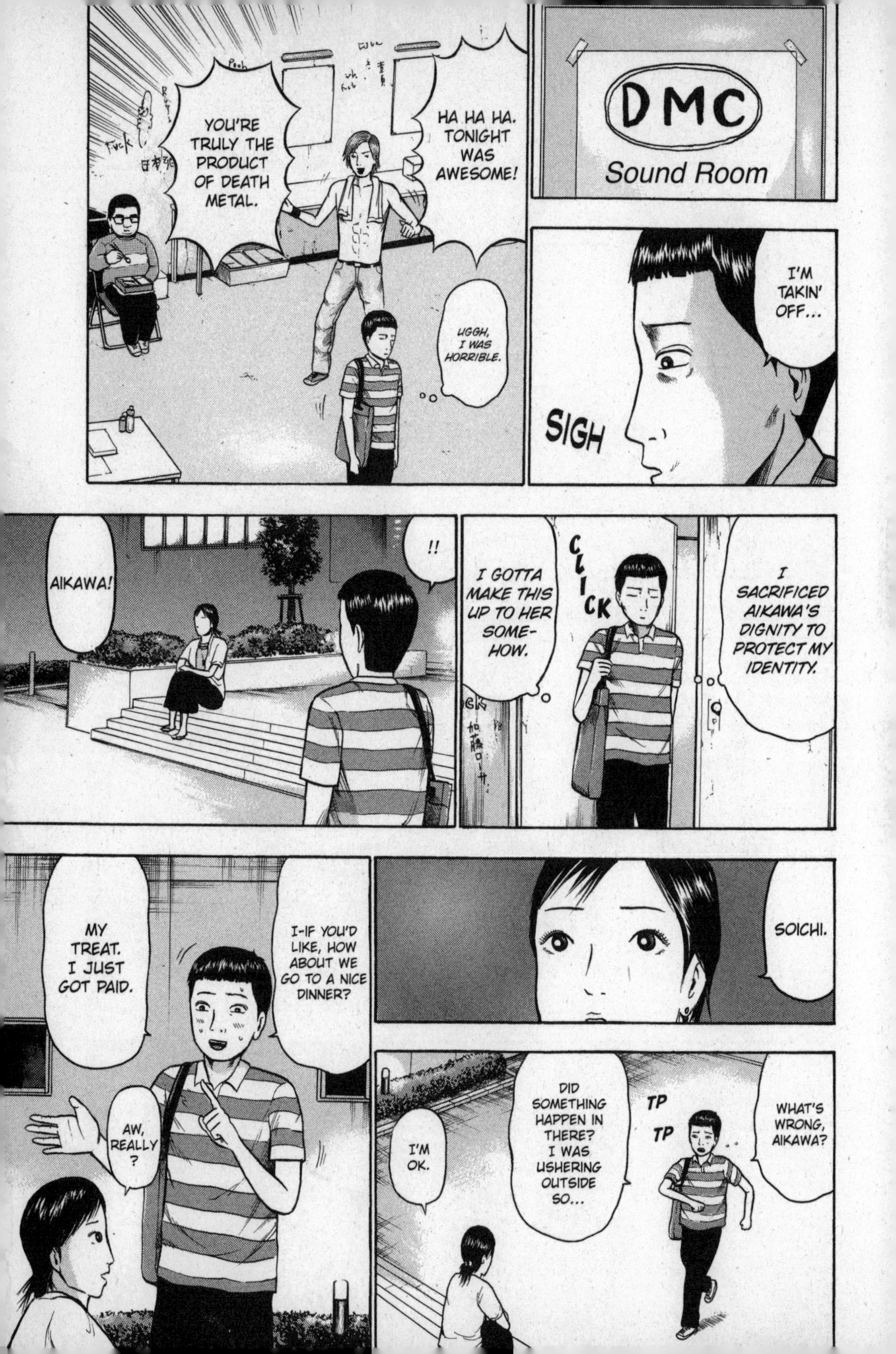
DMC
Sound Room
I'M TAKIN' OFF...
SIGH
HA HA HA. TONIGHT WAS AWESOME!
YOU'RE TRULY THE PRODUCT OF DEATH METAL.
UGGH, I WAS HORRIBLE.
I SACRIFICED AIKAWA'S DIGNITY TO PROTECT MY IDENTITY.
CLICK
I GOTTA MAKE THIS UP TO HER SOME-HOW.
!!
AIKAWA!
SOICHI.
WHAT'S WRONG, AIKAWA?
TP
TP
DID SOMETHING HAPPEN IN THERE? I WAS USHERING OUTSIDE SO...
I'M OK.
I-IF YOU'D LIKE, HOW ABOUT WE GO TO A NICE DINNER?
MY TREAT. I JUST GOT PAID.
AW, REALLY?

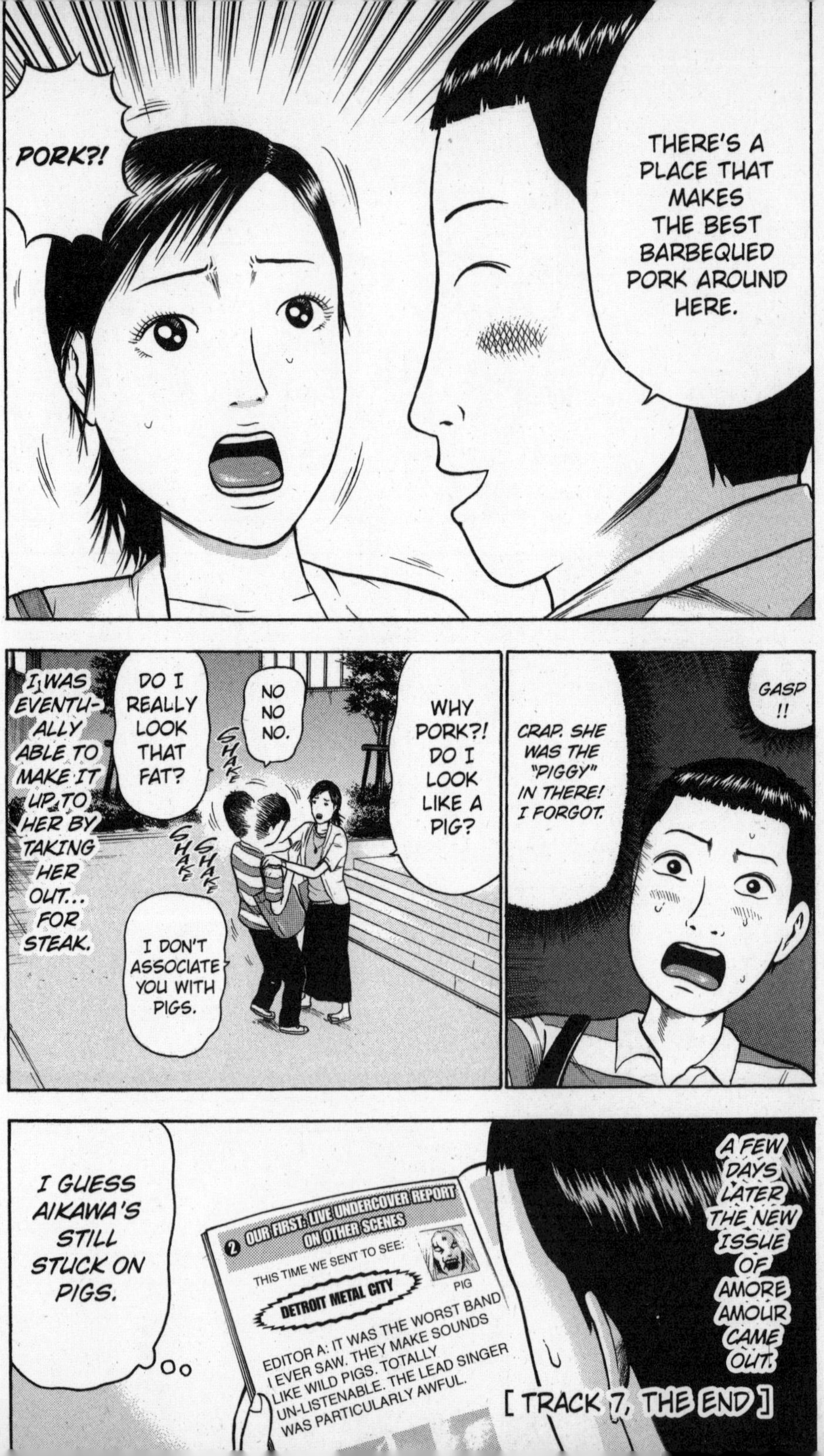
THERE'S A PLACE THAT MAKES THE BEST BARBEQUED PORK AROUND HERE.
PORK?!
GASP !!
CRAP. SHE WAS THE "PIGGY" IN THERE! I FORGOT.
WHY PORK?! DO I LOOK LIKE A PIG?
NO NO NO.
SHAKE
SHAKE
SHAKE
DO I REALLY LOOK THAT FAT?
I DON'T ASSOCIATE YOU WITH PIGS.
I WAS EVENTUALLY ABLE TO MAKE IT UP TO HER BY TAKING HER OUT... FOR STEAK.
A FEW DAYS LATER THE NEW ISSUE OF AMORE AMOUR CAME OUT.
2 OUR FIRST: LIVE UNDERCOVER REPORT ON OTHER SCENES
THIS TIME WE SENT TO SEE:
DETROIT METAL CITY
PIG
EDITOR A: IT WAS THE WORST BAND I EVER SAW. THEY MAKE SOUNDS LIKE WILD PIGS. TOTALLY UN-LISTENABLE. THE LEAD SINGER WAS PARTICULARLY AWFUL.
I GUESS AIKAWA'S STILL STUCK ON PIGS.
[TRACK 7, THE END]

DMC LEXICON

SOW

A disdainful term used against women. Should never be used, and is generally considered an insult. Only Krauser is allowed to say it. He especially likes taunting female superiors with this word.

Usage: I can't believe a career gal like you is such a horny sow underneath it all.

デトロイト・メタル・シティ

Detroit Metal City

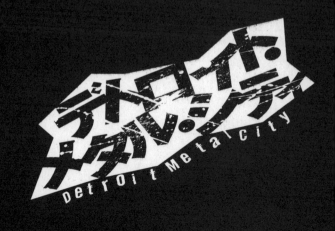

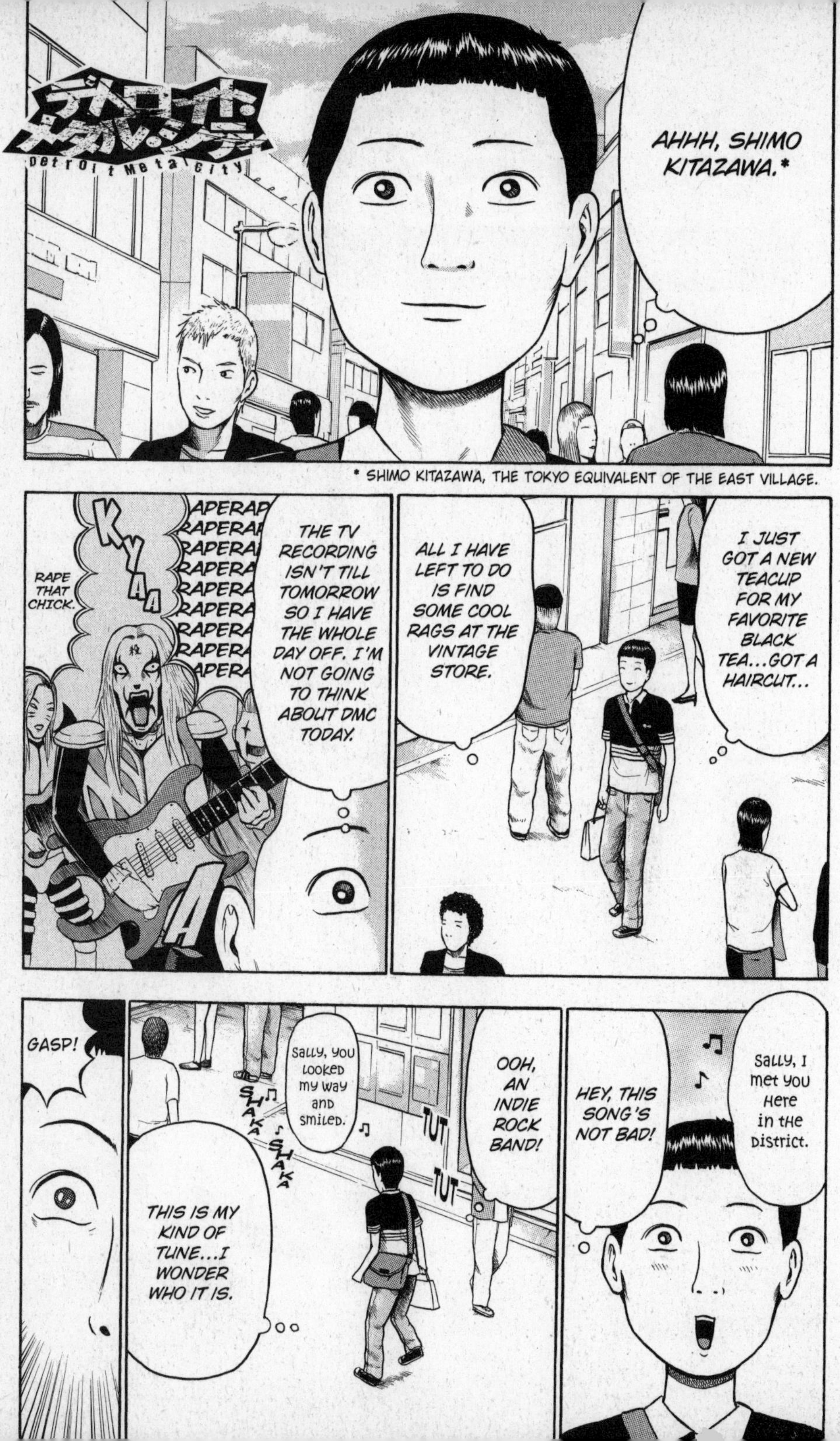
Detroit Metal City
AHHH, SHIMO KITAZAWA.*
* SHIMO KITAZAWA, THE TOKYO EQUIVALENT OF THE EAST VILLAGE.
I JUST GOT A NEW TEACUP FOR MY FAVORITE BLACK TEA...GOT A HAIRCUT...
ALL I HAVE LEFT TO DO IS FIND SOME COOL RAGS AT THE VINTAGE STORE.
THE TV RECORDING ISN'T TILL TOMORROW SO I HAVE THE WHOLE DAY OFF. I'M NOT GOING TO THINK ABOUT DMC TODAY.
KYAAA
RAPERAP RAPERA RAPERA RAPERA RAPERA RAPERA RAPERA RAPERA RAPERA
RAPE THAT CHICK.
Sally, I met you here in the district.
HEY, THIS SONG'S NOT BAD!
OOH, AN INDIE ROCK BAND!
TUT TUT
Sally, you looked my way and smiled.
SHAKA SHAKA
THIS IS MY KIND OF TUNE...I WONDER WHO IT IS.
GASP!

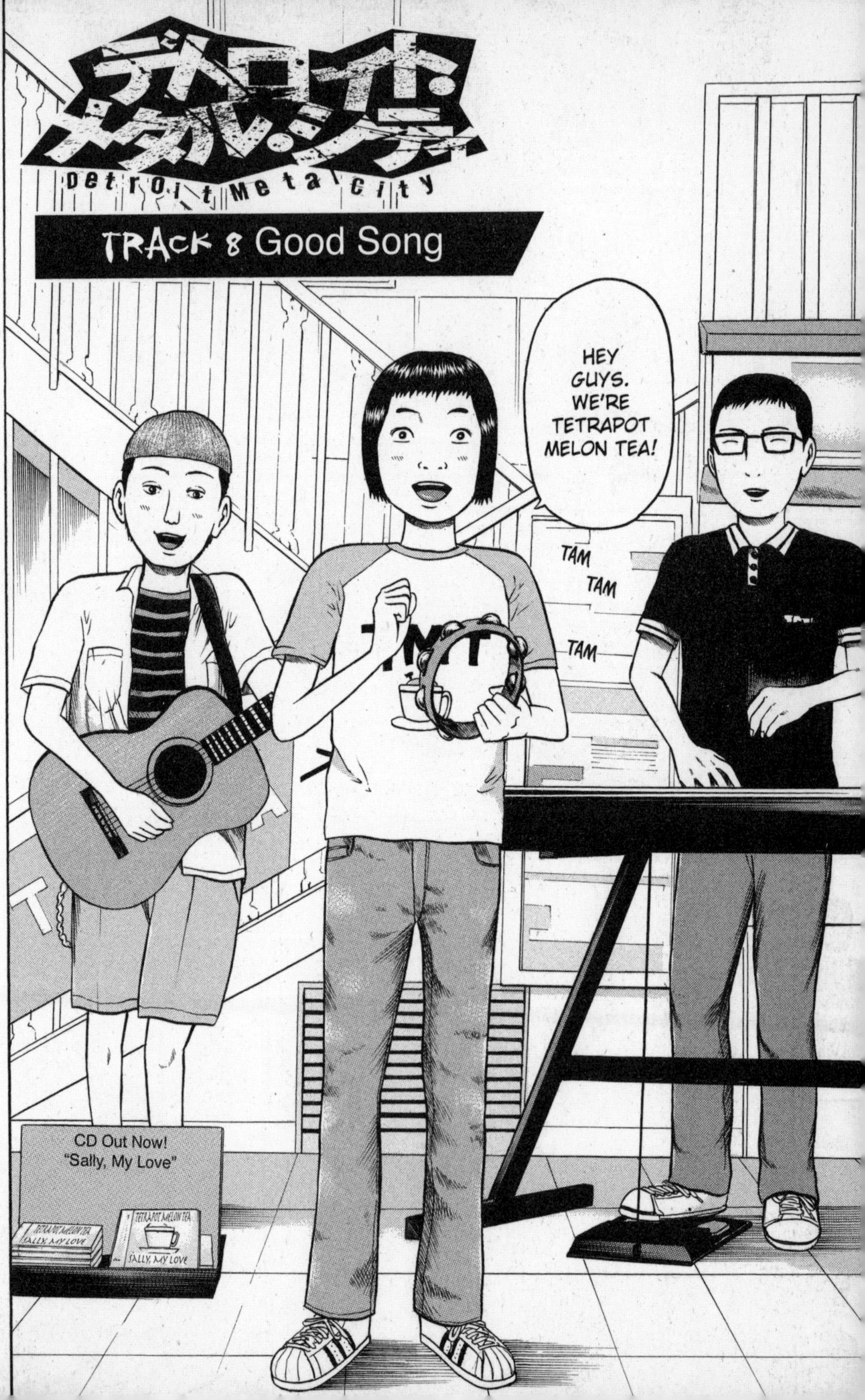

Detroit Metal City
TRACK 8 Good Song
HEY GUYS. WE'RE TETRAPOT MELON TEA!
TAM
TAM
TAM
CD Out Now!
"Sally, My Love"
TETRAPOT MELON TEA
SALLY, MY LOVE

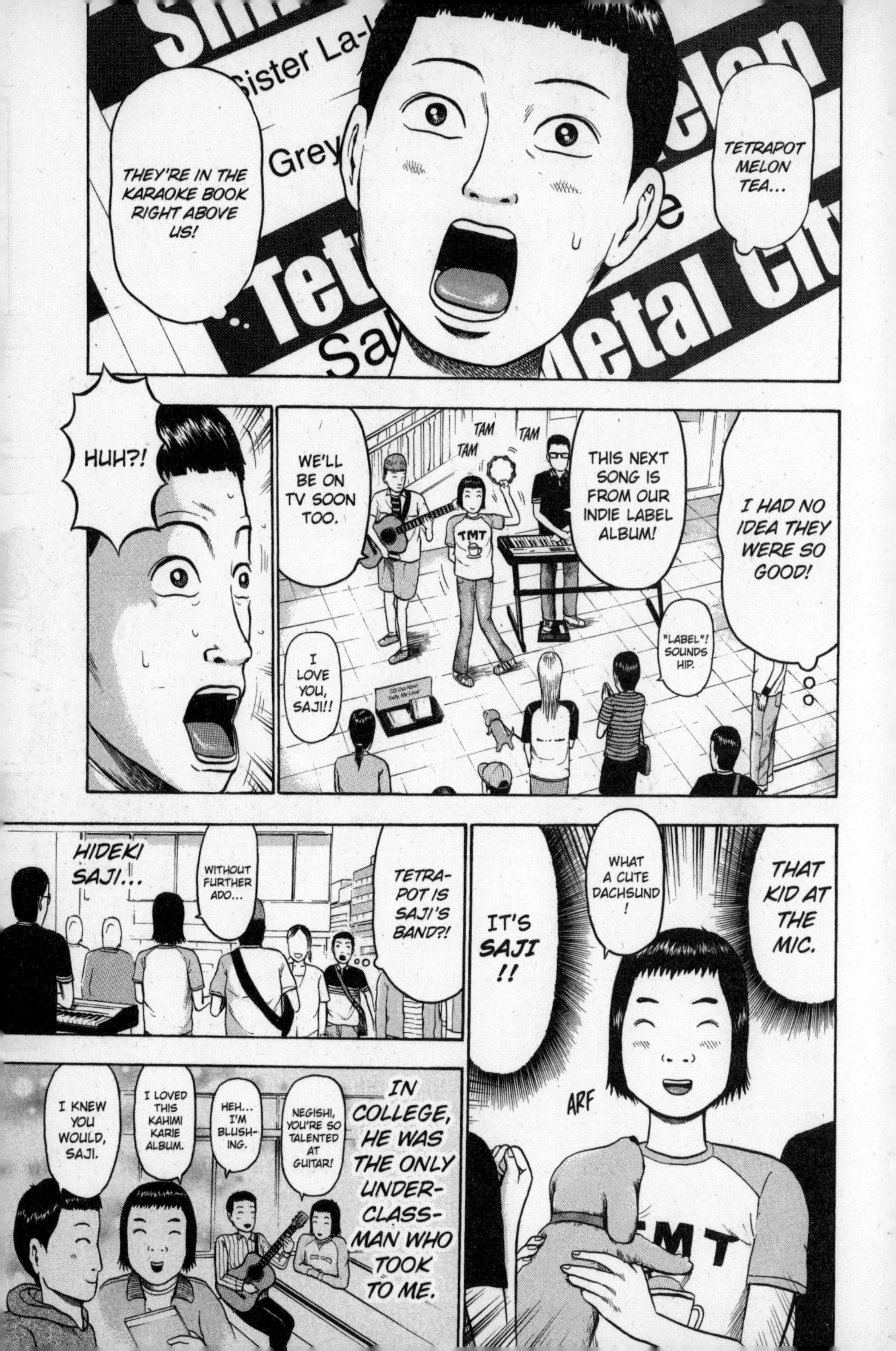

TETRAPOT MELON TEA...
THEY'RE IN THE KARAOKE BOOK RIGHT ABOVE US!
I HAD NO IDEA THEY WERE SO GOOD!
THIS NEXT SONG IS FROM OUR INDIE LABEL ALBUM!
TAM TAM TAM
WE'LL BE ON TV SOON TOO.
"LABEL"! SOUNDS HIP.
I LOVE YOU, SAJI!!
HUH?!
THAT KID AT THE MIC.
WHAT A CUTE DACHSUND!
IT'S SAJI!!
ARF
TETRA-POT IS SAJI'S BAND?!
WITHOUT FURTHER ADO...
HIDEKI SAJI...
IN COLLEGE, HE WAS THE ONLY UNDER-CLASS-MAN WHO TOOK TO ME.
NEGISHI, YOU'RE SO TALENTED AT GUITAR!
HEH... I'M BLUSH-ING.
I LOVED THIS KAHIMI KARIE ALBUM.
I KNEW YOU WOULD, SAJI.

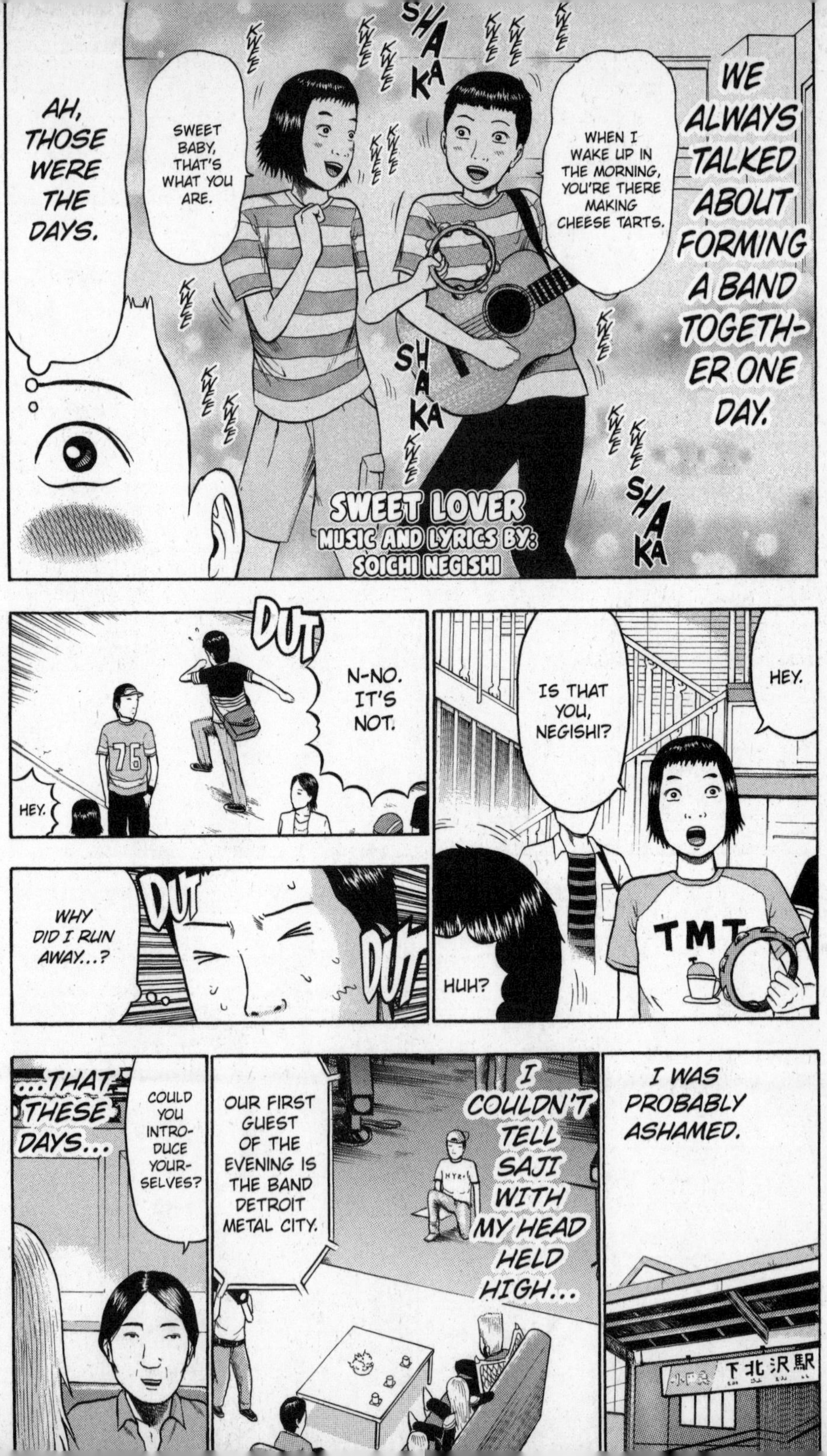
WE ALWAYS TALKED ABOUT FORMING A BAND TOGETH-ER ONE DAY.
WHEN I WAKE UP IN THE MORNING, YOU'RE THERE MAKING CHEESE TARTS.
SHAKA
KWEE KWEE
SWEET BABY, THAT'S WHAT YOU ARE.
KWEE KWEE
AH, THOSE WERE THE DAYS.
SHAKA
KWEE
SHAKA
SWEET LOVER
MUSIC AND LYRICS BY: SOICHI NEGISHI
HEY.
IS THAT YOU, NEGISHI?
HUH?
DUT
N-NO. IT'S NOT.
HEY.
DUT
WHY DID I RUN AWAY...?
DUT
I WAS PROBABLY ASHAMED.
下北沢駅
I COULDN'T TELL SAJI WITH MY HEAD HELD HIGH...
OUR FIRST GUEST OF THE EVENING IS THE BAND DETROIT METAL CITY.
...THAT THESE DAYS...
COULD YOU INTRO-DUCE YOUR-SELVES?

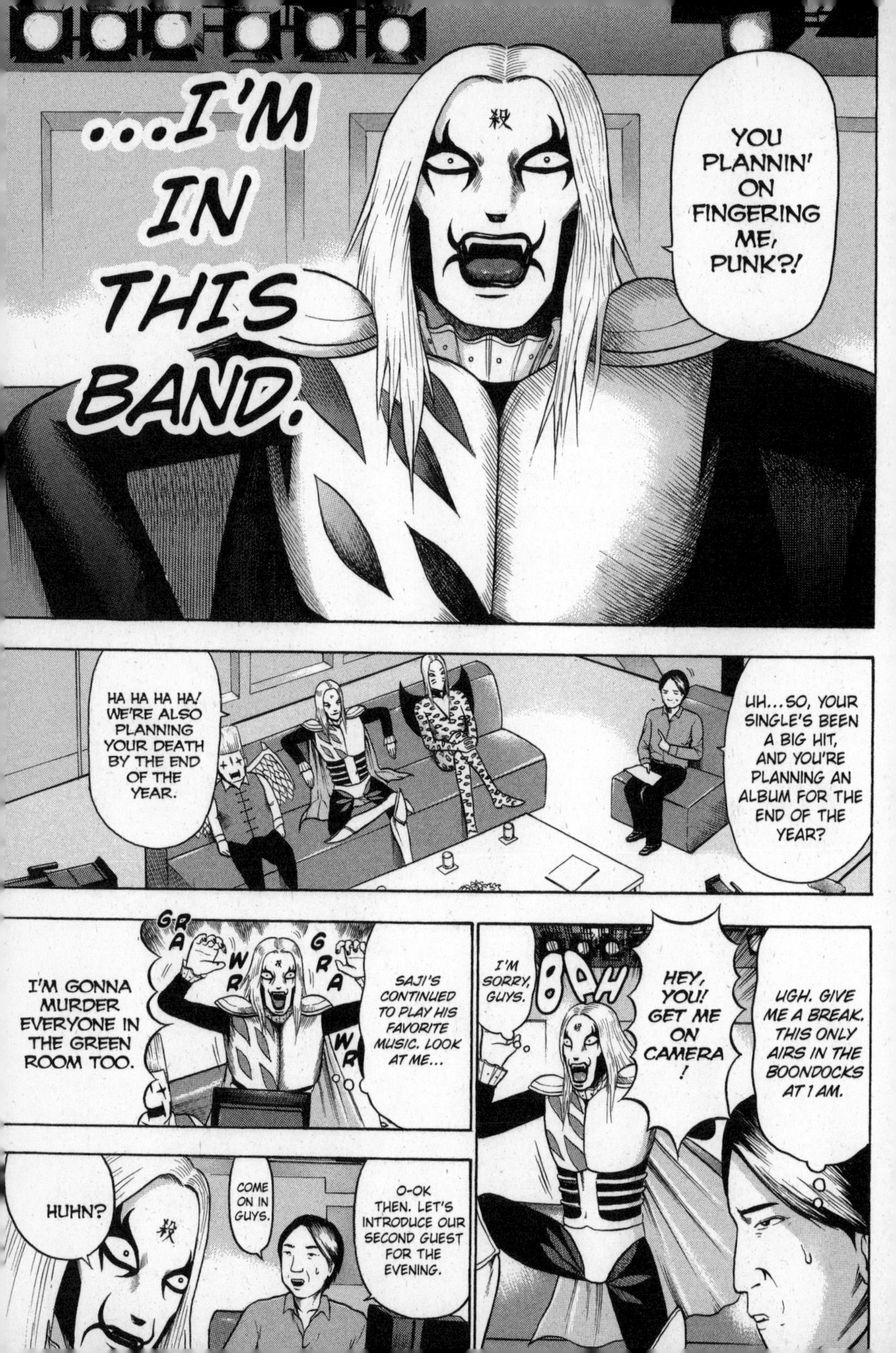
YOU PLANNIN' ON FINGERING ME, PUNK?!
...I'M IN THIS BAND.
UH...SO, YOUR SINGLE'S BEEN A BIG HIT, AND YOU'RE PLANNING AN ALBUM FOR THE END OF THE YEAR?
HA HA HA HA! WE'RE ALSO PLANNING YOUR DEATH BY THE END OF THE YEAR.
UGH. GIVE ME A BREAK. THIS ONLY AIRS IN THE BOONDOCKS AT 1 AM.
HEY, YOU! GET ME ON CAMERA!
BAH
I'M SORRY, GUYS.
SAJI'S CONTINUED TO PLAY HIS FAVORITE MUSIC. LOOK AT ME...
GRA WR
GRA WR
I'M GONNA MURDER EVERYONE IN THE GREEN ROOM TOO.
O-OK THEN. LET'S INTRODUCE OUR SECOND GUEST FOR THE EVENING.
COME ON IN GUYS.
HUHN?

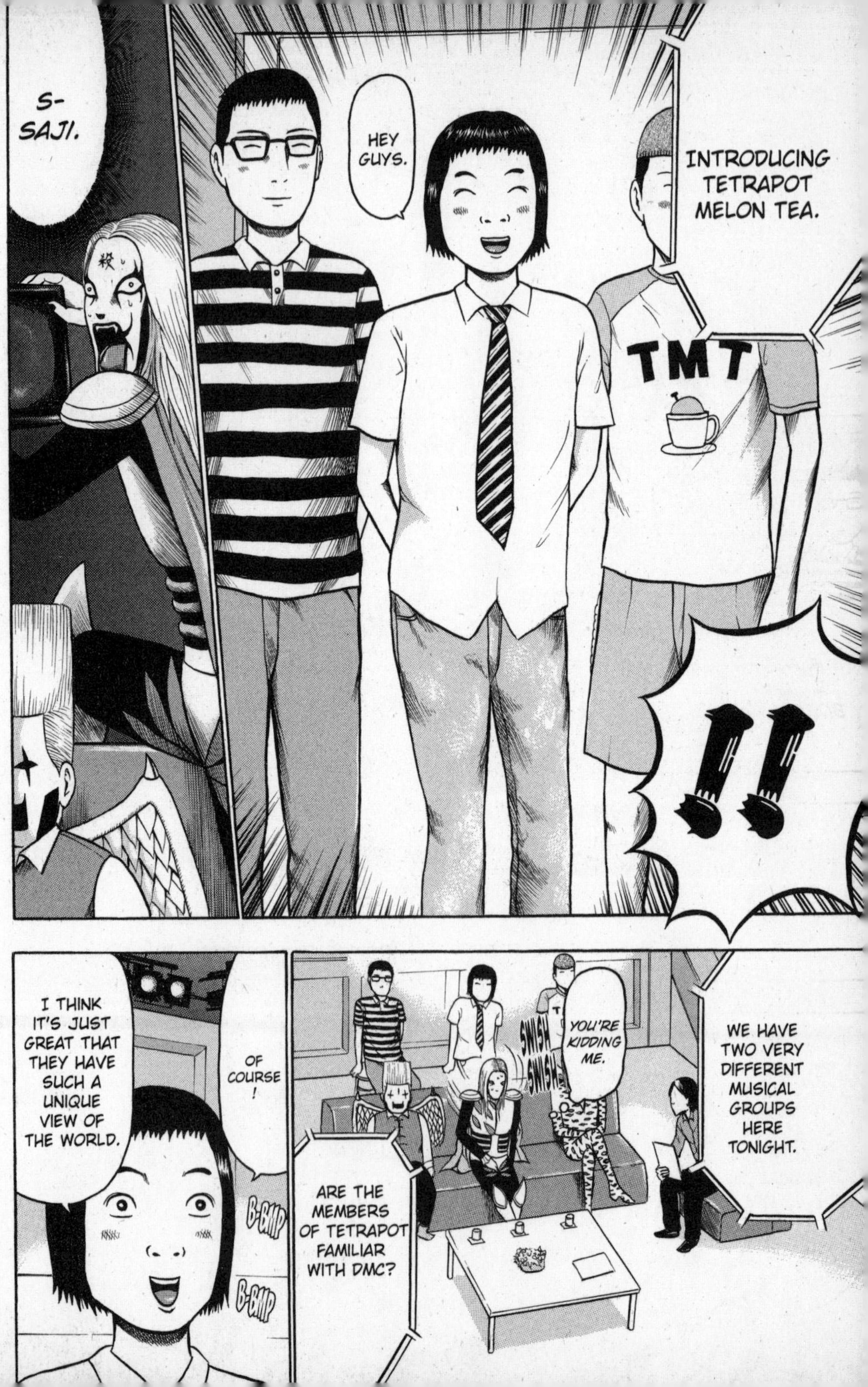
INTRODUCING TETRAPOT MELON TEA.
HEY GUYS.
S- SAJI.
TMT
!!
WE HAVE TWO VERY DIFFERENT MUSICAL GROUPS HERE TONIGHT.
YOU'RE KIDDING ME.
SWISH SWISH
ARE THE MEMBERS OF TETRAPOT FAMILIAR WITH DMC?
OF COURSE!
I THINK IT'S JUST GREAT THAT THEY HAVE SUCH A UNIQUE VIEW OF THE WORLD.
B-BMP
B-BMP

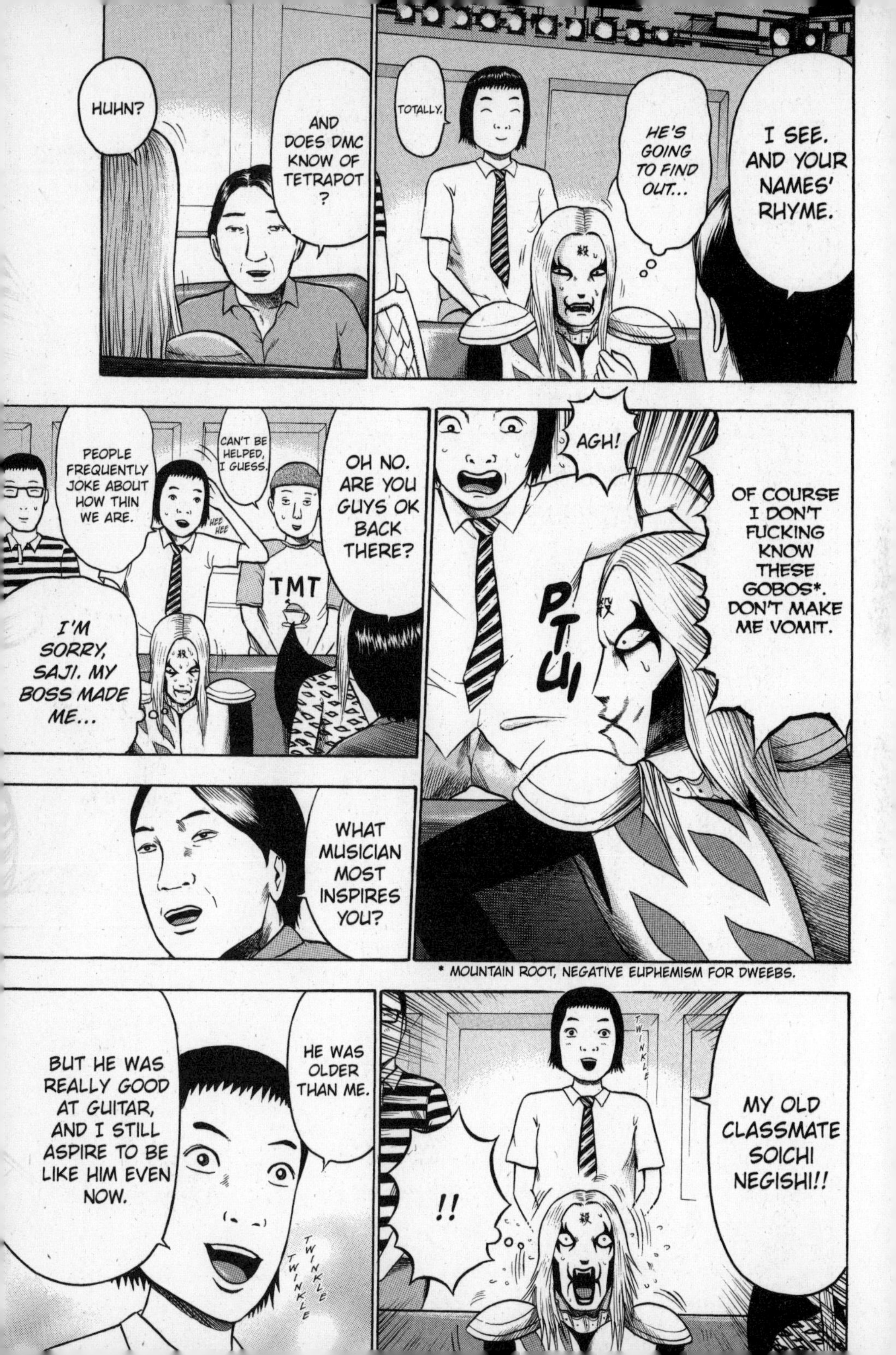
I SEE. AND YOUR NAMES' RHYME.
HE'S GOING TO FIND OUT...
TOTALLY.
AND DOES DMC KNOW OF TETRAPOT?
HUHN?
AGH!
OF COURSE I DON'T FUCKING KNOW THESE GOBOS*. DON'T MAKE ME VOMIT.
PTUI
OH NO. ARE YOU GUYS OK BACK THERE?
CAN'T BE HELPED, I GUESS.
PEOPLE FREQUENTLY JOKE ABOUT HOW THIN WE ARE.
HEE HEE
TMT
I'M SORRY, SAJI. MY BOSS MADE ME...
WHAT MUSICIAN MOST INSPIRES YOU?
MY OLD CLASSMATE SOICHI NEGISHI!!
TWINKLE
!!
HE WAS OLDER THAN ME.
BUT HE WAS REALLY GOOD AT GUITAR, AND I STILL ASPIRE TO BE LIKE HIM EVEN NOW.
TWINKLE TWINKLE

* MOUNTAIN ROOT, NEGATIVE EUPHEMISM FOR DWEEBS.

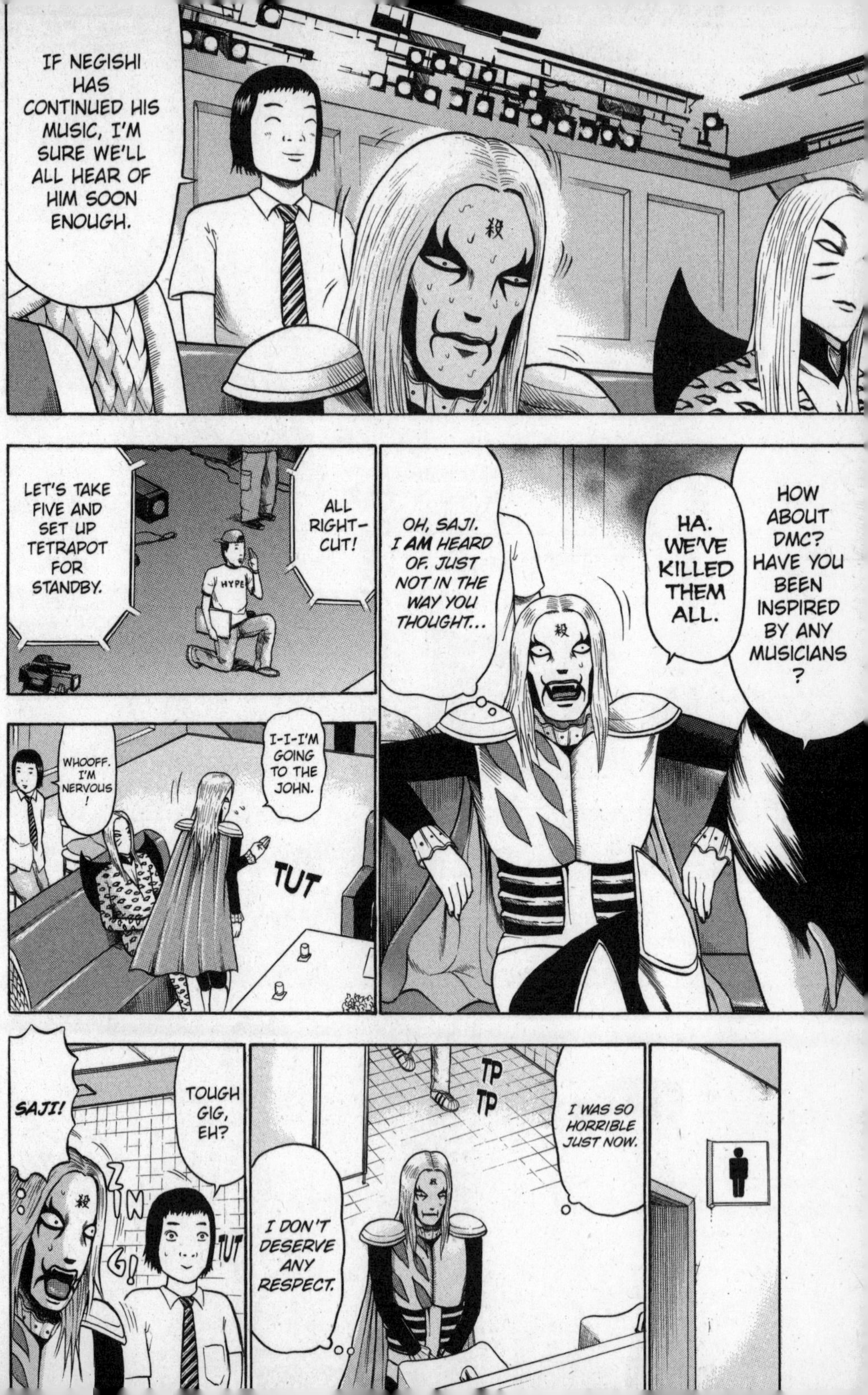
IF NEGISHI HAS CONTINUED HIS MUSIC, I'M SURE WE'LL ALL HEAR OF HIM SOON ENOUGH.
HOW ABOUT DMC? HAVE YOU BEEN INSPIRED BY ANY MUSICIANS?
HA. WE'VE KILLED THEM ALL.
OH, SAJI. I AM HEARD OF. JUST NOT IN THE WAY YOU THOUGHT...
ALL RIGHT-CUT!
LET'S TAKE FIVE AND SET UP TETRAPOT FOR STANDBY.
HYPE
I-I-I'M GOING TO THE JOHN.
WHOOFF. I'M NERVOUS!
TUT
TP TP
I WAS SO HORRIBLE JUST NOW.
I DON'T DESERVE ANY RESPECT.
TOUGH GIG, EH?
SAJI!
ZING!
TUT

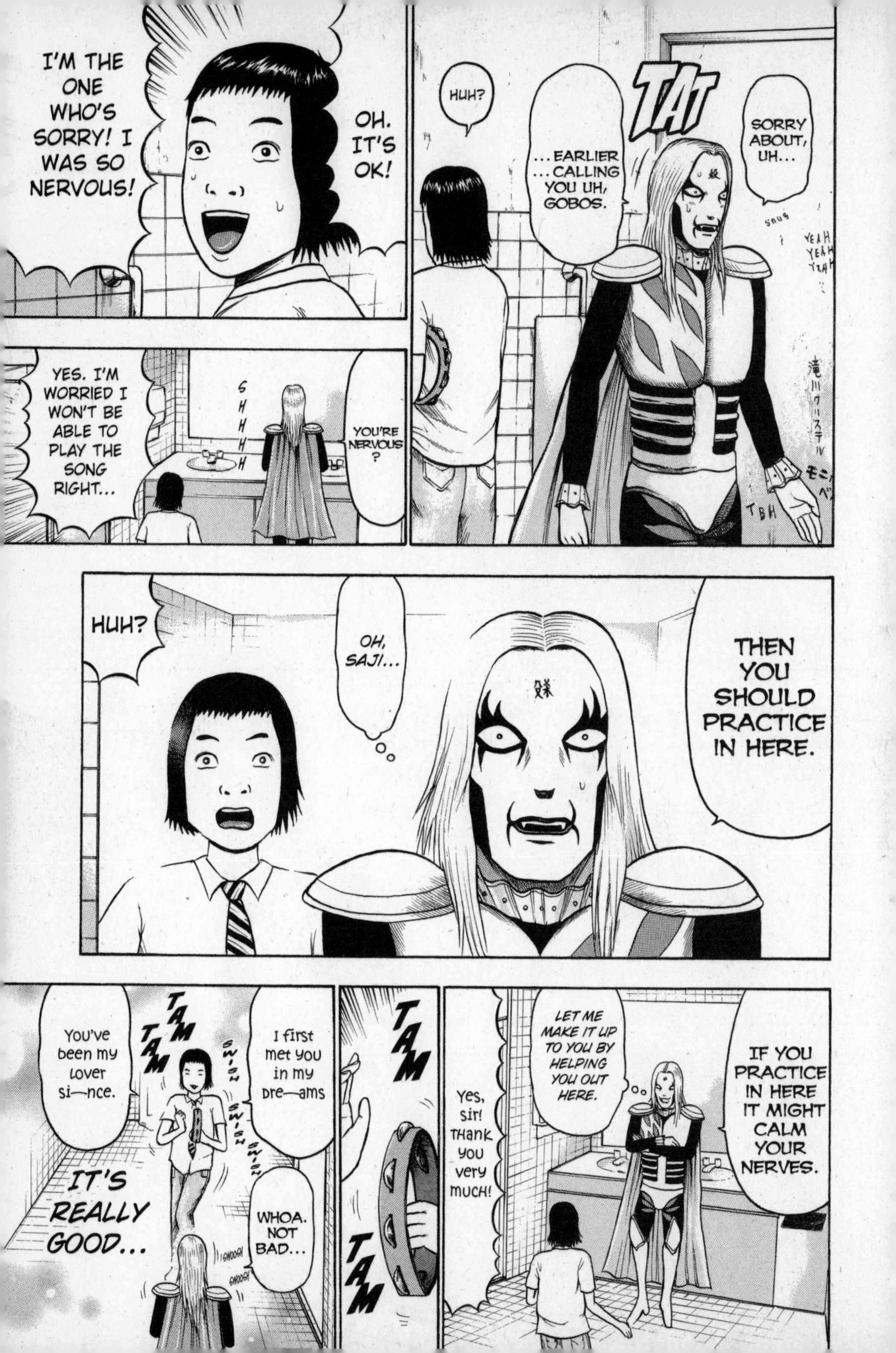
SORRY ABOUT, UH...
TAT
...EARLIER ...CALLING YOU UH, GOBOS.
HUH?
YEAH YEAH YEAH
TBH
OH. IT'S OK!
I'M THE ONE WHO'S SORRY! I WAS SO NERVOUS!
YOU'RE NERVOUS?
SHHHHH
YES. I'M WORRIED I WON'T BE ABLE TO PLAY THE SONG RIGHT...
THEN YOU SHOULD PRACTICE IN HERE.
OH, SAJI...
HUH?
IF YOU PRACTICE IN HERE IT MIGHT CALM YOUR NERVES.
LET ME MAKE IT UP TO YOU BY HELPING YOU OUT HERE.
Yes, sir! Thank you very much!
TAM
TAM
I first met you in my dre—ams
TAM TAM
You've been my lover si—nce.
SWISH SWISH SWISH
WHOA. NOT BAD...
IT'S REALLY GOOD...

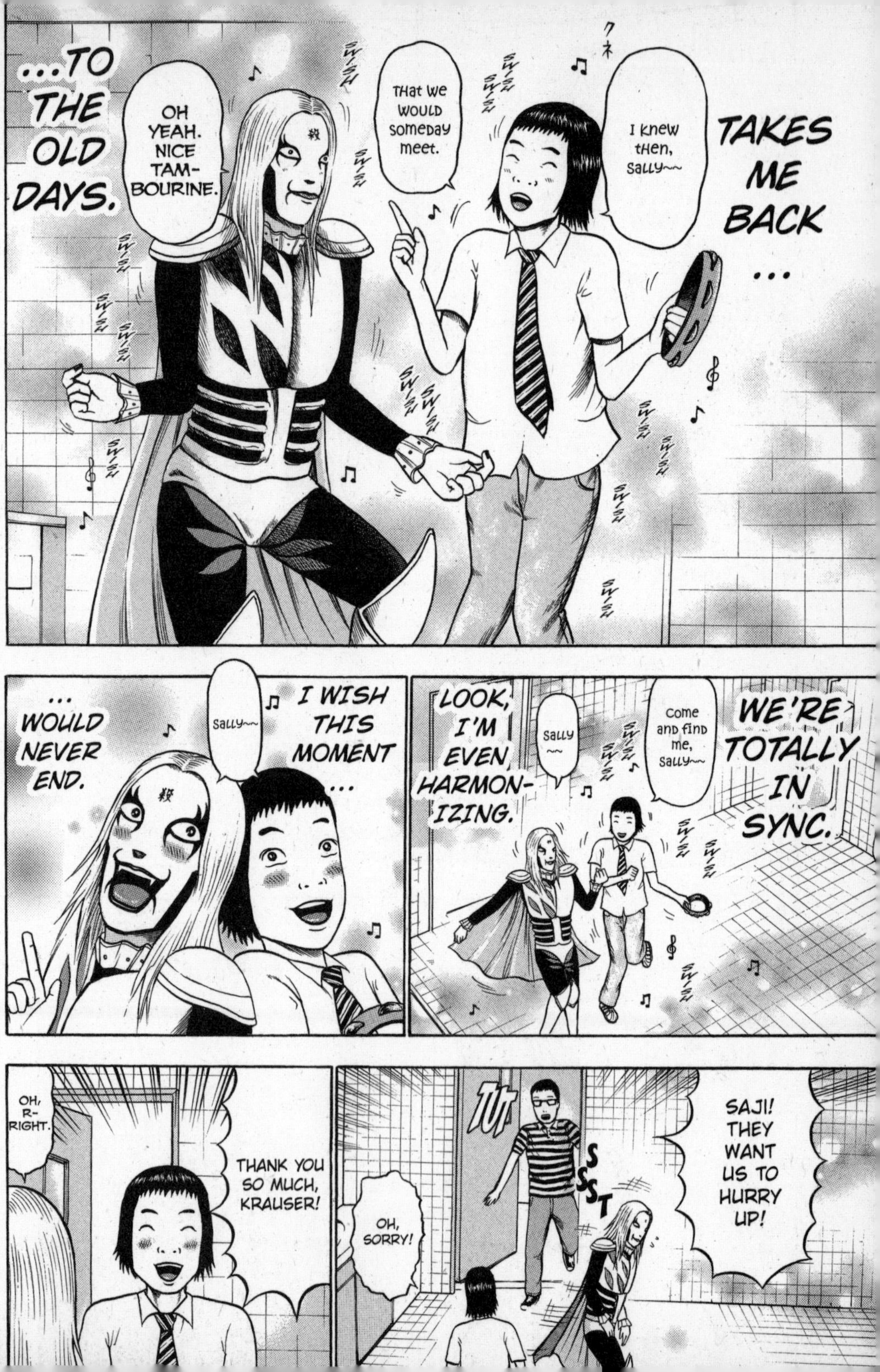
TAKES ME BACK...
I knew then, Sally~~
クネ
That we would someday meet.
SWISH
OH YEAH. NICE TAM-BOURINE.
...TO THE OLD DAYS.
WE'RE TOTALLY IN SYNC.
Come and find me, Sally~~
Sally ~~
LOOK, I'M EVEN HARMON-IZING.
I WISH THIS MOMENT...
Sally~~
...WOULD NEVER END.
SAJI! THEY WANT US TO HURRY UP!
TUT
SSST
OH, SORRY!
THANK YOU SO MUCH, KRAUSER!
OH, R-RIGHT.

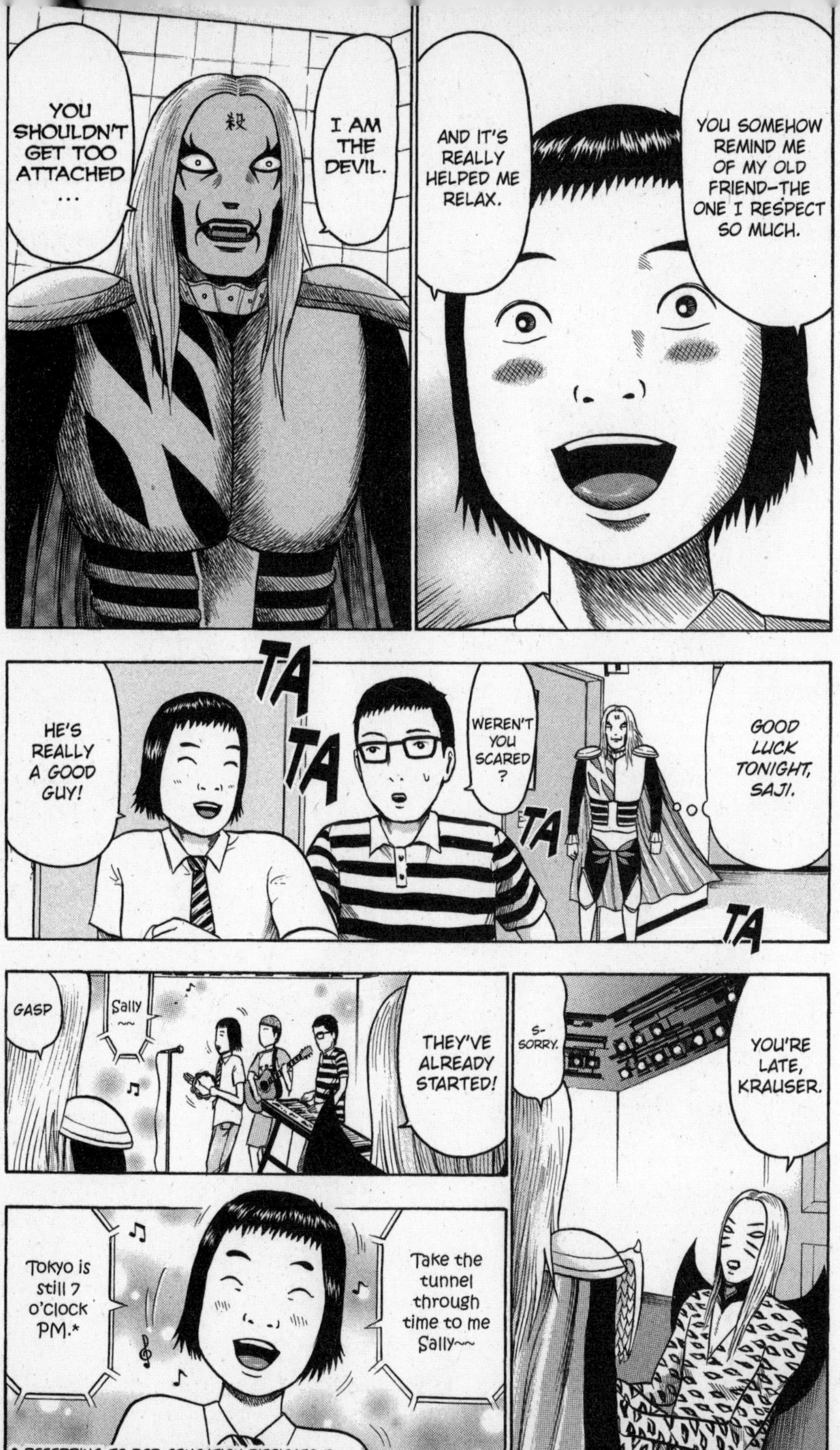
YOU SOMEHOW REMIND ME OF MY OLD FRIEND—THE ONE I RESPECT SO MUCH.
AND IT'S REALLY HELPED ME RELAX.
I AM THE DEVIL.
YOU SHOULDN'T GET TOO ATTACHED ...
GOOD LUCK TONIGHT, SAJI.
TA
TA
WEREN'T YOU SCARED?
TA
TA
HE'S REALLY A GOOD GUY!
YOU'RE LATE, KRAUSER.
S-SORRY.
THEY'VE ALREADY STARTED!
Sally ~~
GASP
Take the tunnel through time to me Sally~~
Tokyo is still 7 o'clock PM.*

* REFERRING TO POP SENSATION PIZZICATO 5.

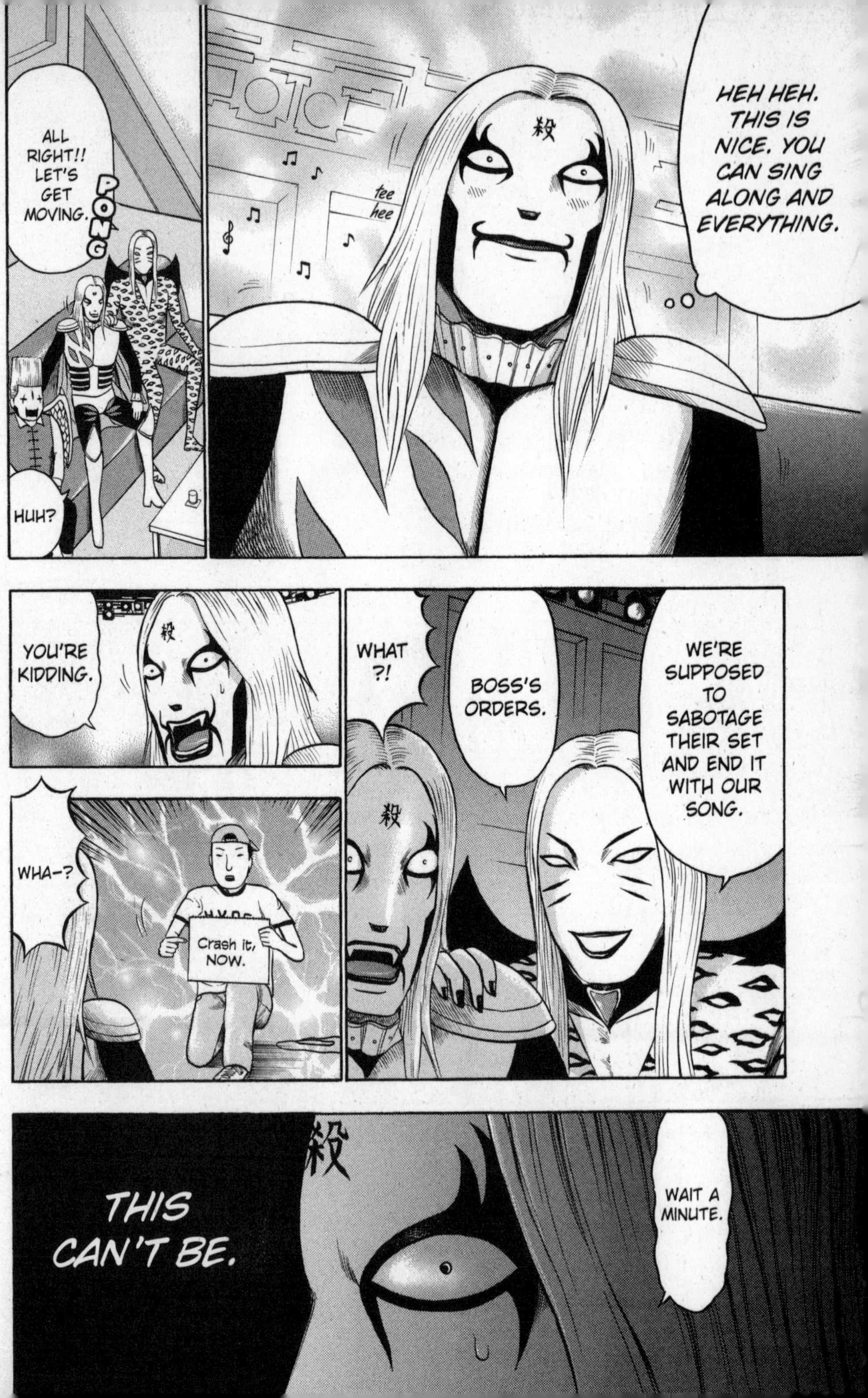
HEH HEH. THIS IS NICE. YOU CAN SING ALONG AND EVERYTHING.
tee hee
ALL RIGHT!! LET'S GET MOVING.
PONG
HUH?
WE'RE SUPPOSED TO SABOTAGE THEIR SET AND END IT WITH OUR SONG.
BOSS'S ORDERS.
WHAT ?!
YOU'RE KIDDING.
WHA-?
Crash it, NOW.
WAIT A MINUTE.
THIS CAN'T BE.

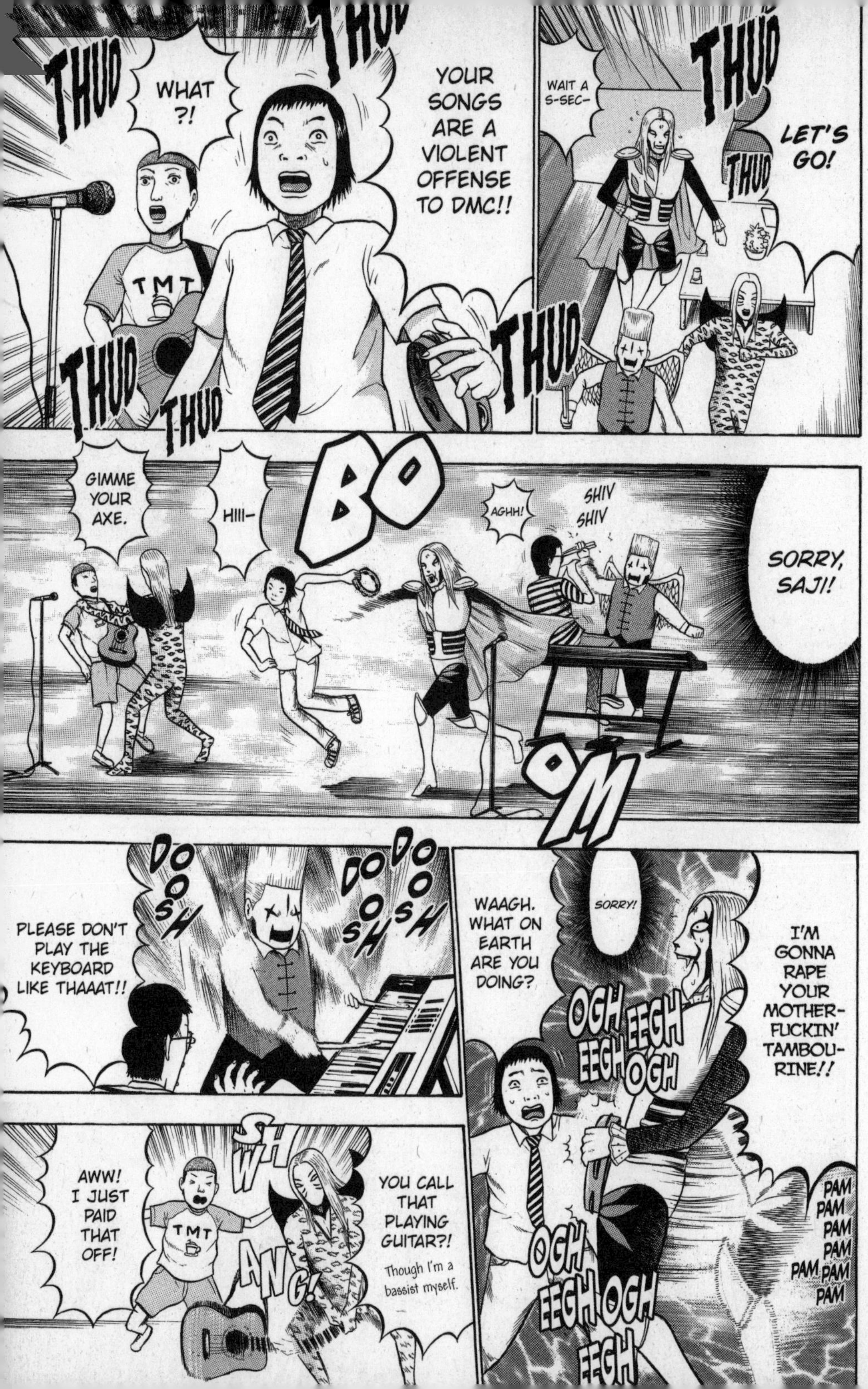
WAIT A S-SEC—
THUD
LET'S GO!
THUD
THUD
THUD
WHAT ?!
THUD
YOUR SONGS ARE A VIOLENT OFFENSE TO DMC!!
THUD
THUD
SORRY, SAJI!
SHIV SHIV
AGHH!
BOOM
HIII—
GIMME YOUR AXE.
SORRY!
I'M GONNA RAPE YOUR MOTHER-FUCKIN' TAMBOURINE!!
WAAGH. WHAT ON EARTH ARE YOU DOING?
OGH EEGH EEGH OGH
PAM PAM PAM PAM PAM PAM PAM PAM
OGH EEGH OGH EEGH
DOOSH
DOOSH DOOSH
PLEASE DON'T PLAY THE KEYBOARD LIKE THAAAT!!
SHWANG!
YOU CALL THAT PLAYING GUITAR?!
Though I'm a bassist myself.
AWW! I JUST PAID THAT OFF!

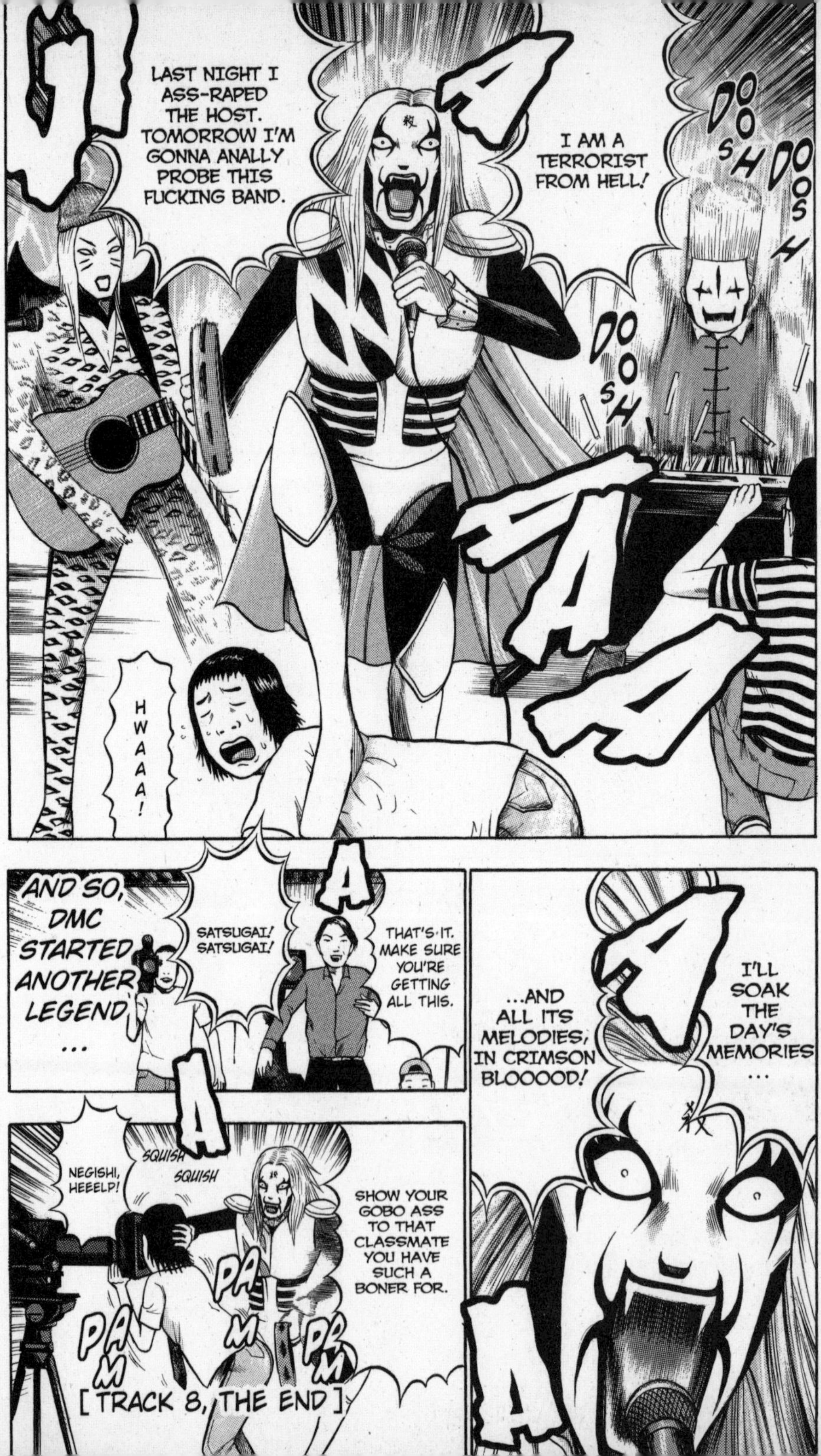

DOOSH DOOSH
I AM A TERRORIST FROM HELL!
A
LAST NIGHT I ASS-RAPED THE HOST. TOMORROW I'M GONNA ANALLY PROBE THIS FUCKING BAND.
DOOSH
AAA
HWAAAA!
I'LL SOAK THE DAY'S MEMORIES...
...AND ALL ITS MELODIES, IN CRIMSON BLOOOOD!
AA
A
THAT'S IT. MAKE SURE YOU'RE GETTING ALL THIS.
SATSUGAI! SATSUGAI!
AND SO, DMC STARTED ANOTHER LEGEND...
A
SHOW YOUR GOBO ASS TO THAT CLASSMATE YOU HAVE SUCH A BONER FOR.
SQUISH SQUISH
NEGISHI, HEEELP!
PAM PAM PAM
[TRACK 8, THE END]

DMC LEXICON

🐱 TAMBOURINE

A simple instrument even a child can play. When you slap it it makes a pretty pam pam sound, with a metallic ring. Since performing with one instantly makes you chic, under no circumstances should it be used in the presence of DMC.

Usage: This tambourine sounds good slapped on your ass. I'm gonna come!

デトロイト・メタル・シティ
Detroit Metal City

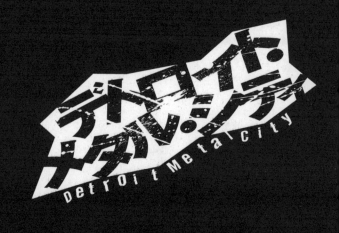

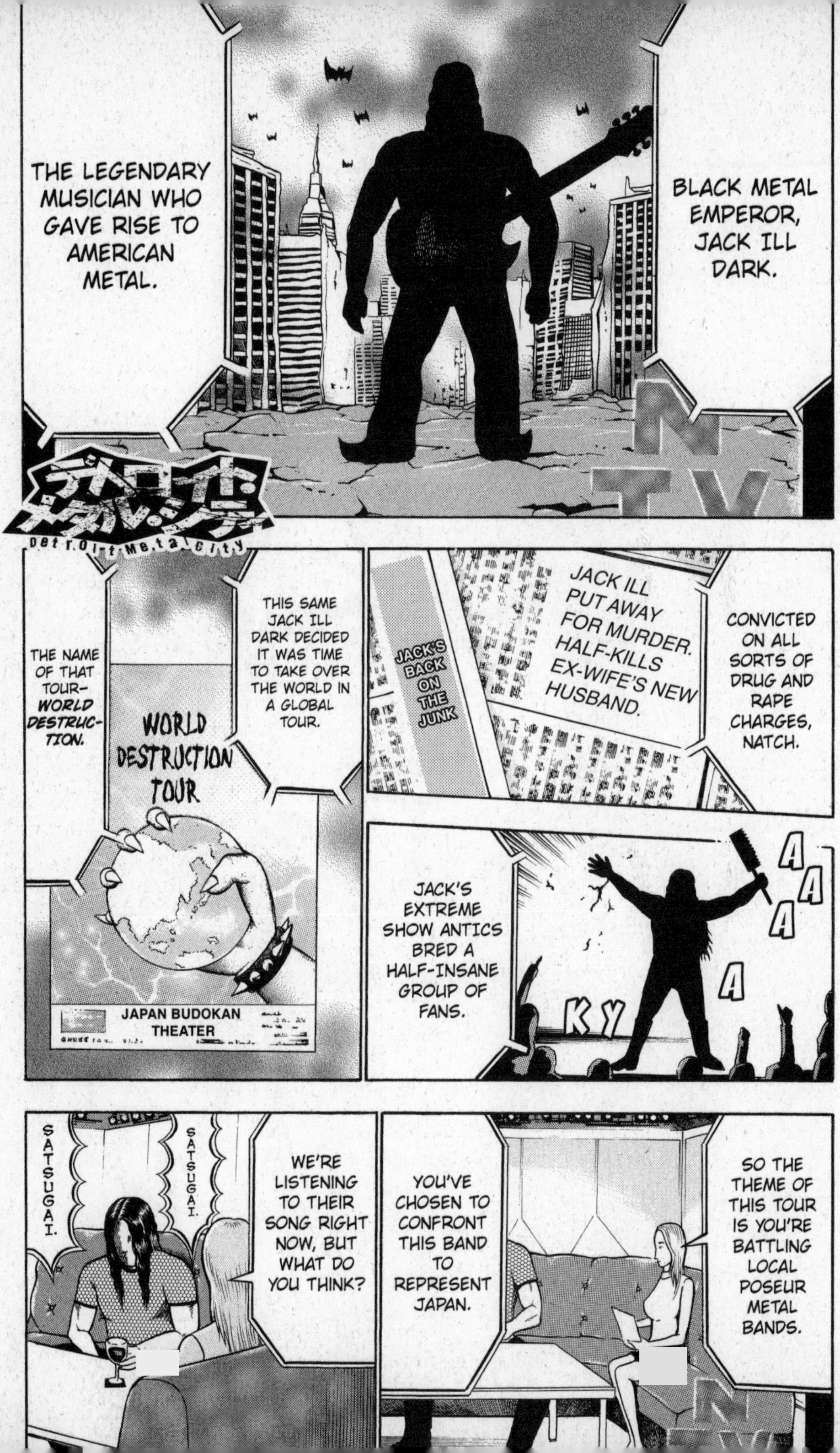
BLACK METAL EMPEROR, JACK ILL DARK.
THE LEGENDARY MUSICIAN WHO GAVE RISE TO AMERICAN METAL.
Detroit Metal City
CONVICTED ON ALL SORTS OF DRUG AND RAPE CHARGES, NATCH.
JACK ILL PUT AWAY FOR MURDER. HALF-KILLS EX-WIFE'S NEW HUSBAND.
JACK'S BACK ON THE JUNK
AAAA
JACK'S EXTREME SHOW ANTICS BRED A HALF-INSANE GROUP OF FANS.
KY
THIS SAME JACK ILL DARK DECIDED IT WAS TIME TO TAKE OVER THE WORLD IN A GLOBAL TOUR.
THE NAME OF THAT TOUR– *WORLD DESTRUCTION.*
WORLD DESTRUCTION TOUR
JAPAN BUDOKAN THEATER
SO THE THEME OF THIS TOUR IS YOU'RE BATTLING LOCAL POSEUR METAL BANDS.
YOU'VE CHOSEN TO CONFRONT THIS BAND TO REPRESENT JAPAN.
WE'RE LISTENING TO THEIR SONG RIGHT NOW, BUT WHAT DO YOU THINK?
SATSUGAI.
SATSUGAI.

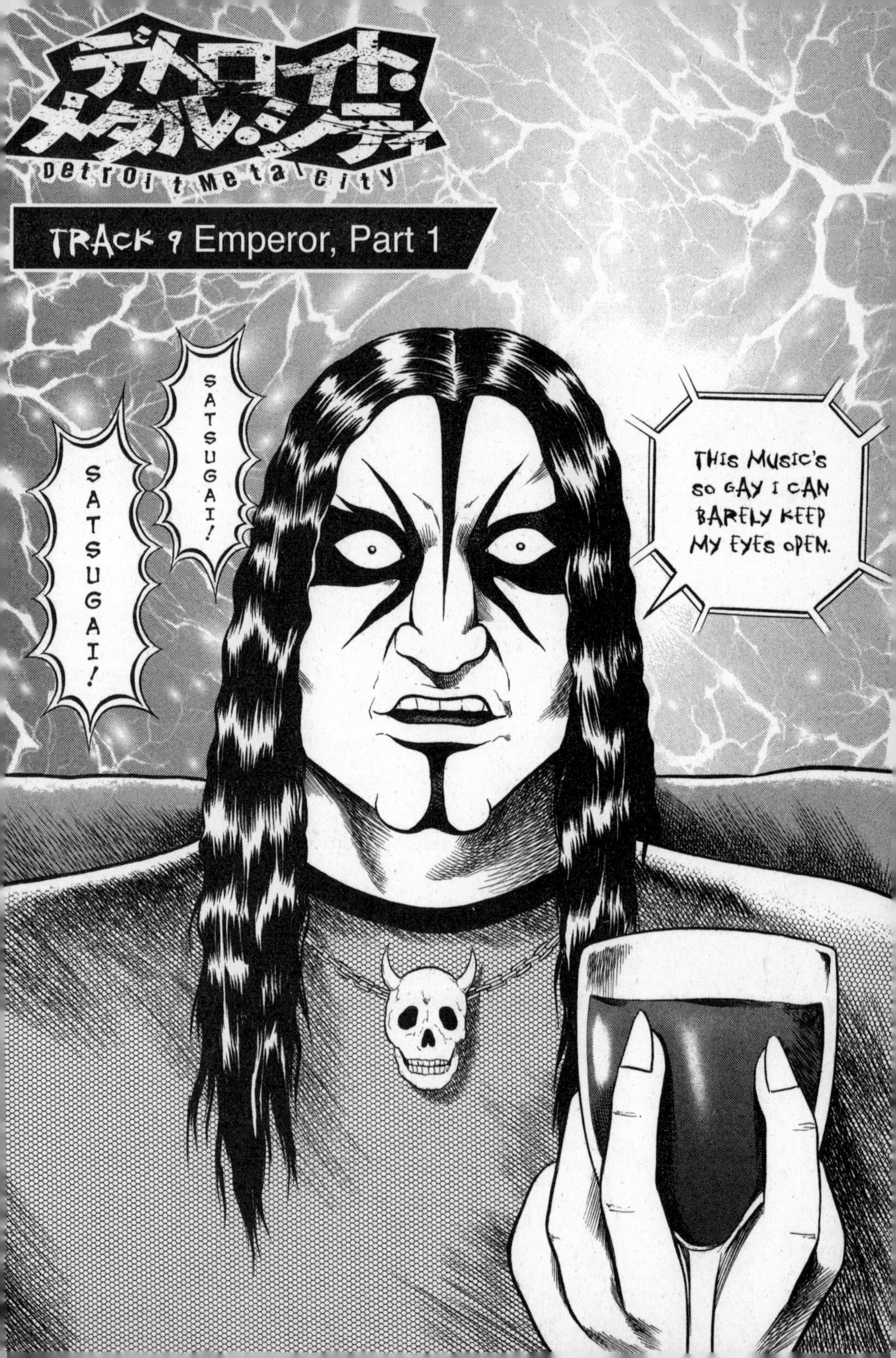
Detroit Metal City
TRACK 9 Emperor, Part 1
THIS MUSIC'S SO GAY I CAN BARELY KEEP MY EYES OPEN.
SATSUGAI!
SATSUGAI!

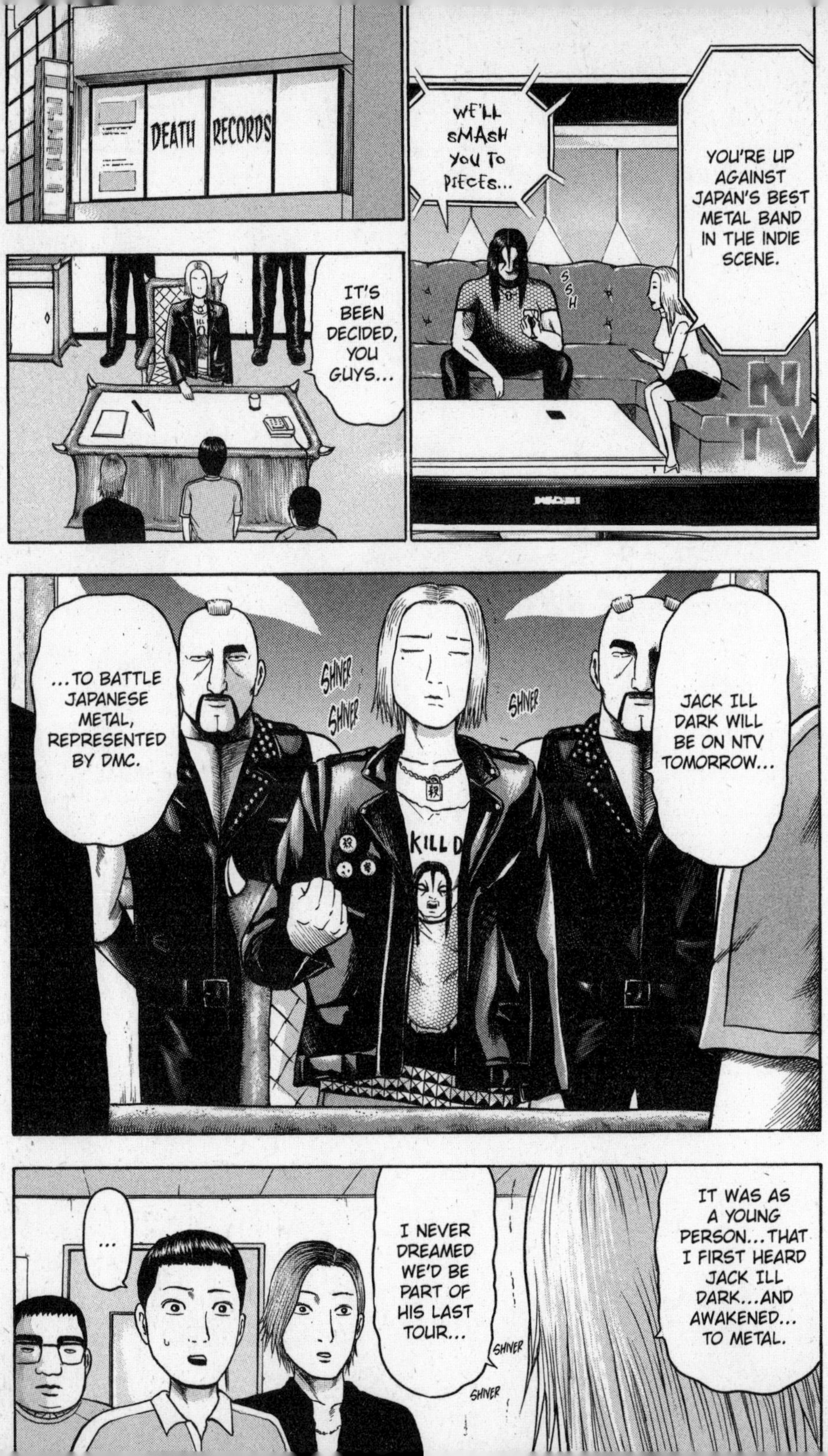
YOU'RE UP AGAINST JAPAN'S BEST METAL BAND IN THE INDIE SCENE.
SSH
WE'LL SMASH YOU TO PIECES...
NTV
DEATH RECORDS
IT'S BEEN DECIDED, YOU GUYS...
JACK ILL DARK WILL BE ON NTV TOMORROW...
SHIVER
SHIVER SHIVER
...TO BATTLE JAPANESE METAL, REPRESENTED BY DMC.
KILL D
IT WAS AS A YOUNG PERSON...THAT I FIRST HEARD JACK ILL DARK...AND AWAKENED...TO METAL.
I NEVER DREAMED WE'D BE PART OF HIS LAST TOUR...
SHIVER
SHIVER
...

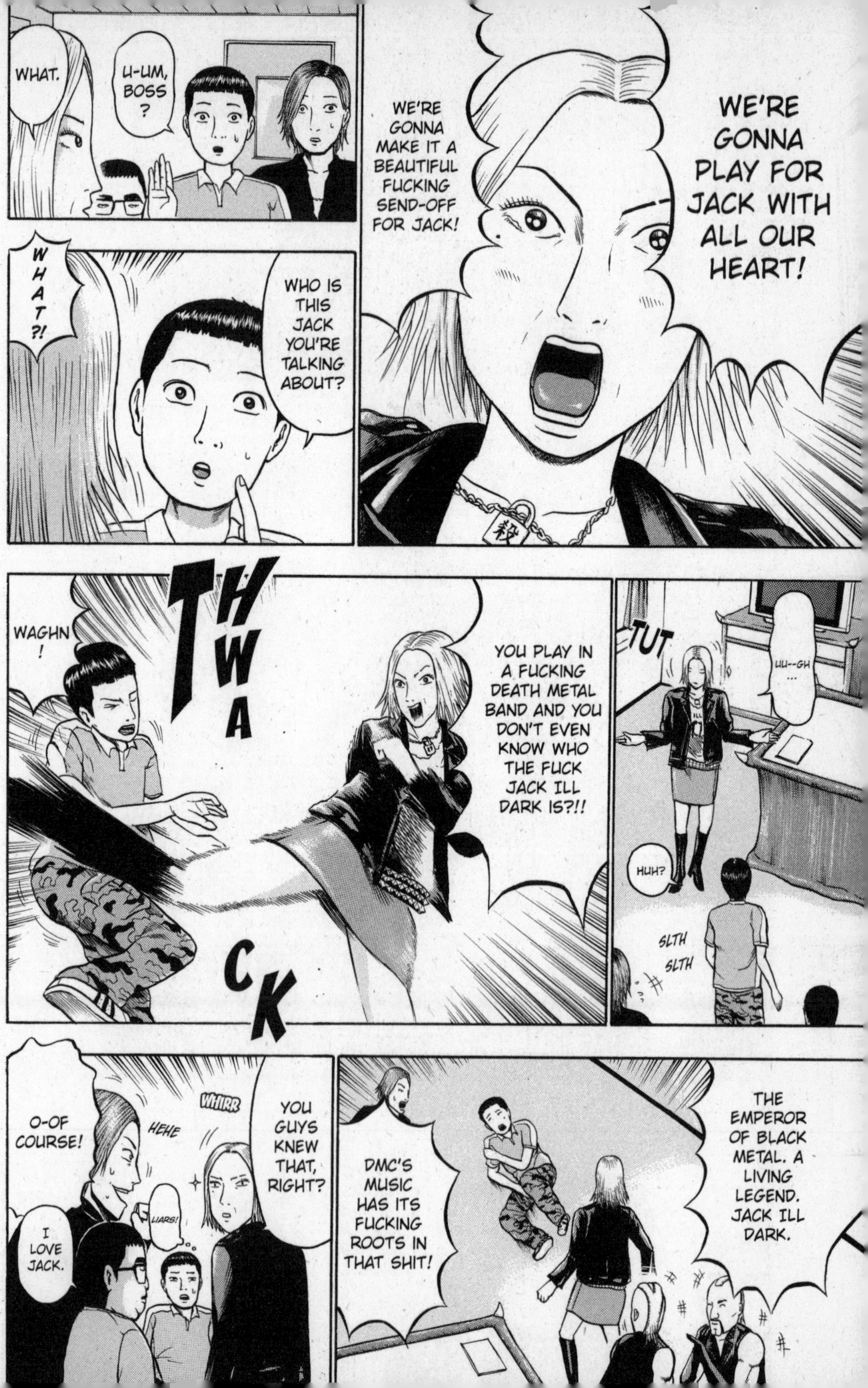
WE'RE GONNA PLAY FOR JACK WITH ALL OUR HEART!
WE'RE GONNA MAKE IT A BEAUTIFUL FUCKING SEND-OFF FOR JACK!
U-UM, BOSS?
WHAT.
WHO IS THIS JACK YOU'RE TALKING ABOUT?
WHAT?!
UU--GH ...
TUT
HUH?
SLTH
SLTH
THWACK
YOU PLAY IN A FUCKING DEATH METAL BAND AND YOU DON'T EVEN KNOW WHO THE FUCK JACK ILL DARK IS?!!
WAGHN!
THE EMPEROR OF BLACK METAL. A LIVING LEGEND. JACK ILL DARK.
DMC'S MUSIC HAS ITS FUCKING ROOTS IN THAT SHIT!
WHIRR
YOU GUYS KNEW THAT, RIGHT?
HEHE
O-OF COURSE!
LIARS!
I LOVE JACK.

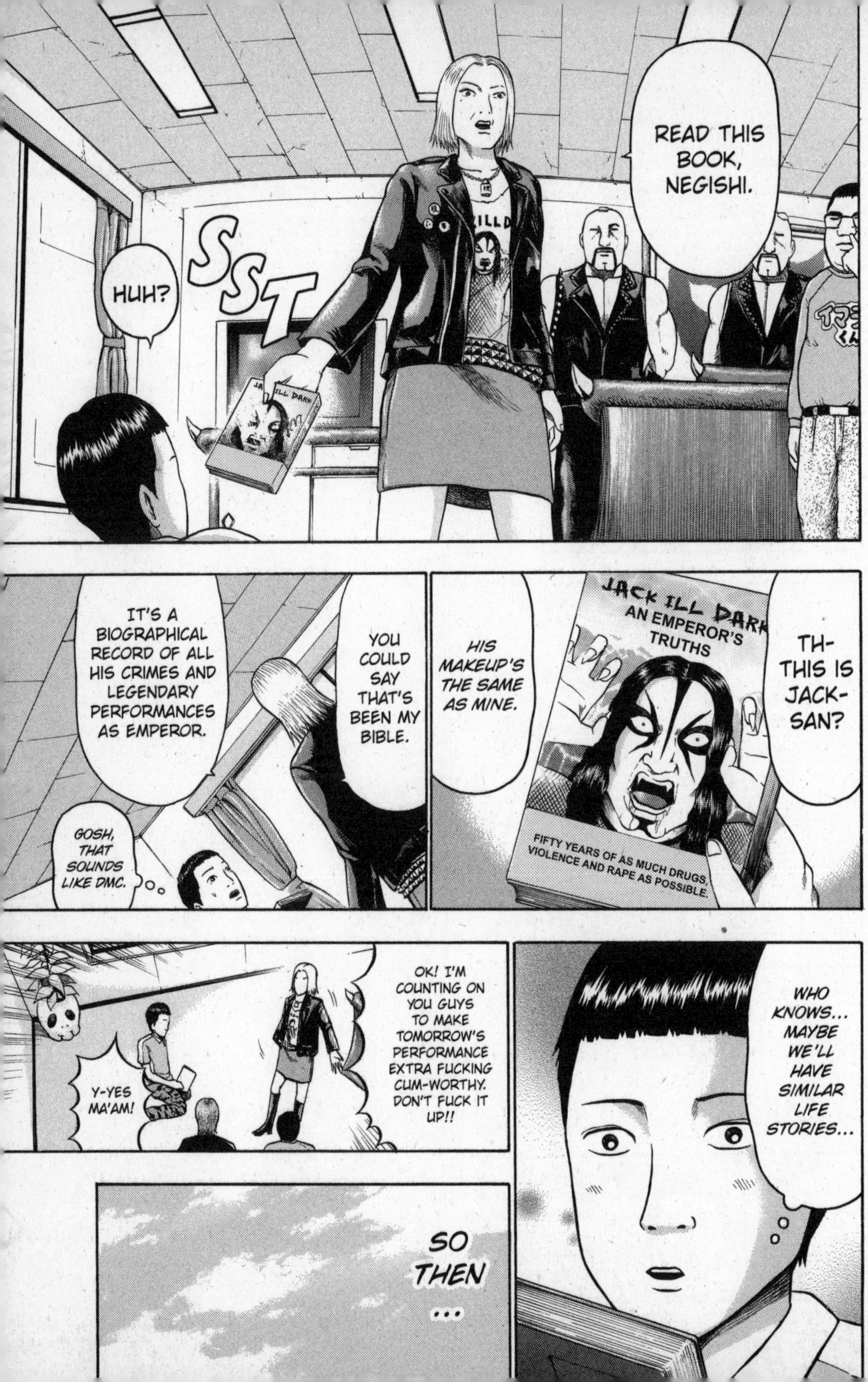

READ THIS BOOK, NEGISHI.
SST
HUH?
TH- THIS IS JACK-SAN?
JACK ILL DARK
AN EMPEROR'S TRUTHS
FIFTY YEARS OF AS MUCH DRUGS, VIOLENCE AND RAPE AS POSSIBLE.
HIS MAKEUP'S THE SAME AS MINE.
YOU COULD SAY THAT'S BEEN MY BIBLE.
IT'S A BIOGRAPHICAL RECORD OF ALL HIS CRIMES AND LEGENDARY PERFORMANCES AS EMPEROR.
GOSH, THAT SOUNDS LIKE DMC.
WHO KNOWS... MAYBE WE'LL HAVE SIMILAR LIFE STORIES...
OK! I'M COUNTING ON YOU GUYS TO MAKE TOMORROW'S PERFORMANCE EXTRA FUCKING CUM-WORTHY. DON'T FUCK IT UP!!
Y-YES MA'AM!
SO THEN ...

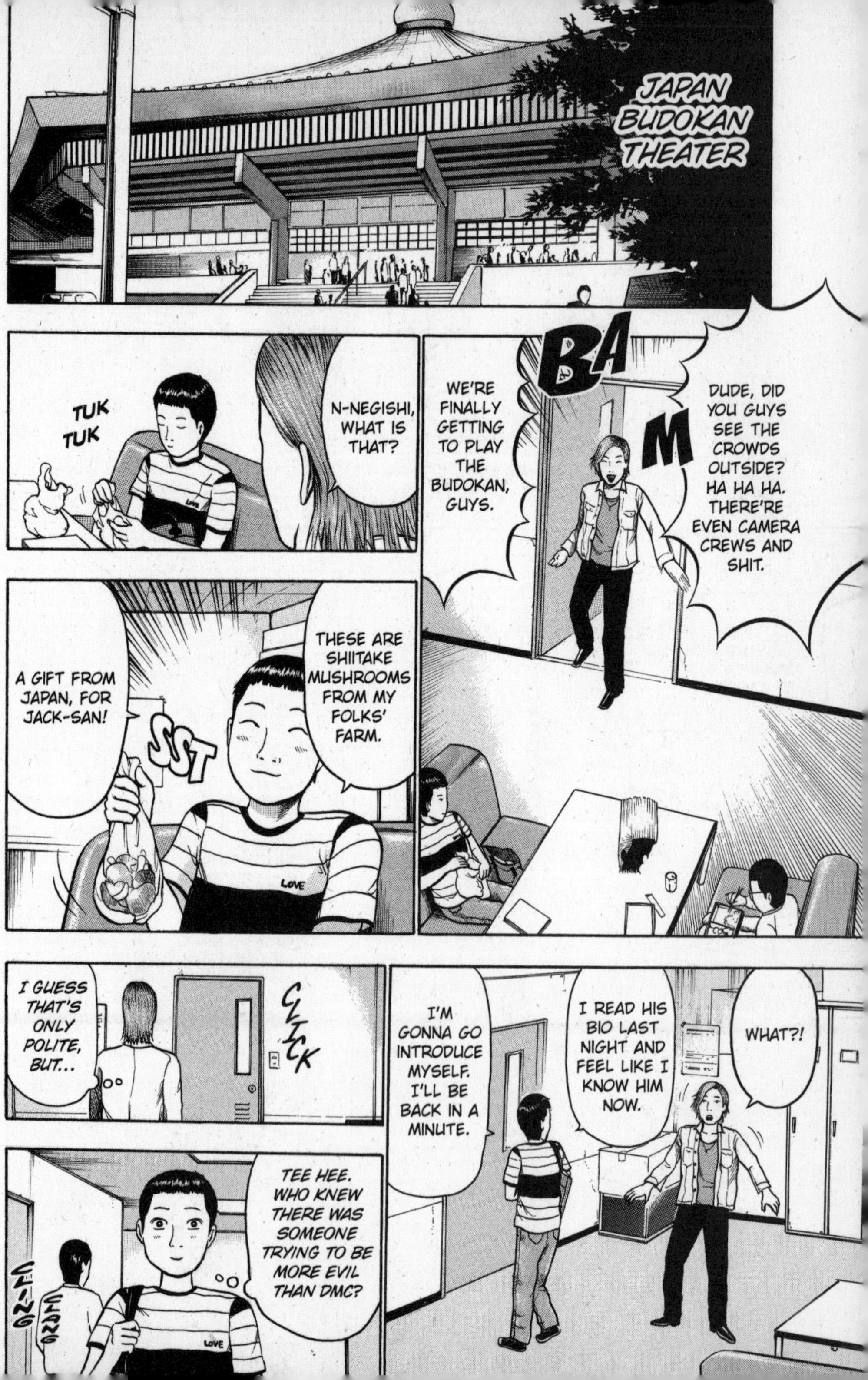
JAPAN BUDOKAN THEATER
BAM
DUDE, DID YOU GUYS SEE THE CROWDS OUTSIDE? HA HA HA. THERE'RE EVEN CAMERA CREWS AND SHIT.
WE'RE FINALLY GETTING TO PLAY THE BUDOKAN, GUYS.
N-NEGISHI, WHAT IS THAT?
TUK TUK
THESE ARE SHIITAKE MUSHROOMS FROM MY FOLKS' FARM.
A GIFT FROM JAPAN, FOR JACK-SAN!
SST
WHAT?!
I READ HIS BIO LAST NIGHT AND FEEL LIKE I KNOW HIM NOW.
I'M GONNA GO INTRODUCE MYSELF. I'LL BE BACK IN A MINUTE.
CLICK
I GUESS THAT'S ONLY POLITE, BUT...
TEE HEE. WHO KNEW THERE WAS SOMEONE TRYING TO BE MORE EVIL THAN DMC?
CLING CLANG

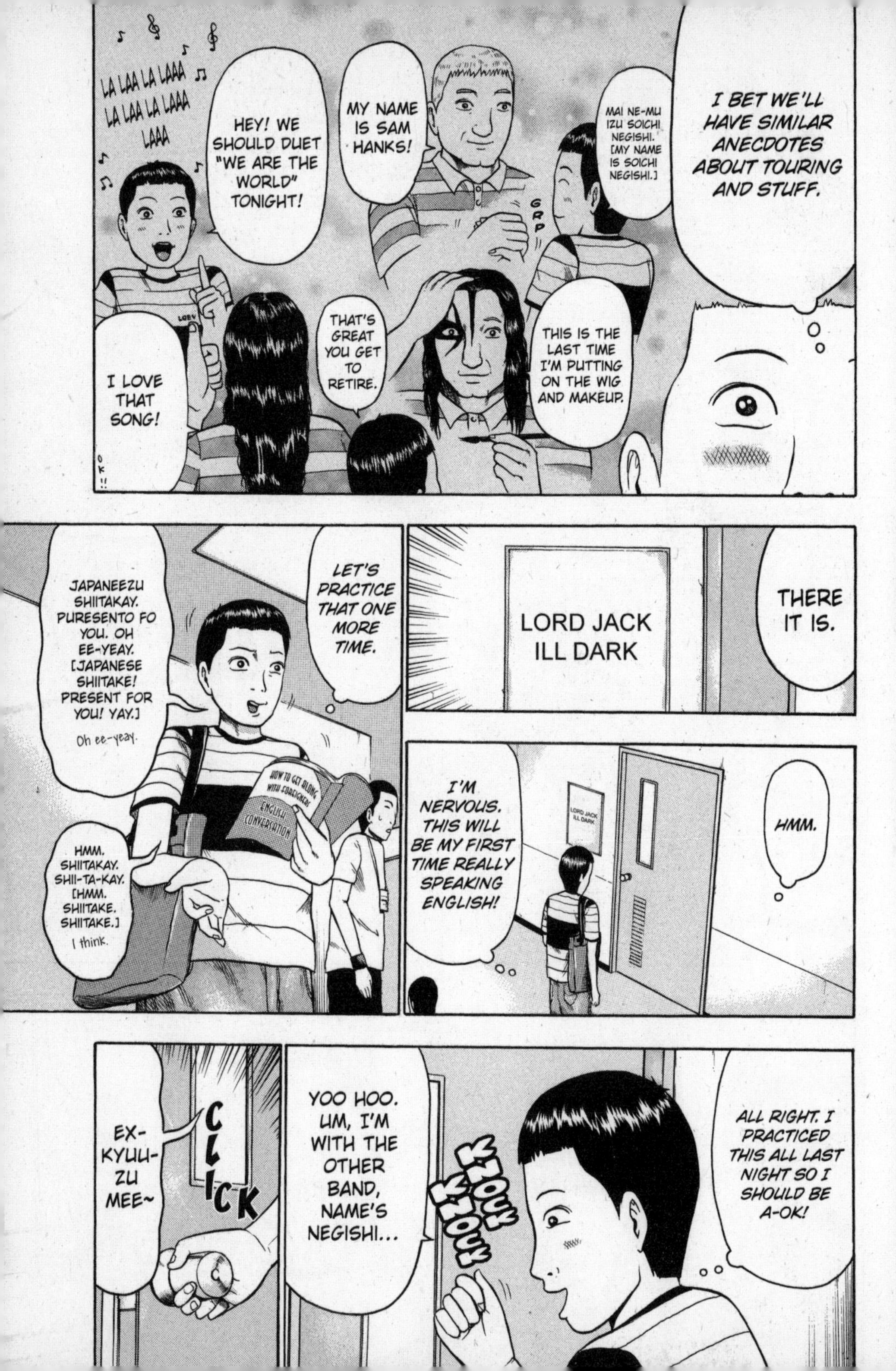
I BET WE'LL HAVE SIMILAR ANECDOTES ABOUT TOURING AND STUFF.
MAI NE-MU IZU SOICHI NEGISHI. [MY NAME IS SOICHI NEGISHI.]
GRP
MY NAME IS SAM HANKS!
HEY! WE SHOULD DUET "WE ARE THE WORLD" TONIGHT!
LA LAA LA LAAA LA LAA LA LAAA LAAA
THIS IS THE LAST TIME I'M PUTTING ON THE WIG AND MAKEUP.
THAT'S GREAT YOU GET TO RETIRE.
I LOVE THAT SONG!
OK!!
THERE IT IS.
LORD JACK ILL DARK
HMM.
I'M NERVOUS. THIS WILL BE MY FIRST TIME REALLY SPEAKING ENGLISH!
LORD JACK ILL DARK
LET'S PRACTICE THAT ONE MORE TIME.
JAPANEEZU SHIITAKAY. PURESENTO FO YOU. OH EE-YEAY. [JAPANESE SHIITAKE! PRESENT FOR YOU! YAY.]
Oh ee-yeay.
HOW TO GET ALONG WITH FOREIGNERS
ENGLISH CONVERSATION
HMM. SHIITAKAY. SHII-TA-KAY. [HMM. SHIITAKE. SHIITAKE.]
I think.
ALL RIGHT. I PRACTICED THIS ALL LAST NIGHT SO I SHOULD BE A-OK!
KNOCK KNOCK
YOO HOO. UM, I'M WITH THE OTHER BAND, NAME'S NEGISHI...
EX-KYUU-ZU MEE~
CLICK

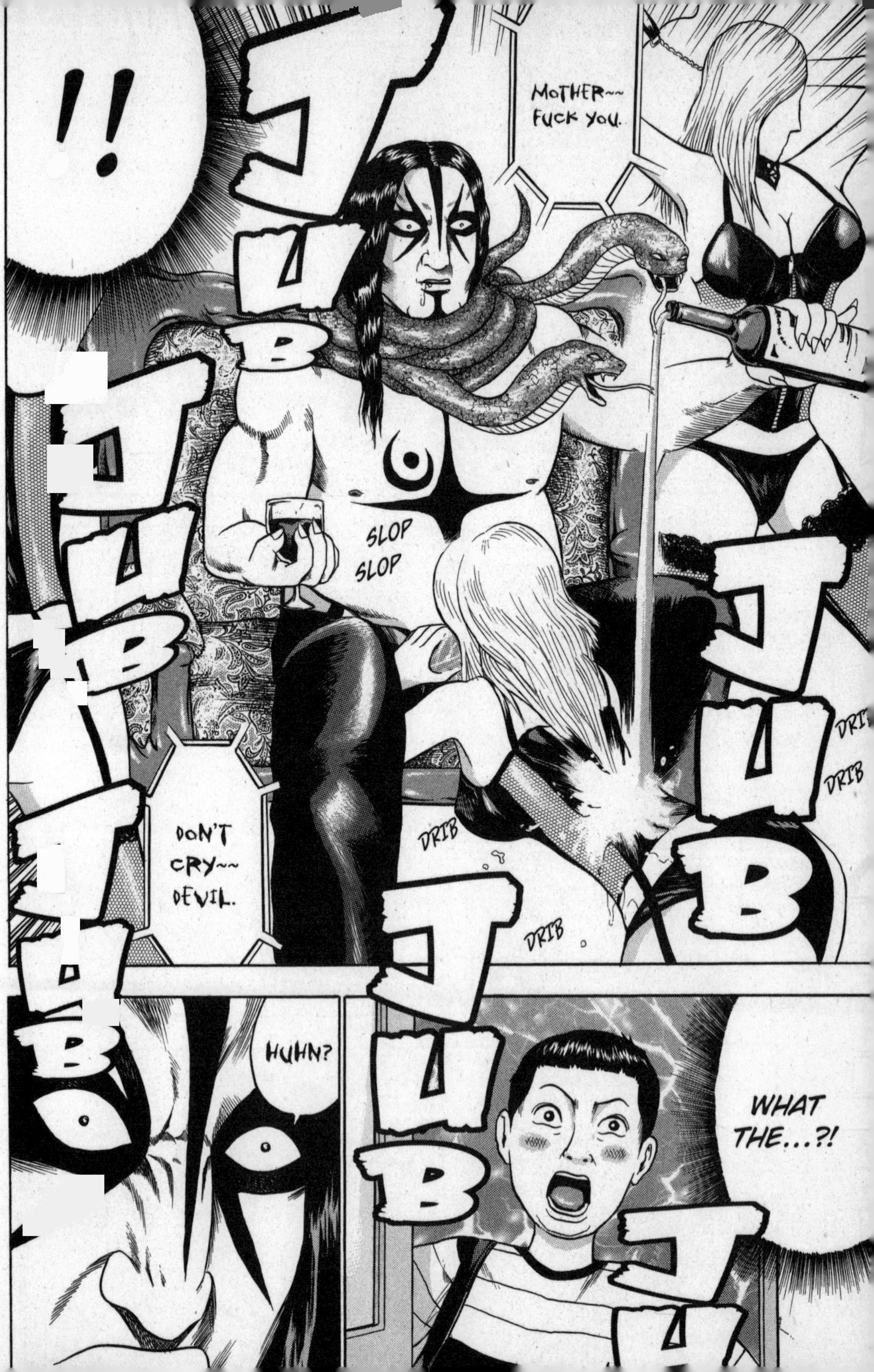
MOTHER~~ FUCK YOU.
JUB
JUB
DRIB
DRIB
SLOP SLOP
DRIB
DRIB
DON'T CRY~~ DEVIL.
!!
WHAT THE...?!
JUB
HUHN?

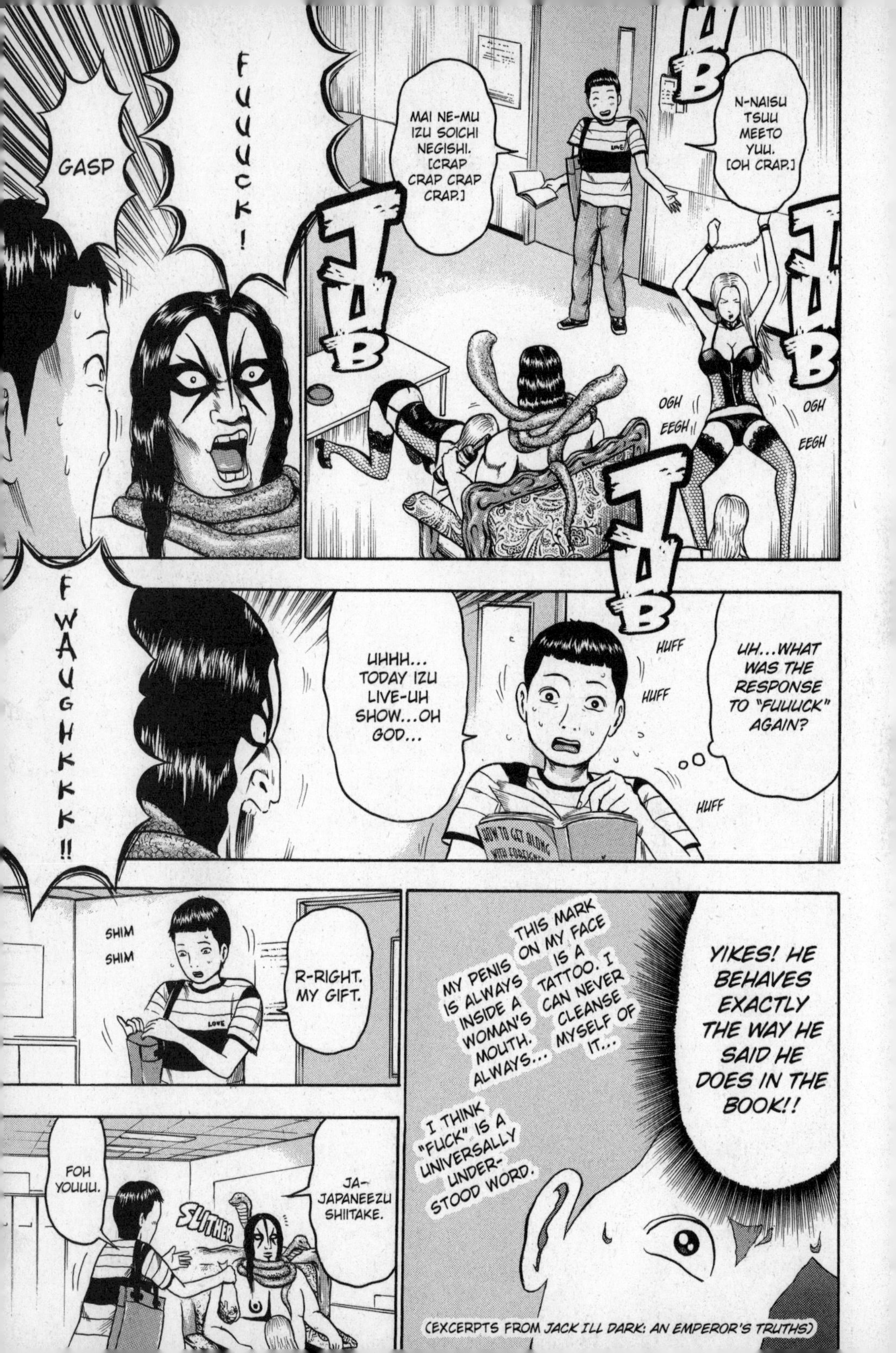
N-NAISU TSUU MEETO YUU. [OH CRAP.]
MAI NE-MU IZU SOICHI NEGISHI. [CRAP CRAP CRAP CRAP.]
JUB
JUB
OGH
EEGH
OGH
EEGH
JUB
JUB
FUUUCK!
GASP
JUB
UH...WHAT WAS THE RESPONSE TO "FUUUCK" AGAIN?
HUFF
HUFF
HUFF
UHHH... TODAY IZU LIVE-UH SHOW...OH GOD...
FWAUGHKKKK!!
YIKES! HE BEHAVES EXACTLY THE WAY HE SAID HE DOES IN THE BOOK!!
THIS MARK ON MY FACE IS A TATTOO. I CAN NEVER CLEANSE MYSELF OF IT...
MY PENIS IS ALWAYS INSIDE A WOMAN'S MOUTH. ALWAYS...
I THINK "FUCK" IS A UNIVERSALLY UNDER-STOOD WORD.
(EXCERPTS FROM JACK ILL DARK: AN EMPEROR'S TRUTHS)
R-RIGHT. MY GIFT.
SHIM
SHIM
JA-JAPANEEZU SHIITAKE.
SLITHER
FOH YOUUU.

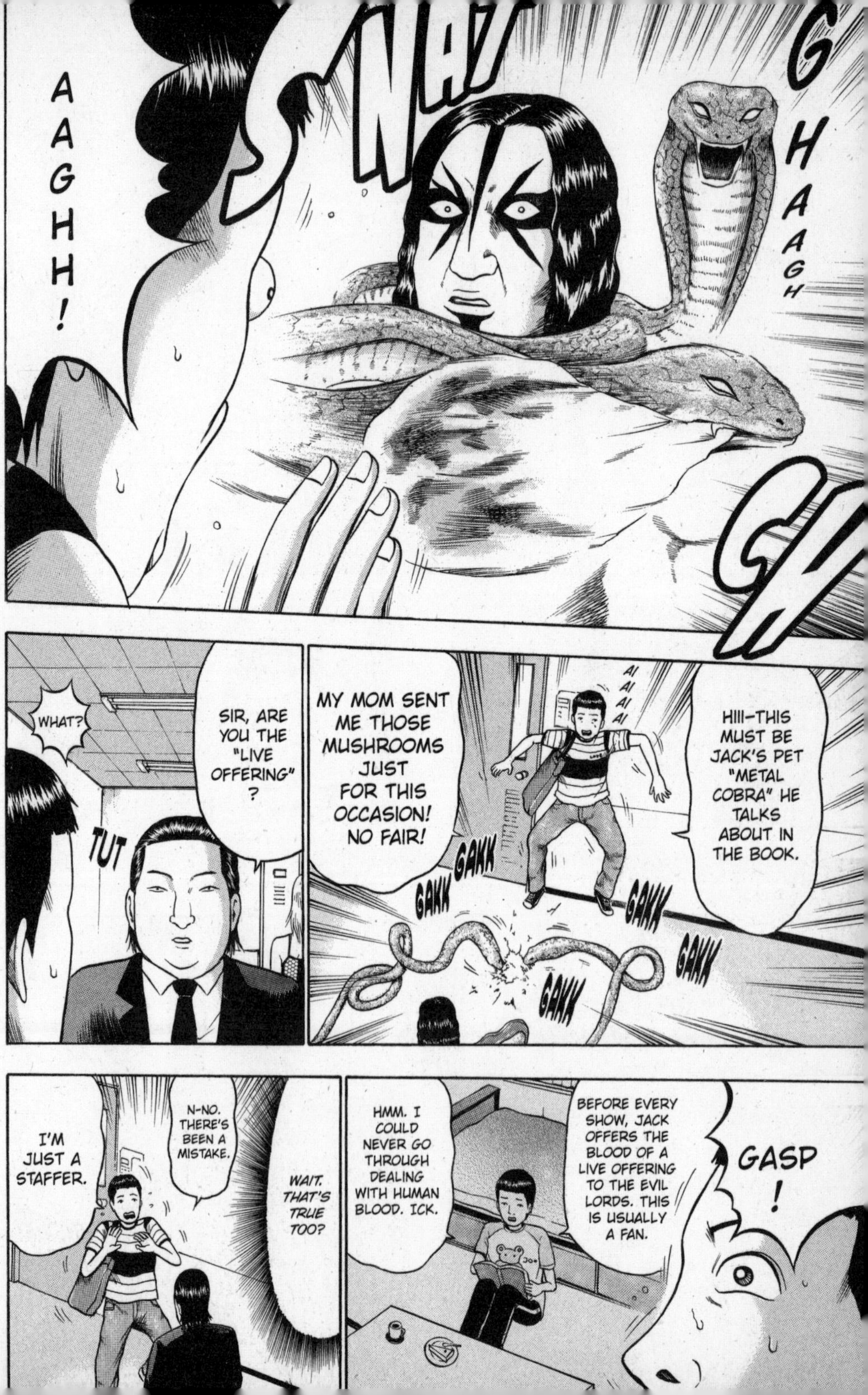
GHAAGH
AAGHH!
HIII—THIS MUST BE JACK'S PET "METAL COBRA" HE TALKS ABOUT IN THE BOOK.
AI AI AI AI
GAKK GAKK GAKK GAKK GAKK GAKK
MY MOM SENT ME THOSE MUSHROOMS JUST FOR THIS OCCASION! NO FAIR!
SIR, ARE YOU THE "LIVE OFFERING"?
WHAT?
TUT
GASP!
BEFORE EVERY SHOW, JACK OFFERS THE BLOOD OF A LIVE OFFERING TO THE EVIL LORDS. THIS IS USUALLY A FAN.
HMM. I COULD NEVER GO THROUGH DEALING WITH HUMAN BLOOD. ICK.
WAIT. THAT'S TRUE TOO?
N-NO. THERE'S BEEN A MISTAKE.
I'M JUST A STAFFER.

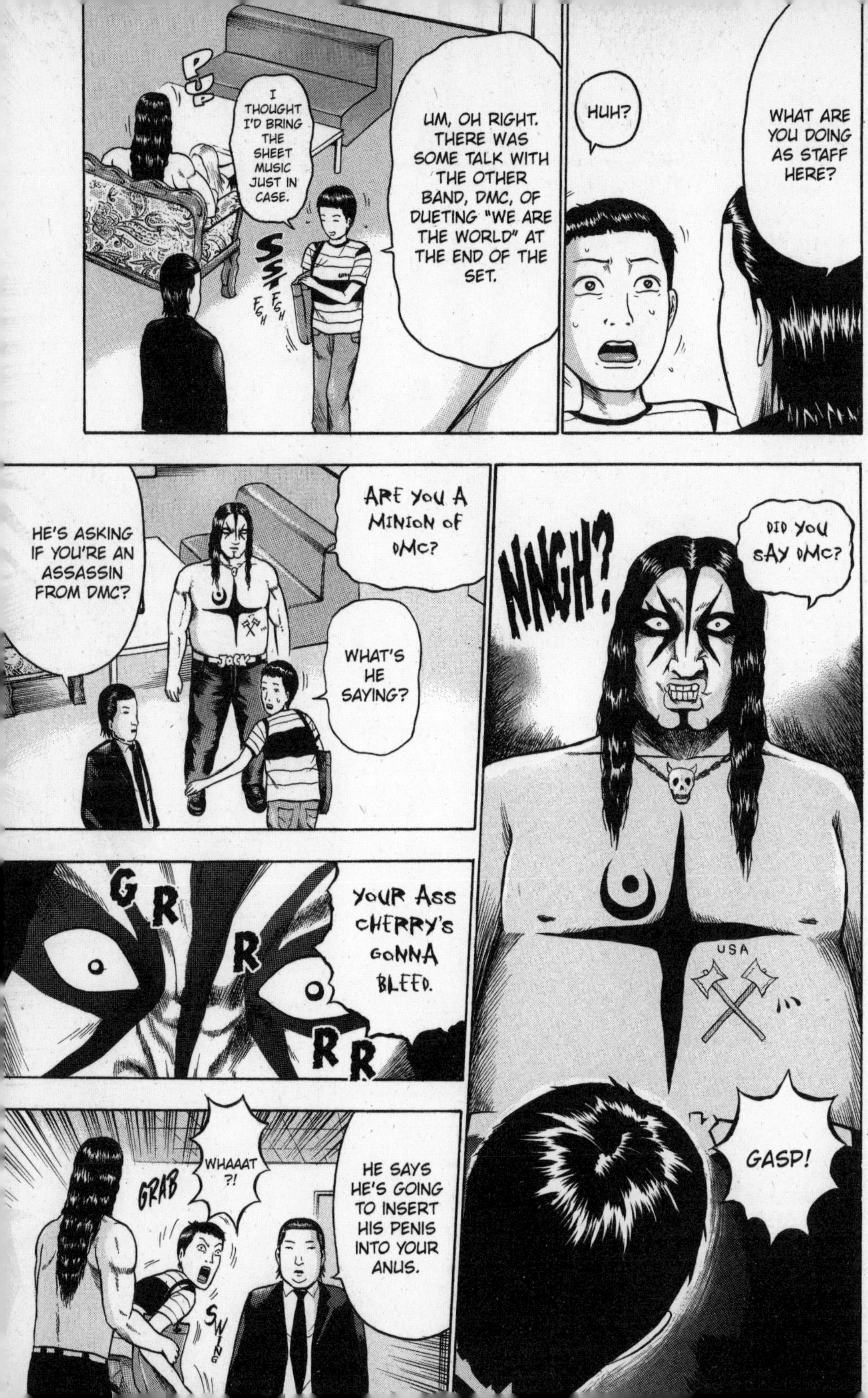
WHAT ARE YOU DOING AS STAFF HERE?
HUH?
UM, OH RIGHT. THERE WAS SOME TALK WITH THE OTHER BAND, DMC, OF DUETING "WE ARE THE WORLD" AT THE END OF THE SET.
I THOUGHT I'D BRING THE SHEET MUSIC JUST IN CASE.
POP
SS
FSH FSH
NNGH?
DID YOU SAY DMC?
GASP!
ARE YOU A MINION OF DMC?
HE'S ASKING IF YOU'RE AN ASSASSIN FROM DMC?
WHAT'S HE SAYING?
YOUR ASS CHERRY'S GONNA BLEED.
GRRRRR
HE SAYS HE'S GOING TO INSERT HIS PENIS INTO YOUR ANUS.
WHAAAT ?!
GRAB
SWING

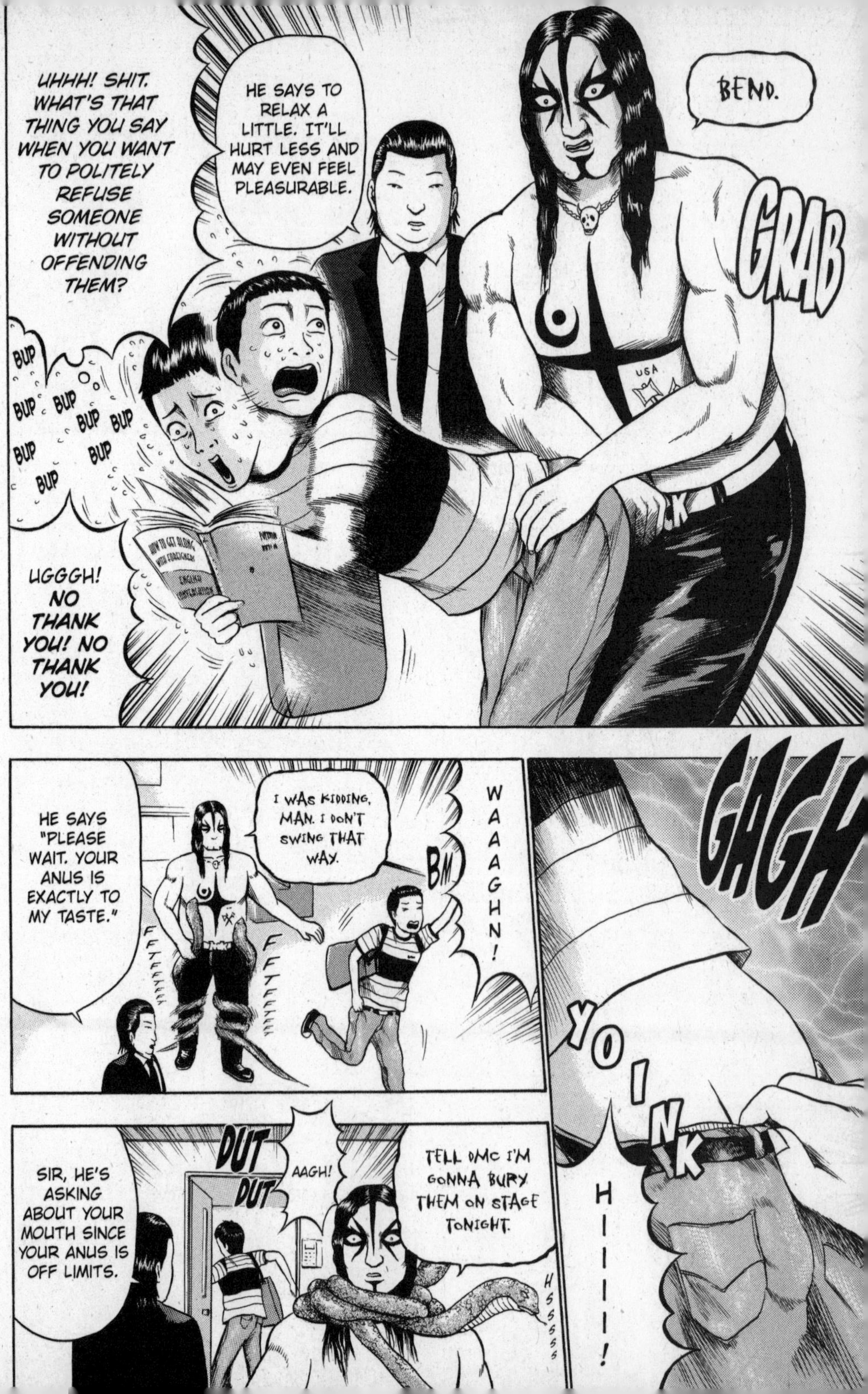
BEND.
GRAB
HE SAYS TO RELAX A LITTLE. IT'LL HURT LESS AND MAY EVEN FEEL PLEASURABLE.
UHHH! SHIT. WHAT'S THAT THING YOU SAY WHEN YOU WANT TO POLITELY REFUSE SOMEONE WITHOUT OFFENDING THEM?
BUP BUP BUP BUP BUP BUP BUP BUP
UGGGH! NO THANK YOU! NO THANK YOU!
GAGH
YOINK
HIIII!
WAAAAGHN!
I WAS KIDDING, MAN. I DON'T SWING THAT WAY.
BM
FFTEEEEE
FFTEEEEE
HE SAYS "PLEASE WAIT. YOUR ANUS IS EXACTLY TO MY TASTE."
TELL DMC I'M GONNA BURY THEM ON STAGE TONIGHT.
AAGH!
DUT DUT
SIR, HE'S ASKING ABOUT YOUR MOUTH SINCE YOUR ANUS IS OFF LIMITS.
HSSSS

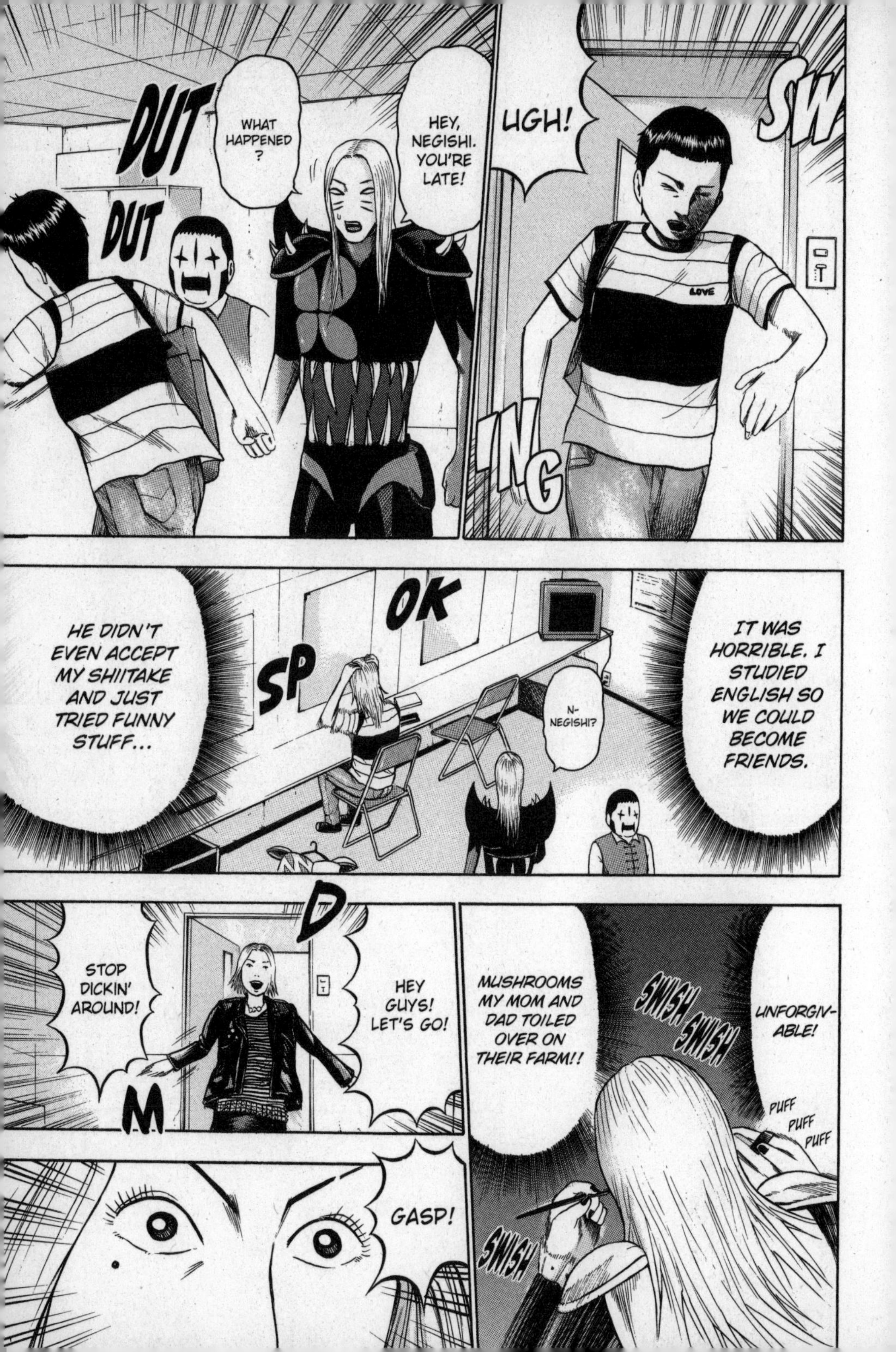
SW
UGH!
ING
HEY, NEGISHI. YOU'RE LATE!
WHAT HAPPENED?
DUT
DUT
IT WAS HORRIBLE. I STUDIED ENGLISH SO WE COULD BECOME FRIENDS.
N-NEGISHI?
OK
SP
HE DIDN'T EVEN ACCEPT MY SHIITAKE AND JUST TRIED FUNNY STUFF...
UNFORGIV-ABLE!
MUSHROOMS MY MOM AND DAD TOILED OVER ON THEIR FARM!!
SWISH SWISH
PUFF PUFF PUFF
SWISH
D
HEY GUYS! LET'S GO!
STOP DICKIN' AROUND!
M
GASP!

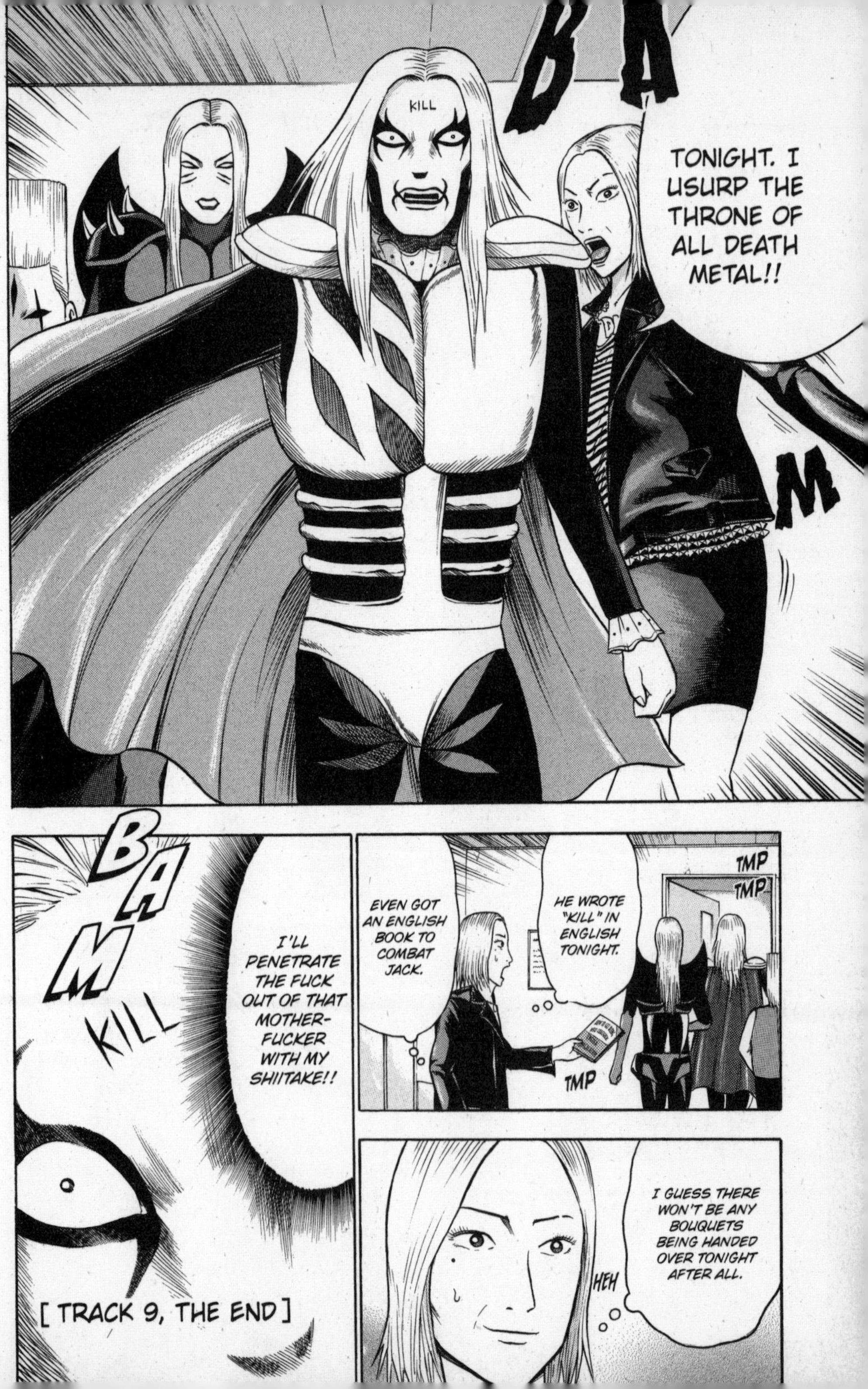
KILL
BAM
TONIGHT. I USURP THE THRONE OF ALL DEATH METAL!!
TMP TMP
HE WROTE "KILL" IN ENGLISH TONIGHT.
EVEN GOT AN ENGLISH BOOK TO COMBAT JACK.
TMP
I GUESS THERE WON'T BE ANY BOUQUETS BEING HANDED OVER TONIGHT AFTER ALL.
HEH
BAM
KILL
I'LL PENETRATE THE FUCK OUT OF THAT MOTHER-FUCKER WITH MY SHIITAKE!!
[TRACK 9, THE END]

DMC LEXICON

☻NO THANK YOU.

Meaning "that's all right," it is an expression used to politely refuse a master's order to fuck you up. If you accidentally omit the "no" in that phrase you will in actuality be "fucked up," and so while convenient as an expression, it is also risky.

Usage: I value and honor our relationship, Captain, but it's not romantic love, so no thank you! No thank you! No thank you!

デトロイト・メタル・シティ
Detroit Metal City

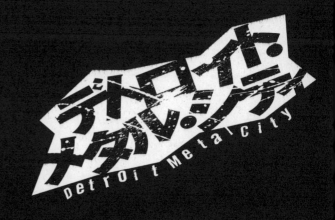

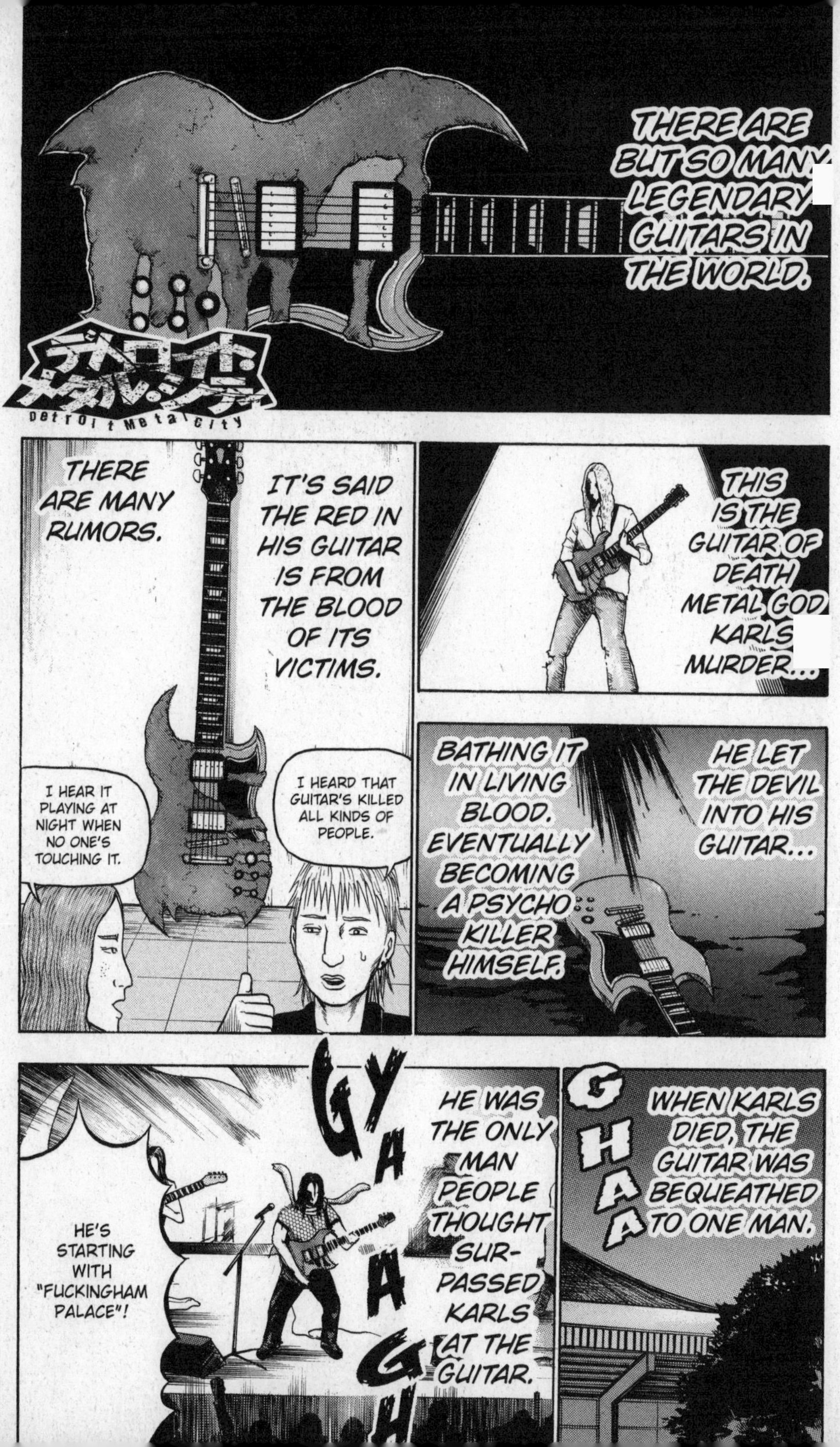
THERE ARE BUT SO MANY LEGENDARY GUITARS IN THE WORLD.
デトロイト・メタル・シティ
Detroit Metal City
THIS IS THE GUITAR OF DEATH METAL GOD KARLS MURDER...
HE LET THE DEVIL INTO HIS GUITAR...
BATHING IT IN LIVING BLOOD. EVENTUALLY BECOMING A PSYCHO KILLER HIMSELF.
IT'S SAID THE RED IN HIS GUITAR IS FROM THE BLOOD OF ITS VICTIMS.
THERE ARE MANY RUMORS.
I HEARD THAT GUITAR'S KILLED ALL KINDS OF PEOPLE.
I HEAR IT PLAYING AT NIGHT WHEN NO ONE'S TOUCHING IT.
GHAA
WHEN KARLS DIED, THE GUITAR WAS BEQUEATHED TO ONE MAN.
HE WAS THE ONLY MAN PEOPLE THOUGHT SUR-PASSED KARLS AT THE GUITAR.
GYAAGH
HE'S STARTING WITH "FUCKINGHAM PALACE"!

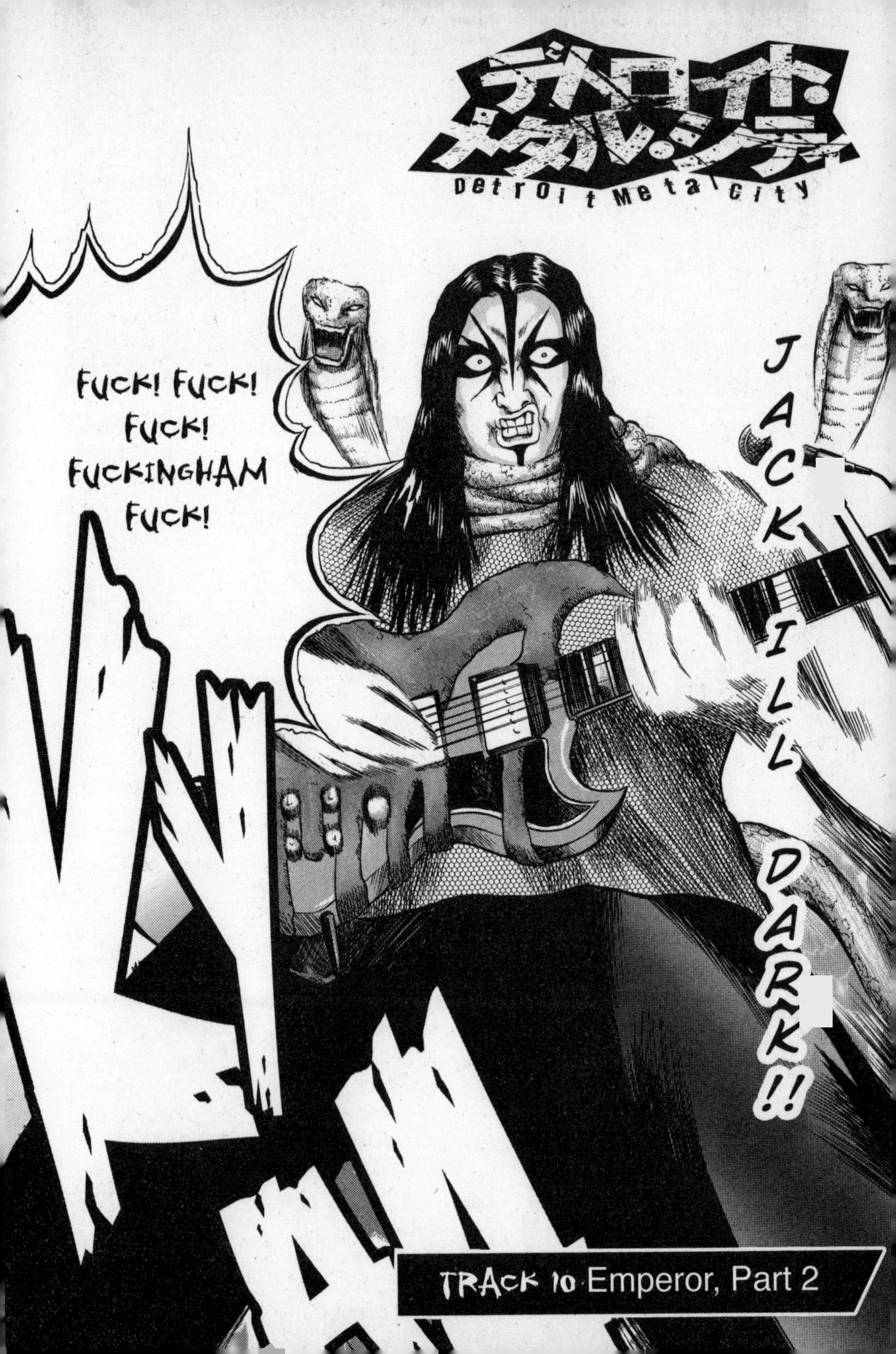
Detroit Metal City
FUCK! FUCK! FUCK! FUCKINGHAM FUCK!
JACK ILL DARK!!
TRACK 10 Emperor, Part 2

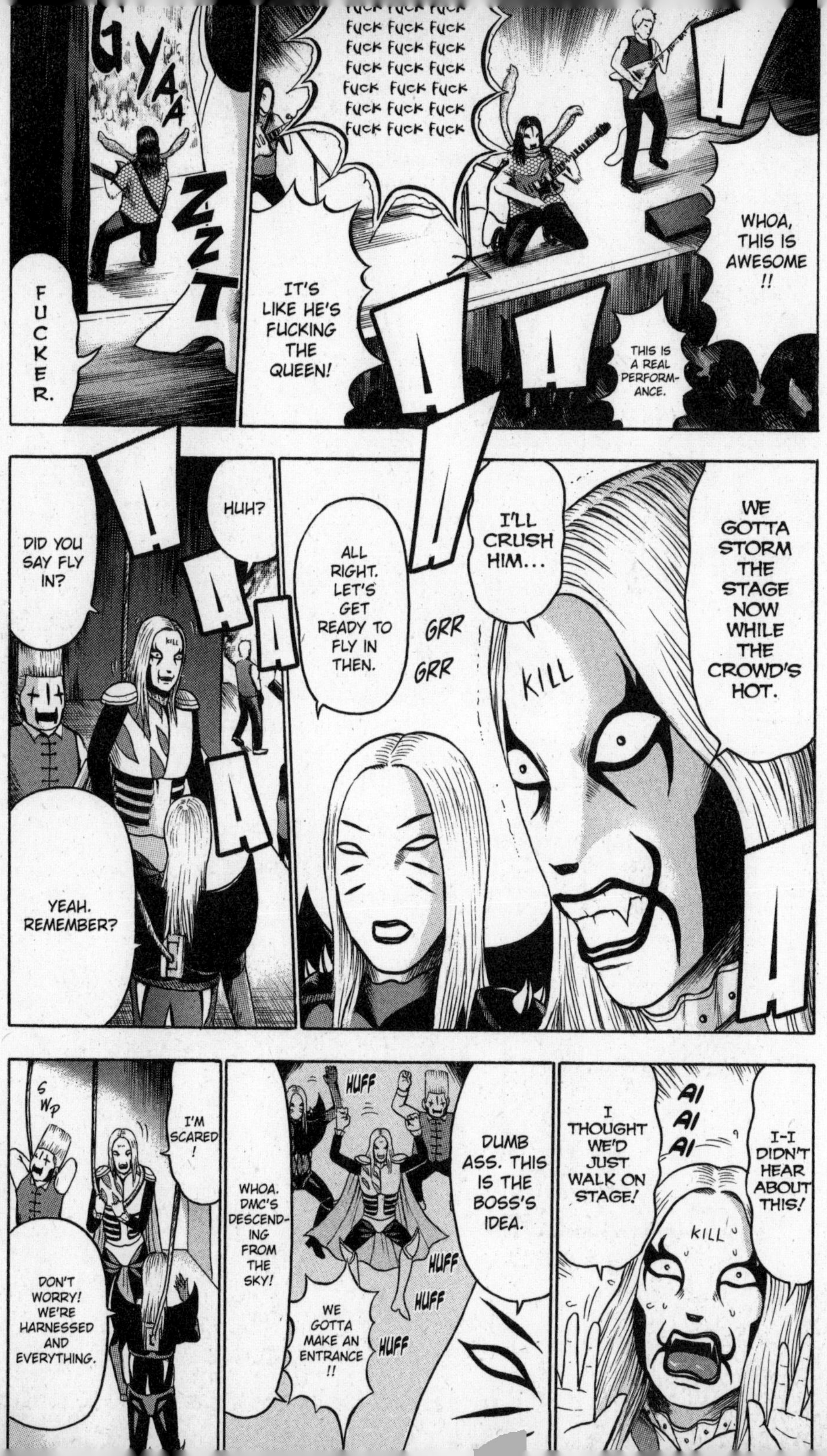
FUCK FUCK FUCK
FUCK FUCK FUCK
FUCK FUCK FUCK
FUCK FUCK FUCK
FUCK FUCK FUCK
FUCK FUCK FUCK
WHOA, THIS IS AWESOME !!
IT'S LIKE HE'S FUCKING THE QUEEN!
THIS IS A REAL PERFORM-ANCE.
AAAA
GYAA
ZZZT
FUCKER.
WE GOTTA STORM THE STAGE NOW WHILE THE CROWD'S HOT.
I'LL CRUSH HIM...
KILL
GRR
GRR
ALL RIGHT. LET'S GET READY TO FLY IN THEN.
AAAAA
HUH?
DID YOU SAY FLY IN?
KILL
YEAH. REMEMBER?
I-I DIDN'T HEAR ABOUT THIS!
AI AI AI
I THOUGHT WE'D JUST WALK ON STAGE!
KILL
DUMB ASS. THIS IS THE BOSS'S IDEA.
HUFF
WHOA. DMC'S DESCEND-ING FROM THE SKY!
HUFF
HUFF
HUFF
WE GOTTA MAKE AN ENTRANCE !!
I'M SCARED!
SWP
DON'T WORRY! WE'RE HARNESSED AND EVERYTHING.

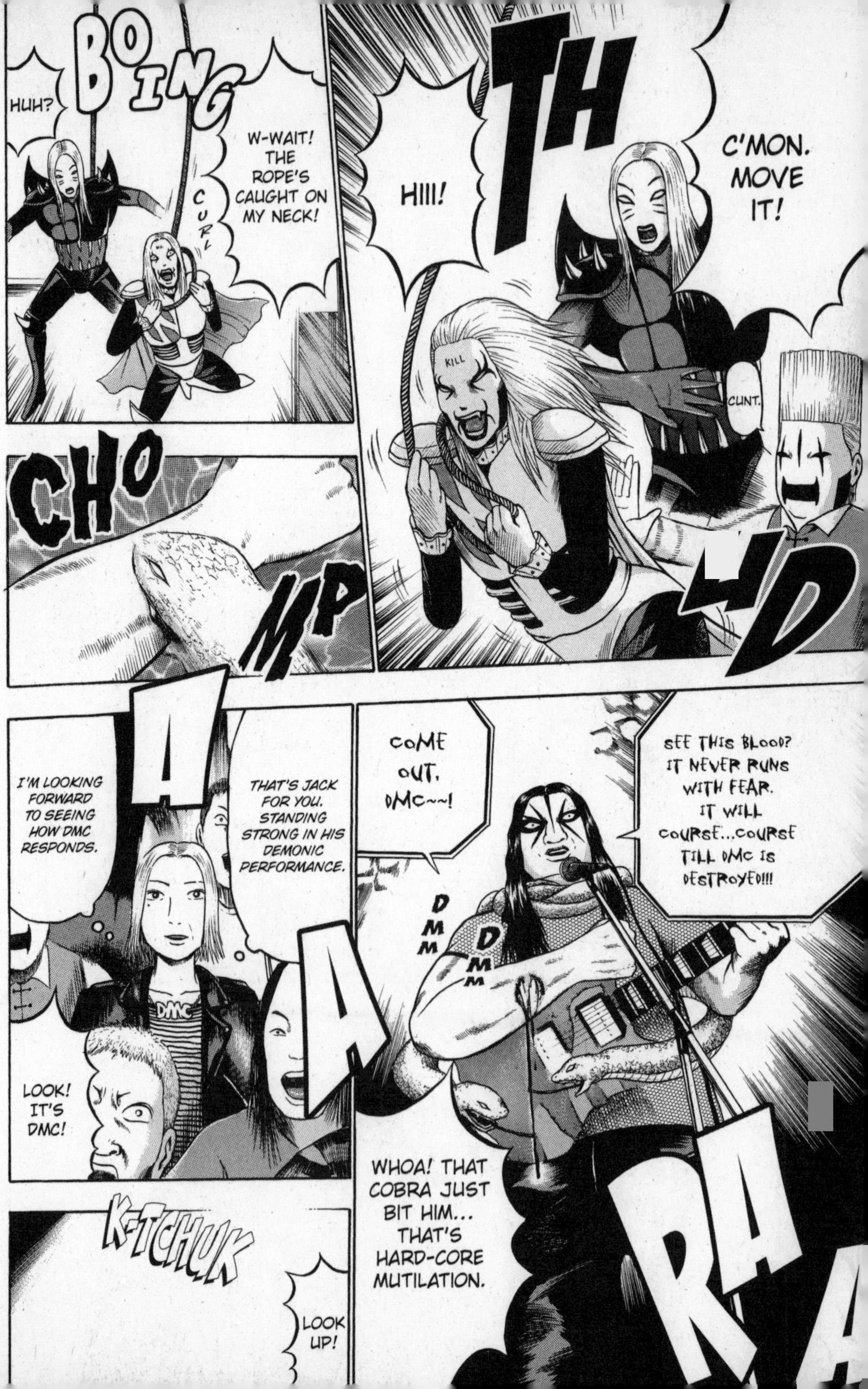
C'MON. MOVE IT!
TH
HIII!
CUNT.
D
BOING
W-WAIT! THE ROPE'S CAUGHT ON MY NECK!
CURL
HUH?
CHO
MP
SEE THIS BLOOD? IT NEVER RUNS WITH FEAR. IT WILL COURSE...COURSE TILL DMC IS DESTROYED!!!
COME OUT, DMC~~!
DMM
DMM
D
WHOA! THAT COBRA JUST BIT HIM... THAT'S HARD-CORE MUTILATION.
RA
A
A
THAT'S JACK FOR YOU. STANDING STRONG IN HIS DEMONIC PERFORMANCE.
I'M LOOKING FORWARD TO SEEING HOW DMC RESPONDS.
A
DMC
LOOK! IT'S DMC!
K-TCHUK
LOOK UP!

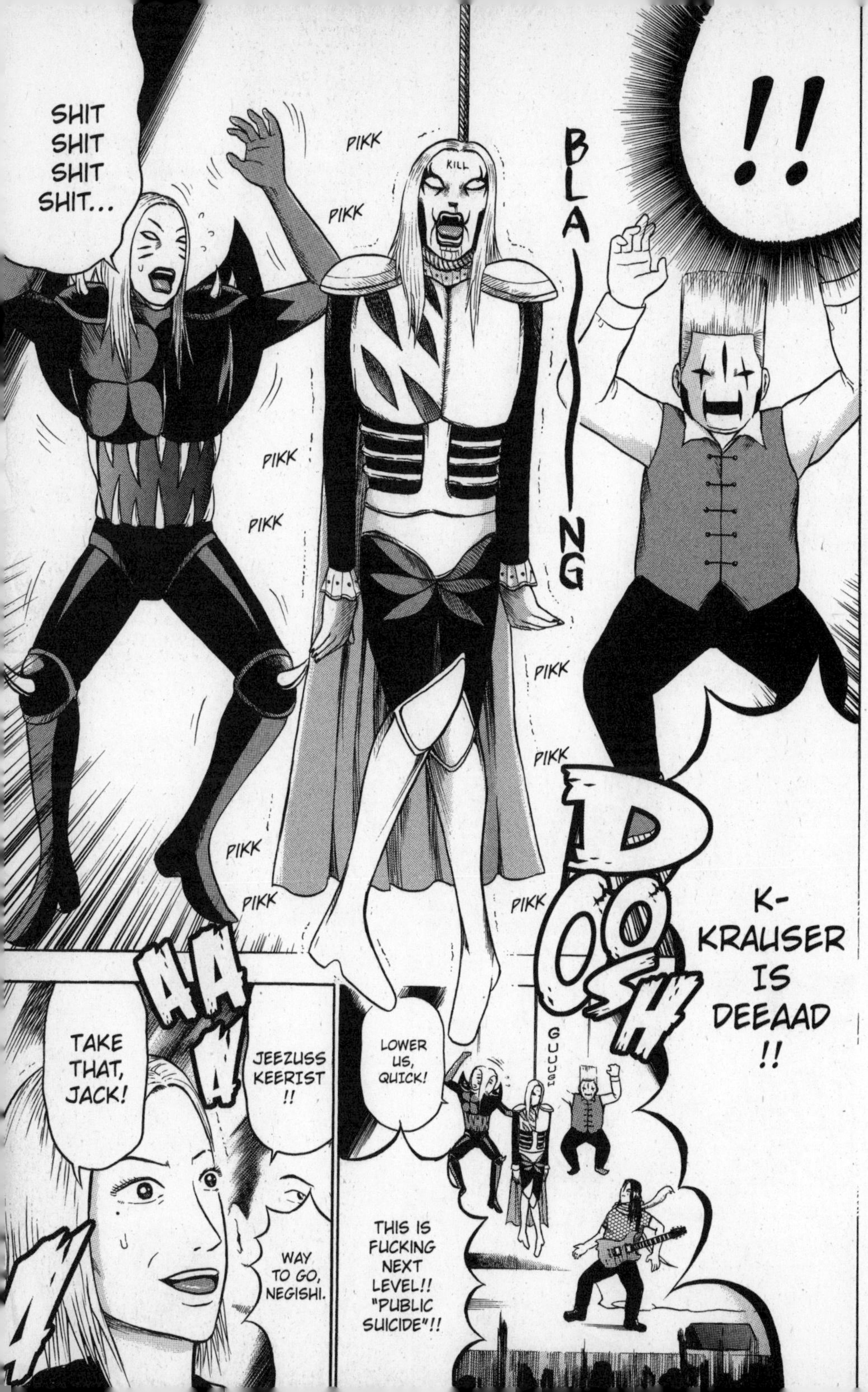
!!
BLA—NG
PIKK
PIKK
SHIT SHIT SHIT SHIT...
PIKK
PIKK
PIKK
PIKK
PIKK
PIKK
DOOSH
K-KRAUSER IS DEEAAD!!
GUUSH
LOWER US, QUICK!
THIS IS FUCKING NEXT LEVEL!! "PUBLIC SUICIDE"!!
AAA
JEEZUSS KEERIST!!
TAKE THAT, JACK!
WAY TO GO, NEGISHI.

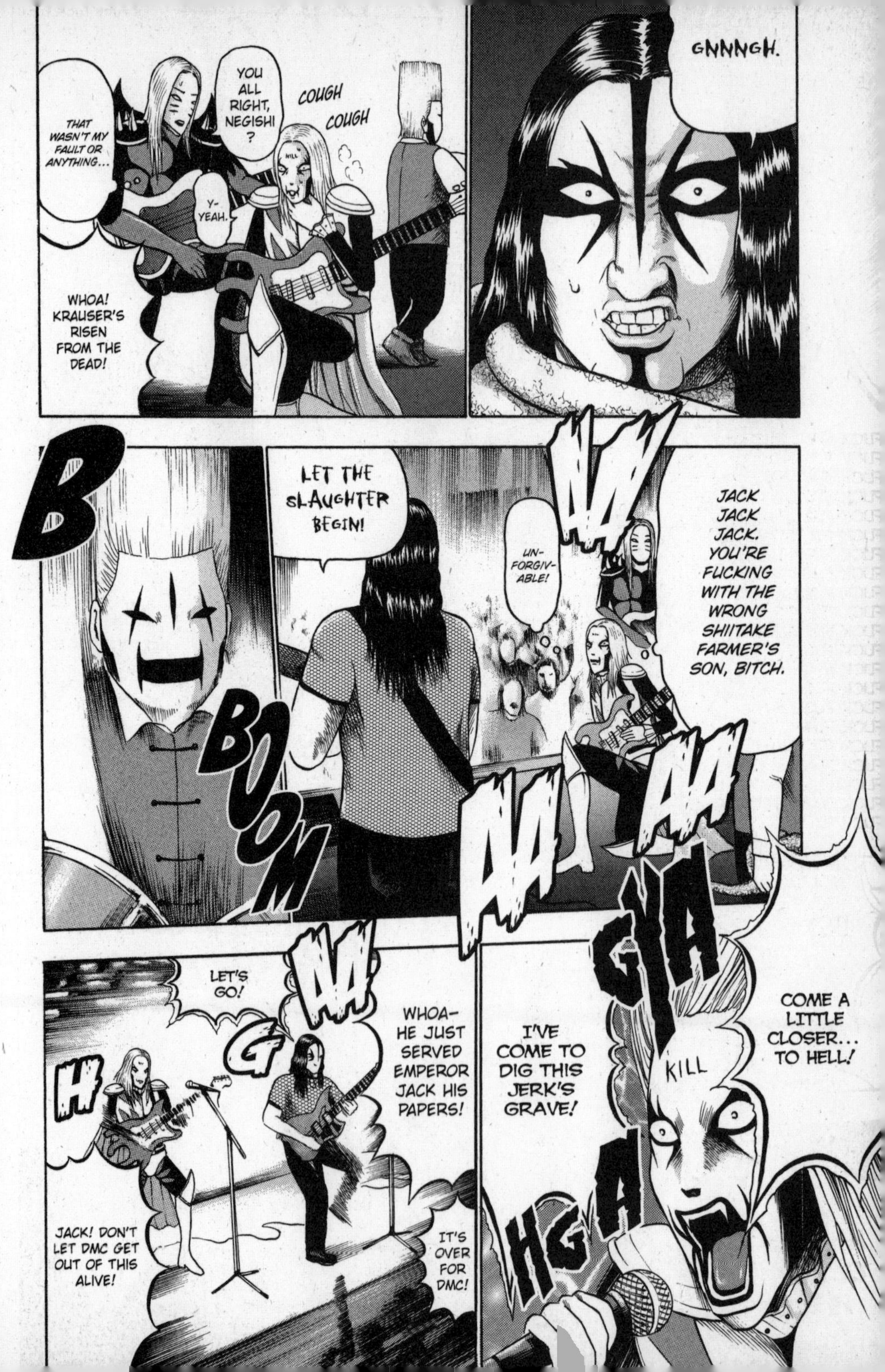
GNNNGH.
COUGH COUGH
YOU ALL RIGHT, NEGISHI?
Y-YEAH.
THAT WASN'T MY FAULT OR ANYTHING...
WHOA! KRAUSER'S RISEN FROM THE DEAD!
AAA
JACK JACK JACK. YOU'RE FUCKING WITH THE WRONG SHIITAKE FARMER'S SON, BITCH.
UN-FORGIVABLE!
AA AA
LET THE SLAUGHTER BEGIN!
BOOM
B
GIA
COME A LITTLE CLOSER... TO HELL!
KILL
I'VE COME TO DIG THIS JERK'S GRAVE!
HGA
AA
WHOA- HE JUST SERVED EMPEROR JACK HIS PAPERS!
LET'S GO!
G
H
IT'S OVER FOR DMC!
JACK! DON'T LET DMC GET OUT OF THIS ALIVE!

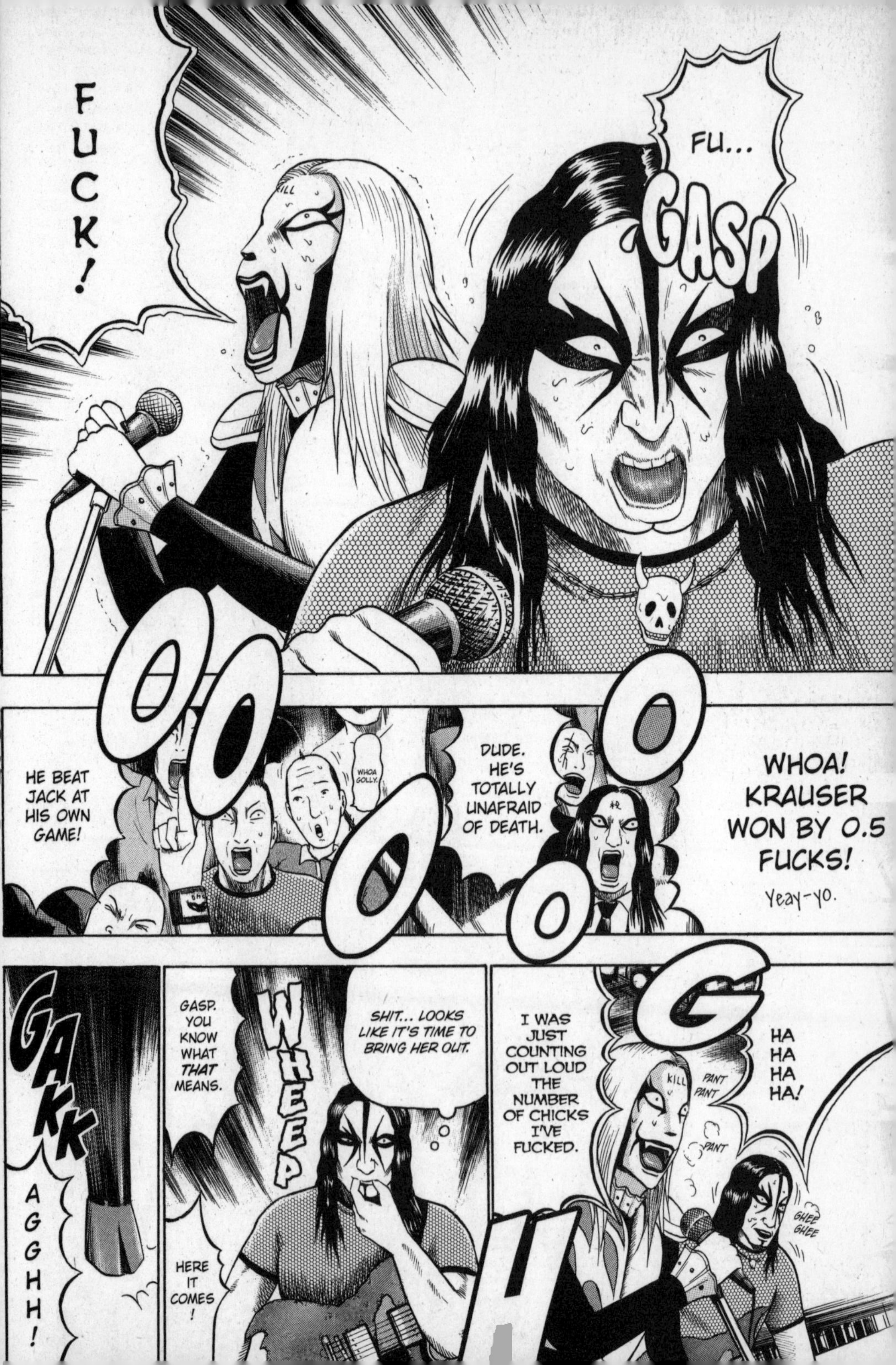
FU...
GASP
FUCK!
WHOA! KRAUSER WON BY 0.5 FUCKS!
Yeay-yo.
OOOOO
DUDE. HE'S TOTALLY UNAFRAID OF DEATH.
WHOA GOLLY.
HE BEAT JACK AT HIS OWN GAME!
HA HA HA HA!
GHEE GHEE
PANT PANT
PANT
I WAS JUST COUNTING OUT LOUD THE NUMBER OF CHICKS I'VE FUCKED.
GH
SHIT... LOOKS LIKE IT'S TIME TO BRING HER OUT.
WHEEP
GASP. YOU KNOW WHAT *THAT* MEANS.
HERE IT COMES!
GAKK
AGGHH!

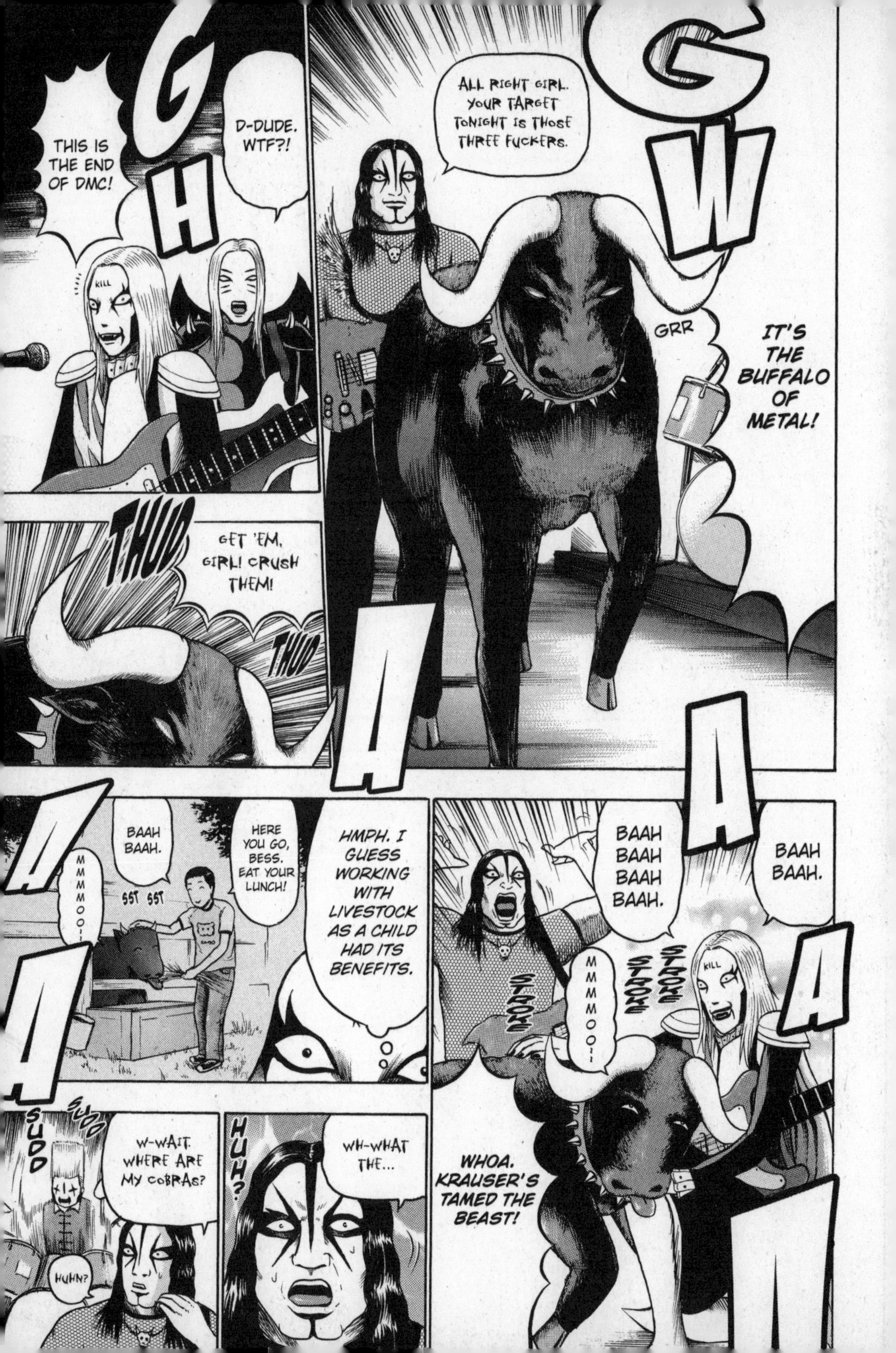
G
W
ALL RIGHT GIRL. YOUR TARGET TONIGHT IS THOSE THREE FUCKERS.
GRR
IT'S THE BUFFALO OF METAL!
G
H
D-DUDE. WTF?!
THIS IS THE END OF DMC!
THUD
GET 'EM, GIRL! CRUSH THEM!
THUD
A
A
A
BAAH BAAH.
BAAH BAAH BAAH BAAH.
STROKE
STROKE
STROKE
MMMMOO!!
WHOA. KRAUSER'S TAMED THE BEAST!
HMPH. I GUESS WORKING WITH LIVESTOCK AS A CHILD HAD ITS BENEFITS.
HERE YOU GO, BESS. EAT YOUR LUNCH!
BAAH BAAH.
SST SST
MMMMOO!!
A
A
WH-WHAT THE...
HUH?
W-WAIT. WHERE ARE MY COBRAS?
SUDD
SUDD
HUHN?

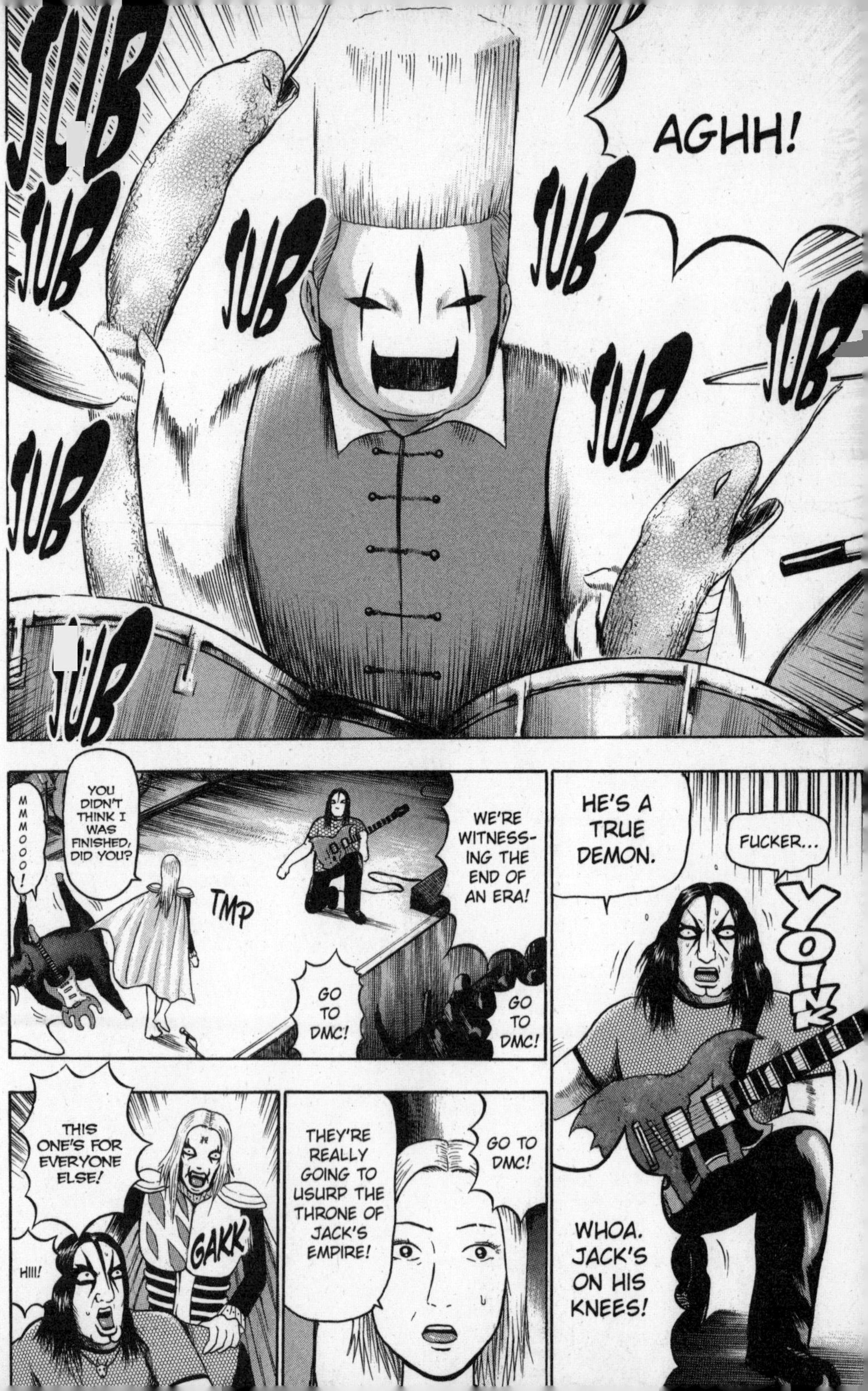
AGHH!
SUB
SUB
SUB
SUB
SUB
SUB
SUB
SUB
HE'S A TRUE DEMON.
FUCKER...
YOINK
WHOA. JACK'S ON HIS KNEES!
WE'RE WITNESSING THE END OF AN ERA!
YOU DIDN'T THINK I WAS FINISHED, DID YOU?
MMMOOOO!
TMP
GO TO DMC!
GO TO DMC!
GO TO DMC!
THEY'RE REALLY GOING TO USURP THE THRONE OF JACK'S EMPIRE!
THIS ONE'S FOR EVERYONE ELSE!
GAKK
HIII!

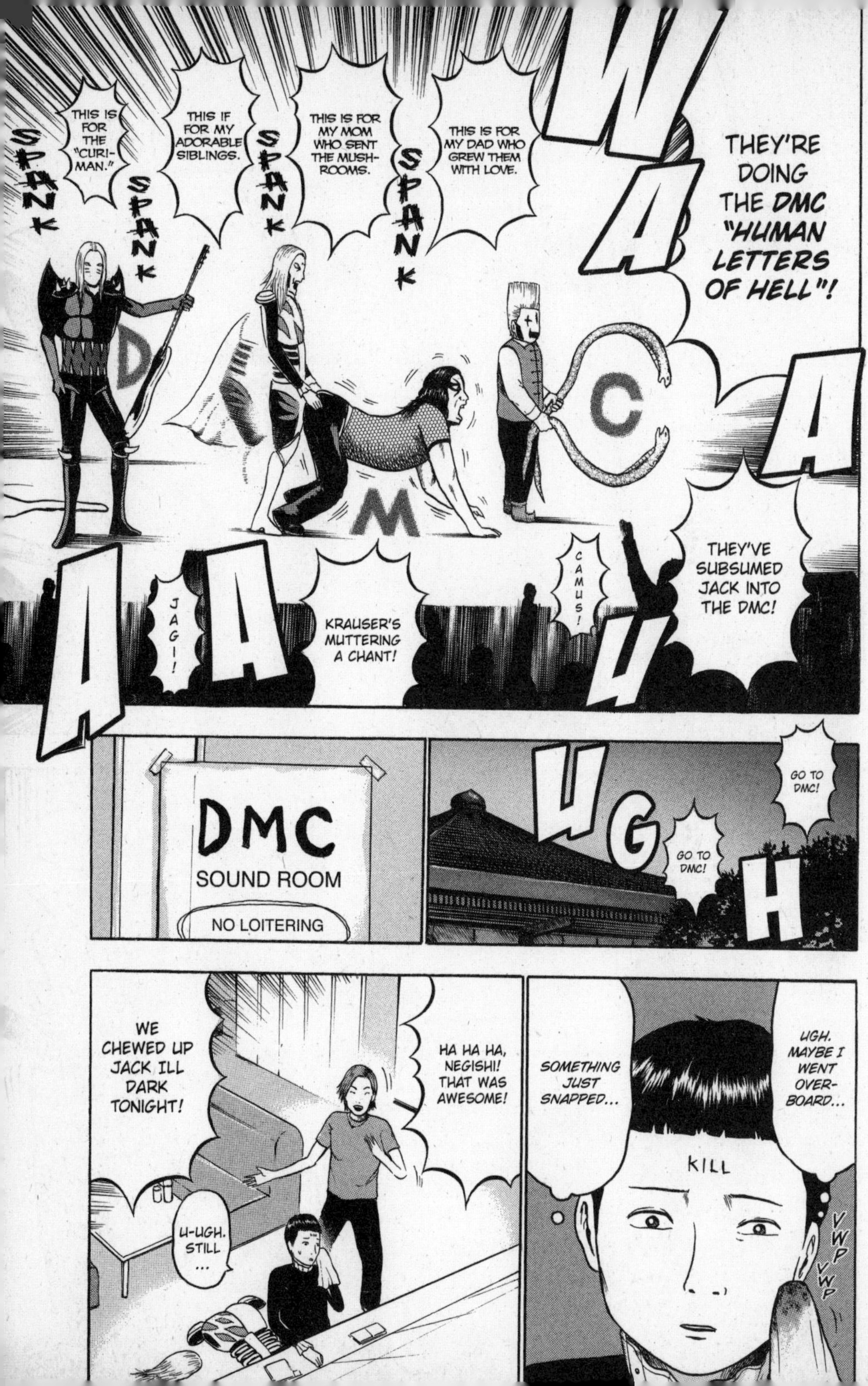
WA
THEY'RE DOING THE DMC "HUMAN LETTERS OF HELL"!
THIS IS FOR MY DAD WHO GREW THEM WITH LOVE.
SPANK
THIS IS FOR MY MOM WHO SENT THE MUSH-ROOMS.
SPANK
THIS IF FOR MY ADORABLE SIBLINGS.
SPANK
THIS IS FOR THE "CURI-MAN."
SPANK
SPANK
A
THEY'VE SUBSUMED JACK INTO THE DMC!
CAMUS!
KRAUSER'S MUTTERING A CHANT!
JAGI!
AAU
GO TO DMC!
GO TO DMC!
UGH
DMC
SOUND ROOM
NO LOITERING
UGH. MAYBE I WENT OVER-BOARD...
SOMETHING JUST SNAPPED...
KILL
VWP VWP
HA HA HA, NEGISHI! THAT WAS AWESOME!
WE CHEWED UP JACK ILL DARK TONIGHT!
U-UGH. STILL ...

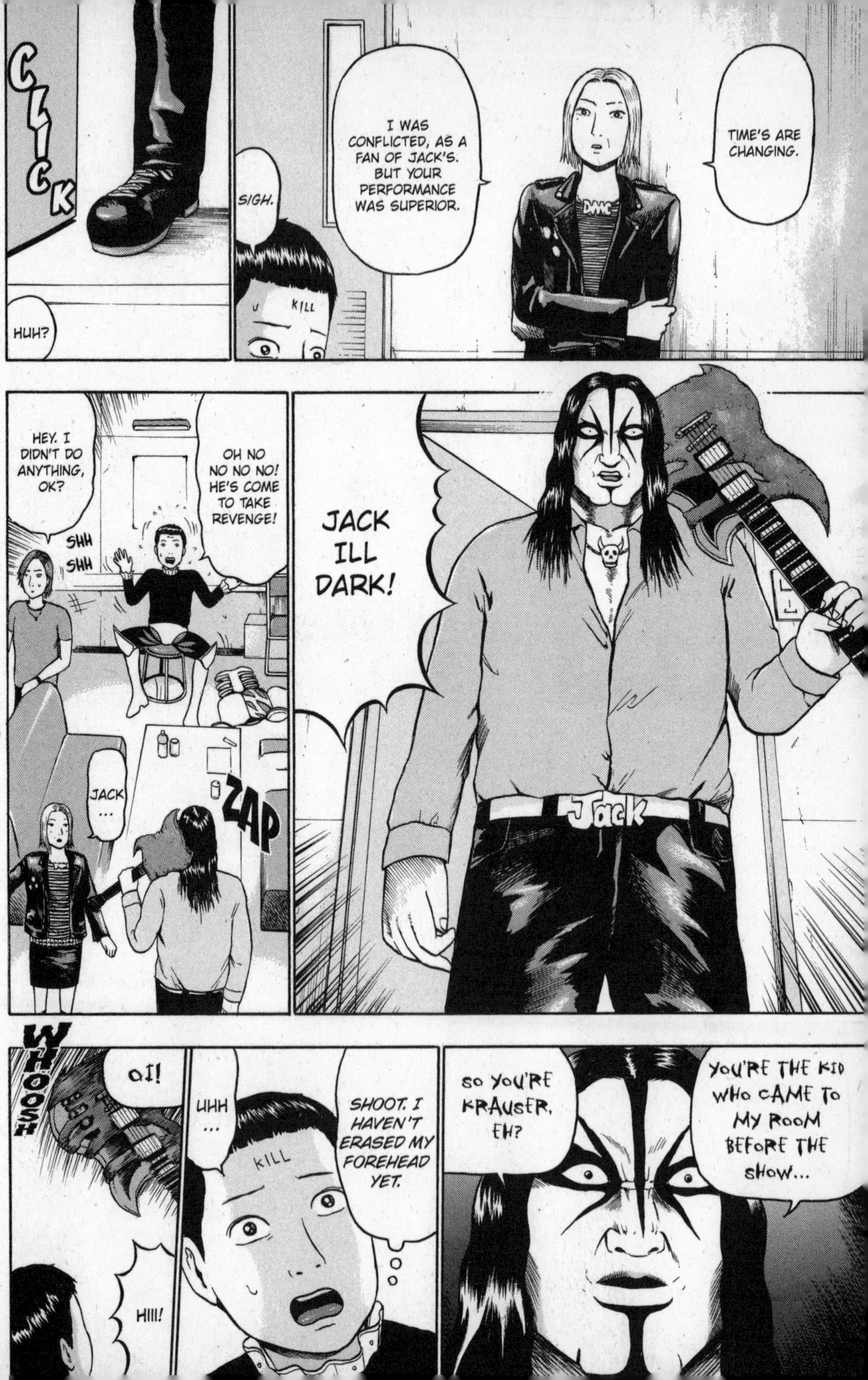

TIME'S ARE CHANGING.
I WAS CONFLICTED, AS A FAN OF JACK'S. BUT YOUR PERFORMANCE WAS SUPERIOR.
DMC
SIGH.
KILL
CLICK
HUH?
JACK ILL DARK!
Jack
OH NO NO NO NO! HE'S COME TO TAKE REVENGE!
HEY. I DIDN'T DO ANYTHING, OK?
SHH SHH
JACK ...
ZAP
YOU'RE THE KID WHO CAME TO MY ROOM BEFORE THE SHOW...
SO YOU'RE KRAUSER, EH?
SHOOT. I HAVEN'T ERASED MY FOREHEAD YET.
UHH ...
KILL
WHOOSH
OI!
HIII!

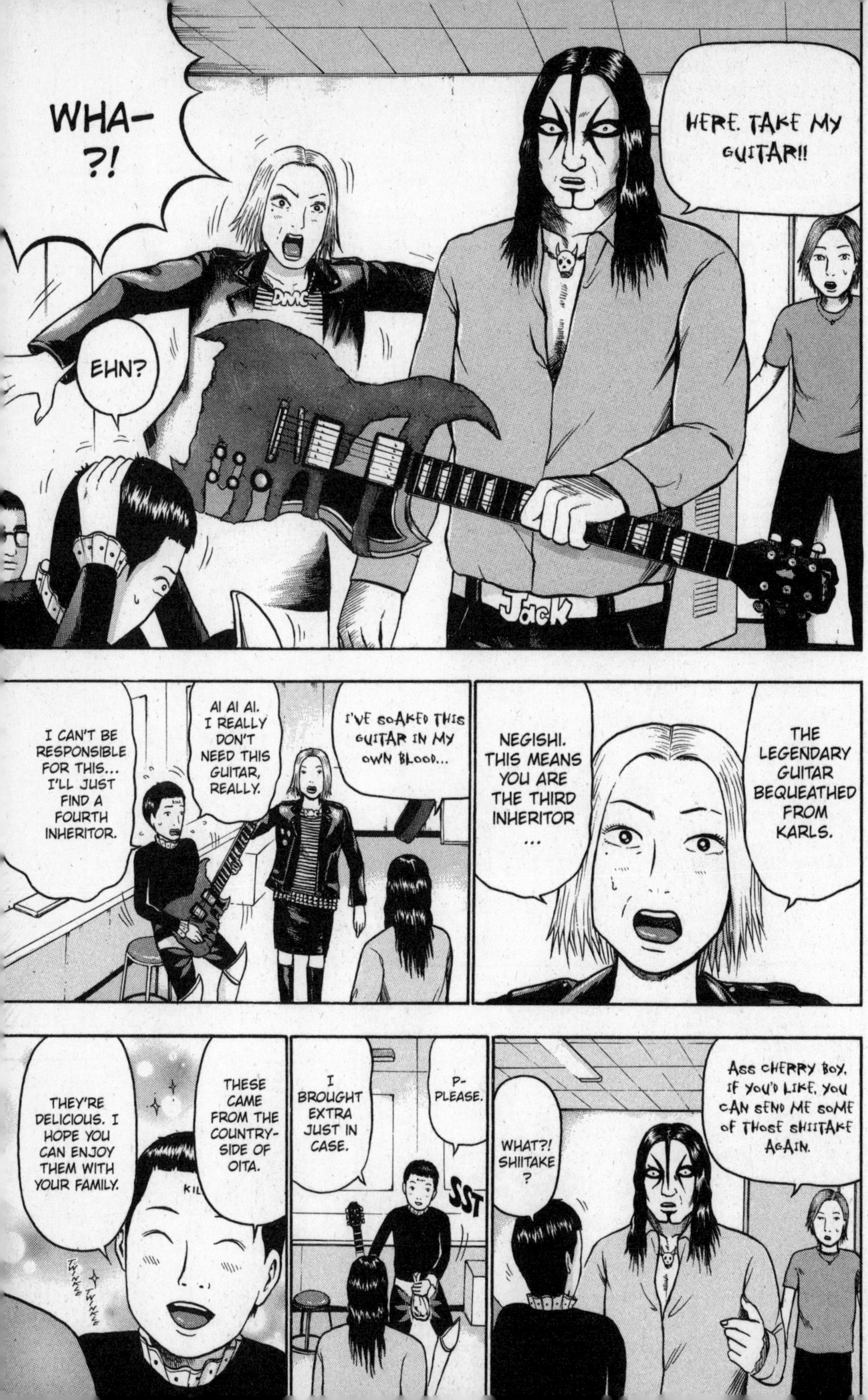
HERE. TAKE MY GUITAR!!
WHA- ?!
DMC
EHN?
Jack
THE LEGENDARY GUITAR BEQUEATHED FROM KARLS.
NEGISHI. THIS MEANS YOU ARE THE THIRD INHERITOR ...
I'VE SOAKED THIS GUITAR IN MY OWN BLOOD...
AI AI AI. I REALLY DON'T NEED THIS GUITAR, REALLY.
I CAN'T BE RESPONSIBLE FOR THIS... I'LL JUST FIND A FOURTH INHERITOR.
ASS CHERRY BOY, IF YOU'D LIKE, YOU CAN SEND ME SOME OF THOSE SHIITAKE AGAIN.
WHAT?! SHIITAKE ?
P- PLEASE.
I BROUGHT EXTRA JUST IN CASE.
SST
THESE CAME FROM THE COUNTRY-SIDE OF OITA.
THEY'RE DELICIOUS. I HOPE YOU CAN ENJOY THEM WITH YOUR FAMILY.
TWINKLE TWINKLE

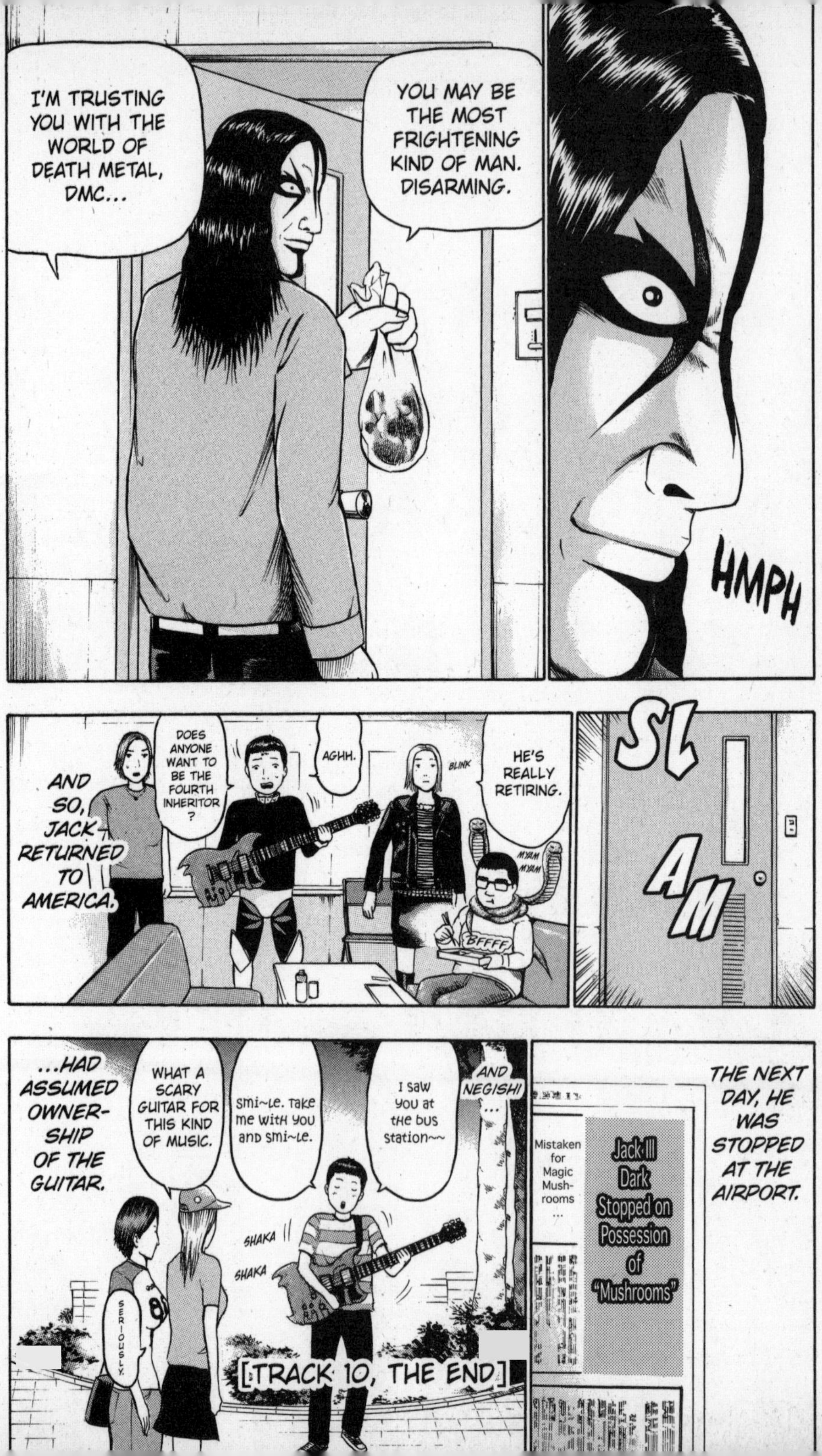
HMPH
YOU MAY BE THE MOST FRIGHTENING KIND OF MAN. DISARMING.
I'M TRUSTING YOU WITH THE WORLD OF DEATH METAL, DMC...
SLAM
HE'S REALLY RETIRING.
BLINK
AGHH.
DOES ANYONE WANT TO BE THE FOURTH INHERITOR ?
MYAM MYAM
BFFFF
AND SO, JACK RETURNED TO AMERICA.
THE NEXT DAY, HE WAS STOPPED AT THE AIRPORT.
Jack III Dark Stopped on Possession of "Mushrooms"
Mistaken for Magic Mushrooms ...
AND NEGISHI ...
I saw you at the bus station~~
smi~le. take me with you and smi~le.
WHAT A SCARY GUITAR FOR THIS KIND OF MUSIC.
...HAD ASSUMED OWNERSHIP OF THE GUITAR.
SHAKA
SHAKA
SERIOUSLY.
[TRACK 10, THE END]

DMC LEXICON

🎭 SHIITAKE

Of the tricholomataceae family of fungi. Taxonomically speaking, it is generally considered an edible product, and hence differs from the penis. English renderings include such variations as "shiitake" and "shitake."

Usage: Mt. Fuji, sushi, shiitake.

デトロイト・メタル・シティ
Detroit Metal City

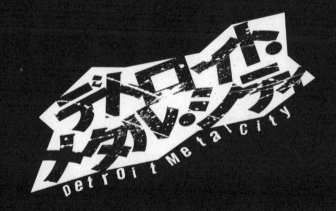

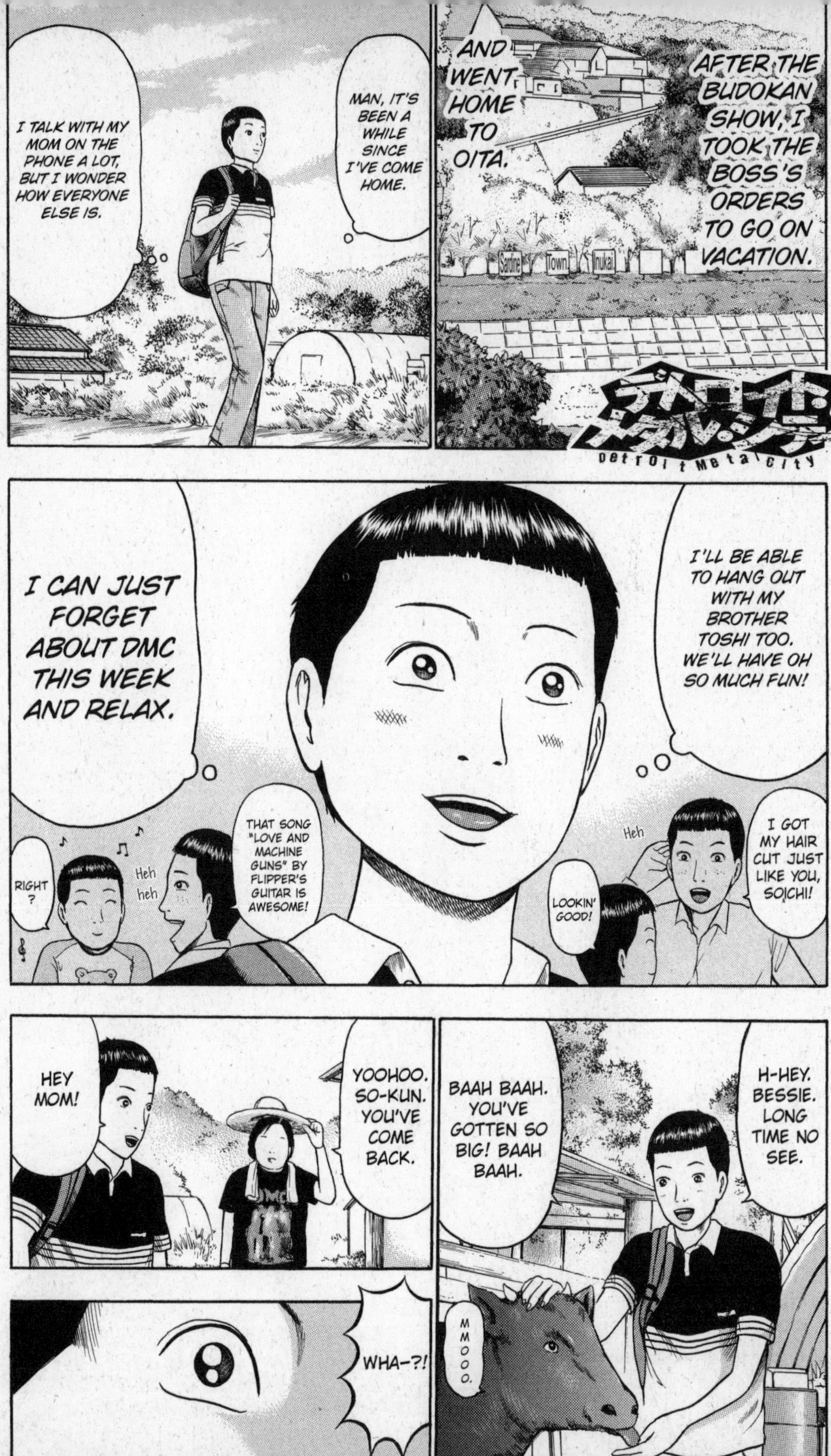
AFTER THE BUDOKAN SHOW, I TOOK THE BOSS'S ORDERS TO GO ON VACATION.
AND WENT HOME TO OITA.
Sardine
Town
Inukai
Detroit Metal City
MAN, IT'S BEEN A WHILE SINCE I'VE COME HOME.
I TALK WITH MY MOM ON THE PHONE A LOT, BUT I WONDER HOW EVERYONE ELSE IS.
I'LL BE ABLE TO HANG OUT WITH MY BROTHER TOSHI TOO. WE'LL HAVE OH SO MUCH FUN!
I CAN JUST FORGET ABOUT DMC THIS WEEK AND RELAX.
I GOT MY HAIR CUT JUST LIKE YOU, SOICHI!
Heh
LOOKIN' GOOD!
THAT SONG "LOVE AND MACHINE GUNS" BY FLIPPER'S GUITAR IS AWESOME!
Heh heh
RIGHT?
H-HEY. BESSIE. LONG TIME NO SEE.
BAAH BAAH. YOU'VE GOTTEN SO BIG! BAAH BAAH.
MMOOO.
YOOHOO. SO-KUN. YOU'VE COME BACK.
HEY MOM!
WHA-?!

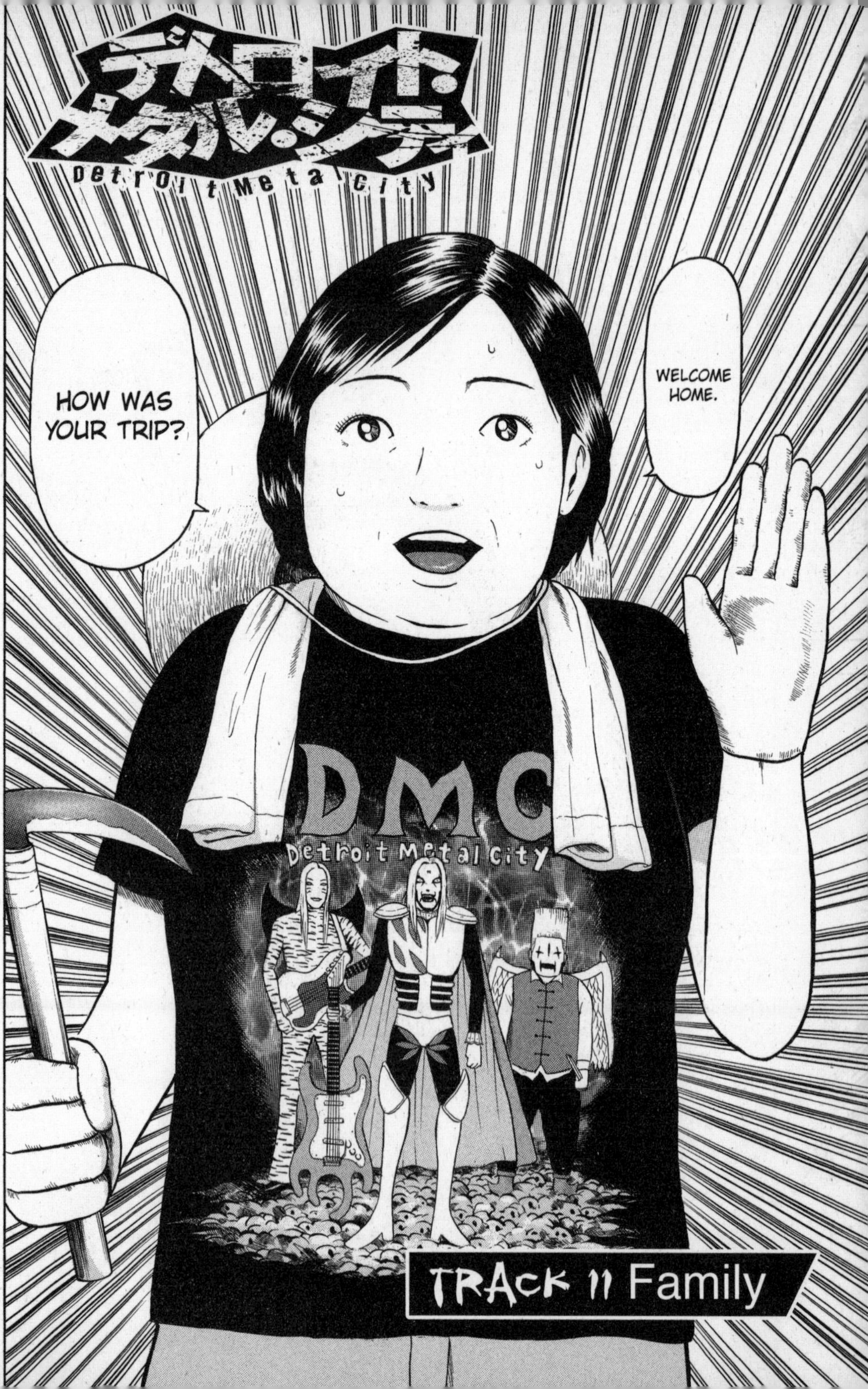

デトロイト・メタル・シティ
Detroit Metal City
WELCOME HOME.
HOW WAS YOUR TRIP?
DMC
Detroit Metal City
TRACK 11 Family

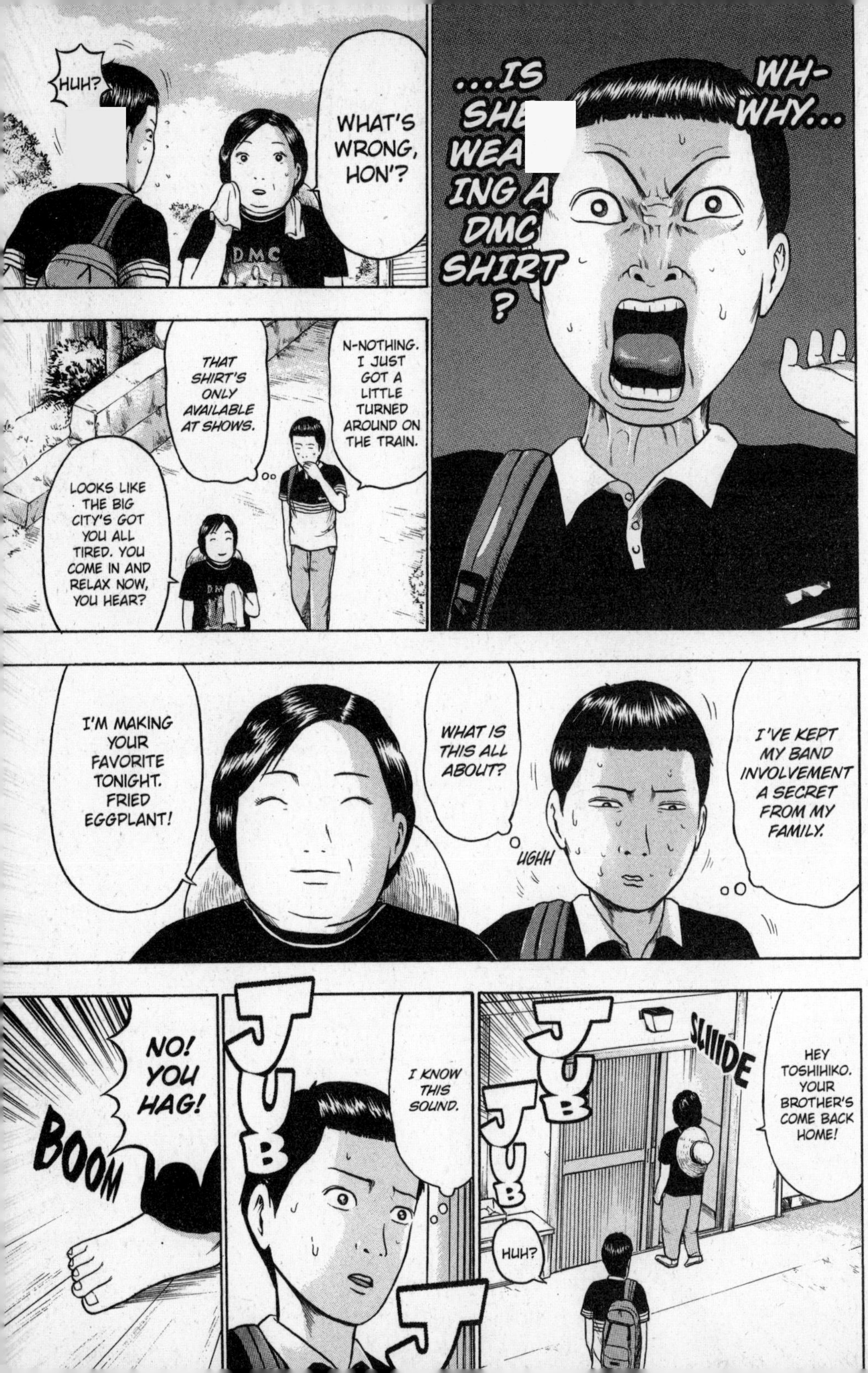
WH- WHY...
...IS SHE WEA ING A DMC SHIRT?
WHAT'S WRONG, HON'?
HUH?
N-NOTHING. I JUST GOT A LITTLE TURNED AROUND ON THE TRAIN.
THAT SHIRT'S ONLY AVAILABLE AT SHOWS.
LOOKS LIKE THE BIG CITY'S GOT YOU ALL TIRED. YOU COME IN AND RELAX NOW, YOU HEAR?
I'VE KEPT MY BAND INVOLVEMENT A SECRET FROM MY FAMILY.
WHAT IS THIS ALL ABOUT?
UGHH
I'M MAKING YOUR FAVORITE TONIGHT. FRIED EGGPLANT!
HEY TOSHIHIKO. YOUR BROTHER'S COME BACK HOME!
SLIIIDE
JUB
JUB
HUH?
JUB
I KNOW THIS SOUND.
NO! YOU HAG!
BOOM

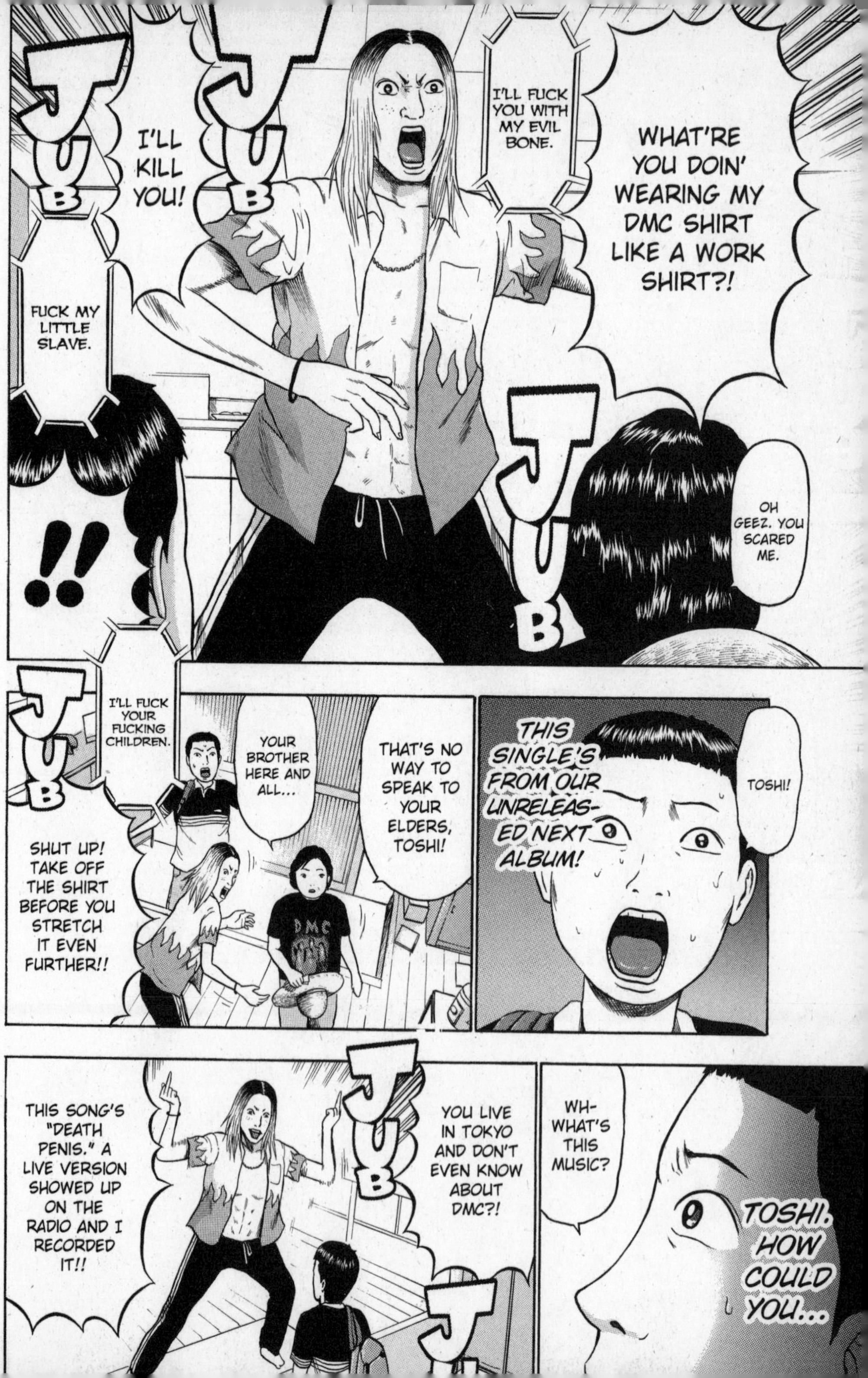
WHAT'RE YOU DOIN' WEARING MY DMC SHIRT LIKE A WORK SHIRT?!
I'LL FUCK YOU WITH MY EVIL BONE.
JUB
I'LL KILL YOU!
JUB
FUCK MY LITTLE SLAVE.
OH GEEZ. YOU SCARED ME.
JUB
!!
TOSHI!
THIS SINGLE'S FROM OUR UNRELEAS-ED NEXT ALBUM!
THAT'S NO WAY TO SPEAK TO YOUR ELDERS, TOSHI!
YOUR BROTHER HERE AND ALL...
I'LL FUCK YOUR FUCKING CHILDREN.
JUB
SHUT UP! TAKE OFF THE SHIRT BEFORE YOU STRETCH IT EVEN FURTHER!!
TOSHI. HOW COULD YOU...
WH- WHAT'S THIS MUSIC?
YOU LIVE IN TOKYO AND DON'T EVEN KNOW ABOUT DMC?!
JUB
THIS SONG'S "DEATH PENIS." A LIVE VERSION SHOWED UP ON THE RADIO AND I RECORDED IT!!
J

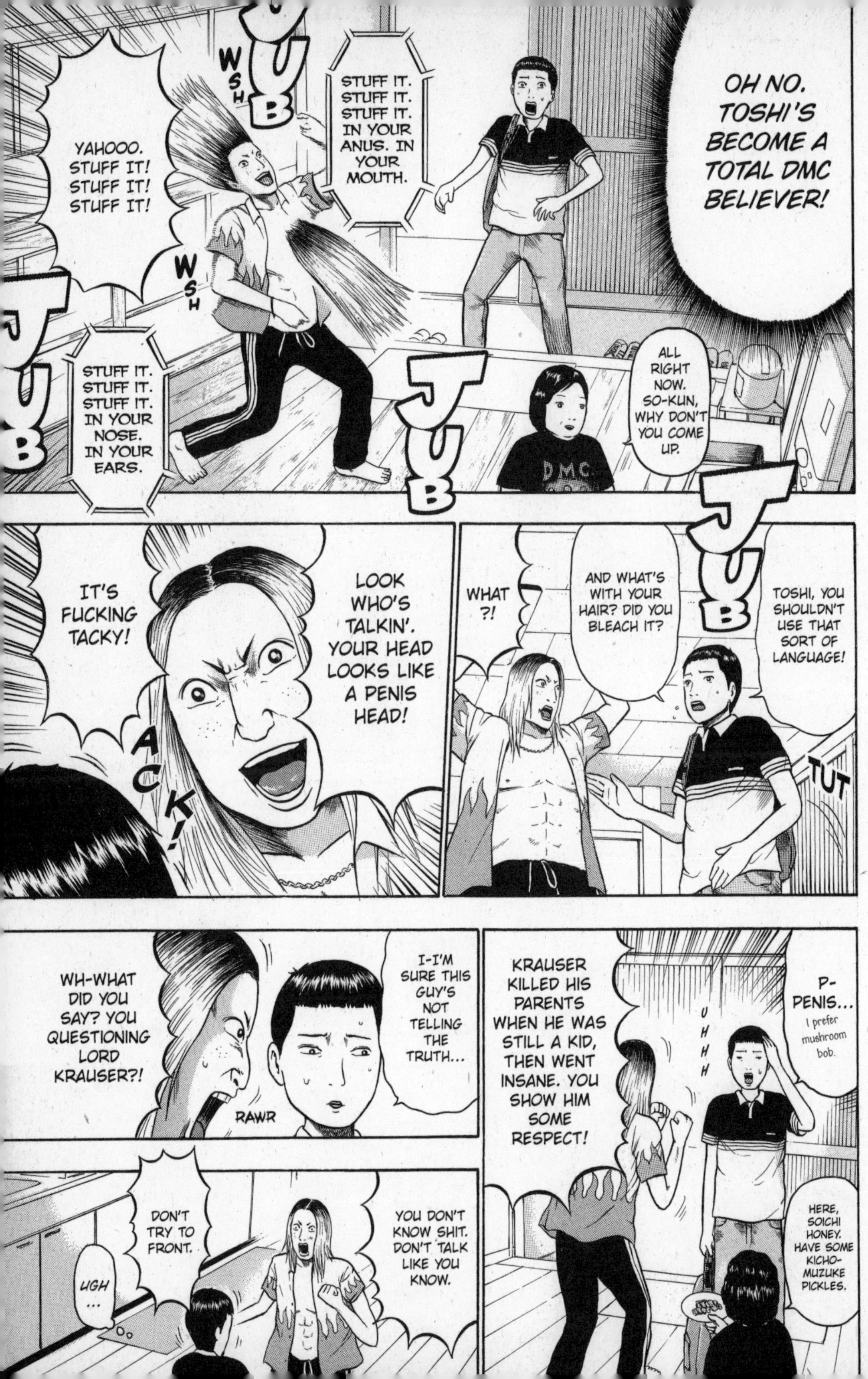
OH NO. TOSHI'S BECOME A TOTAL DMC BELIEVER!
STUFF IT. STUFF IT. STUFF IT. IN YOUR ANUS. IN YOUR MOUTH.
JUB
WSH
YAHOOO. STUFF IT! STUFF IT! STUFF IT!
WSH
ALL RIGHT NOW. SO-KUN, WHY DON'T YOU COME UP.
JUB
STUFF IT. STUFF IT. STUFF IT. IN YOUR NOSE. IN YOUR EARS.
JUB
JUB
TOSHI, YOU SHOULDN'T USE THAT SORT OF LANGUAGE!
AND WHAT'S WITH YOUR HAIR? DID YOU BLEACH IT?
WHAT ?!
TUT
LOOK WHO'S TALKIN'. YOUR HEAD LOOKS LIKE A PENIS HEAD!
IT'S FUCKING TACKY!
ACK!
P- PENIS...
I prefer mushroom bob.
UHHH
KRAUSER KILLED HIS PARENTS WHEN HE WAS STILL A KID, THEN WENT INSANE. YOU SHOW HIM SOME RESPECT!
HERE, SOICHI HONEY. HAVE SOME KICHO-MUZUKE PICKLES.
I-I'M SURE THIS GUY'S NOT TELLING THE TRUTH...
WH-WHAT DID YOU SAY? YOU QUESTIONING LORD KRAUSER?!
RAWR
YOU DON'T KNOW SHIT. DON'T TALK LIKE YOU KNOW.
DON'T TRY TO FRONT.
UGH ...

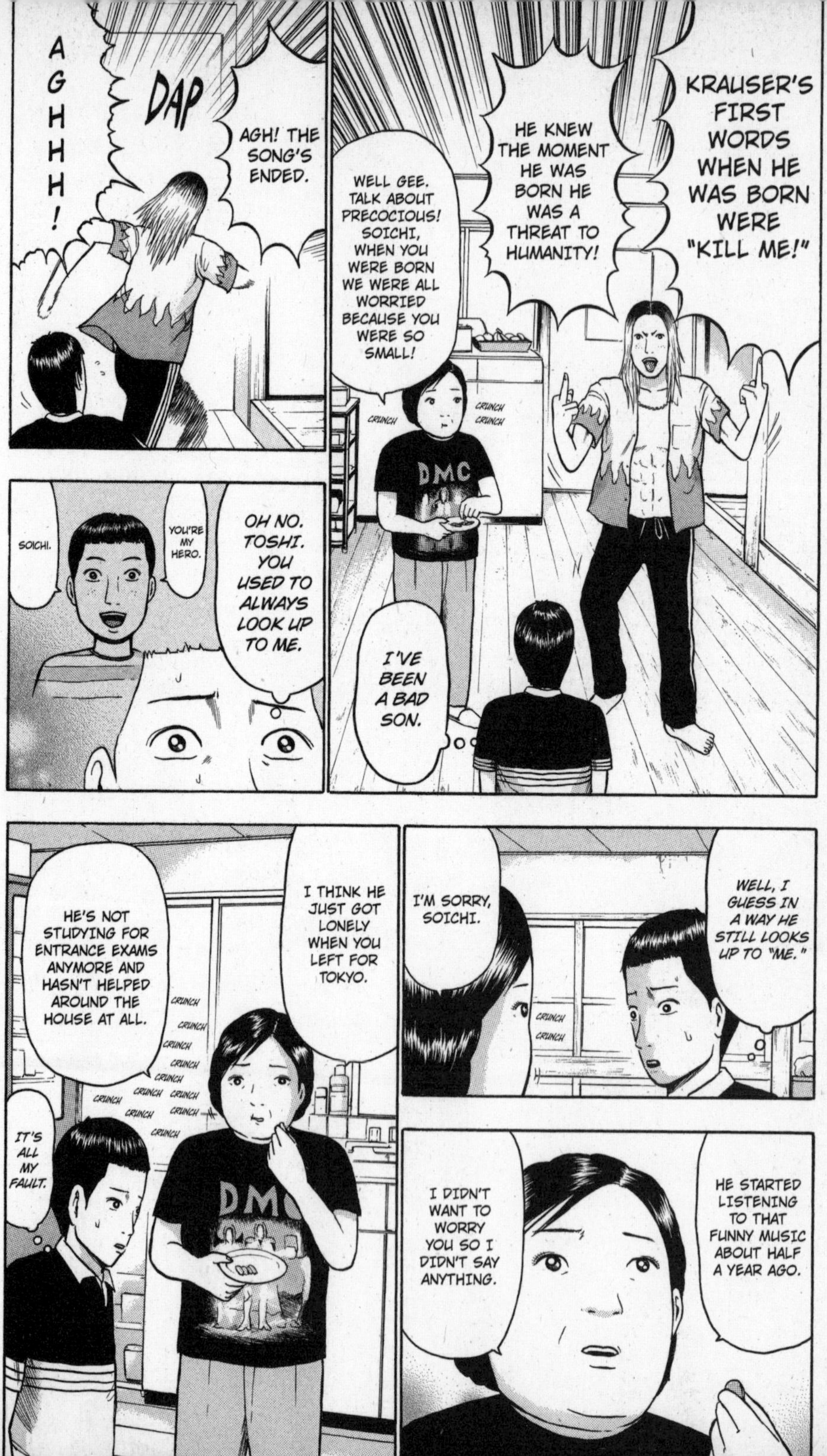
KRAUSER'S FIRST WORDS WHEN HE WAS BORN WERE "KILL ME!"
HE KNEW THE MOMENT HE WAS BORN HE WAS A THREAT TO HUMANITY!
WELL GEE. TALK ABOUT PRECOCIOUS! SOICHI, WHEN YOU WERE BORN WE WERE ALL WORRIED BECAUSE YOU WERE SO SMALL!
CRUNCH CRUNCH
CRUNCH
I'VE BEEN A BAD SON.
AGHHH!
DAP
AGH! THE SONG'S ENDED.
OH NO. TOSHI. YOU USED TO ALWAYS LOOK UP TO ME.
YOU'RE MY HERO.
SOICHI.
WELL, I GUESS IN A WAY HE STILL LOOKS UP TO "ME."
CRUNCH CRUNCH
I'M SORRY, SOICHI.
HE STARTED LISTENING TO THAT FUNNY MUSIC ABOUT HALF A YEAR AGO.
I DIDN'T WANT TO WORRY YOU SO I DIDN'T SAY ANYTHING.
I THINK HE JUST GOT LONELY WHEN YOU LEFT FOR TOKYO.
HE'S NOT STUDYING FOR ENTRANCE EXAMS ANYMORE AND HASN'T HELPED AROUND THE HOUSE AT ALL.
CRUNCH CRUNCH CRUNCH CRUNCH CRUNCH CRUNCH CRUNCH CRUNCH CRUNCH CRUNCH CRUNCH
IT'S ALL MY FAULT.

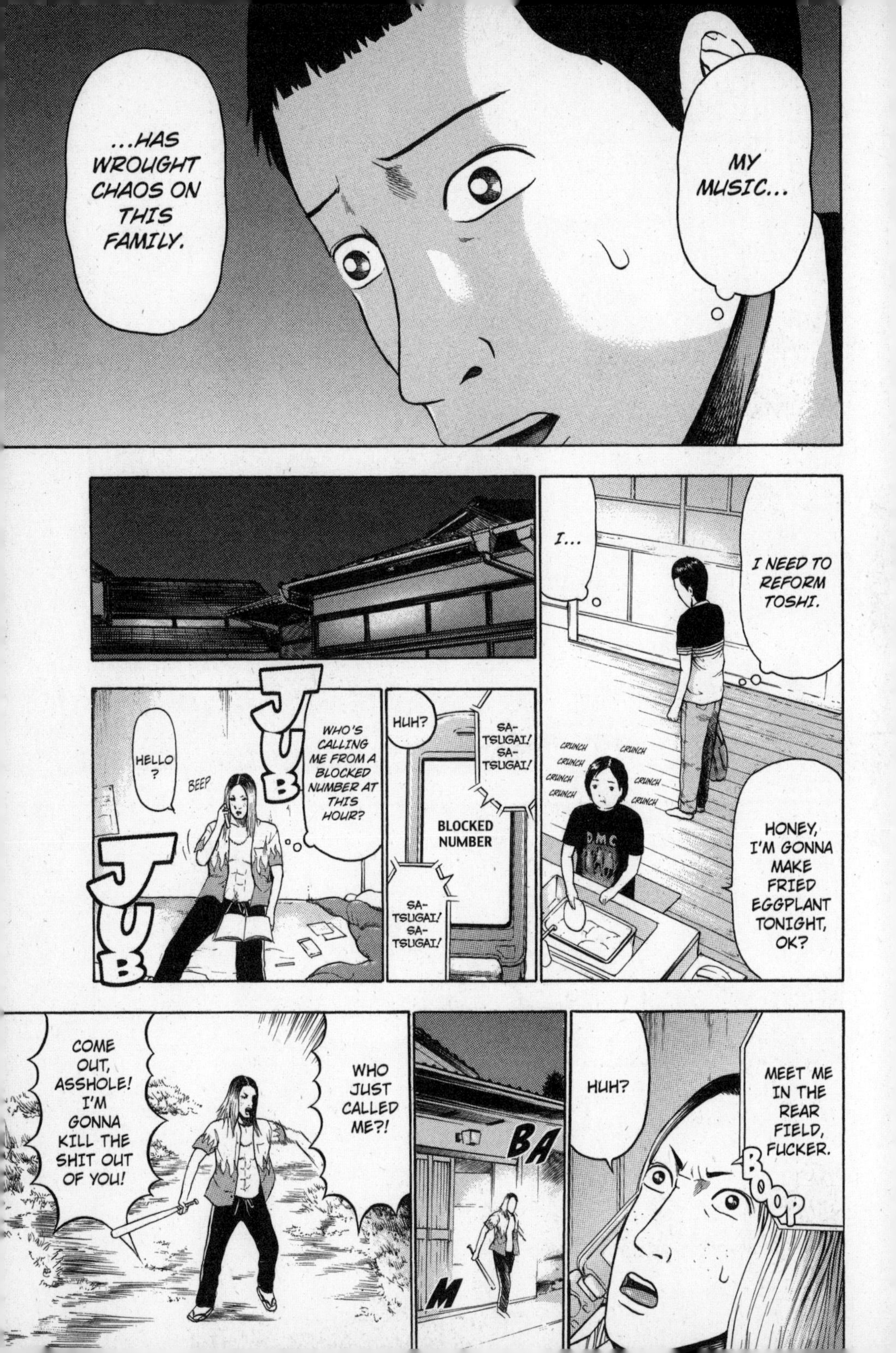
MY MUSIC...
...HAS WROUGHT CHAOS ON THIS FAMILY.
I...
I NEED TO REFORM TOSHI.
CRUNCH CRUNCH CRUNCH CRUNCH CRUNCH CRUNCH CRUNCH
HONEY, I'M GONNA MAKE FRIED EGGPLANT TONIGHT, OK?
HUH?
SA-TSUGAI! SA-TSUGAI!
BLOCKED NUMBER
SA-TSUGAI! SA-TSUGAI!
JUB
WHO'S CALLING ME FROM A BLOCKED NUMBER AT THIS HOUR?
HELLO?
BEEP
JUB
MEET ME IN THE REAR FIELD, FUCKER.
BOOP
HUH?
BAM
WHO JUST CALLED ME?!
COME OUT, ASSHOLE! I'M GONNA KILL THE SHIT OUT OF YOU!

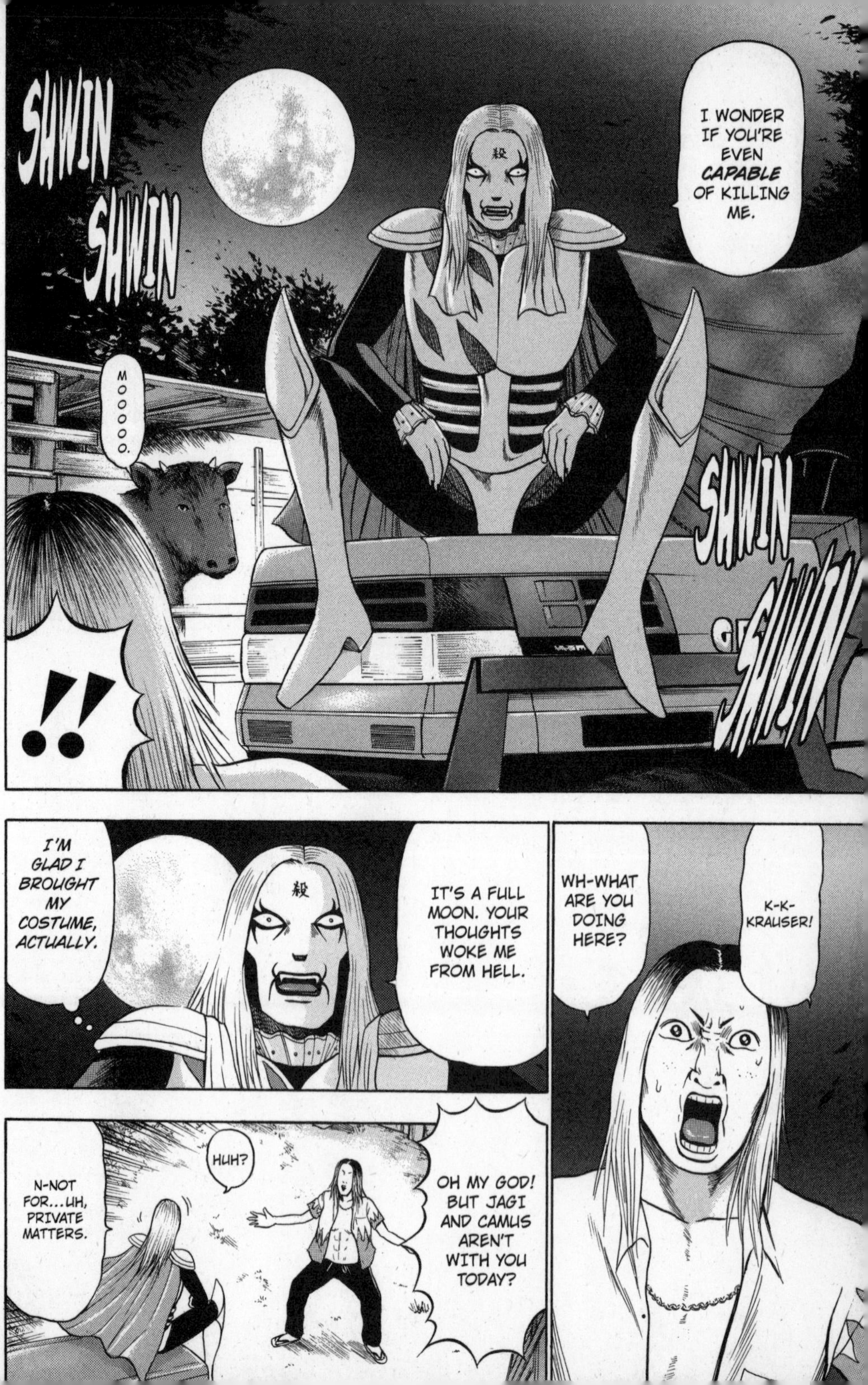
I WONDER IF YOU'RE EVEN CAPABLE OF KILLING ME.
SHWIN
SHWIN
MOOOOO.
SHWIN
SHWIN
!!
K-K-KRAUSER!
WH-WHAT ARE YOU DOING HERE?
IT'S A FULL MOON. YOUR THOUGHTS WOKE ME FROM HELL.
I'M GLAD I BROUGHT MY COSTUME, ACTUALLY.
OH MY GOD! BUT JAGI AND CAMUS AREN'T WITH YOU TODAY?
HUH?
N-NOT FOR...UH, PRIVATE MATTERS.

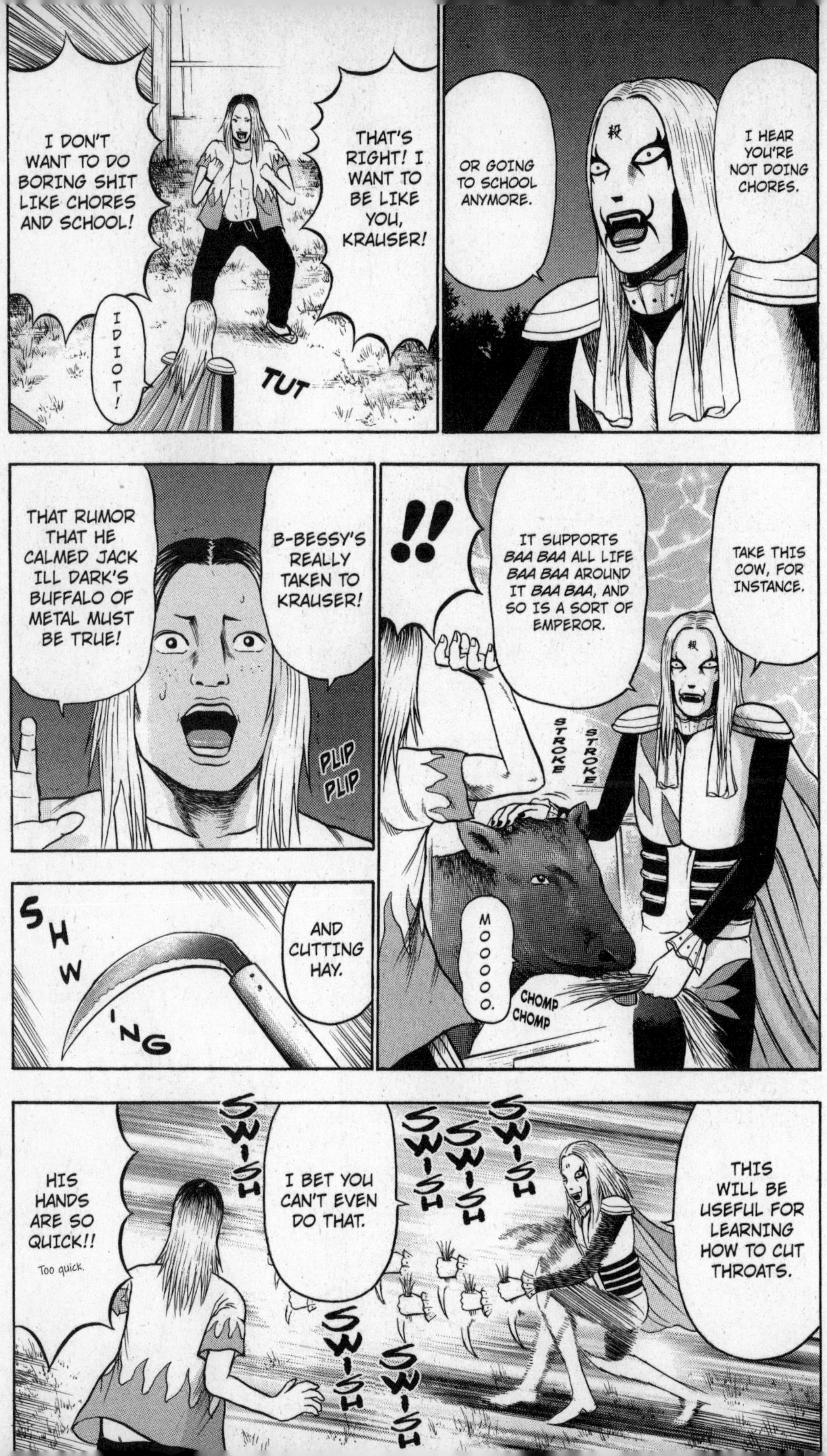
I HEAR YOU'RE NOT DOING CHORES.
OR GOING TO SCHOOL ANYMORE.
THAT'S RIGHT! I WANT TO BE LIKE YOU, KRAUSER!
I DON'T WANT TO DO BORING SHIT LIKE CHORES AND SCHOOL!
IDIOT!
TUT
TAKE THIS COW, FOR INSTANCE.
IT SUPPORTS *BAA BAA* ALL LIFE *BAA BAA* AROUND IT *BAA BAA*, AND SO IS A SORT OF EMPEROR.
!!
STROKE STROKE
MOOOOO.
CHOMP CHOMP
B-BESSY'S REALLY TAKEN TO KRAUSER!
THAT RUMOR THAT HE CALMED JACK ILL DARK'S BUFFALO OF METAL MUST BE TRUE!
PLIP PLIP
AND CUTTING HAY.
SHWING
THIS WILL BE USEFUL FOR LEARNING HOW TO CUT THROATS.
SWISH SWISH SWISH
I BET YOU CAN'T EVEN DO THAT.
SWISH
HIS HANDS ARE SO QUICK!!
Too quick.
SWISH SWISH

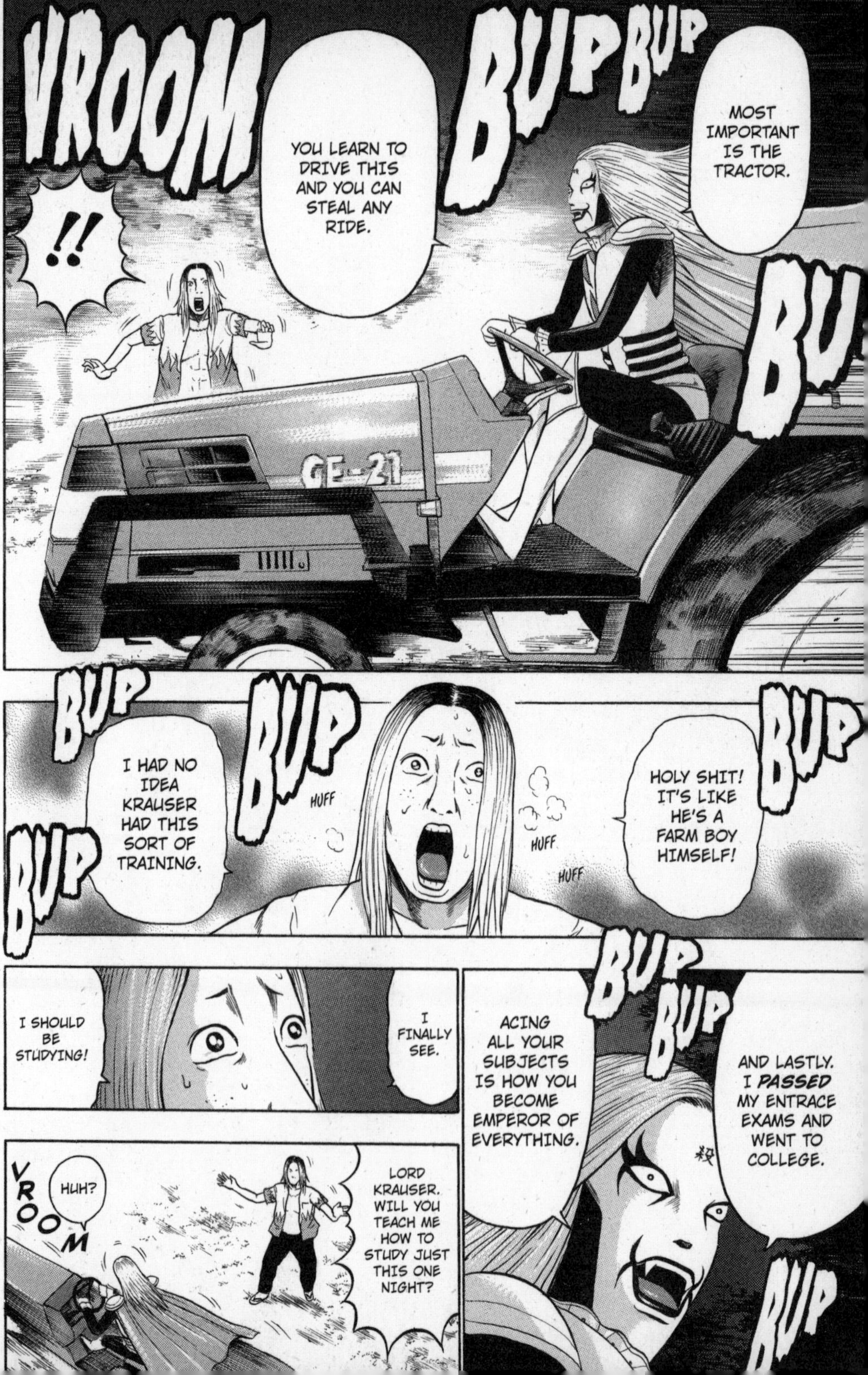
BUP BUP
MOST IMPORTANT IS THE TRACTOR.
YOU LEARN TO DRIVE THIS AND YOU CAN STEAL ANY RIDE.
VROOM
!!
BU
GE-21
BUP
HOLY SHIT! IT'S LIKE HE'S A FARM BOY HIMSELF!
HUFF
HUFF
HUFF
BUP
I HAD NO IDEA KRAUSER HAD THIS SORT OF TRAINING.
BUP
BUP
BUP BUP
AND LASTLY. I **PASSED** MY ENTRACE EXAMS AND WENT TO COLLEGE.
ACING ALL YOUR SUBJECTS IS HOW YOU BECOME EMPEROR OF EVERYTHING.
BUP
I FINALLY SEE.
I SHOULD BE STUDYING!
LORD KRAUSER. WILL YOU TEACH ME HOW TO STUDY JUST THIS ONE NIGHT?
HUH?
VROOM

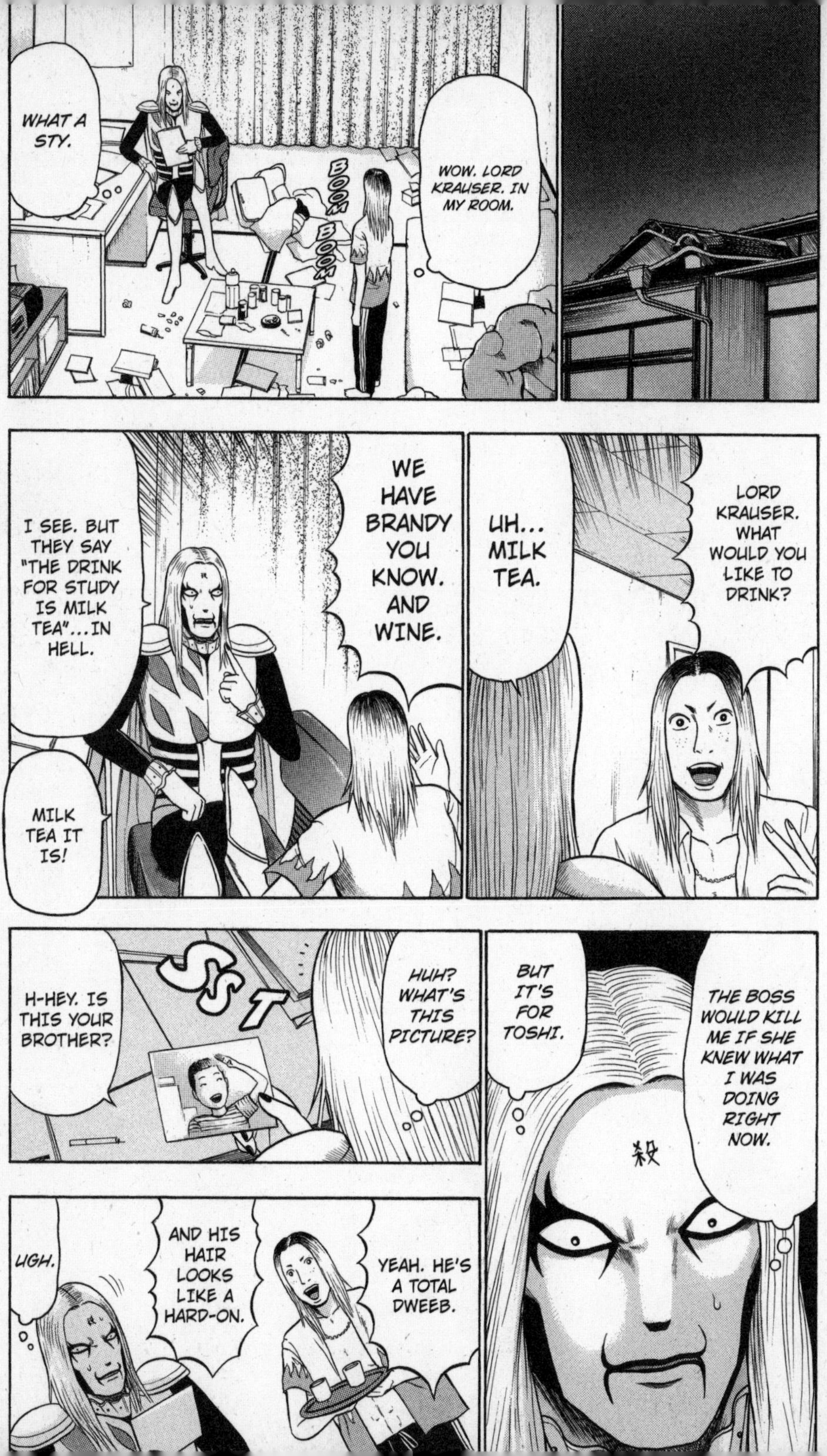
WOW. LORD KRAUSER. IN MY ROOM.
BOOM BOOM
WHAT A STY.
LORD KRAUSER. WHAT WOULD YOU LIKE TO DRINK?
UH... MILK TEA.
WE HAVE BRANDY YOU KNOW. AND WINE.
I SEE. BUT THEY SAY "THE DRINK FOR STUDY IS MILK TEA"...IN HELL.
MILK TEA IT IS!
THE BOSS WOULD KILL ME IF SHE KNEW WHAT I WAS DOING RIGHT NOW.
BUT IT'S FOR TOSHI.
殺
HUH? WHAT'S THIS PICTURE?
SST
H-HEY. IS THIS YOUR BROTHER?
YEAH. HE'S A TOTAL DWEEB.
AND HIS HAIR LOOKS LIKE A HARD-ON.
UGH.

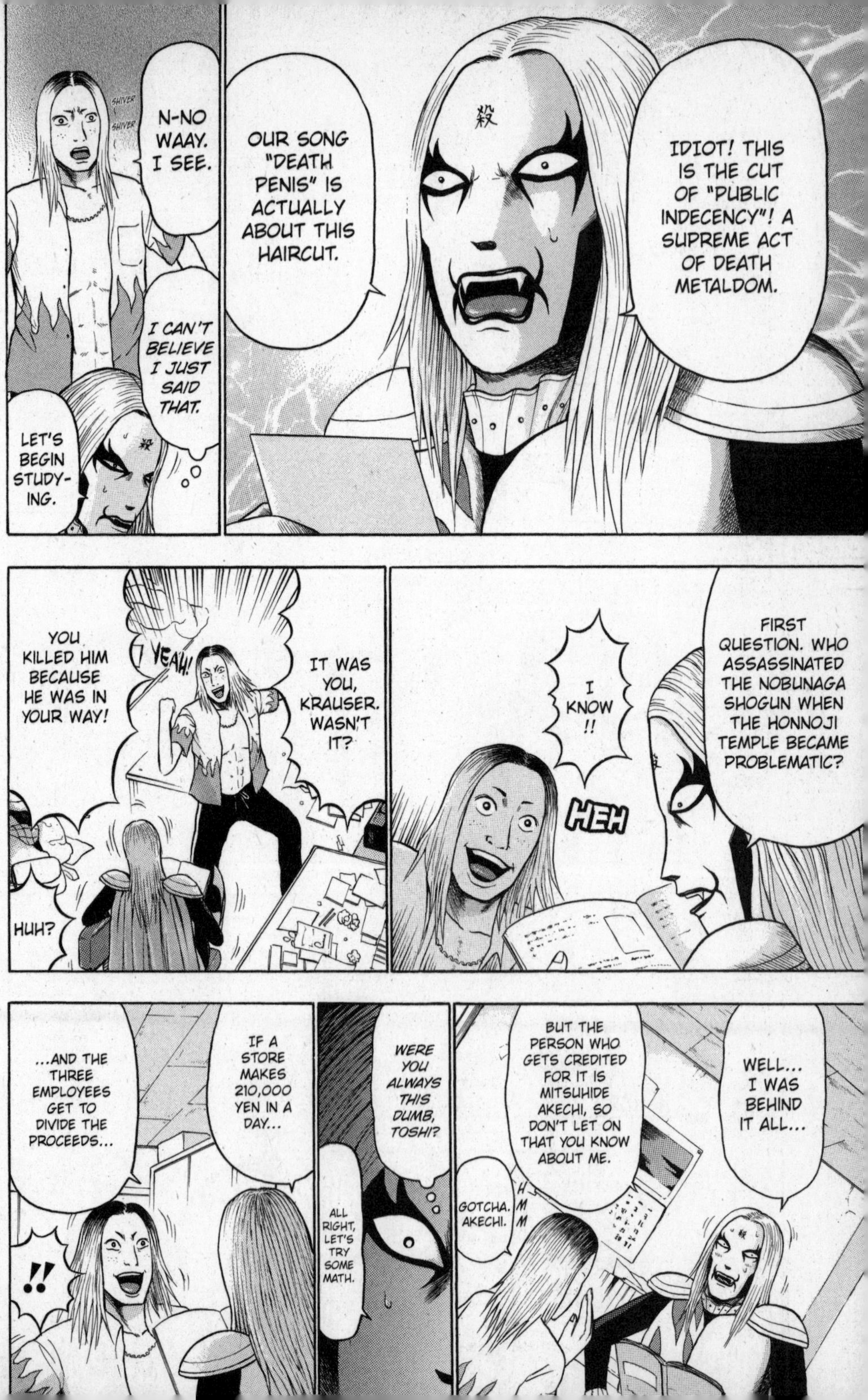
IDIOT! THIS IS THE CUT OF "PUBLIC INDECENCY"! A SUPREME ACT OF DEATH METALDOM.
OUR SONG "DEATH PENIS" IS ACTUALLY ABOUT THIS HAIRCUT.
SHIVER
SHIVER
N-NO WAAY. I SEE.
I CAN'T BELIEVE I JUST SAID THAT.
LET'S BEGIN STUDY-ING.
FIRST QUESTION. WHO ASSASSINATED THE NOBUNAGA SHOGUN WHEN THE HONNOJI TEMPLE BECAME PROBLEMATIC?
I KNOW !!
HEH
IT WAS YOU, KRAUSER. WASN'T IT?
YEAH!
YOU KILLED HIM BECAUSE HE WAS IN YOUR WAY!
HUH?
WELL... I WAS BEHIND IT ALL...
BUT THE PERSON WHO GETS CREDITED FOR IT IS MITSUHIDE AKECHI, SO DON'T LET ON THAT YOU KNOW ABOUT ME.
HMM
GOTCHA. AKECHI.
WERE YOU ALWAYS THIS DUMB, TOSHI?
ALL RIGHT, LET'S TRY SOME MATH.
IF A STORE MAKES 210,000 YEN IN A DAY...
...AND THE THREE EMPLOYEES GET TO DIVIDE THE PROCEEDS...
!!

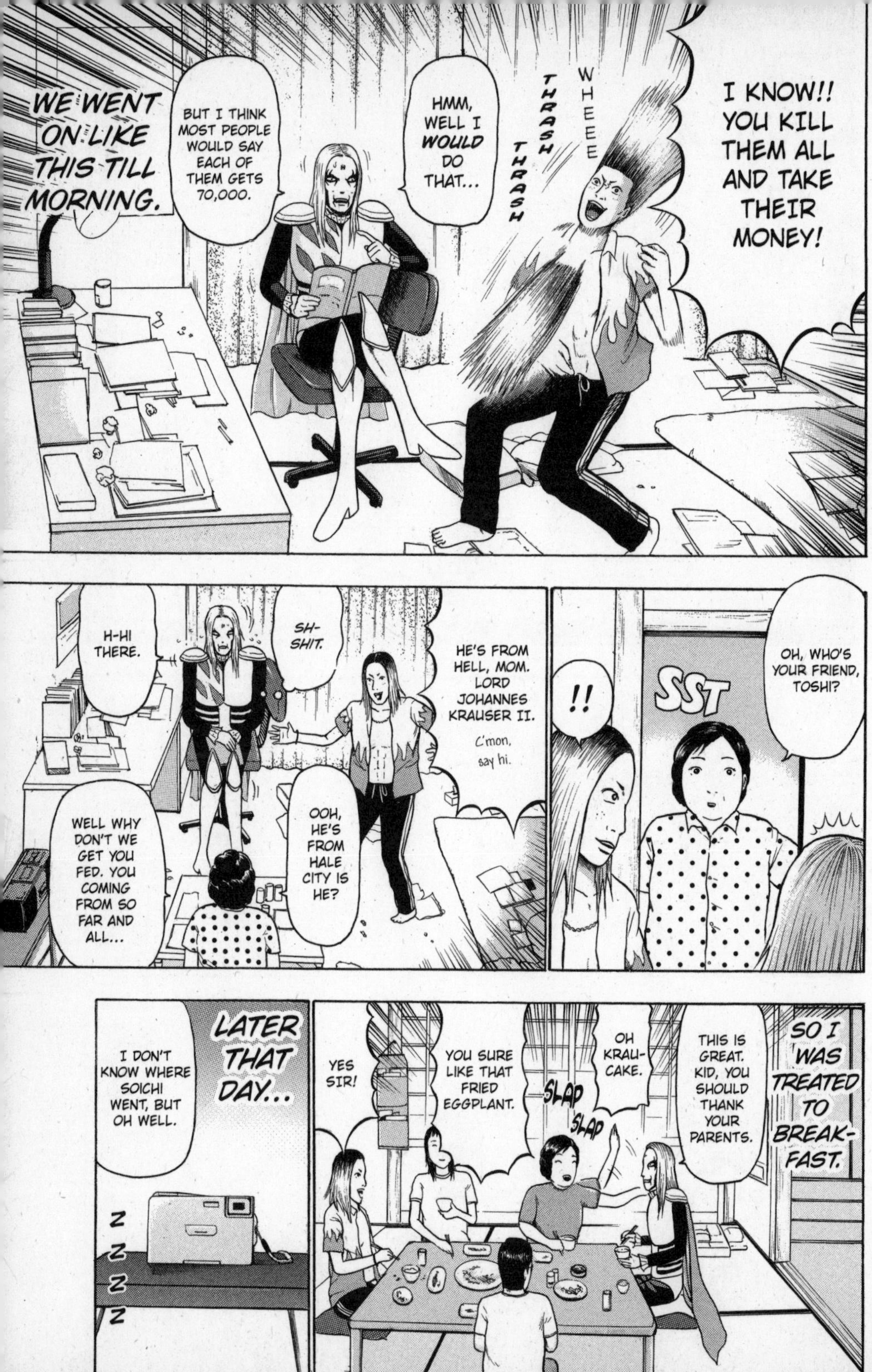

I KNOW!! YOU KILL THEM ALL AND TAKE THEIR MONEY!
WHEEE
THRASH THRASH
HMM, WELL I *WOULD* DO THAT...
BUT I THINK MOST PEOPLE WOULD SAY EACH OF THEM GETS 70,000.
WE WENT ON LIKE THIS TILL MORNING.
OH, WHO'S YOUR FRIEND, TOSHI?
SST
!!
HE'S FROM HELL, MOM. LORD JOHANNES KRAUSER II.
C'mon, say hi.
SH-SHIT.
H-HI THERE.
OOH, HE'S FROM HALE CITY IS HE?
WELL WHY DON'T WE GET YOU FED. YOU COMING FROM SO FAR AND ALL...
SO I WAS TREATED TO BREAKFAST.
THIS IS GREAT. KID, YOU SHOULD THANK YOUR PARENTS.
OH KRAUCAKE.
SLAP SLAP
YOU SURE LIKE THAT FRIED EGGPLANT.
YES SIR!
LATER THAT DAY...
I DON'T KNOW WHERE SOICHI WENT, BUT OH WELL.
Z Z Z Z

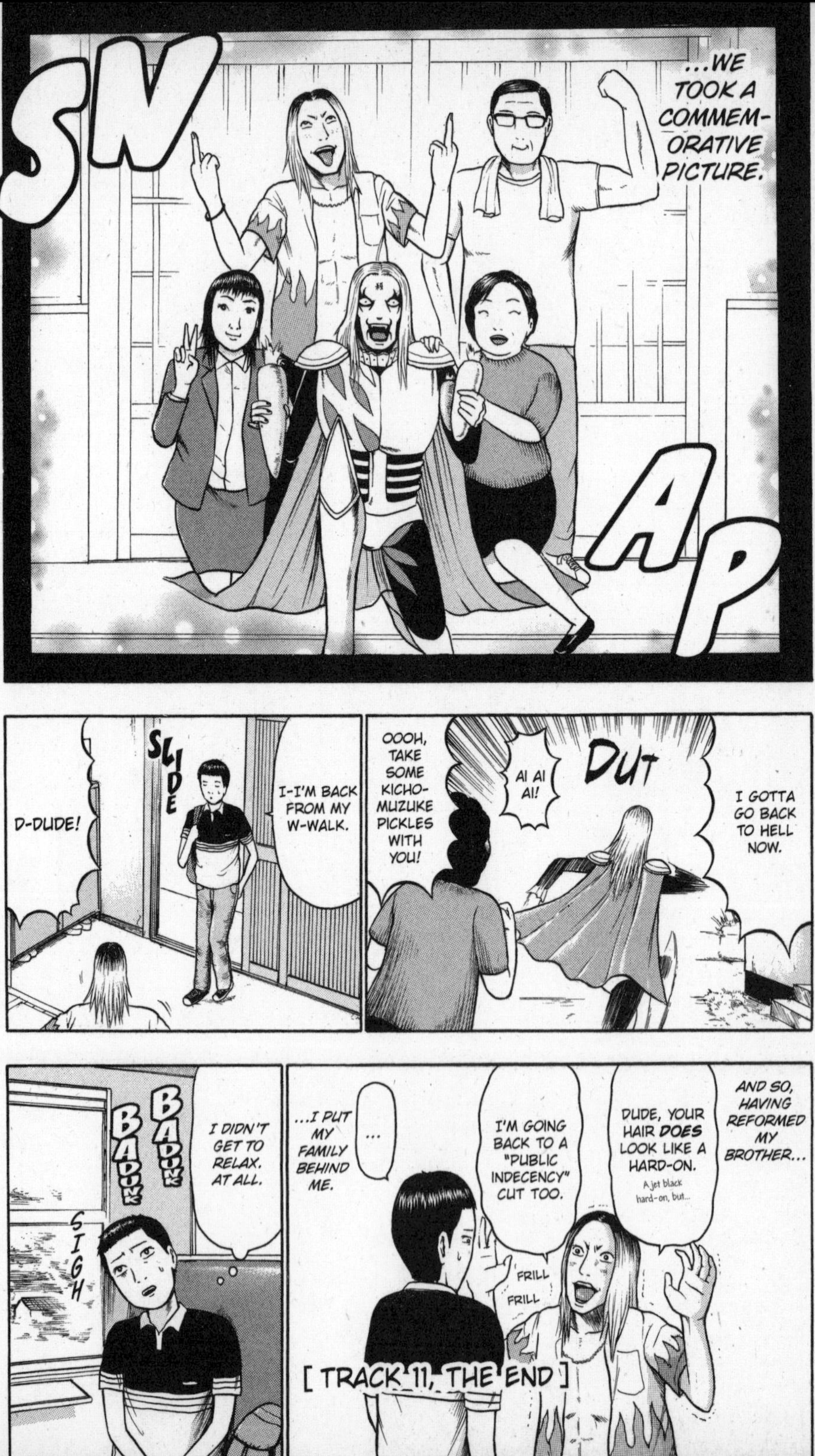
...WE TOOK A COMMEM-ORATIVE PICTURE.
SN
AP
I GOTTA GO BACK TO HELL NOW.
DUT
AI AI AI!
OOOH, TAKE SOME KICHO-MUZUKE PICKLES WITH YOU!
I-I'M BACK FROM MY W-WALK.
SLIDE
D-DUDE!
AND SO, HAVING REFORMED MY BROTHER...
DUDE, YOUR HAIR DOES LOOK LIKE A HARD-ON.
A jet black hard-on, but...
I'M GOING BACK TO A "PUBLIC INDECENCY" CUT TOO.
...
FRILL
FRILL
...I PUT MY FAMILY BEHIND ME.
[TRACK 11, THE END]
I DIDN'T GET TO RELAX. AT ALL.
BADUNK
BADUNK
SIGH

DMC LEXICON

KICHOMUZUKE PICKLES

Famous pickles from Oita Prefecture, made by pickling daikon radish, cucumber, or carrots, in a fermented broth with soy sauce. Wonderful consistency and taste. A great way to meet your daily intake of vegetables, especially if you don't like your greens.

Usage: Kichomuzuke Pickles are deeelish. Chomp chomp chomp chomp.

デトロイト・メタル・シティ

Detroit Metal City

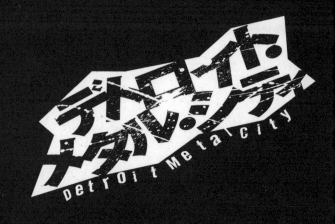

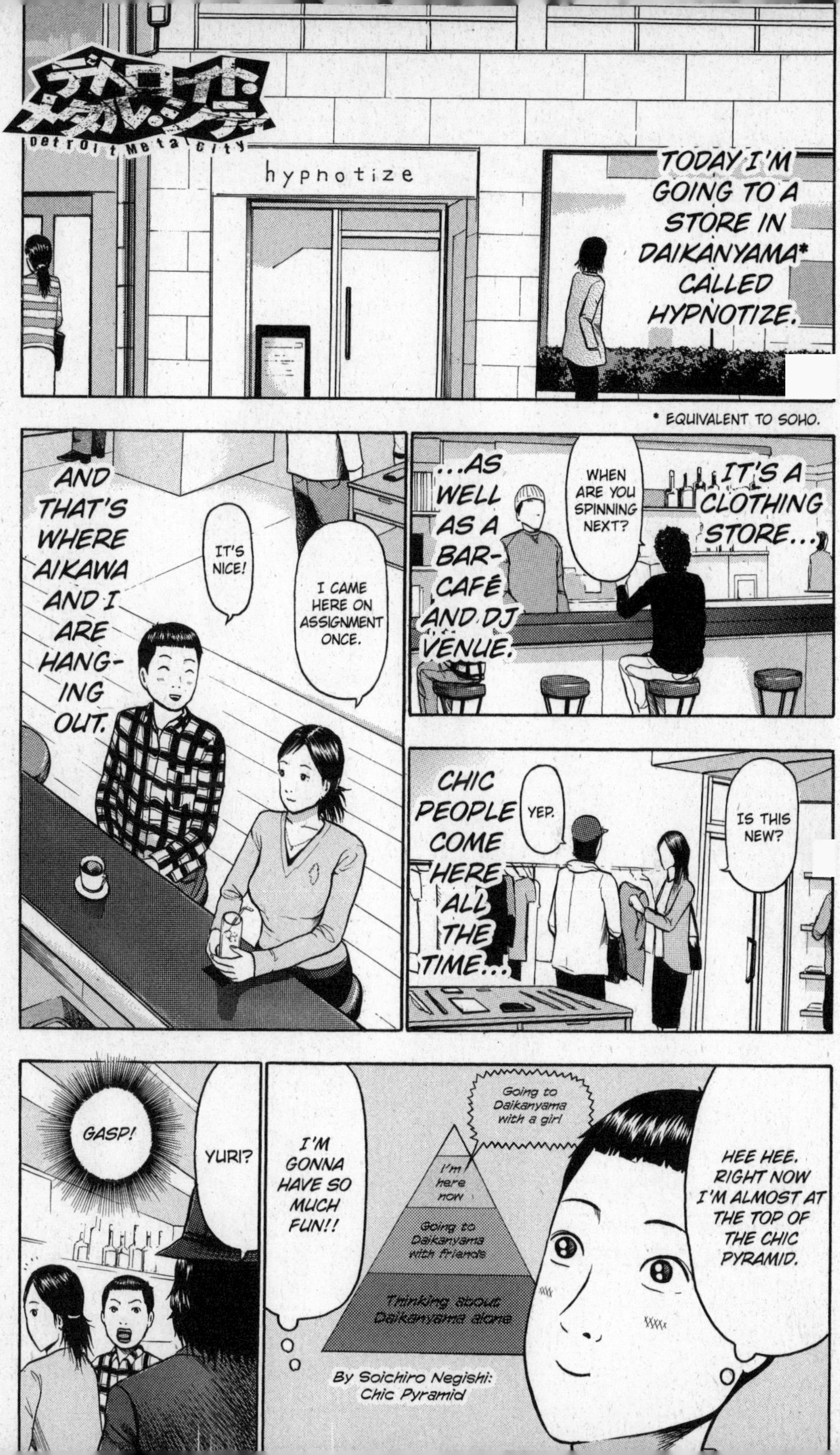
Detroit Metal City
hypnotize
TODAY I'M GOING TO A STORE IN DAIKANYAMA* CALLED HYPNOTIZE.
IT'S A CLOTHING STORE...
...AS WELL AS A BAR-CAFÉ AND DJ VENUE.
WHEN ARE YOU SPINNING NEXT?
IS THIS NEW?
CHIC PEOPLE COME HERE ALL THE TIME...
YEP.
AND THAT'S WHERE AIKAWA AND I ARE HANGING OUT.
I CAME HERE ON ASSIGNMENT ONCE.
IT'S NICE!
HEE HEE. RIGHT NOW I'M ALMOST AT THE TOP OF THE CHIC PYRAMID.
Going to Daikanyama with a girl
I'm here now
Going to Daikanyama with friends
Thinking about Daikanyama alone
By Soichiro Negishi: Chic Pyramid
I'M GONNA HAVE SO MUCH FUN!!
YURI?
GASP!
* EQUIVALENT TO SOHO.

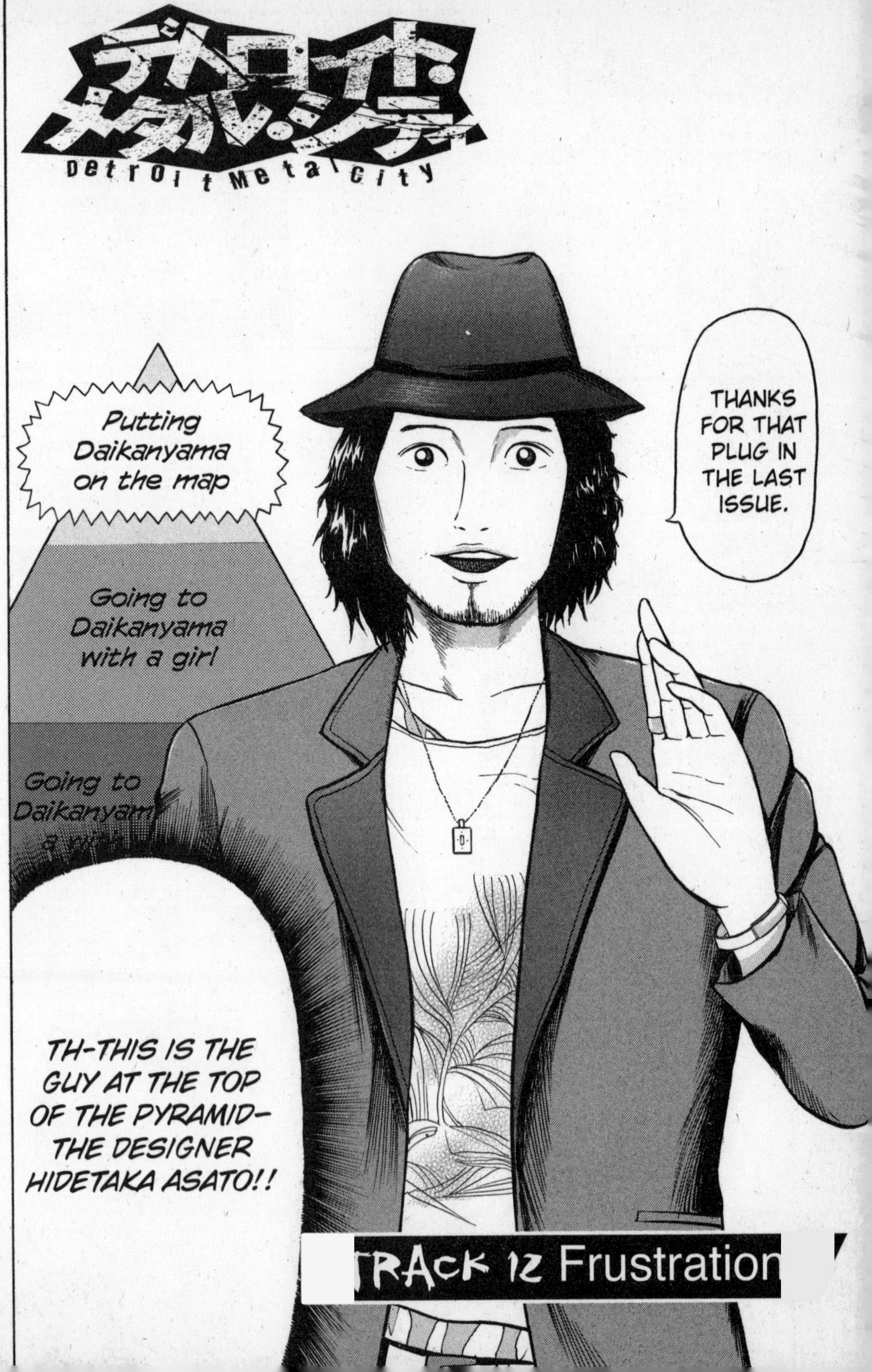
DetrOit Metal city
THANKS FOR THAT PLUG IN THE LAST ISSUE.
Putting Daikanyama on the map
Going to Daikanyama with a girl
Going to Daikanyam
TH-THIS IS THE GUY AT THE TOP OF THE PYRAMID- THE DESIGNER HIDETAKA ASATO!!

TRACK 12 Frustration

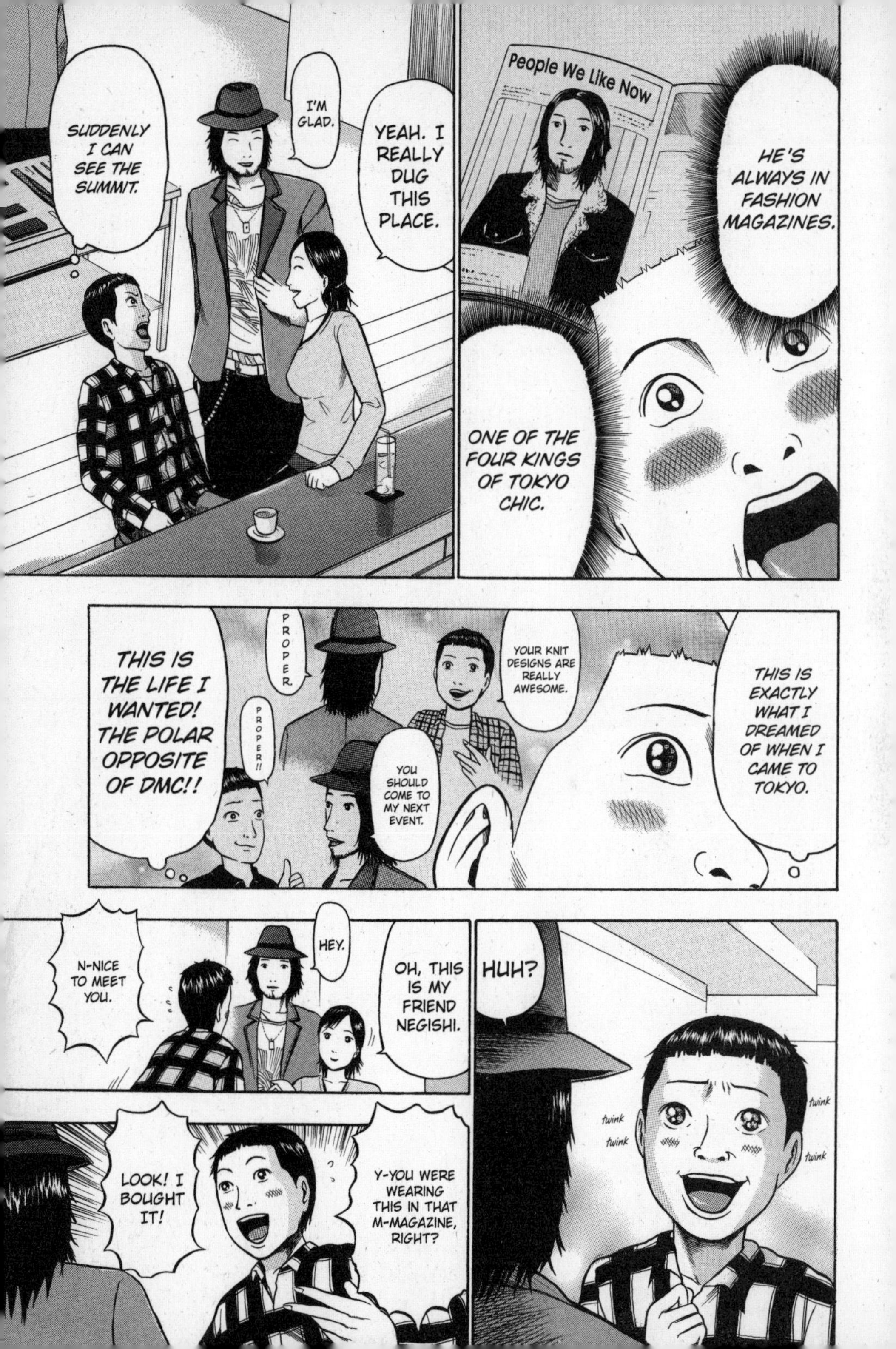
People We Like Now
HE'S ALWAYS IN FASHION MAGAZINES.
ONE OF THE FOUR KINGS OF TOKYO CHIC.
YEAH. I REALLY DUG THIS PLACE.
I'M GLAD.
SUDDENLY I CAN SEE THE SUMMIT.
THIS IS EXACTLY WHAT I DREAMED OF WHEN I CAME TO TOKYO.
YOUR KNIT DESIGNS ARE REALLY AWESOME.
PROPER.
PROPER!!
YOU SHOULD COME TO MY NEXT EVENT.
THIS IS THE LIFE I WANTED! THE POLAR OPPOSITE OF DMC!!
HUH?
twink
twink
twink
twink
OH, THIS IS MY FRIEND NEGISHI.
HEY.
N-NICE TO MEET YOU.
Y-YOU WERE WEARING THIS IN THAT M-MAGAZINE, RIGHT?
LOOK! I BOUGHT IT!

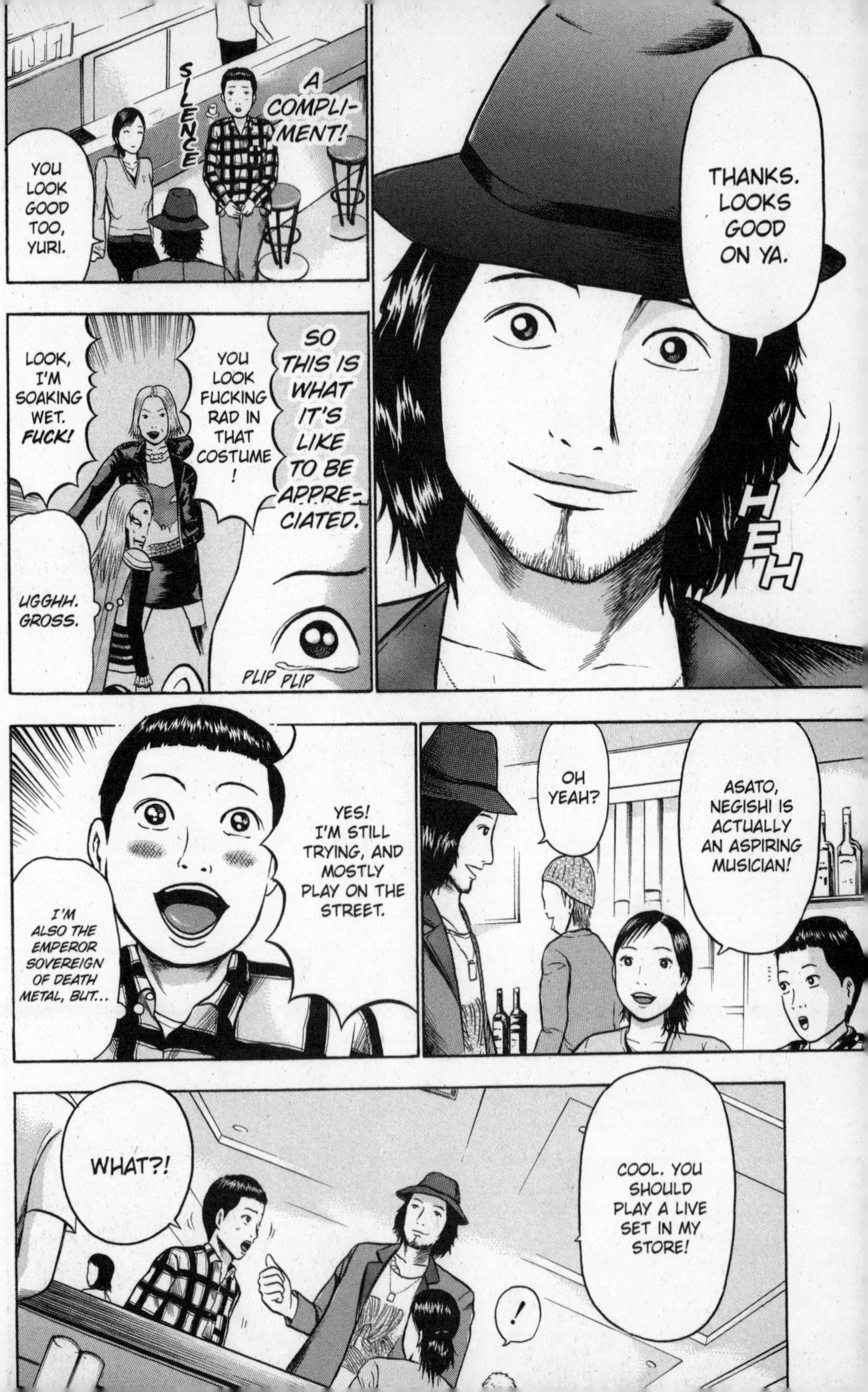
THANKS. LOOKS GOOD ON YA.
HEH
A COMPLIMENT!
SILENCE
YOU LOOK GOOD TOO, YURI.
SO THIS IS WHAT IT'S LIKE TO BE APPRECIATED.
YOU LOOK FUCKING RAD IN THAT COSTUME!
LOOK, I'M SOAKING WET. FUCK!
UGGHH. GROSS.
PLIP PLIP
ASATO, NEGISHI IS ACTUALLY AN ASPIRING MUSICIAN!
OH YEAH?
YES! I'M STILL TRYING, AND MOSTLY PLAY ON THE STREET.
I'M ALSO THE EMPEROR SOVEREIGN OF DEATH METAL, BUT...
COOL. YOU SHOULD PLAY A LIVE SET IN MY STORE!
!
WHAT?!

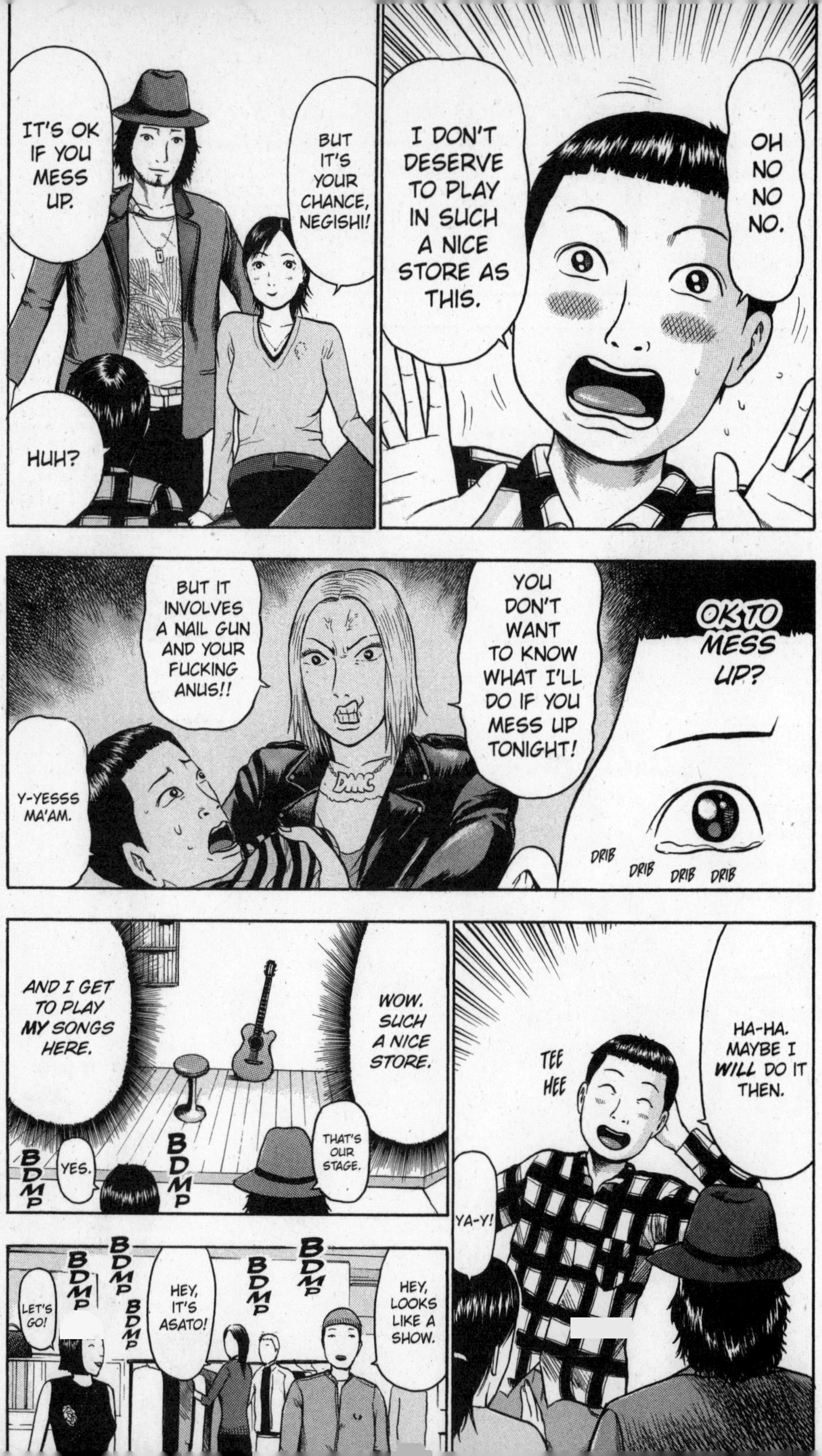
OH NO NO NO.
I DON'T DESERVE TO PLAY IN SUCH A NICE STORE AS THIS.
BUT IT'S YOUR CHANCE, NEGISHI!
IT'S OK IF YOU MESS UP.
HUH?
OK TO MESS UP?
DRIB DRIB DRIB DRIB
YOU DON'T WANT TO KNOW WHAT I'LL DO IF YOU MESS UP TONIGHT!
BUT IT INVOLVES A NAIL GUN AND YOUR FUCKING ANUS!!
Y-YESSS MA'AM.
HA-HA. MAYBE I WILL DO IT THEN.
TEE HEE
YA-Y!
WOW. SUCH A NICE STORE.
AND I GET TO PLAY MY SONGS HERE.
THAT'S OUR STAGE.
BDMP
YES.
BDMP
BDMP
HEY, LOOKS LIKE A SHOW.
BDMP
HEY, IT'S ASATO!
BDMP
BDMP
LET'S GO!

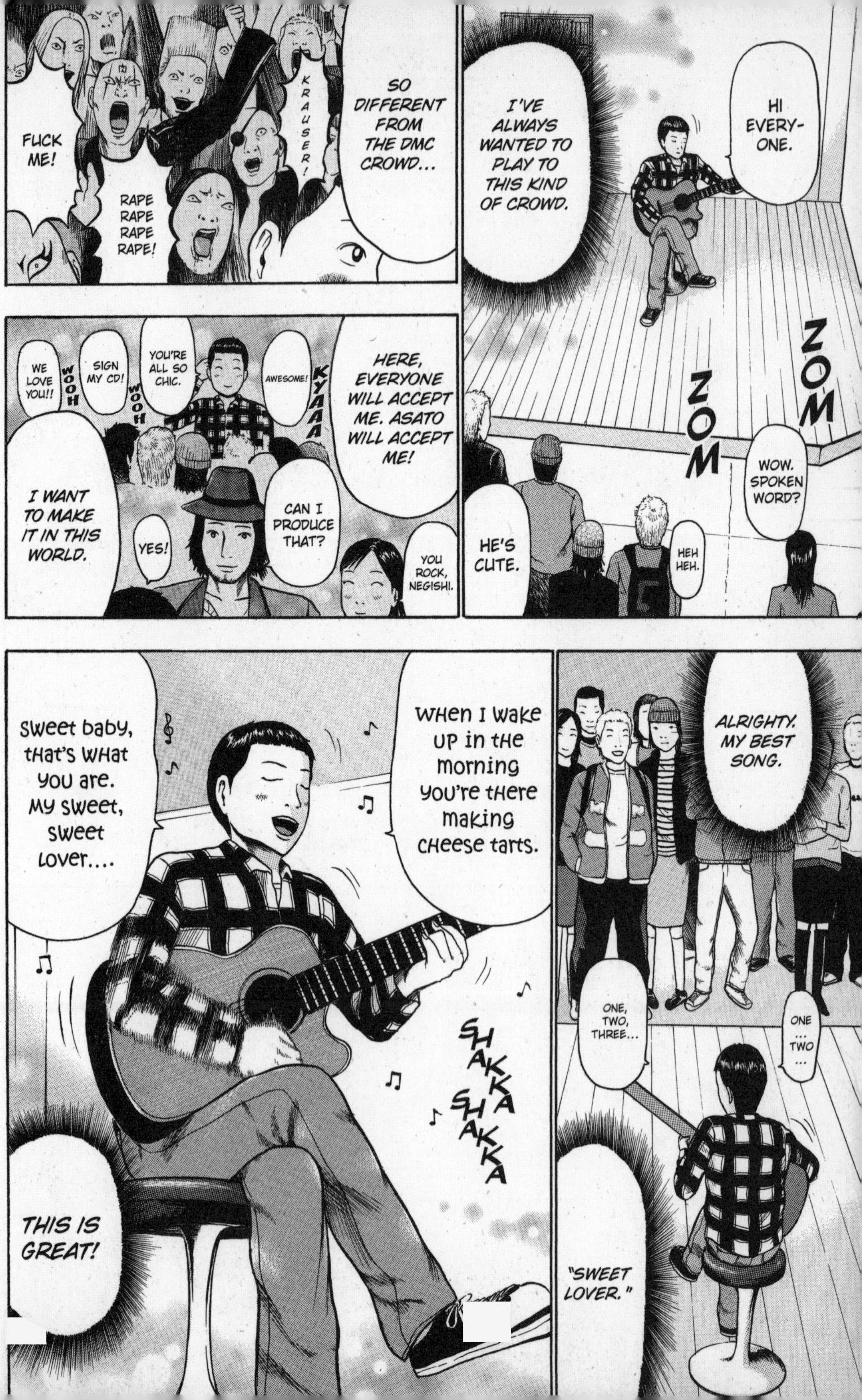
HI EVERY-ONE.
I'VE ALWAYS WANTED TO PLAY TO THIS KIND OF CROWD.
ZOM
ZOM
WOW. SPOKEN WORD?
HEH HEH.
HE'S CUTE.
SO DIFFERENT FROM THE DMC CROWD...
KRAUSER!
RAPE RAPE RAPE RAPE!
FUCK ME!
HERE, EVERYONE WILL ACCEPT ME. ASATO WILL ACCEPT ME!
KYAAA
AWESOME!
YOU'RE ALL SO CHIC.
WOOH
SIGN MY CD!
WOOH
WE LOVE YOU!!
CAN I PRODUCE THAT?
YOU ROCK, NEGISHI.
YES!
I WANT TO MAKE IT IN THIS WORLD.
ALRIGHTY. MY BEST SONG.
ONE ... TWO ...
ONE, TWO, THREE...
"SWEET LOVER."
When I wake up in the morning you're there making cheese tarts.
Sweet baby, that's what you are. My sweet, sweet lover....
SHAKKA SHAKKA
THIS IS GREAT!

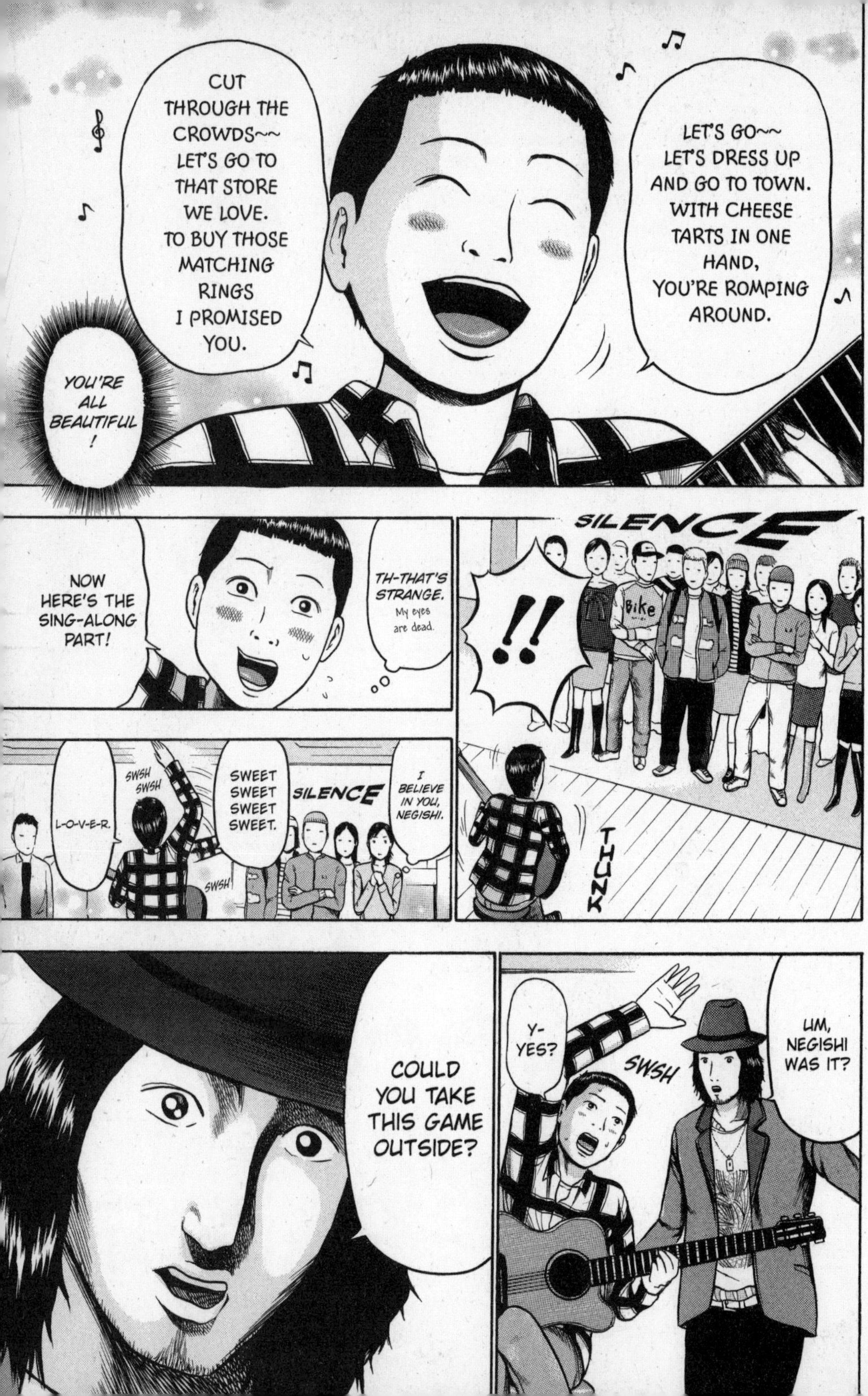
LET'S GO~~ LET'S DRESS UP AND GO TO TOWN. WITH CHEESE TARTS IN ONE HAND, YOU'RE ROMPING AROUND.
CUT THROUGH THE CROWDS~~ LET'S GO TO THAT STORE WE LOVE. TO BUY THOSE MATCHING RINGS I PROMISED YOU.
YOU'RE ALL BEAUTIFUL!
SILENCE
!!
THUNK
TH-THAT'S STRANGE. My eyes are dead.
NOW HERE'S THE SING-ALONG PART!
I BELIEVE IN YOU, NEGISHI.
SILENCE
SWEET SWEET SWEET SWEET.
SWSH SWSH
L-O-V-E-R.
SWSH
UM, NEGISHI WAS IT?
SWSH
Y-YES?
COULD YOU TAKE THIS GAME OUTSIDE?

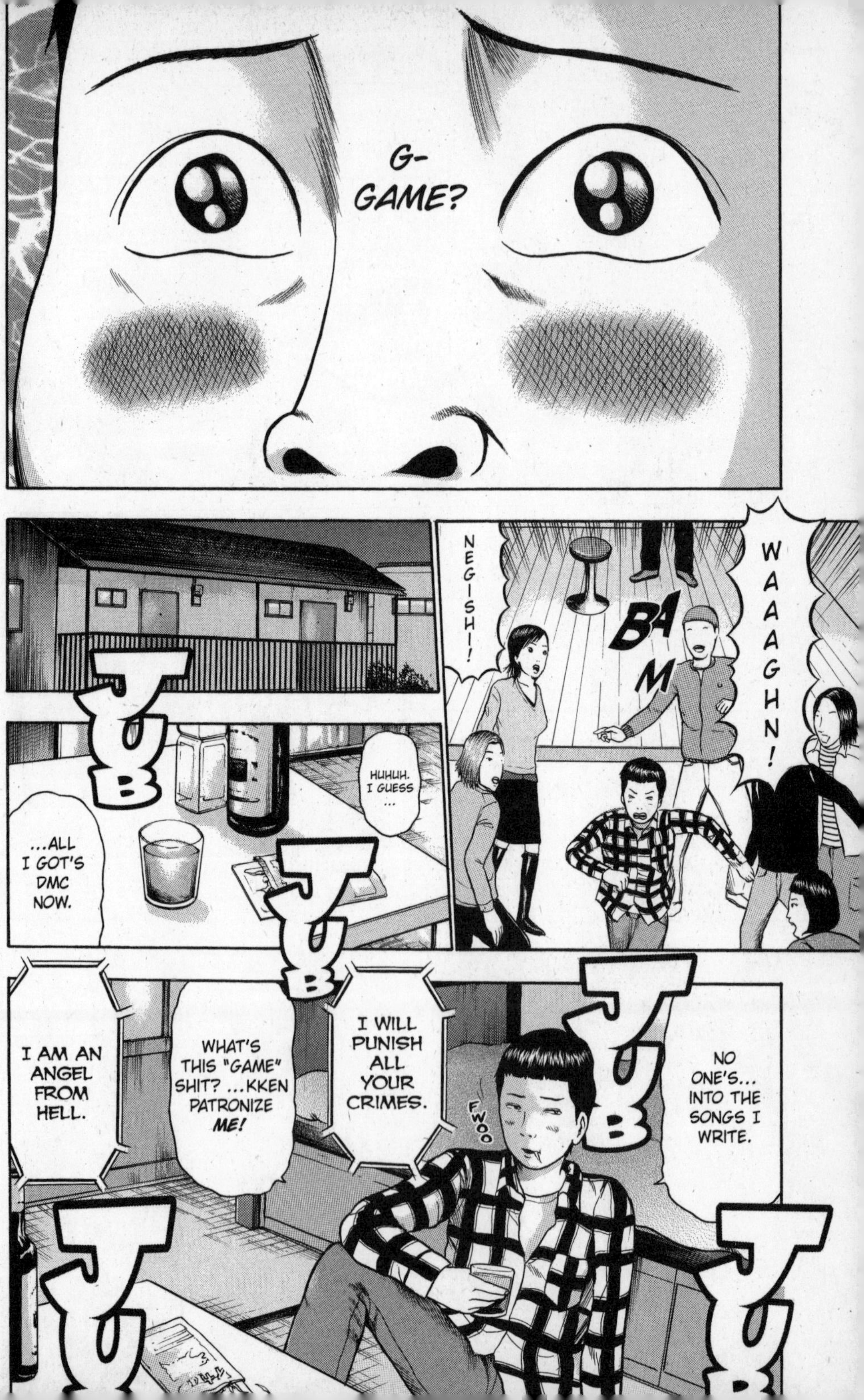
G- GAME?
WAAAGHN!
BAM
NEGISHI!
JUB
HUHUH. I GUESS ...
...ALL I GOT'S DMC NOW.
JUB
JUB
NO ONE'S... INTO THE SONGS I WRITE.
FWOO
I WILL PUNISH ALL YOUR CRIMES.
WHAT'S THIS "GAME" SHIT? ...KKEN PATRONIZE *ME!*
I AM AN ANGEL FROM HELL.
JUB
JUB

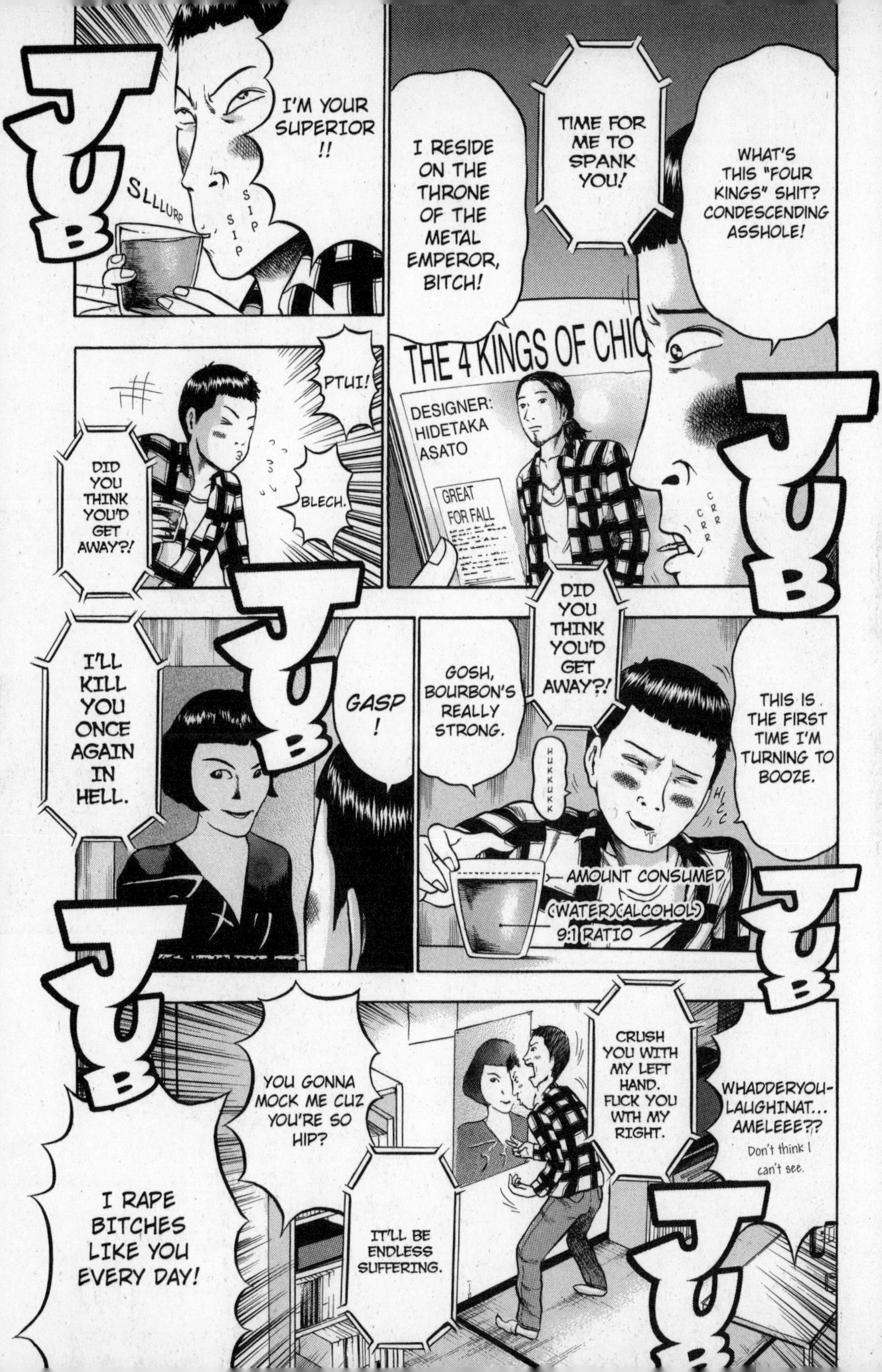
WHAT'S THIS "FOUR KINGS" SHIT? CONDESCENDING ASSHOLE!
TIME FOR ME TO SPANK YOU!
I RESIDE ON THE THRONE OF THE METAL EMPEROR, BITCH!
THE 4 KINGS OF CHIC
DESIGNER: HIDETAKA ASATO
GREAT FOR FALL
JUB
CRR CRR
JUB
I'M YOUR SUPERIOR!!
SLLLURP
SIP SIP
PTUI!
BLECH.
DID YOU THINK YOU'D GET AWAY?!
JUB
THIS IS THE FIRST TIME I'M TURNING TO BOOZE.
DID YOU THINK YOU'D GET AWAY?!
GOSH, BOURBON'S REALLY STRONG.
HUKKUKK
HIC
AMOUNT CONSUMED
(WATER)(ALCOHOL) 9:1 RATIO
JUB
GASP!
I'LL KILL YOU ONCE AGAIN IN HELL.
JUB
WHADDERYOU-LAUGHINAT... AMELEEE??
Don't think I can't see.
CRUSH YOU WITH MY LEFT HAND. FUCK YOU WTH MY RIGHT.
YOU GONNA MOCK ME CUZ YOU'RE SO HIP?
IT'LL BE ENDLESS SUFFERING.
I RAPE BITCHES LIKE YOU EVERY DAY!
JUB

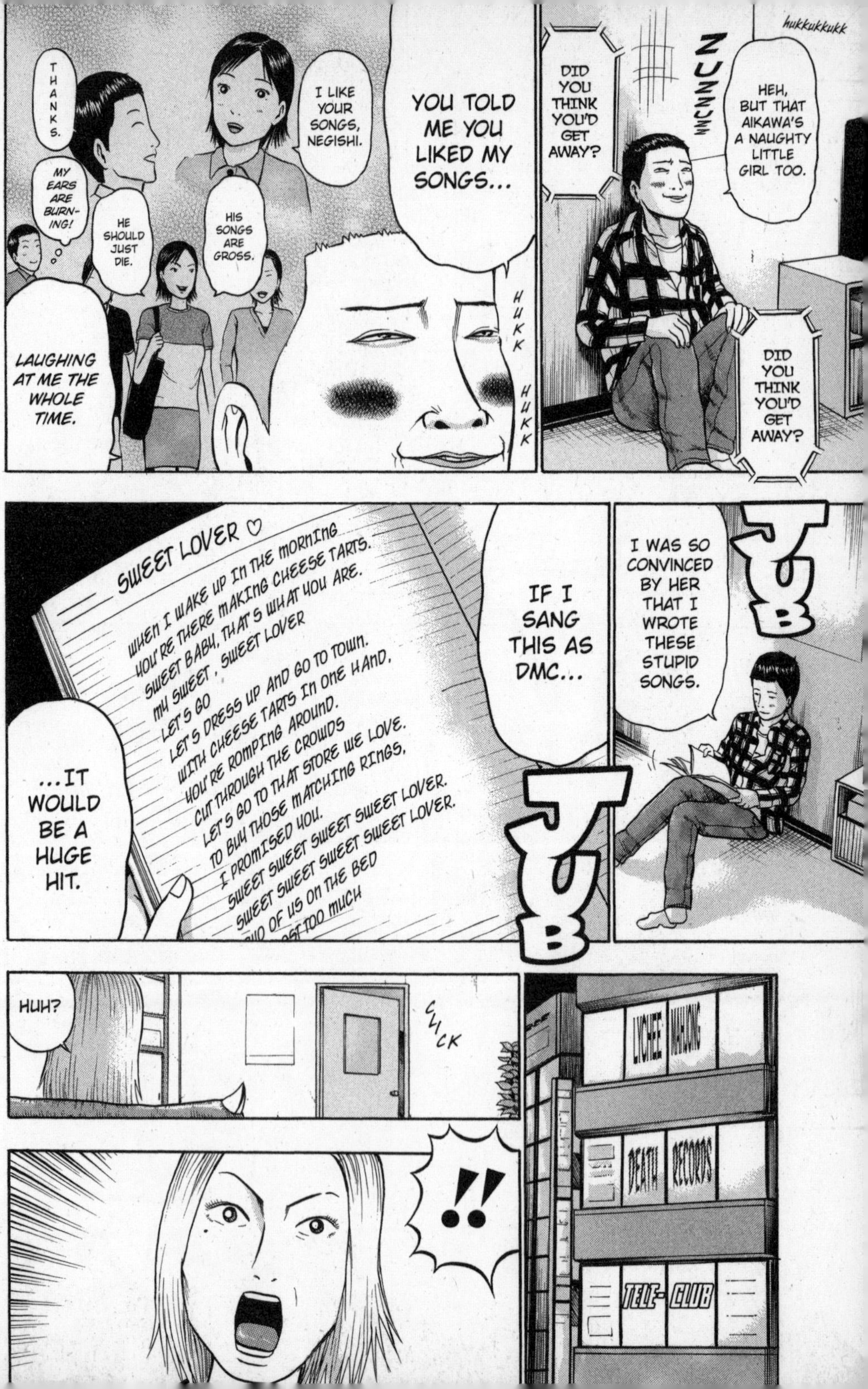
hukkukkukk
HEH, BUT THAT AIKAWA'S A NAUGHTY LITTLE GIRL TOO.
DID YOU THINK YOU'D GET AWAY?
DID YOU THINK YOU'D GET AWAY?
YOU TOLD ME YOU LIKED MY SONGS...
HUKK HUKK
I LIKE YOUR SONGS, NEGISHI.
THANKS.
MY EARS ARE BURNING!
HIS SONGS ARE GROSS.
HE SHOULD JUST DIE.
LAUGHING AT ME THE WHOLE TIME.
JUB
I WAS SO CONVINCED BY HER THAT I WROTE THESE STUPID SONGS.
JUB
IF I SANG THIS AS DMC...
SWEET LOVER ♡
WHEN I WAKE UP IN THE MORNING
YOU'RE THERE MAKING CHEESE TARTS.
SWEET BABY, THAT'S WHAT YOU ARE.
MY SWEET, SWEET LOVER
LET'S GO
LET'S DRESS UP AND GO TO TOWN.
WITH CHEESE TARTS IN ONE HAND,
YOU'RE ROMPING AROUND.
CUT THROUGH THE CROWDS
LET'S GO TO THAT STORE WE LOVE.
TO BUY THOSE MATCHING RINGS,
I PROMISED YOU.
SWEET SWEET SWEET SWEET LOVER.
SWEET SWEET SWEET SWEET LOVER.
...IT WOULD BE A HUGE HIT.
LYCHEE
MAHJONG
DEATH
RECORDS
TELE-CLUB
HUH?
CLICK
!!

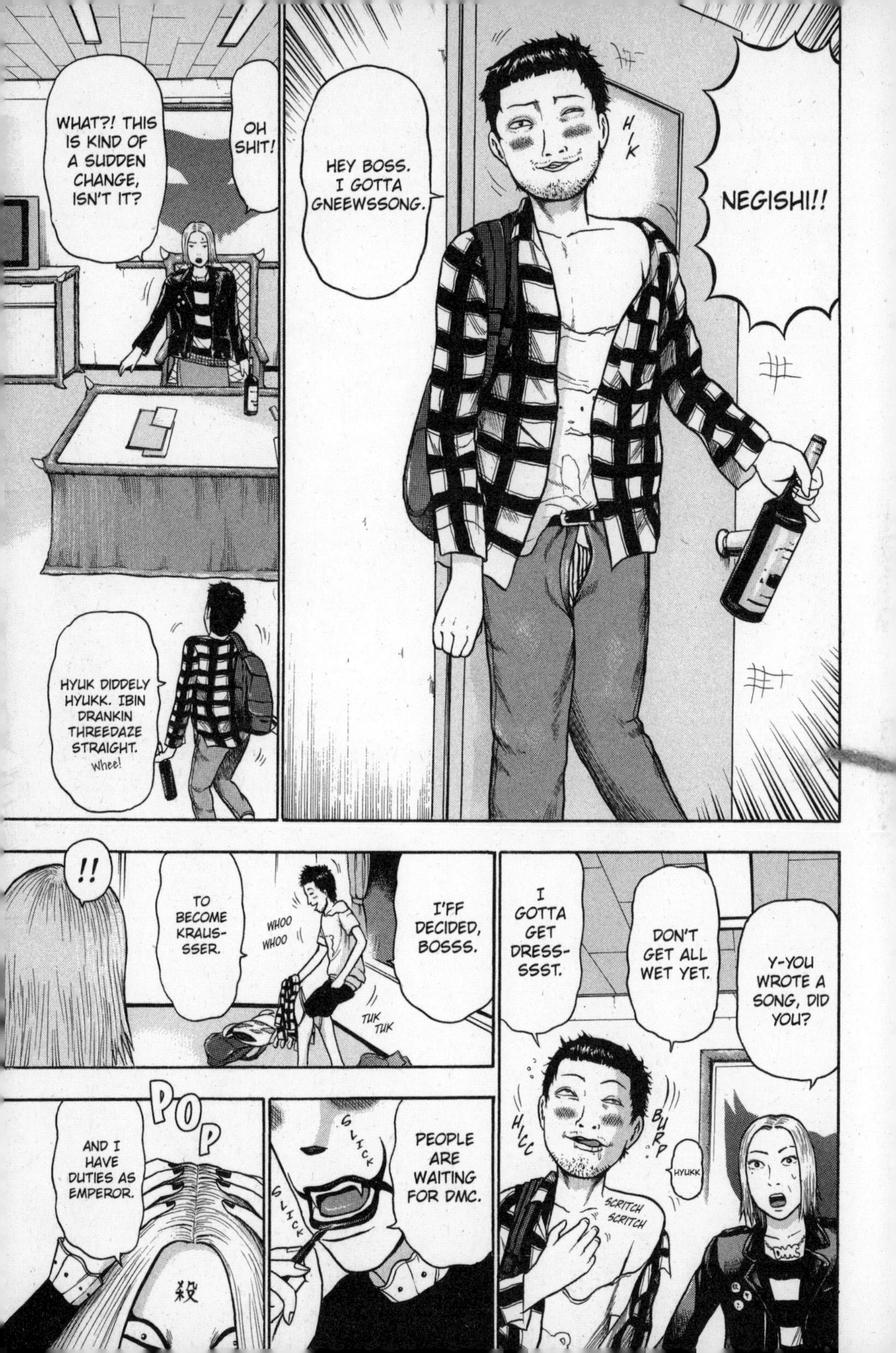
NEGISHI!!
HIK
HEY BOSS. I GOTTA GNEEWSSONG.
OH SHIT!
WHAT?! THIS IS KIND OF A SUDDEN CHANGE, ISN'T IT?
HYUK DIDDELY HYUKK. IBIN DRANKIN THREEDAZE STRAIGHT.
Whee!
Y-YOU WROTE A SONG, DID YOU?
DON'T GET ALL WET YET.
I GOTTA GET DRESS-SSST.
BURP
HYUKK
HICC
SCRITCH SCRITCH
I'FF DECIDED, BOSSS.
WHOO WHOO
TO BECOME KRAUS-SSER.
TUK TUK
!!
PEOPLE ARE WAITING FOR DMC.
SLICK
SLICK
POP
AND I HAVE DUTIES AS EMPEROR.
殺

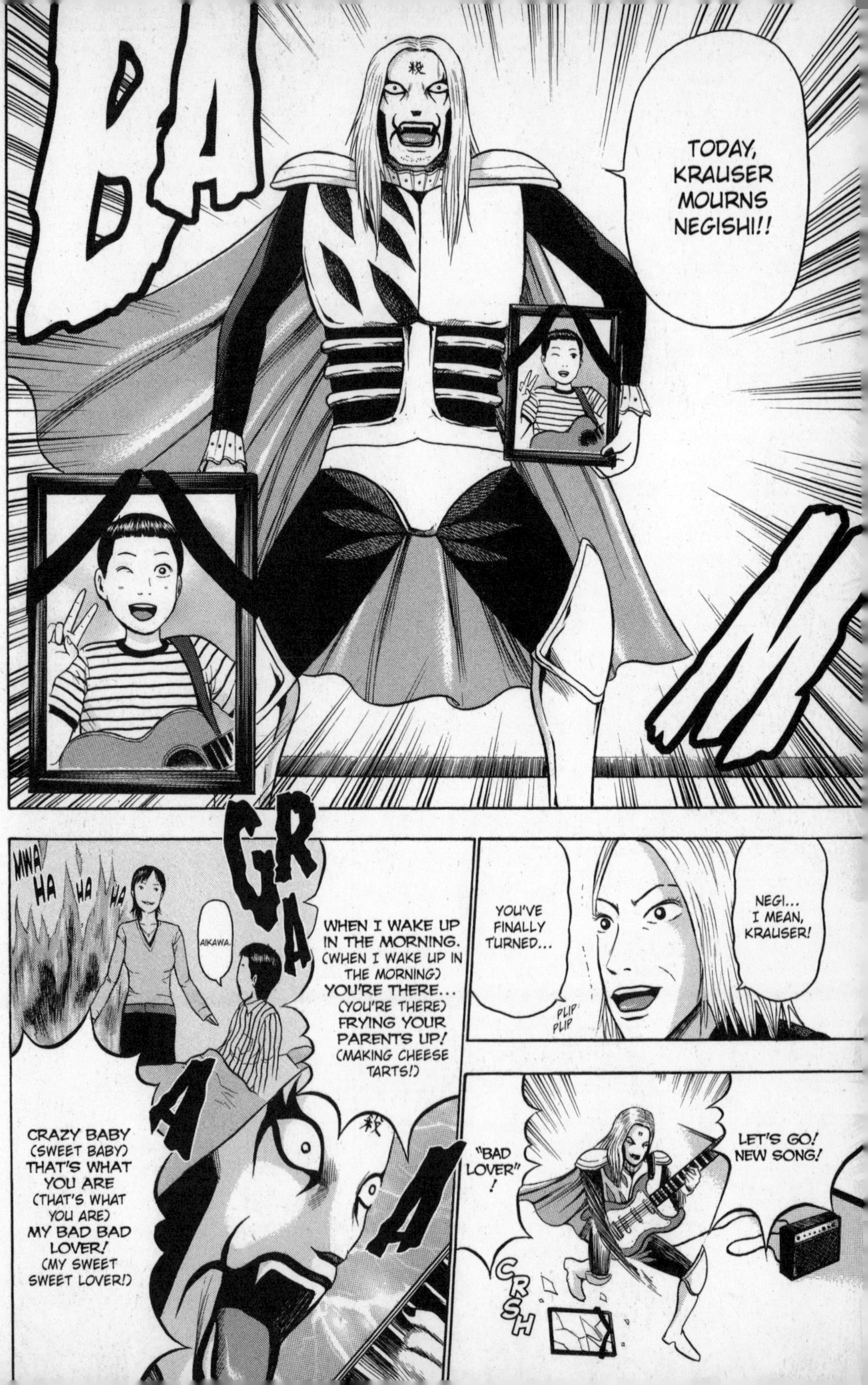
BAM
TODAY, KRAUSER MOURNS NEGISHI!!
NEGI... I MEAN, KRAUSER!
YOU'VE FINALLY TURNED...
PLIP PLIP
LET'S GO! NEW SONG!
"BAD LOVER"!
CRSH
MWA HA HA HA
AIKAWA.
GRAAA
WHEN I WAKE UP IN THE MORNING. (WHEN I WAKE UP IN THE MORNING) YOU'RE THERE... (YOU'RE THERE) FRYING YOUR PARENTS UP! (MAKING CHEESE TARTS!)
CRAZY BABY (SWEET BABY) THAT'S WHAT YOU ARE (THAT'S WHAT YOU ARE) MY BAD BAD LOVER! (MY SWEET SWEET LOVER!)

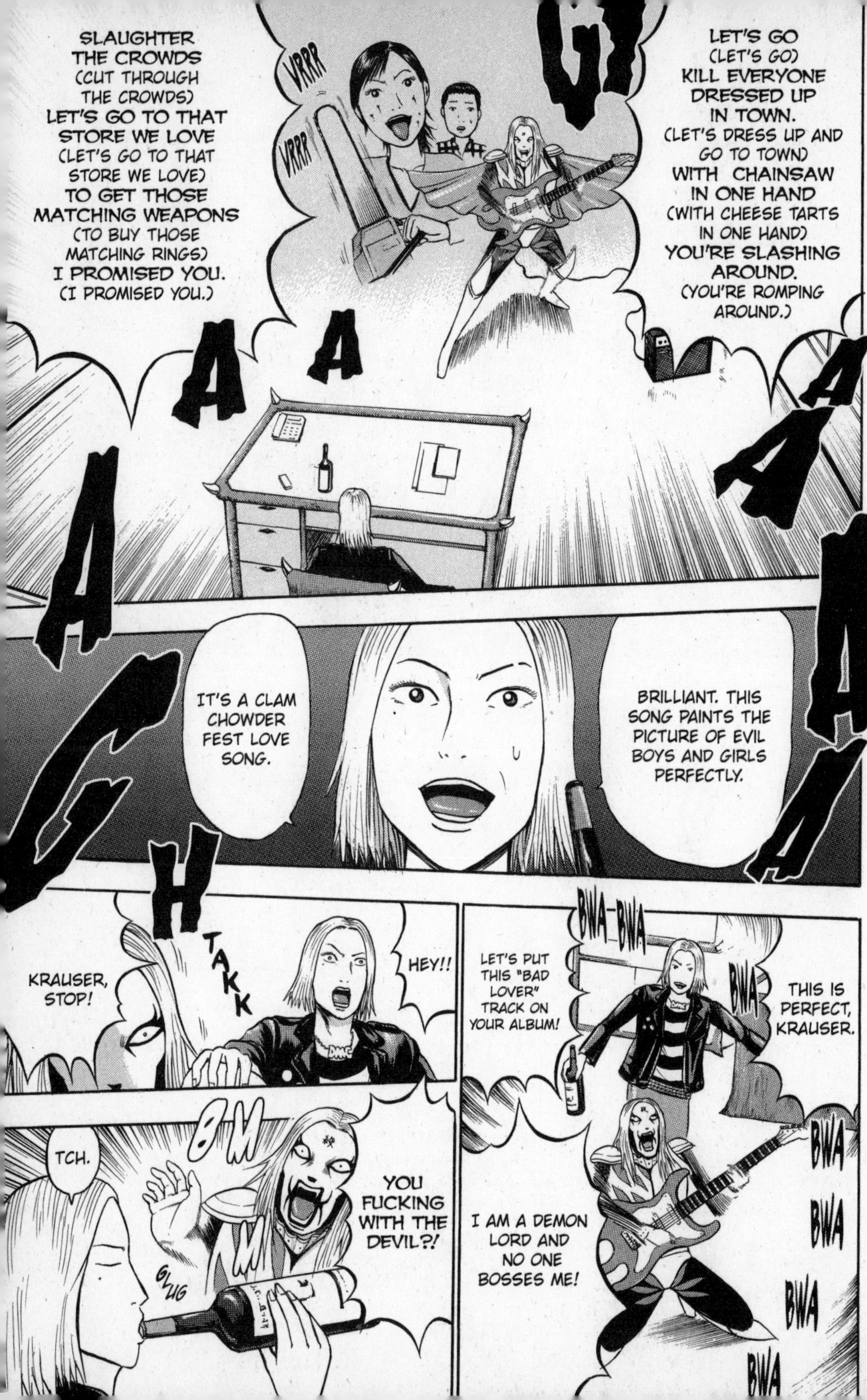
LET'S GO (LET'S GO) KILL EVERYONE DRESSED UP IN TOWN. (LET'S DRESS UP AND GO TO TOWN) WITH CHAINSAW IN ONE HAND (WITH CHEESE TARTS IN ONE HAND) YOU'RE SLASHING AROUND. (YOU'RE ROMPING AROUND.)
VRRR
VRRR
SLAUGHTER THE CROWDS (CUT THROUGH THE CROWDS) LET'S GO TO THAT STORE WE LOVE (LET'S GO TO THAT STORE WE LOVE) TO GET THOSE MATCHING WEAPONS (TO BUY THOSE MATCHING RINGS) I PROMISED YOU. (I PROMISED YOU.)
GYAAAAAAAGH
BRILLIANT. THIS SONG PAINTS THE PICTURE OF EVIL BOYS AND GIRLS PERFECTLY.
IT'S A CLAM CHOWDER FEST LOVE SONG.
BWA BWA
BWA
THIS IS PERFECT, KRAUSER.
LET'S PUT THIS "BAD LOVER" TRACK ON YOUR ALBUM!
I AM A DEMON LORD AND NO ONE BOSSES ME!
BWA
BWA
BWA
BWA
HEY!!
TAKK
KRAUSER, STOP!
YOU FUCKING WITH THE DEVIL?!
TCH.
GLUG

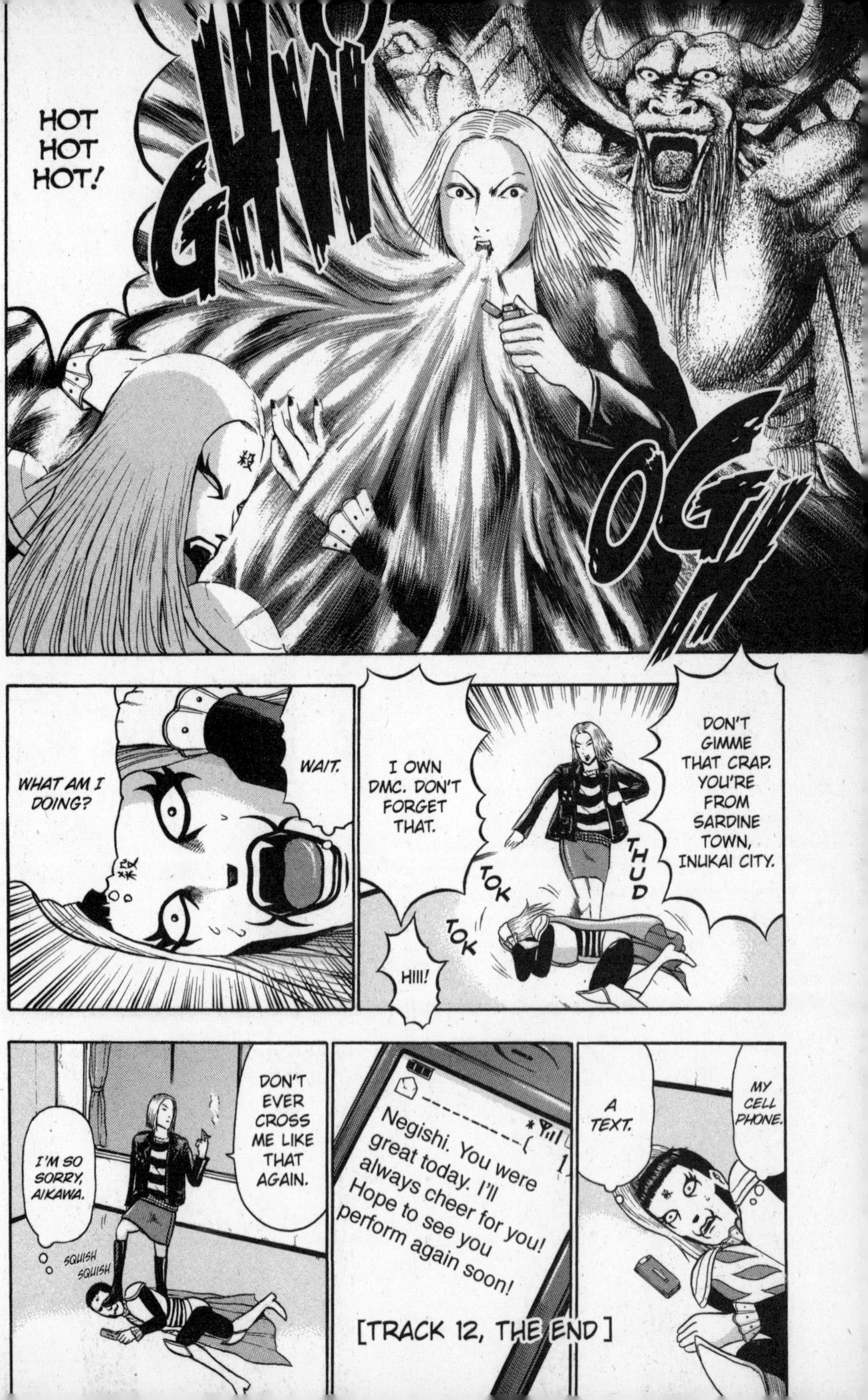
HOT HOT HOT!
DON'T GIMME THAT CRAP. YOU'RE FROM SARDINE TOWN, INUKAI CITY.
THUD
I OWN DMC. DON'T FORGET THAT.
TOK
TOK
HIII!
WAIT.
WHAT AM I DOING?
MY CELL PHONE.
A TEXT.
Negishi. You were great today. I'll always cheer for you! Hope to see you perform again soon!
[TRACK 12, THE END]
DON'T EVER CROSS ME LIKE THAT AGAIN.
I'M SO SORRY, AIKAWA.
SQUISH SQUISH

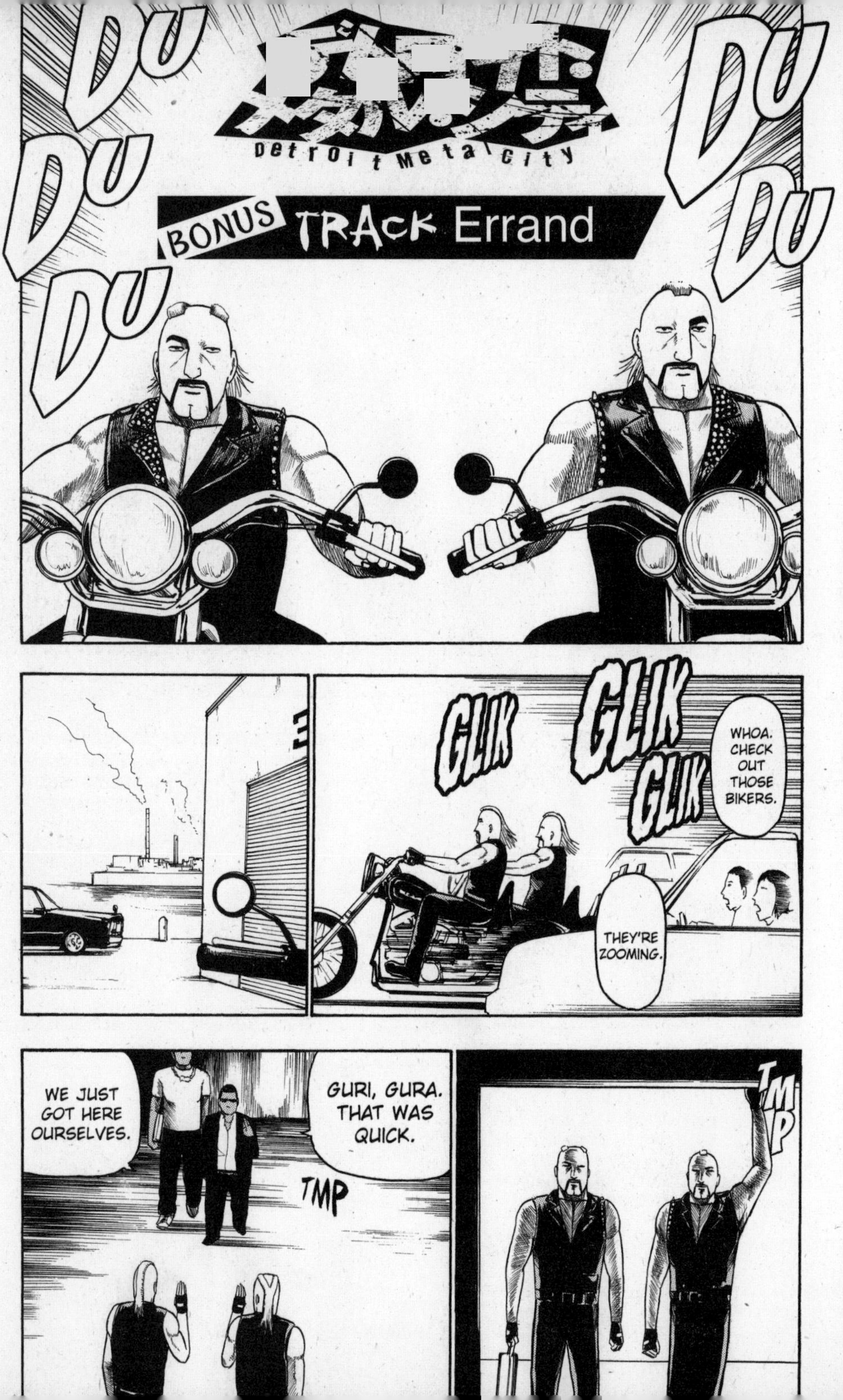
DU DU DU
DU DU DU
Detroit Metal City
BONUS TRACK Errand
GLIK GLIK GLIK
WHOA. CHECK OUT THOSE BIKERS.
THEY'RE ZOOMING.
TMP
GURI, GURA. THAT WAS QUICK.
WE JUST GOT HERE OURSELVES.
TMP

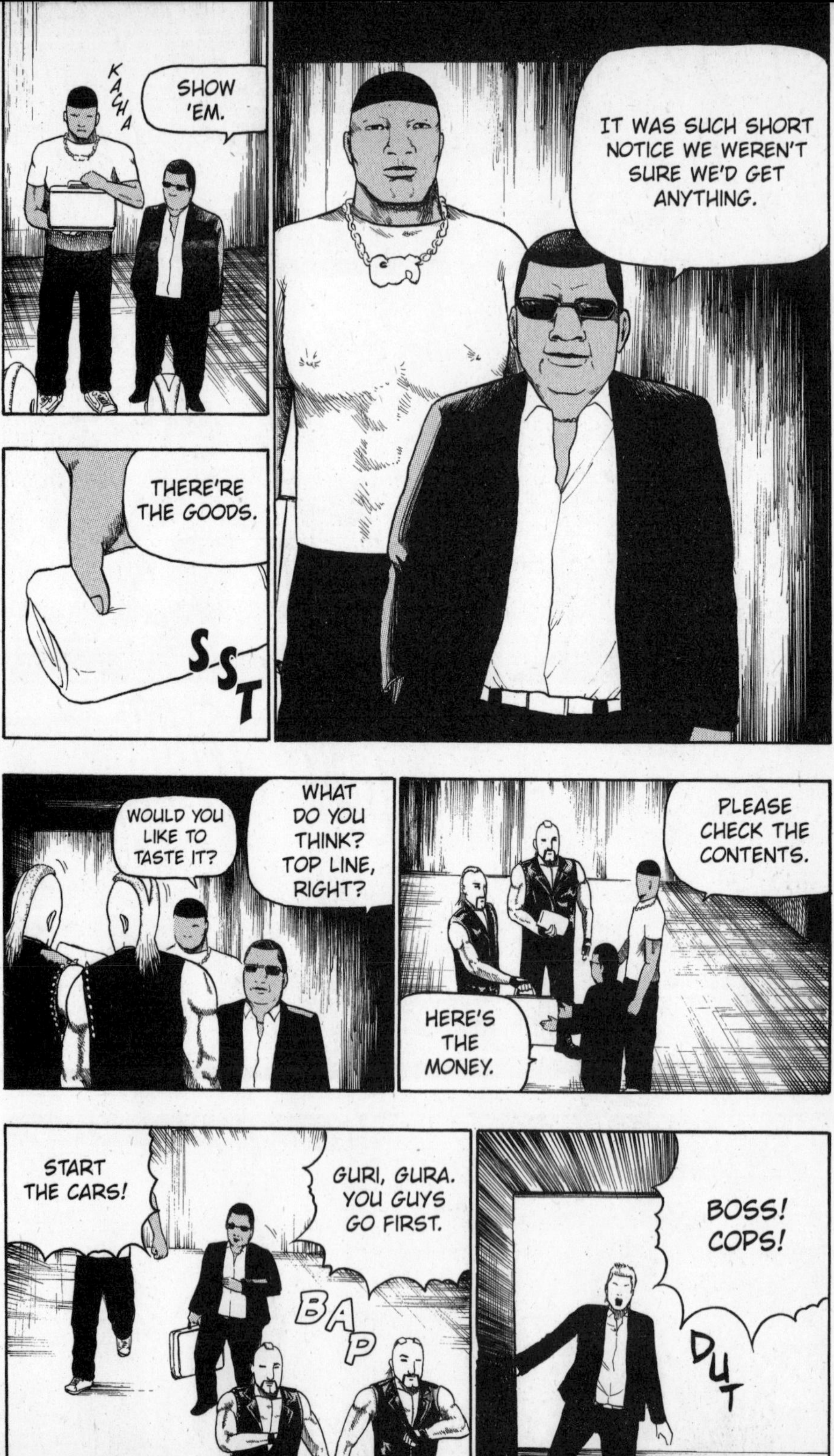
IT WAS SUCH SHORT NOTICE WE WEREN'T SURE WE'D GET ANYTHING.
KACHA
SHOW 'EM.
THERE'RE THE GOODS.
SSST
PLEASE CHECK THE CONTENTS.
HERE'S THE MONEY.
WHAT DO YOU THINK? TOP LINE, RIGHT?
WOULD YOU LIKE TO TASTE IT?
BOSS! COPS!
DUT
GURI, GURA. YOU GUYS GO FIRST.
START THE CARS!
BAP

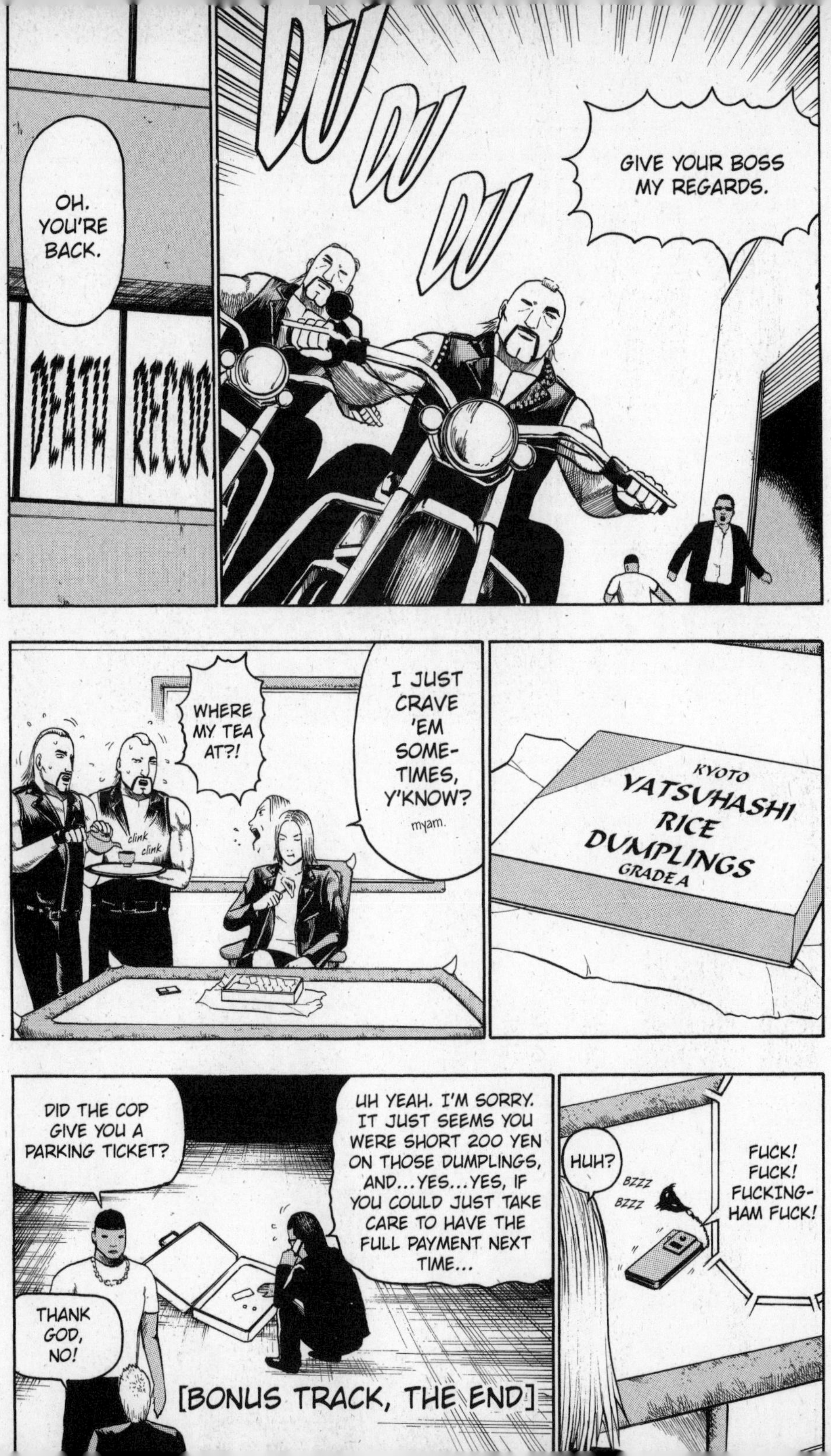
GIVE YOUR BOSS MY REGARDS.
OH. YOU'RE BACK.
DEATH RECOR
KYOTO
YATSUHASHI RICE DUMPLINGS
GRADE A
I JUST CRAVE 'EM SOME-TIMES, Y'KNOW?
myam.
WHERE MY TEA AT?!
clink
clink
FUCK! FUCK! FUCKING-HAM FUCK!
HUH?
BZZZ
BZZZ
UH YEAH. I'M SORRY. IT JUST SEEMS YOU WERE SHORT 200 YEN ON THOSE DUMPLINGS, AND...YES...YES, IF YOU COULD JUST TAKE CARE TO HAVE THE FULL PAYMENT NEXT TIME...
DID THE COP GIVE YOU A PARKING TICKET?
THANK GOD, NO!
[BONUS TRACK, THE END]

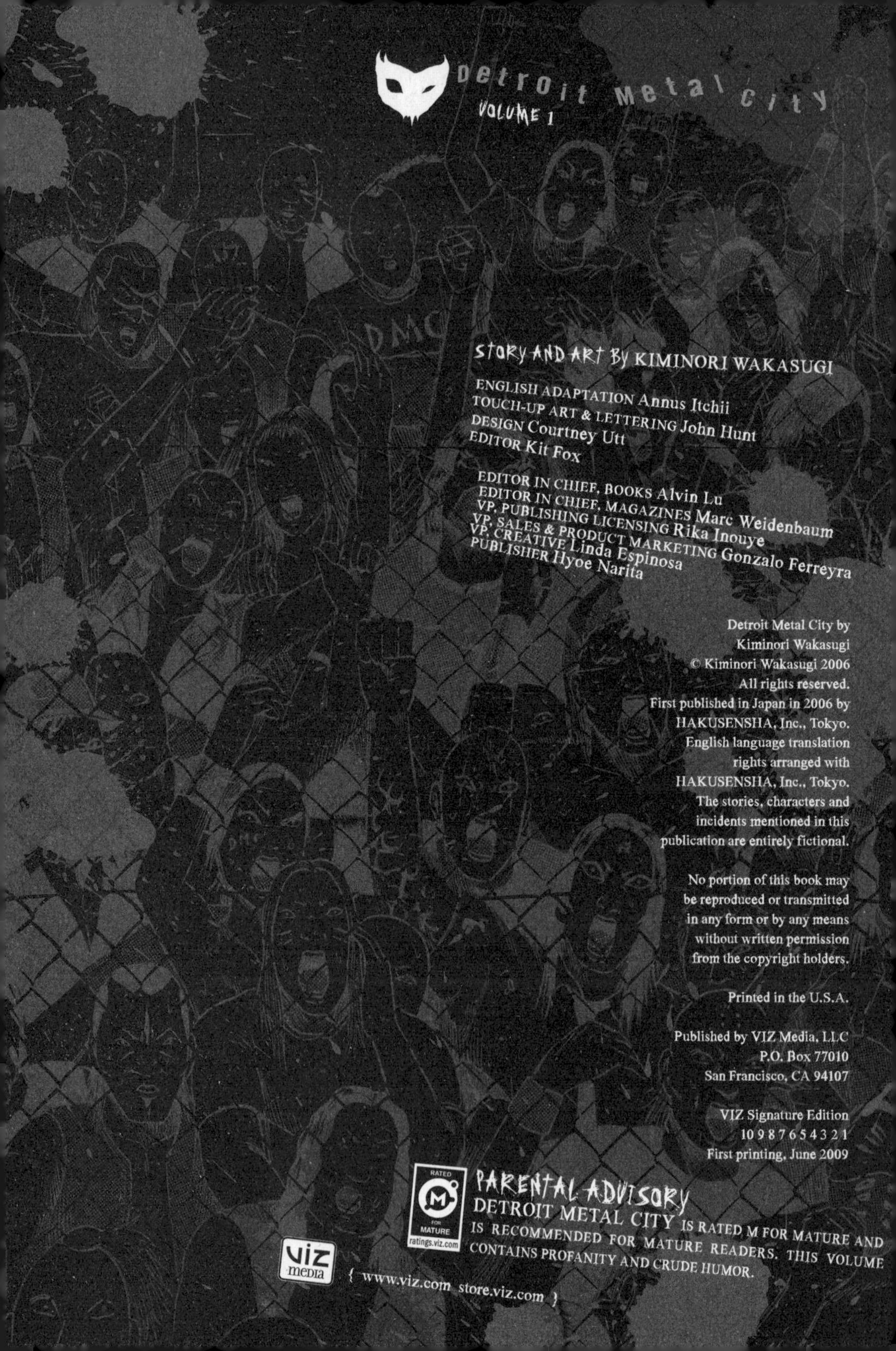

Detroit Metal City

VOLUME 1

STORY AND ART BY KIMINORI WAKASUGI

ENGLISH ADAPTATION Annus Itchii
TOUCH-UP ART & LETTERING John Hunt
DESIGN Courtney Utt
EDITOR Kit Fox

EDITOR IN CHIEF, BOOKS Alvin Lu
EDITOR IN CHIEF, MAGAZINES Marc Weidenbaum
VP, PUBLISHING LICENSING Rika Inouye
VP, SALES & PRODUCT MARKETING Gonzalo Ferreyra
VP, CREATIVE Linda Espinosa
PUBLISHER Hyoe Narita

Printed in the U.S.A.

Published by VIZ Media, LLC
P.O. Box 77010
San Francisco, CA 94107

VIZ Signature Edition
10 9 8 7 6 5 4 3 2 1
First printing, June 2009

RATED M FOR MATURE
ratings.viz.com

PARENTAL ADVISORY
DETROIT METAL CITY IS RATED M FOR MATURE AND IS RECOMMENDED FOR MATURE READERS. THIS VOLUME CONTAINS PROFANITY AND CRUDE HUMOR.